THE RED AND THE BLACK

THE RED AND THE BLACK

AMERICAN FILM NOIR IN THE 1950S

ROBERT MIKLITSCH

**UNIVERSITY OF
ILLINOIS PRESS**
Urbana, Chicago, and Springfield

Library of Congress Cataloging-in-Publication Data
Names: Miklitsch, Robert, 1953- author.
Title: The red and the black : American film noir in the
    1950s / Robert Miklitsch.
Description: Urbana : University of Illinois Press, 2016. |
    Includes bibliographical references and index.
Identifiers: LCCN 2016026159 (print) | LCCN 2016042419
    (ebook) | ISBN 9780252040689 (hardback) | ISBN
    9780252082191 (paperback) | ISBN 9780252099120
    (e-book)
Subjects: LCSH: Film noir—United States—History and
    criticism. | BISAC: PERFORMING ARTS / Film & Video
    / History & Criticism. | PERFORMING ARTS / Film &
    Video / Direction & Production. | HISTORY / Social
    History.
Classification: LCC PN1995.9.F54 M545 2016 (print) | LCC
    PN1995.9.F54 (ebook) | DDC 791.43/6556—dc23
LC record available at https://lccn.loc.gov/2016026159

For Red Badge Detective readers everywhere
and for my mother, Catherine B. Miklitsch (1925–2016),
a native of Niagara Falls, who instilled in me an appreciation,
deep as life itself, of poetry and the love that moves the sun
and all the stars

But the problem of film criticism, like art criticism, arises because it is a genre which does not exist in its own right. All great art critics have been poets.

—*Jean-Luc Godard*

I see a red door and I want it painted black
No colors anymore, I want them to turn black

—*"Paint It Black," Rolling Stones (Mick Jagger and Keith Richards, 1966)*

CONTENTS

ACKNOWLEDGMENTS

I want to begin by expressing my gratitude to Danny Nasset for his early enthusiasm for this book. He's a prince of an editor and prescient to boot. In addition, I want to thank all the staff at the University of Illinois Press—especially Angela Burton, Marika Christofides, Kevin Cunningham, Tad Ringo, and Roberta Sparenberg—for shepherding *The Red and the Black* through the publication process and beyond. Their labor is anything but invisible to this writer.

I'm also grateful to Daryl Malarry Davidson, a devotee of '50s American cinema, who was gracious enough to proofread the manuscript before it was submitted to the press, and to Jill R. Hughes, who was incredibly clement about my jazz-fueled queries about how far I could push "house style" and grammatical etiquette. Listening to early "Blue Note" Miles Davis while reviewing the copy may not have been the wisest decision, but, needless to say, all the "blue notes" are mine. I'm beholden, in addition, to Evan Shaw, award-winning documentary filmmaker at WOUB, for taking time out of his busy schedule to make 4K images for me, and Sheila Bodell, for compiling the index and graciously agreeing to defer payment.

Thanks to the marketing and publicity department at Illinois, I'm pleased to be able to give a shout-out here to the Mystery Writers of America for nominating my previous Illinois book, *Kiss the Blood Off My Hands: On Classic Noir*, for an Edgar Allan Poe Award and to the American Library Association for naming it a "Choice" Outstanding Academic Title of 2015.

Chapter 1 appeared in *Camera Obscura* and chapter 9 in the *Journal of Film and Video*, respectively, and I am very appreciative of the editors with whom I collaborated at these journals, Sharon Willis and Stephen Tropiano. I'd also like to tip my fedora to Felicia Campbell at the *Popular Culture Review* and James Distefano at the *Journal of Popular Film and Television*.

In the course of writing this book, I've tried to review the extant criticism on 1950s noir and am therefore indebted to all of the writers whom I cite. In addition to Mark Osteen, whose essay on "nuclear noir" provided a template for my own take on the subject, I want to single out Jeff Smith, who, unbeknownst to me, was writing about anticommunist noir—in particular, *The Woman on Pier 13*—around the same time that I was. I was therefore both surprised and delighted to discover how fraternal our readings are, which not only confirmed my considered sense of these "red" films but, happily, that the act of interpretation is less subjective than it is sometimes made out to be.

At Ohio University, Brian McCarthy, associate dean of the College of Arts and Sciences, has generously provided funds for the index, and the Research Support Fund has been instrumental in acquiring illustrations. In the English department, Sherrie Gradin has been a wonderfully supportive chair; the faculty, unfailingly collegial colleagues; and the students in my film noir class, "Kiss Me Deadly," spirited and engaging interlocutors. I'm much obliged as well to Beth Quitslund and Ghirmai Negash for their continued support of the last noir course, without which this book would certainly be poorer.

In the same spirit, I want to express my deep appreciation to Ann Douglas, whose intellectual companionship and profound knowledge of classic American noir have been a real gift. I can only hope that *The Red and the Black* lives up, at least in part, to her imprimatur.

Mille grazie to Hedy and Joe Ruffalo, new friends from outside of "the 6," who are not only super, salt-of-the-earth people but "very proud of me," like my father (another native of NF) as well as my brother and sisters—Cathy (Nyack, New York), Dave (Colorado Springs), Tre (Buffalo), Fran (Washington, D.C.), and Rose (Toronto/Santa Monica)—who may be geographically distant from me but remain as close as a heartbeat.

Finally, I'm most indebted to Jessica "Jayne" Burchard, whose mad lyrical skills and sing-along singing continue to amaze and delight me. Luck is not, contrary to Ian Fleming in *Casino Royale* (1953), a woman, but I'm lucky to have her in my life. Bartender, two martinis, si'l vous plaît: "Three measures of Gordon's, one of vodka, half a measure of Kina Lillet. Shake it very well until it's ice-cold, then add a large thin slice of lemon peel. Got it?" (James Bond, "Rouge et Noir," *Casino Royale*).

PRISE DE POSITION

FOR '50S NOIR, OR CONFESSIONS OF A FILM NOIR ADDICT

Our true passions are selfish.
—Stendahl, *The Red and the Black* (1830)

Nineteen fifties noir is, like Disney noir, something of an oxymoron.[1] The stereotypical conception of "the Fifties"—whether it's Elvis or Eisenhower, Lucy or *Ozzie and Harriet*, Chevies or gray flannel suits, Sputnik or Levittown-style suburbia—just doesn't jibe with the stereotypical notions about film noir (private eye, femme fatale, chiaroscuro, etc.).

The major premise of *The Red and the Black: American Film Noir in the 1950s*—that there is such a thing as '50s noir, that it's not a contradiction in terms—is therefore counterintuitive. More to the point, perhaps, this book sets out to disprove the received, declensionist argument about the "fall" of '50s noir as opposed to its "rise" in the 1940s. Since I am wary about—for, I think, good philosophical reasons—the conventional valorization of the general over the particular (theme [+]/example [−]) as well as overarching arguments about both '50s and historical noir, the deconstructive thesis of *The Red and the Black* (example [+]/theme [−]) can be said to be, à la Adorno, a negative or anti-thesis.

This said, the minor premise of *The Red and the Black* is that '50s noirs are more complex, both formally and thematically speaking, than generalizations about the period suggest and that this complexity is frequently a function of a specific film's contradictory or performative character. In order to demonstrate this premise, it's imperative, I believe, to attend to the heterogeneity of texts. Accordingly, although *The Red and the Black* is structured around general thematic motifs, I have felt free—within discursive reason—to follow the films where they take me. This means trying to do justice to the particularity of texts while respecting larger, more abstract imperatives. The philosophical presupposition here is that all texts are exorbitant vis-à-vis whatever topic is utilized to interpret them and, moreover, that this exorbitance is itself constitutive and can tell us just as much, sometimes more, about a film than its ostensible theme. Put another way, the book's performative form or mode of argumentation strives to do justice to Paul Schrader's observation that in film noir the "theme is hidden in the style."[2] The task, in short, has been to strike a balance between close reading and argumentation, a position that's especially important when dealing with a topic such as '50s noir that has been subject to so many generalities.

But let me be more specific still with respect to the style and address of *The Red and the Black*. First, I'm tempted to say—thank you, Magritte!—that *This is not a book* (*Ceci n'est pas une pipe*). Which is to say, whether for good or ill, that it's not addressed simply or only to film scholars. Second, inasmuch as this book is addressed to fans *and* scholars, film buffs *and* common readers (which designations are not, of course, mutually exclusive), it's by definition a hybrid, even heterogeneous text, not unlike classic noir itself. This means, among other things, not assuming that readers are familiar with all of the films discussed in the following pages, many of which may be obscure even for noir aficionados. Hence my considered decision to adopt a detailed, novelistic approach to a strictly analytical one. My rationale is not merely philosophical or practical. Although attending to a film's narrative provides readers with an entrée to a given picture and is also intended to produce a heightened, critical sense of mimesis (as exemplified in certain moments in my readings of *The Thief* [1952] and *Kiss Me Deadly* [1955] where I revert to something like slow motion), I have discovered in the process of writing this book that rack-focusing on a film's form has frequently had the surprising effect of defamiliarizing or "making strange" what, for many, are generic or "bad objects," whether it's "programmers" like *The Whip Hand* (1951), *Shack Out on 101* (1955), and *City of Fear* (1959) or controversial subgenres such as the anticommunist noir.

A classic example of the latter subgenre is *Big Jim McLain* (1952), a film whose rhetoric, as I elucidate in chapter 2, is more complicated than its ideologically conservative address might suggest. For instance, it's worth noting that *Big Jim McLain* was released in a number of European markets where the communist angle was traded out, reversing *Kiss Me Deadly*, for a drug-smuggling plot. (See the Italian foglio for the film, titled *Marijuana: La droga infernale*. Is that sweet Nancy Olson, John Wayne's love interest in *Big Jim McLain*, her outsized face looming like a ghost in the background of the poster, her head thrown back, eyes closed, lost in the intoxicating plumes of smoke trailing from the lit cannabis stick in the foreground?) The wonderfully exploitative artwork for the Italian poster for *Big Jim McLain* highlights for me the issue of rhetoric or style in the restricted sense.

Given the book's multiple address, I have occasionally opted to employ a colloquial, vernacular register that's more commonly associated today with commercial or trade books. An unwritten but stringently enforced rule in the academy is that you should never, upon the pain of disciplinary expulsion, approximate the language of the object of analysis. Critical and creative writing are different, and never the twain shall meet. However, my model here is Jean-Luc Godard, who in an interview with *Cahiers du cinéma* once observed: "I think of myself as an essayist. . . . Were the cinema to disappear, I would simply accept the inevitable and turn to television; were television to disappear, I would simply revert to pen and paper. For there is a clear continuity between all forms of expression."[3]

The films themselves are another model. Although I can't claim to match, say, Ernest Lehman and Clifford Odets's inspired screenplay for *Sweet Smell of Success* (1957)—J. J. Hunsecker (Burt Lancaster) to Sidney Falco (Tony Curtis), "Match me"—the vibrancy of their dialogue, a distinct part of which is a direct result of the subatomic-like collision of the high and low, the demotic and the sublime, catches the peculiar tonality of '50s noir. A random sample (*sortes Virgilianae!*) from *Sweet Smell of Success*. As the supremely venal Broadway columnist and his press-agent votary are strolling down Fifty-Second Street in New York City, a black Lincoln Continental discreetly trailing them, Hunsecker inquires whether "Sidalee" has sabotaged, as promised, the budding romance between his sister and a modern jazz musician: "Conjugate me a verb, Sidney. For instance, *to promise!*" Rather than attempt to distance myself from this sort of "gutter poetry"—there are worse afflictions for me than Stendahl's syndrome—I have tried instead to reenact it and, in the diabolical-alchemical process that is writing, wrest something of the performativity of '50s film noir.

In conclusion, I'd be remiss if I didn't note that my passionate aim for this book is a simple, selfish one: more readers. If it's a sin today, when Twitter has become the new Republic of Letters, to desire a larger audience (but see @filmnoirforever), I happily plead nolo contendere. Having long since sprouted hellfire-red horns and a pointy tail, I hereby confess that my pen is a pitchfork and my soul as black as the inkiest film noir.

Courteous, and, I hope, indulgent reader . . . having accompanied
me thus far, now let me request you move onwards.

—Thomas De Quincey, *Confessions of an English Opium-Eater*
(1821)

PREFACE

> [Art] only becomes universally eloquent in the
> specific impulse, by its opposition to the universal.
>
> —Theodor Adorno, *Aesthetic Theory*

In 1955, in *A Panorama of American Film Noir*, Étienne Chaumeton and Raymond Borde declared, "From 1949, the career of the noir genre, properly so called, comes to an end."[1] In 1972, in "Notes on Film Noir," Paul Schrader stated that the "third and final phase of film noir" is "from 1949 to 1953."[2] And in 2002, in *Film Noir*, Andrew Spicer referred to 1952 to 1958 as the period of "fragmentation and decay."[3] From this brief chronological review, it's clear that the periodization of classic noir has changed considerably over the years.[4]

Critics have differed about when exactly the classic era of American film noir concluded, but there is little disagreement that the genre began to decline sometime in the early 1950s. The reasons that have been cited for the fall of film noir are almost as various as definitions of the genre.[5] As I elaborate in more detail in the introductory synopsis, "Coming Attractions," and in the body of *The Red and the Black*, these reasons include, in addition to color and television, the 1948 Paramount Decree, the increasing influence of the teen and foreign markets, and the gradual loosening of censorship and self-regulation in the wake of the U.S. Supreme Court's 1952 "Miracle Decision."

For example, in *Film and Politics in America*, Brian Neve remarks that the "divorcement of the studios of their exhibition wings, a process begun by the successful antitrust suit in 1948, meant the beginning of the end for the double bill and the heyday of the B *noir*."[6] Other critics have argued that the decline of classic noir should be attributed less to the above legal and industrial changes than to the hearings held by the House Committee on Un-American Activities (HUAC) in 1947 and 1951. The influence of the HUAC investigations on classic noir can be seen in the rash of "red menace" films that appeared between 1947 and 1954 as well as the related, precipitous decline of the "social problem" picture epitomized by films such as *Crossfire* (1947) and *Force of Evil* (1949).[7]

More generally, the argument for the fall of American film noir has tended to focus on the rise of authority figures. Whereas the accent in the first decade of the genre is, according to the stock reading, on the individual—say, a private detective who has an adversarial relation with the law as, for instance, Sam Spade classically does in *The Maltese Falcon* (1941)—the emphasis in the second decade is ostensibly on the "institutional forces" of law and order: "The characteristic 1950s noir is the pared-down, tautly scripted thriller, which focuses on organized professional criminals in their battle with the authorities."[8] This description of the characteristic 1950s noir has in fact become a commonplace.[9] Hence in the introduction to *The Rough Guide to Film Noir*, Alexander Ballinger and Danny Graydon reiterate that the "1950s saw a distinct shift towards tightly plotted, grittier fare, showcasing an increasing focus on organized criminals engaged in fierce battles with the authorities."[10]

This shift in plot, theme, and character is coupled, so the narrative goes, with a corresponding mutation in style. In the late 1940s and 1950s, as a result of, among other things, technological advances occasioned by the Second World War such as faster film stock and portable recording equipment, the studio-bound expressionism of the first phase of the genre began to give way to the "mean," naturalistically rendered "streets" associated with neorealism: "Expressionist stylization is downplayed or avoided altogether in many 1950s noirs. . . . Location shooting becomes more routine and flatly naturalistic."[11]

One consequence of the above rise-and-fall "narrative" or *grand récit* about classic American noir is that the 1950s have become something of an afterthought, a reaction that's registered in the tendency on the part of certain critics to cherry-pick a few diamonds out of the dross and consign the rest of the decade to the dustbin of history. This practice is illustrated by the consecration of a few isolated jewels such as Robert Aldrich's *Kiss Me Deadly*, which Paul Schrader in 1972 referred to as a "masterpiece" and which Borde and Chaumeton in the 1979 "Postface" to *A Panorama of American Film Noir* called a "point of no return," as if no film noirs appeared after it.[12] Yet *Kiss Me Deadly* did not materialize in a generic or even authorial vacuum. In addition to Aldrich's Hollywood exposé, *The Big Knife*, 1955 saw the release of a number of key film noirs such as Joseph H. Lewis's *The Big Combo*, Samuel Fuller's *House of Bamboo*, Stanley Kubrick's *Killer's Kiss*, Charles Laughton's *Night of the Hunter*, and Phil Karlson's *The Phenix City Story*.

Nineteen fifty-five is a significant point in time not simply because it's the year that *Kiss Me Deadly* theoretically atomized the genre but also because it's the moment that critics have retrospectively seized upon as being the crux or turning point of the decade—the moment, that is, when the 1950s starts to become indistinguishable from "the Fifties." So in the section on "The 1950s" in *The Rough Guide to Film Noir*, Ballinger and Graydon write, in the context of the 1955 publication of Borde and Chaumeton's *Panorama of American Film Noir*: "At this point, film noir was clearly on the decline, its essential qualities of anxiety and despair at odds with the more upbeat mood brought about by greater economic prosperity."[13] Not so incidentally, Ballinger and Graydon's rendition of the moment when the "age of anxiety" becomes the "age of affluence" echoes Schrader's commentary on the demise of classic noir in his "Notes on Film Noir": "As the rise . . . of Eisenhower demonstrated, Americans were eager to see a more bourgeois view of themselves. . . . Any attempt at social criticism had to be cloaked in ludicrous affirmations of the American way of life."[14]

Despite the received critical wisdom about the genre at mid-century, both the beginning and the end of the decade suggest that there may be more to '50s noir than meets the eye and ear. For instance, much has been made of the aforementioned decline of the "social problem" film and the concurrent rise of the anticommunist noir. But as Thom Andersen essays in "Red Hollywood," a "new genre of Hollywood films," so-called *film gris*, appeared "between the first HUAC hearings of October 1947 and the second of May 1951."[15] While film gris has been referred to as the "most radically leftist cycle of Hollywood pictures,"[16] the anticommunist thriller, has, by contrast, tended "to be discounted as a 'noir cycle' because of its overt political orientation."[17] This said, it may be more accurate to say that the real problem with the anticommunist thriller has been not so much its politics as its retrograde, conservative character. Bluntly, rather than argue that there can be no such thing, strictly speaking, as anticommunist noir, it makes more sense to recognize that the "right-wing cycle" of classic American noir exists and, moreover, that it's the dialectical other of film gris, proffering a unique perspective on the genre at a critical moment in its historical evolution and the cultural-political "structure of feeling" of the United States in the first part of the 1950s.

Although anticommunism is one of the "foremost socio-political influences on the post–World World II film industry,"[18] what a character in *Split Second* (1953) calls the "bright red bomb" is also part of the texture of everyday life in the early 1950s. As Nicholas Christopher remarks in *Somewhere in the Night*: "Noir not only traces its roots to the dawn of the Atomic Age" but "displays an ongoing obsession with all things nuclear. And communist."[19] The "red scare" is itself incarnated—to cross sci-fi with the anticommunist noir—with the invasion of the mind snatchers:

"They are everywhere suddenly, repopulating the noir underside of the big city and restoking the basic fuels of angst, alienation, and paranoia. . . . And what are they obsessed with night and day, above all else? What is it that drives them in their every move, large or small? The atom bomb."[20]

Yet if it's true that the "Big Secret," in conjunction with "Big Communism," spawned the "alienating, twin darknesses" of dread and paranoia that dominated the American political unconscious during the Cold War,[21] the way that this atomic *Stimmung* is dramatized in '50s noir varies considerably from picture to picture. Thus, in the introduction to *Film Noir: An Encyclopedic Reference to the American Style*, the editors write: "The potential hazards of the atomic bomb, and after 1949 the threat of nuclear war may have been most explicitly . . . depicted in the science fiction genre; but such concepts also altered the narratives of film noir."[22]

A classic example of this "sublimation" is Fritz Lang's *The Big Heat* (1953), a "rogue cop"/"syndicate" picture that, despite the "absence of direct signifiers of atomic materials," is "thoroughly imbued with nuclear trauma."[23] In "Keep the Coffee Hot, Hugo," Walter Metz delineates how *The Big Heat*'s brutal exposé of American culture and politics in the early 1950s is a direct function of its indirect representation of the ubiquitous "non-presentness" of the nuclear threat.[24] Metz's primary example is the car bomb that the crime syndicate has planted in Det. Dave Bannion's (Glenn Ford) car that inadvertently kills his wife, Katie (Jocelyn Brando): "the explosion is filmed from inside Bannion's house as he is putting his daughter Joyce to bed," and, "as if it were an atomic blast, we see only the white flash of the bomb through the bedroom window."[25]

Just as film noir at the beginning of the 1950s is a complex discursive formation, the end or terminus of the classical era is equally complex. Although *Touch of Evil* (1958) has traditionally been seen as closing the classical period of the genre,[26] Borde and Chaumeton do not reference Orson Welles's film in the initial edition of *A Panorama of American Film Noir* nor, somewhat surprisingly (since it "enjoyed a two-year run in Paris" from 1959 to 1960), in the 1979 "Postface."[27] However, in "Notes on Film Noir" Schrader refers to *Touch of Evil* as "film noir's epitaph,"[28] and Spicer contends that the "baroque expressionism" of *Touch of Evil* represents the "culmination of [the] most popular version" of the "noir style."[29] More recently, critics have assiduously explored the film's transgressive cultural politics, concentrating on its racial and sexual, ethnic and transnational thematics.[30] In fact, it might not be too much to say that, pitched as it is on the border between tragedy and farce, *Touch of Evil* deconstructs the sort of binary oppositions that subtend the '40s social problem film, not to mention the strict identitarian political interpretation (left versus right wing) of classic noir itself.

Odds against Tomorrow (1959), the current candidate for the honorific title as the final film noir of the classical period, is instructive here.[31] Robert Wise's picture, at least from the vertiginous perspective of *Touch of Evil*, appears like an old-fashioned "social problem" film, a perception that's partly due to the fact that it was scripted by one of the auteurs of film gris, Abe Polonsky, who was blacklisted at the time. At the same time, in its overtly liberal orientation, *Odds against Tomorrow* suggests that the politics of race is one of the key tropes of late '50s noir, a topic that I explore in the conclusion to *The Red and the Black*, where I take up Samuel Fuller's *Crimson Kimono*, which was released in October 1959, the same month as *Odds against Tomorrow*.

In addition to, among other things, HUAC and the Paramount Decree, the decline of American film noir in the 1950s has been attributed to color and television. So in "Notes on Film Noir" Schrader writes that "television, with its demands for full lighting and close-ups, undercut the German influence and color cinematography was, of course, the final blow to the noir look."[32] Although Schrader's recourse to the locution "of course" speaks to the supposed incontrovertibility of his claim, as I demonstrate in Part Three of *The Red and the Black*, there are more color noirs in the 1950s than is generally acknowledged, and, moreover, a number of filmmakers, working closely with certain talented cinematographers such as John Alton, Lucien Ballard, and Joe MacDonald, were able to translate the subtle gradations of black-and-white into the prismatic medium of color.

Two late noirs considered peripheral to the classical noir canon, Alfred Hitchcock's *Vertigo* (1958) and Nicholas Ray's *Party Girl* (1958), are central to the genre when viewed from this perspective. In "Paint It Black" (1970), Raymond Durgnat, foreshadowing Schrader's rhetoric in "Notes on Film Noir," refers to *Vertigo* as a "beautiful" "late straggler."[33] Similarly, Nicholas Ray's *Party Girl*, a "pioneering" Metrocolor picture that marries "noir themes and stylistics" with the "visual splash" of an M-G-M musical, appears like *Vertigo* at the "tail end of the classic noir cycle" and anticipates the angularity and self-reflexivity of neo-modernist noir.[34] And here I hasten to add that the colors named in the title of this book, as in Stendahl's *Le Rouge et le noir*, do not possess a simple, one-to-one symbolic correspondence. While the color red connotes, say, the atomic bomb or anticommunism and the color black film noir or the "blacklist," these titular hues are also intended to prompt other, more fleeting cinephilic codes or moments such as the two-toned ensemble—the incarnadine-red dress and sable-black fur—that Vicki Gaye (Cyd Charisse) wears in *Party Girl*. (It's not irrelevant, I think, that Ray's splashily colored Metro gangster noir has been read as "one of America's most devastating critiques of McCarthyism."[35])

As color noirs like *Vertigo* and *Party Girl* attest, '50s noirs responded, sometimes tacitly, sometimes tangibly, to new media and technologies. Film noirs about the motion picture industry—see, for instance, *Sunset Blvd.* (1950), *In a Lonely Place* (1950), and *The Big Knife*[36]—are only the most obvious example that classical

Hollywood cinema is always in some sense, to some degree, about the medium itself. Accordingly, the relation between film noir and TV is not, pace Schrader, merely antagonistic; as *The Glass Web* (1953), a 3-D picture about the production of a live, true-crime television show, testifies, it's productive as well. Indeed, Jack Arnold's "B" TV movie exemplifies how "late" '50s noirs actively engaged new media and technologies, a creative reappropriation that points to the resurgence of the genre in neo-noir and, not so incidentally, its robust, myriad remediation in mass popular culture.[37]

INTRODUCTION

COMING ATTRACTIONS, OR THE PARTICULARS

The dialectical postulate that the particular is the
universal has its model in art.

—Theodor Adorno, *Aesthetic Theory*

The Red and the Black is composed of three parts, each of which is devoted to a particular topic: anticommunism, "atomic noir," and new media/technologies. Each part also has a slightly different configuration given my sense of how intensive or extensive the play of the theme is in '50s noir. Cognizant as I am of the variable experience of watching previews, I have endeavored in what follows to offer a fresh, animated take on the various films discussed in more detail and at greater length in the body of the book.

*   *   *

Part One of *The Red and the Black* takes as its subject that peculiar '50s phenomenon the "red menace." Chapter 1 presents a case history on *The Woman on Pier 13*, which was released in 1950. The fact that the film was originally released by RKO in 1949 as *I Married a Communist* suggests that it was intended to exploit the American public's fascination with and dread about the red scare. Although the rather more generic title, *The Woman on Pier 13*, points a long, incriminating finger at the communist infiltration of American labor, in particular West Coast longshoremen, the original title better captures what I call the "romance of communism."

The heterosexual romance narrative is central to the melo-noir, and *The Woman on Pier 13* is, as its original title suggests, just as much about marriage as communism. While the conventional wisdom is that the institution of marriage was enjoying a halcyon period in the 1950s, *The Woman on Pier 13* paints a revealing picture, under the guise of anticommunist agitprop, of the cultural contradictions surrounding gender and sexuality at the beginning of the atomic age. Moreover, precisely because of its generic reversibility (melodrama/film noir), *The Woman on Pier 13* complicates the received wisdom about the "bad romance" or "unhappy marriage" between film noir and anticommunism. In other words, if the reflexive, knee-jerk critique of anticommunist noir has conventionally been predicated on its regressive politics, not to mention bad form, a close reading of *The Woman on Pier 13* highlights not only its ideological mutability—for example, ex-communist Brad Collins (Robert Ryan) as a victim of the witch hunt instigated by the House Un-American Activities Committee (HUAC)—but its very real aesthetic interest, which is especially on exhibit, true to Paul Schrader's dictum in "Notes on Film Noir," in the waterfront scenes.

In *The RKO Story* author Richard Jewell remarks that 1948, the year before *The Woman on Pier 13* was first released, "was the beginning of the plague years for RKO."[1] "Plague years" is an especially apt catchphrase because it points to the beginning of the fall of the "house of noir" as well as the "red plague" that so exercised Howard Hughes, who assumed controlling interest of RKO in 1948. *The Whip Hand*, which opens the general discussion of anticommunist noir in chapter 2, combines Hughes's hysterical fear of germs with his equally hysterical fear of communism. In the original script for *The Whip Hand*, the villains were ex-Nazis and Hitler himself was alive and well. After the film was in the can, however, Hughes decided to ditch the "Hitler angle": in the "new and improved" version, the communists "have taken over a fortress-like lodge where they conduct germ-warfare experiments" and are "plotting the destruction of the US population through biological means."[2]

Although *The Whip Hand* may well be, as this plot synopsis hints, "overheated and preposterous," it vividly conveys the paranoia and apocalypticism of the 1950s, a "structure of feeling" that characterizes other, more canonical '50s noirs such as *Kiss Me Deadly*. Wheeler Winston Dixon rightly praises William Cameron Menzies's "customary visual brio," but if Menzies is responsible for the "nightmarish, forced-perspective sets," the "sheer frenzy" of the film's "violent, aggressive camerawork" should be credited to the film's director of photography, Nicholas Musuraca, who is one of the missing links between classic, pre-1948 RKO noirs such as *Out of the Past* (1947) and '50s anticommunist noirs such as *The Woman on Pier 13* and *The Whip Hand*.[3]

Another reflex of the critical literature on film noir is that in the aftermath of HUAC and the anticommunist hysteria provoked by Senator Joe McCarthy, the genre took a not so classic swerve to the right, one that coincides with its decline. This demise can be attributed, according to Raymond Borde and Étienne Chaumeton in *A Panorama of American Film Noir*, to the influence of an international movement, neorealism, and a subgenre, the police semidocumentary.[4] From this dual perspective, *I Was a Communist for the F.B.I.* (1951), featuring Frank Lovejoy as FBI undercover agent Matt Cvetic, is one of the principal films of the anticommunist noir cycle.

As with *The Whip Hand*, the producing studio is critical. In other words, if RKO's *The Whip Hand*, mirroring Hughes's mania, switches out Nazis for Commies, Warner Bros.' *I Was a Communist for the F.B.I.* replaces—in a paradigmatic substitution—Original Gangsters with Communists. At the same time, since the protagonist's undercover work with the Communist Party is tangled up with his family life, *I Was a Communist for the F.B.I.* is not simply a docu-noir but a docu-melo-noir, a portmanteau term that reflects the film's ideological complexity. This complexity is exemplified by the fact that, unusual for an early 1950s noir, *I Was a Communist for the F.B.I.* traffics in the fear of both a red and black planet.

If the emphasis on race relations in *I Was a Communist for the F.B.I.* underscores the word "black" in "black film," one of the working premises of *The Red and the Black* is that film noir may be associated with black-and-white film stock, but because of its investment in melodrama (itself understood as a complex genre), the sort of issues raised in the films cannot be reduced to a black-and-white calculus. This is true even of a seemingly straightforward docu-noir such as Alfred L. Werker's *Walk East on Beacon!* (1952), which was based on a *Reader's Digest* article, "Crime of the Century," authored by J. Edgar Hoover. Louis de Rochemont, the film's producer, collaborated with the FBI on the picture, and the bureau went so far as to recommend rabid anticommunist and future Republican senator George Murphy, whose later career invites invidious comparison with Ronald Reagan's, for the role of lead federal investigator Inspector James Belden.[5] Throw in an otherworldly scenario, a secret interplanetary space project that anticipates "Star Wars," and you have the recipe for another run-of-the-mill anticommunist exposé.

But not unlike ex-commie turned shipping executive Brad Collins in *The Woman on Pier 13* and double agent Matt Cvetic in *I Was a Communist for the F.B.I.*, Vincent/Malvin Foss (Jack Manning) in *Walk East on Beacon!* is a supremely conflicted character whose predicament sheds light on a number of issues central to the ideological consensus of the 1950s. For example, if *Walk East on Beacon!* foregrounds the tension between civil liberties and the tele-cinematic surveillance associated with the burgeoning national security state, Vincent's backstory involves a secret that was far less of a concern for the U.S. government than it was for the motion picture industry: color film stock. This "color" question, like the race one in *I Was a Communist for the F.B.I.*, is so pronounced in *Walk East on Beacon!* because so peripheral, it appears, to the film's espionage plot. That *Walk East on Beacon!* denotes the use-value of new emergent technologies like television is not surprising. (In this it echoes the glorification of modern technology in Werker's earlier, seminal semidocumentary noir, *He Walked by Night* [1948].) The interest of *Walk East on Beacon!*, though, is that it can be said to rehearse the history of cinema in order to manage the considerable anxiety aroused by the new mass medium of TV. How else explain the fact that Vincent's romance with communism pivots on his possession of the secret of color emulsion?

Just as *Walk East on Beacon!* was produced with the FBI's imprimatur, *Big Jim McLain* was made with the cooperation of HUAC, as the concluding title card indicates: "The incidents in this motion picture are based on the files of the Committee on Un-American Activities. . . . We gratefully acknowledge the cooperation of the Committee." However, when Carl Milliken Jr., the head of the research department at Warner Bros., initially vetted the script, he complained that there appeared to be no relationship between the source material, a *Saturday Evening Post* article about the HUAC investigation of the 1949 International Longshoremen's and Warehousemen's strike, and Eric Taylor, Richard English, and James Edward Grant's screenplay."[6]

Milliken also complained that the HUAC investigators in the film, Jim McLain (John Wayne) and Mal Baxter (James Arness), were portrayed as "low-caliber" individuals prone to committing "illegal and offensive" acts in order to extract information.[7] In response, the film's producer, James Fellows, bragged that HUAC not only approved "the business of BUGGING THE PREMISES and the ILLEGAL ENTRY" but urged the filmmakers "not to eliminate it."[8] There's no little irony, then, that Fellows and Wayne's production company was originally titled The Fifth Corp. after the communists' abuse of the Fifth Amendment, which is dramatized at both the beginning and the end of Edward Ludwig's film.

As Milliken's critique suggests, *Big Jim McLain* is, generically speaking, not so much a hybrid as a mishmash. Still, despite or perhaps because of the motley cloth out of which it was woven, *Big Jim McLain* proved to be the most commercially successful anticommunist picture of the period, activating its generic parts—romance, melodrama, semidocumentary, picture-postcard travelogue—to recycle the dominant motifs of the anticommunist thriller.[9] For example, as in *The Whip Hand*, *Big Jim McLain* mobilizes the trope of contamination to evoke the deadly contagious specter of communism. So, in the course of the film, Big Jim travels to the leper colony on the island of Molokai to interview Mrs. Nomaka (Madame Soo Yong), the ex-wife of the party's former treasurer; in addition, party honcho Sturak (Alan Napier) instructs bacteriologist Dr. Mortimer to be ready—"when the word comes"—to create an epidemic by unleashing his "rodents" on the island of Hawaii.

Big Jim McLain also reprises the theme of union subversion that propels the plot of *The Woman on Pier 13*. In *Big Jim McLain* a rising young labor leader named Edwin White (Robert Keys) appears to be committed to ridding the longshoremen's union of the "red menace." In reality, he's one of the seventh cell's three essential members whom Sturak asks, along with Mortimer, to be prepared to act—in White's case, to call for a waterfront strike that will paralyze the island's shipping and communications. Not unlike the Kafers in *Walk East on Beacon!*, who are political refugees from Communist East Germany now happily ensconced in Boston, Massachusetts, White's parents, the Lexiters, are émigrés from Poland living the good life in Hawaii—"free and in the sun"—on Mr. Lexiter's union pension. Since Mr. Lexiter (Paul Hurst) is a Christian and good, because anti-communist, union man, the Lexiters kicked their son Edwin to the curb when he "turned [his] back on God" after a high school study-abroad trip to the Soviet Union.

But perhaps the most surprising reiteration of anticommunist symbology (as White's nickname, "Whitey," insinuates) is that *Big Jim McLain*, like *I Was a Communist for the F.B.I.*, casts communists as affluent, dyed-in-the-wool racists, albeit country-club ones. While Big Jim is prototypically "quick to punch and slow to think,"[10] in the concluding action of the film he suppresses his desire to punch out commie psychoanalyst Dr. Gelster (Gayne Whitman) until one of the country-club communists utters the "n" word. In *Big Jim McLain* the classic image of communism as the party of the expropriated is turned on its head, and it's the rich, not the black or working-class poor, who are the standard-bearers of the hammer-and-sickle-figured red flag.

Chapter 3, "*Pickup on South Street*: Out of the Red and Into the Black," book-ends the breakout chapter on *The Woman on Pier 13* that commences Part One. I discuss *Pickup on South Street* (1953) in the section on film noir and anticommu-nism rather than in the following section on atomic noir because when Samuel Fuller's film was first released, it was considered both anticommunist and, as it were, *anti*-anticommunist: "FBI boss J. Edgar Hoover was mortified at the film's disdain for flag waving," while "from the opposite corner" (boxing, I show, is one of the constitutive tropes of *Pickup on South Street*), "Fuller was criticized for joining the anti-communist Hollywood bandwagon."[11]

That the latter opinion still has some legs can be seen in Peter Lev's conten-tion in "Anticommunist Noir" that the film's "silly premise allows Fuller to make a fast moving crime picture with no attention to defining or describing commu-nism."[12] Although this is essentially the same critique that Lev levels against *The Woman on Pier 13*, *Pickup on South Street*, despite its "McCarthy era potboiler" of a plot,[13] is an altogether different sort of picture. For one thing, it's a one-off. That is to say, it's not a genre picture, even in the complicated way that *The Woman on Pier 13* is a melo-noir. Nor is it a docu-noir like *Walk East on Beacon!* "*Pickup on South Street* has elements of anti-Communist films like *I Married a Communist* and *I Was a Communist for the F.B.I.* but, unlike these pictures, it does not equate

Communists with organized crime."[14] Rather (and this is doubtlessly one of the reasons why Hoover put a stop to the FBI's involvement in the film), Fuller's film equates the Reds with the Feds *and* with the "men in blue," a subversive deconstruction of the anticommunist formula whereby communists are new-fashioned gangsters. The antiheroes of *Pickup on South Street* are not G-men or policemen but a prostitute and pickpocket, Candy (Jean Peters) and Skip McCoy (Richard Widmark), who, living on the margins of "underworld, U.S.A.," are motivated less by grand abstractions than by the daily struggle for self-preservation.

Fuller's sexual politics are just as idiosyncratic as his take on capitalism versus communism. Candy may be a hooker with a heart of gold, but on the black side of the ledger, she's not a femme fatale or pushover. Indeed, one of the very real virtues of *Pickup on South Street* is that sex is not written off—as it all too often is in anticommunist films—as something only Reds practice (when, of course, they're not hiding under beds). "*Pickup* is hardly conventional noir," Alexander Ballinger and Danny Graydon observe,[15] and it's a better picture for that. Antinomian to its core, Fuller's film is a true test for any critic with an ideological axe to grind.

The MacGuffin of *Pickup on South Street*—a stolen strip of microfilm that, according to Fuller, "contains a new patent for a chemical formula"[16]—provides a neat segue to Part Two of *The Red and the Black*, "'50s Noir in the Atomic Age." The subject of chapter 4, Rudolph Maté's *D.O.A.*, appeared in 1950 and, like *Sunset Blvd.* (1950), is told primarily in flashback, a classic noir device that imports a classic noir theme: that fate, to cite the doomed protagonist of *Detour* (1945), "can put its finger on you or me for no reason at all." In *D.O.A.* fate intervenes in the form of a toxic "Mickey Finn" that Frank Bigelow (Edmond O'Brien) imbibes at the Fisherman club. While the subsequent labyrinthine plot could be lifted from any number of '40s noirs, including its theme of errant masculine desire, what makes *D.O.A.* a quintessential '50s noir is that the toxin—a luminous one—is radioactive. Consequently, the film's most resonant scenario is as representative of the period as witch hunts and pumpkin patches: "The radioactive man, running out of time, inventories the mundane daily activities that could be atomically annihilated in an eye blink. Bigelow stares into the sun, bright as a bomb blast, and contemplates Armageddon as he knows it."[17]

True to the anamorphic character of certain '50s noirs, the atomic subtext of *D.O.A.* (and it remains a fecund one) also comments on the film's primary narrative about sexual infidelity, so much so that the picture can be seen, like *The Woman on Pier 13*, as a covert meditation on the fate of sexuality in the post-Hiroshima period. In 1951, speaking about the deleterious effects of "the bomb" on social mores, Charles Walter Clarke, executive director of the American Social Hygiene Association, warned about the "potential for sexual chaos" where "moral standards would relax and promiscuity would prevail."[18] If anticommunist noirs such as *The Woman on Pier 13*, *I Was a Communist for the F.B.I.*, and *Pickup on South Street* convey social anxiety about women as peculiarly "susceptible to the seductions of Communism,"[19] *D.O.A.*, which notably does not feature a full-fledged femme fatale, dramatizes the perils of the '50s everyman cut off from small-town America and let loose in San Francisco, one of the quintessential dark cities of classic noir, like New York and Los Angeles.

Chapter 5, "'Black Film' and the Bomb," examines a quartet of '50s nuclear noirs: *The Thief* (1952), *The Atomic City* (1952), *Shack Out on 101* (1955), and *City of Fear* (1959). In the aftermath of the Soviet Union's detonation of an atomic device in 1949, President Harry Truman's instruction to the Atomic Energy Commission (AEC) to develop a hydrogen bomb in 1950, and the inception of atomic testing in the continental United States in 1951, 1952 became the "catalytic year of the 'atom spy film.'"[20] Russell Rouse's *The Thief*, starring Ray Milland as a nuclear physicist who works at the AEC, represents a dynamic fusion—like *D.O.A.*, which was co-scripted by Rouse—of realism and expressionism. Although the studio's promotional material is slightly hyperbolic ("THE ONLY MOTION PICTURE OF ITS KIND—Not a word is spoken . . . !"), the absence of dialogue in *The Thief* brilliantly mimes both the film's audiovisual registers and the utter alienation of its protagonist, Dr. Allan Fields.

A formally audacious film, *The Thief* also departs from classical Hollywood cinema in that there is no obvious motivation for Fields's treasonous behavior. The poster for the film features a stereotypical noir scenario: in the left "white" panel, a dark-haired woman seductively lounges, legs wide open, on a bed; in the right "black" panel, a slouch-hatted Fields appears to be gazing at the woman, a cigarette dangling from his lip, a flaming match poised in midair. However, since Fields never reciprocates the raven-haired woman's blatant interest, his sexual identity remains as mysterious as his motivation. In *Film Noir Guide*, Michael F. Keaney comments: "Why this film is called *The Thief* instead of *The Traitor* or *The Spy* is as big a mystery as why it was filmed without dialogue."[21] Question: is it possible that, in addition to referencing Fields's theft of top-secret government documents, the title is an oblique allusion to Jean Genet's *The Thief's Journal* (1949)? Additionally, is it possible that the Soviet agents are using Fields's sexual orientation to blackmail him? Regardless of how one answers these questions, the mystery at the heart of *The Thief* reflects the way national security discourses in the 1950s exploited Americans' fear of the Other, whether that Other was a Martian, a communist, or a homosexual.

While *The Thief* is set in the East—New York City and Washington, D.C.—another "atomic espionage noir," *The Atomic City*, is set in the Southwest—specifically, Los Alamos, New Mexico. The fact that *The Atomic City* is about a family as opposed to, as in *The Thief*, a single individual (Fields has no discernible family or circle of friends) renders Jerry Hopper's film an "exemplary site for cultural and ideological analysis due to its deliberate infusion of documentary realism with traditional family melodrama."[22] As in another "state-sanctioned" picture, *Walk East on Beacon!*, the semidocumentary elements of *The Atomic City* are apparent in the FBI's active involvement in the film's production and, as in Werker's film, the melodrama centers on communist agents who have kidnapped a scientist's son in order to blackmail him into betraying atomic secrets.

Yet in contradistinction to the East Coast noirs *The Thief* and *Walk East on Beacon!*, *The Atomic City* makes full use of its Los Alamos setting to mobilize the rhetoric of the Western. This "cowboys and Indians" motif surfaces when, in order to find out where his son Tommy (Lee Aaker) has been hidden, Dr. Frank Addison (Gene Barry) beats up a suspect whom the FBI has taken into custody, thereby becoming a "cowboy." It arises again when, in the film's climactic sequence, the Feds discover that the Reds are holding Tommy in the Puye ruins of New Mexico. Since the Reds in *The Atomic City* are disguised as park rangers and therefore coded as Feds, the figuration of the kidnappers as "Indians" speaks volumes about the highly charged, constellatory character of communists in the 1950s.

Similarly, Dr. Addison's coding as a cowboy points up the vexed, problematic status of scientists in the atomic age as "savior-detectives" and Dr. Frankensteins.[23] Accordingly, one of the many ironies of *The Atomic City* is that despite the fact that Dr. Addison is not a rogue scientist like Allan Fields in *The Thief*, he's still imprisoned at the center of a vortex of conflicting discourses—the cold-blooded, murderous demands of the communists, the almost equally cold-blooded, institutional imperatives of the FBI and, last but decidedly least (from the perspective of the national security state), the veritable but subordinate claims of the nuclear family.

Unlike *D.O.A.*, *The Thief*, *The Atomic City*, and *Pickup on South Street*, all of which appeared between 1950 and 1953 and were produced or distributed by, respectively, United Artists, Paramount, and Twentieth Century-Fox, *Shack Out on 101* released in 1955 and distributed by Allied Artists. The year 1955 has commonly been seen to mark both the beginning of the end of classic noir and the beginning of the "exploitation era," the second, post–"classical double bill" phase of the B picture, which vanished not simply because of economic reasons but social reasons as well: "The upward social mobility of the 1950s and the transition of the dominant social group in America to middle and upper middle class coincided with the end of the conventional double bill."[24]

When the Poverty Row studio Monogram metamorphosed into Allied Artists in 1953, Allied Artists was attempting to compete in the "temporarily more open feature film market" (the province of the A or "adult" picture) at the same time that it pursued the "newly emergent and younger market for exploitation films."[25] This A/B strategy was itself a response to the "Korea-A bomb-McCarthy era," which, "as much as anything else," drove the audience inside to watch television—for example, the 1954 Army-McCarthy Senate hearings.[26]

In *The Eighteenth Brumaire of Louis Bonaparte*, Karl Marx famously wrote, tweaking Hegel, that history repeats itself—"the first time as tragedy, the second time as farce."[27] Although *Shack Out on 101* has been described as a "bizarre mix of Clifford Odets 'realism' and hysterical McCarthy-era red baiting,"[28] Edward Dein's film, like McCarthy's performance in the 1954 Senate hearings, is more farcical than not. The vanishing mediator here is Frank Lovejoy, who appeared in both *I Was a Communist for the F.B.I.* and *Shack Out on 101*. But if *I Was a Communist for the F.B.I.* is played for tragedy or, at least, melodrama, *Shack Out on 101* is played mostly for laughs. (See, for example, the truly kooky body-building scene that features the diner's owner, George Bater [Keenan Wynn], and his short-order cook, Slob, aka Leo, aka Mr. Gregory [Lee Marvin].)

In *Shack Out on 101* Lovejoy's character, Professor Sam Bastion, is a nuclear physicist who's selling secret formulas to Slob, an apparatchik (his confederate's name is Perch [Len Lesser]), who's desperate to be a big fish in the party. What neither Slob nor the other habitués of the shack realize is that Sam, like Professor Kafer (Finlay Currie) in *Walk East on Beacon!*, is working undercover for the FBI. That the "red" angle is patently bait is demonstrated by the fact that Terry Moore, not Lovejoy, received top billing in the publicity for *Shack Out on 101*. Moore's "bombshell" sexuality is foregrounded in the film's first, "exploitative" sequence, in which her character, Kotty, is lying out on a California beach in a bikini. In other words, the atomic anticommunist plot can be seen, as in *D.O.A.*, as a screen for a searching rumination on gender and sexuality—in particular, masculinity—in postwar, mid-century America.

However, just as the historical subtext of *Shack Out on 101* is not Korea but World War II, the axial character in the film is not Kotty or Sam, George or Slob, but Eddie (Whit Bissell), a traveling salesman still suffering from D-Day-induced posttraumatic stress syndrome. Although the most pungent metaphor in *Shack Out on 101* conjures a red planet overrun by apes, the film's prevailing conceit is distinctly piscine: can Eddie overcome his disabling anxiety about bloodshed to spear not a trophy like the sailfish hung on the wall of George's shack but a communist masquerading as a cook, a fishy she-man?

City of Fear, directed by Irving Lerner and released in 1959 at the butt end of the classic noir cycle, circles back to the existential thematics of *D.O.A.* by way of the escaped con-on-the-lam premise of another atomic noir, *Split Second* (1953). As in *Split Second*, two men, Vince Ryker and a prison buddy, have escaped from a penitentiary. But whereas Sam Hurley (Stephen McNally) in *Split Second* jacks a couple of cars and takes the passengers hostage, in *City of Fear* Ryker, having already stolen an ambulance, forces a car off the road and then torches it with the driver's body inside. Furthermore, whereas Hurley, befitting an old-school gangster, has a soft spot for his seriously wounded partner, the body of Ryker's partner is later discovered inside the burned-out car.

City of Fear's resemblance to *D.O.A.* is by turns proximate and distant: in *D.O.A.* Bigelow's death-in-life is the result of an "atomic cocktail" that's spiked with iridium; in *City of Fear* Ryder is fatally contaminated by a canister full of Cobalt-60, a radioactive substance that prison authorities have been using to test "volunteers." (The inmates have been told it's heroin.) In addition to this rich allusiveness (compare, for example, the Nazi-experimental subplot of *The Whip Hand* or the atomic-narcotic subtext in *Pickup on South Street* and *Kiss Me Deadly*), *City of Fear* is distinguished by a stark black-and-white tele-cinematic style—it's not for nothing that Ryker is played by Vince Edwards, who's best remembered today as a '60s TV star—and its pre-counterculture critique of '50s carceral society.

Lerner deftly employs a "parallel structure of twin threats"—Ryker and the radioactive canister—that locates the real criminality not in the hoodlum Vince but in institutions such as the state, the police, and the federal government that "enable the nuclear threat."[29] If *City of Fear* is the B side of the more socially con-scious *Odds against Tomorrow* (unlike Robert Wise's film, it ends not with a bang but a whimper), at eighty minutes and photographed on the fly on the glamour-free streets of Los Angeles, it's reminiscent of the bottom-of-the-bill pictures that ostensibly disappeared in the wake of the 1948 Paramount "divorcement."

In the final, breakout chapter of Part Two, "*Kiss Me Deadly:* The X Factor, or The 'Great Whatsit,'" I turn my attention to one of the most heralded and dissected films in the classic noir canon, *Kiss Me Deadly* (1955). One reason for the film's extraordinary reputation is that it has been viewed as detonating the hard-boiled, private-eye tradition exemplified by John Huston's *Maltese Falcon*. (The sexed-up, violence-addicted character of Mike Hammer derives from the sensational series of Mickey Spillane novels published in the late 1940s and early 1950s.) Another reason that *Kiss Me Deadly* has remained so canonical is that the film's ending—"a dirty bomb *avant la lettre*"—metaphorically spells the "end of 'classic' noir" even as it serves up the "secularized doomsday of techné."[30]

Aldrich himself has talked about the picture's "hard-hitting, short-cut, staccato" style,[31] though the most striking aspect of *Kiss Me Deadly*'s audiovisual rhetoric is the recurring X figure. In the classic detective narrative, motored as it is by the protagonist's desire to plumb the mystery, the narrative is a romance quest and the detective is Galahad. In *Kiss Me Deadly* Hammer is an anti-Galahad and the X signifies the mysterious object that everyone in the film appears to be searching for, what Hammer's secretary, Velda (Maxine Cooper), calls—not without sarcasm—the "Great Whatsit." In the end, the Great Whatsit turns out to be a strongbox, hidden inside of which is some form of atomic matter, itself figured by blinding white light. In *D.O.A.* Bigelow's sexuality is placed under the repressive sign of radioactivity. In *Kiss Me Deadly*, by contrast, the hot "Pandora's box" is associated not simply with mass destruction but female sexuality, a conceit that explosively reconfigures '50s anxieties about the sort of bombshell femininity signified by Terry Moore and Marilyn Monroe.

In Part Three of *The Red and the Black*, "New Media and Technologies," I turn my attention to the impact of color film stock on '50s noir as well as another new technology that the motion picture industry adopted, like widescreen and stereophonic sound, to combat the increasing influence of television: 3-D. As I remark at the end of my discussion of *Walk East on Beacon!* in Part One, it seems strange, narratively speaking, that a "red" character's relationship to the Communist Party should turn on his job at Eastman Kodak and the secret of color emulsion. However, for the motion picture industry in the early 1950s, color technology was one answer, like CinemaScope and 3-D, to the problem of declining movie attendance. If the Paramount decision of 1948 is a well-known landmark, less well known is the consent decree that Eastman Kodak signed with Technicolor in 1950, in which Eastman would "license all its patents on the open market, with no priority given to Technicolor."[32] On the minus side, the decree spelled the end to the "glorious era" of Technicolor: "In 1947, 90 percent of 35mm color was Technicolor; ten years later, the firm met only half the industry's color needs."[33] On the plus side, the introduction of Eastmancolor, a single-film "color process that did not need a special camera" like Technicolor,[34] precipitated the production of color motion pictures across a wide spectrum of genres.

The opening chapter of Part Three, *"Noir en couleur*: Color and Widescreen," surveys four '50s color noirs: *Black Widow* (1954), *House of Bamboo* (1955), *Slightly Scarlet* (1956), and *A Kiss before Dying* (1956). A widescreen whodunit, *Black Widow* illustrates the transitional character of color noir in the first, tumultuous part of the 1950s. While Gene Tierney appears in a supporting role in the film as the wife of the narrator-protagonist Peter Denver (Van Heflin), she represents an important link between *the* color noir of the 1940s, *Leave Her to Heaven* (1945), and '50s color noir. *Black Widow*, like *Leave Her to Heaven*, is based on a literary property—Patrick Quentin's 1952 novel of the same name—and references one of the most popular incarnations of the femme fatale, the black widow. Despite the fact that *Black Widow* remains in retrospect something of a compromise formation (reflected in the casting of George Raft and Ginger Rogers), the filmmakers' endeavor to use DeLuxe color and CinemaScope to infuse life into a subgenre, the "murder mystery," that was itself becoming antiquated in the late 1930s is nonetheless illustrative and points to the potential of both widescreen and color film stock.

House of Bamboo, like *Black Widow*, was made at Twentieth Century-Fox and was shot in CinemaScope with DeLuxe color and four-track stereo. The resemblance ends there, however. Whereas *Black Widow* is straitjacketed by its fusty, formulaic plot and polite, drawing-room cinematography—with respect to the latter, Charles G. Clarke once opined, "There are two kinds of cinematographers, those who know and those who put on a show"—*House of Bamboo*, directed by Sam Fuller and Bausch + Lomb–lensed by Joe MacDonald, puts on a show and is a motion picture that, true to Darryl Zanuck's 1953 promise about CinemaScope, *moves*.[35] In addition, *House of Bamboo* is a riot of primary colors and characterized by, in contrast to the prototypical saturnine tonalities of classic noir, bright, high-key lighting.

Although the film's DNA can be traced to its source material, William Keighley's *The Street with No Name* (1948), *House of Bamboo* is a gangster noir that roughly trades on Fuller's go-to genre, the war film. The protagonist Eddie Spanier/Kenner (Robert Stack) is an army policeman who "acts like a gangster," while the expat gang headed by ex-army, "five-star general" Sandy Dawson (Robert Ryan) "behaves like the Army."[36] If *House of Bamboo* samples the war, noir, and gangster genres, it also broaches the element of romance, per Zanuck's wishes, in the form of not one but two romantic subplots. The first, explicit, as well as forbidden love story is between Kenner and Mariko (Shirley Yamaguchi), the secret widow of a former member of Dawson's crew, Webber (Biff Elliot), who was executed—on Dawson's orders—when he was wounded in combat. The second, covert, and even more forbidden love story is between Eddie and Sandy (note the latter's gender-ambiguous name), a homosexual subtext that can be said to trump the film's manifest heterosexual romance narrative.

The climax of *House of Bamboo*, not to mention the bad blood between Kenner and Dawson, is played out on a Saturn-shaped ride that consists of a "central globe surrounded by a horizontal, ring-like walkway" that rotates in the opposite direction of the slowly revolving globe.[37] This "whirligig," as Fuller refers to it in his chapter on *House of Bamboo* in *A Third Face*, becomes the main "element within the CinemaScope frame," offering as it does ample "potential for dynamic graphic play."[38] Whereas the walkway highlights the horizontality of Japanese landscape and architecture as well as the wideness of the motion picture screen, the opposing motions of the ring and globe dramatize the antagonism between the previously obscured relations between Dawson's gang and the forces of law and order. The fact that Kenner and Dawson are playing a deadly game of hide and seek on the roof of the Matsuma department store focalizes, moreover, the corrupting influence of the postwar American occupation of Japan, as if—and here the globe imagery actively comes into play[39]—the United States in all its newly acquired, hegemonic power were itself a character, "the ugly American."

In this imperial context, the conclusion of *House of Bamboo*, in which the uniformed Eddie and kimonoed Mariko can be seen strolling in the ornamental gardens toward a pagoda in the distance, may appear to be a sentimental sop thrown to both the studio and the American, if not Japanese, audience. However, not only was *House of Bamboo* the first Hollywood feature film to be shot on location in Japan, but the interracial romance between the gaijin detective and the "kimono girl" was considered strictly taboo in 1955. "In those rare films with interracial couples," as Fuller observes in "Cherry Blossoms and Whirligigs," "the ending was usually tragic."[40] In *House of Bamboo* the lovers—or, as the director puts it, employing the possessive pronoun, "*my* lovers"—meet a different, rather more beneficent fate: a genuinely happy ending.[41]

If the potentiality of "noir in color" promised by *Black Widow* is expressively realized in *House of Bamboo*, it's spectacularly exceeded in Alan Dwan's *Slightly Scarlet*, which was photographed by noir maestro John Alton. During his "periodic vacations from M-G-M during the mid-1950s," Alton worked on a series of films with Dwan at RKO.[42] (Production on *Slightly Scarlet* began the same day—July 18, 1955—that General Teleradio purchased RKO from Howard Hughes, terminating his disastrous tenure.[43]) In *Painting with Light* (1949) Alton wrote that the "most beautiful photography is in low key, with rich blacks."[44] Alton had previously been criticized for his aggressive, uncompromising manner (he quit the American Society of Cinematographers in 1944), but his painterly style fits the melo-noir gangster picture *Slightly Scarlet* like a glove. In fact, *Slightly Scarlet*—"a gangster film that challenged the restrictions of the Production Code . . . by absorbing elements of the adult melodrama"[45]—is a provocative synthesis of melodrama and dark crime film. The melodramatic strain is conveyed via two sisters—one "good," June Lyons (Rhonda Fleming), one "bad," Dorothy (Arlene Dahl)—whose "red heads" visually deflect the attention away from the presumptive male protagonist, Ben Grace (John Payne), and toward the more than "slightly scarlet" sister, "Dor," whose outlaw femininity flaunts the social roles proscribed for women in the mystique-ridden 1950s.

Like *Slightly Scarlet*, Gerd Oswald's *A Kiss before Dying* features two sisters, but unlike the Lyons sisters, Dorothy (Joanne Woodward) and Ellen Kingship (Virginia Leith) are "good girls," "daughters and sole heirs of a copper magnate."[46] Femmes fatales, of course, are a staple of classic film noir, although the absence of a "bad girl" in *A Kiss before Dying* is more than made up for by the lethally charming Bud Corliss (Robert Wagner), who romances "Dorrie," then, after giving her the big kiss-off (in a startling sequence that foreshadows *Vertigo* [1958]), ensnares Ellen. In *American Film Noir* Robert Ottoson states that *A Kiss before Dying* employs a "familiar noir device—the unscrupulous male who will marry and/or kill for wealth" and, therefore, is a "film noir by virtue of its theme more than its stylistics."[47]

It's true that Bud Corliss is a classic homme fatal, but the character's charisma arguably has more to do with the film's widescreen CinemaScope compositions and ravishing array of warm and cool colors (Bud, naturally, is associated with aquamarine blues). As supervised by Lucien Ballard, the film's "prevailing aesthetic"—"detached, medium-length two-shots"—all but precludes "viewer identification" and "emotional involvement,"[48] a perspective that effectively aligns us with Bud's "cool," acquisitive point of view. (It's not insignificant that Bud's aspirational class fantasies represent a compelling, if twisted, version of the American dream.)

Shot in Twentieth Century-Fox DeLuxe color in and around Tucson, Arizona, the film's desert setting contributes, as in *Leave Her to Heaven*, to its chromaticism so that the oranges and reds "appear even more infernal than they might in a metropolitan setting."[49] The key color, however, is not orange or red but copper, the net effect of which emphasis is that the palette of *A Kiss before Dying* can be said to conspire with Bud's scheme to marry his way by hook or by crook into the Kingship copper fortune. In *Black Widow* Ginger Rogers's character appears to be the femme fatale by default; in *A Kiss before Dying* Bud Corliss is a real homme fatal, the spider-man at the center of a copper-colored web of his own deviously ingenious making.

Gerd Oswald was assistant director on *Niagara* (1953), so it should come as no surprise that Henry Hathaway's transnational color noir, the subject of chapter 8, anticipates *Vertigo* even more so than *A Kiss before Dying*. While Hathaway established his reputation in film noir as a "master of location" in semidocumentaries such as *The House on 92nd Street* (1945) and *Call Northside 777* (1948), Joe MacDonald's extraordinary location shooting in Niagara Falls (on both the American and Canadian sides) betrays Hathaway's continuing fascination with documentary-style neorealism.[50] In *Niagara* Hathaway not only "recruits the icon of the falls themselves" but also enlists another "natural wonder," Marilyn Monroe, then a rising star at Twentieth Century-Fox.[51]

Color psychological thrillers like *Leave Her to Heaven* notwithstanding, film noir in 1945 was wedded to black-and-white, a practice reiterated in the genre's stereotypical, black-and-white representation of women as either "good" or "bad girls," femmes fatales or domestic goddesses. By 1953, though, color was beginning to displace monochrome in the motion picture industry even as the Kinsey Report was challenging prevailing attitudes about female fantasy and sexuality. In *Niagara* the red-letter character of Rose Loomis is ultimately in dramatic tension with Monroe's star persona, whose eroticism has more in common with life—as the word "eros" suggests—than death. In fact, Monroe's hot-pink dress in the celebrated, popular-song sequence "Kiss" suggests that her character is not quite as monochromatic as she appears; that Rose Loomis, inflected by Monroe's persona—an arresting combination of vulnerability and self-possession—represents the colorful evolution of the femme fatale in the 1950s.

3-D, like color, is a component of the late, classical period of film noir. In an effort to capitalize on this new technology, 3-D noirs were set in exotic locales (*Second Chance* [1953]) or amusement parks (*Man in the Dark* [1953]). Set in the then "exotic" world of live TV and revolving around the production of a true-crime television show called "Crime of the Week," *The Glass Web* appeared in 1953, the annus mirabilis of 3-D movies. But as Ray Zone comments about *The Glass Web* in "Deep Black and White," "It's paradoxical to see a 3-D movie about television, which by 1953 had . . . diminished the motion picture audience and was the most compelling reason why the studios had decided to make 3-D films in the first place."[52]

This particular paradox illuminates the contradictory character of classic noir in the early 1950s. For example, although Jack Arnold, the director of *The Glass Web*, began his career in the U.S. Army Signal Corps as an assistant cameraman for famed documentary filmmaker Robert Flaherty, his film owes less to semidocumentary noirs such as *The Naked City* (1948) than to TV series such as *Dragnet* (NBC, 1951–1959). Thus, despite certain expressionist passages in 3-D, the visual style of *The Glass Web* tends toward the "zero degree," reflecting the postwar trend toward television and neorealism. At the same time, the iconic presence of Edward G. Robinson, who plays exacting production researcher Henry Hayes in Arnold's film and whose performance echoes his star turn as Barton Keyes in *Double Indemnity* (1944), benefits from its belatedness via-à-vis '40s noir.

The same might be said of model/actress Paula Ranier, with whom both Henry and his arch-enemy, the show's writer Don Newell (John Forsythe), are inextricably involved. As the putative femme fatale, Paula is—to quote the film's publicity—"bad, beautiful, and bold as sin." Played by "3-D girl" Kathleen Hughes, she also gets all the best angles, as in the de rigueur scene where she puts on her nylon stockings, "the precise adjustment of the point of convergence projecting her shapely legs perfectly out of the screen."[53] Of such scopic pleasures are 3-D movies made.

And yet, as in *A Kiss before Dying* and despite the above "classical" scopophilia, the spider in *The Glass Web* is not a femme but a homme. In a postmodern twist, Henry lures his prey to a broadcast studio where the spider-man himself becomes the object of the televisual gaze when his confession is unwittingly broadcast live to another studio. The LAPD detective watching there spells the end of Henry's story and punctuates his Pirandellian fate: a '40s noir character lost in a '50s 3-D/TV world.

As I noted in the preface, there has been considerable debate about the demise or fall of classic American noir. In the conclusion to *The Red and the Black*, I propose that Samuel Fuller's *Crimson Kimono* is, like *Touch of Evil* and *Odds against Tomorrow*, a critical late '50s noir. As opposed to Fuller's *House of Bamboo*, which is set in Japan and composed in color and CinemaScope, *The Crimson Kimono*, which is shot in black-and-white and set in the "robust community" of Little Tokyo, is part *policier*, part melodrama.[54] In fact, in *The Crimson Kimono*, the director, deploying the sort of self-reflexive devices associated with Douglas Sirk's '50s melodramas, "destroys the limits of the crime picture."[55]

The Crimson Kimono is about two detectives—Det. Sgt. Charlie Bancroft (Glenn Corbett) and Det. Joe Kojaku (James Shigeta)—who fall for the same woman, Christine Downes (Victoria Shaw). The melodramatic twist, according to Fuller, is that "one of the detectives is white and the other is a Nisei, a Japanese American. . . . The girl goes for the Nisei cop, not the white one."[56] Fuller's trademark "sensational" style is extravagantly on display in the climactic sequence of *The Crimson Kimono* in the startling cutaways to a series of black theatrical masks. Here, Fuller's film foregrounds the black-and-white moral calculus of melodrama even as it italicizes the racial difference that has been a part, however occluded, of the history of "black film." Equally or more importantly, by refiguring Kojaku as the "hero" of the narrative who solves the case *and* "gets the girl,"[57] *The Crimson Kimono* refashions one of the constitutive tropes of the genre, the "Shanghai gesture,"[58] a trope that can be traced back to *The Maltese Falcon* and the origins of classic film noir itself.

PART ONE

'50S NOIR AND ANTICOMMUNISM

I had to sell out my own girl—SO WOULD YOU!

I was under the toughest orders a guy could get! I stood by and watched my brother slugged . . . I started a riot that ran red with terror . . . I learned every dirty rule in their book—and had to use them—**because I was a communist**—but "**I WAS A COMMUNIST FOR THE F.B.I.**"

—Warner Bros. publicity for *I Was a Communist for the F.B.I.*

I *was* mad. I *was* a killer and *was* looking forward to killing . . . every one of them from bottom to top and especially the one at the top even if I had to go to the Kremlin to do it. The time for that wouldn't be now. . . . But some day, maybe, some day I'd stand on the steps of the Kremlin with a gun in my fist and I'd yell for them to come out and if they wouldn't I'd go in and get them and when I had lined them up against the wall I'd start shooting until all I had left was a row of corpses that bled on the cold floors and in whose thick red blood would be the promise of a peace that would stick for more generations than I'd live to see.

—Mickey Spillane, *One Lonely Night*

1

THE WOMAN ON PIER 13

I MARRIED A COMMUNIST!

> The political agents of the Kremlin abroad
> continue to beat out the feminist drums in full
> awareness of its disruptive influence among the
> potential enemies of the Soviet Union.
>
> —Ferdinand Lundberg and Marynia F. Farnham,
>   *Modern Woman: The Lost Sex*

In the wake of the 1947 investigation of communist infiltration of the motion picture industry by the House Committee on Un-American Activities, a series of anticommunist films began to appear in the United States. Although a cycle of silent pictures had appeared in 1919 and 1920 that "painted in lurid colors the threat posed by Bolshevism,"[1] the anticommunist pictures produced by Hollywood in the late 1940s and early 1950s are those that have become associated in the public imagination, like some Pavlovian reflex, with the "red menace."

A subset of this second cycle of "red scare" films includes a number of noir-inflected features such as *Walk a Crooked Mile* (1948); *I Married a Communist*, aka *The Woman on Pier 13* (1949/1950); *I Was a Communist for the F.B.I.* (1951); *The Whip Hand* (1951); *Big Jim McLain* (1952); and *Walk East on Beacon!* (1952). Since these films tended to be made "on the cheap," they have been derogated by critics for their aesthetic quality. Since they appeared to promote a right-wing agenda unlike left, progressive pre-1948 noir, they have also been excoriated for their politics. In a word, these anticommunist films are—to invoke Daniel Leab's verdict on *I Married a Communist*—"awful."[2]

In the following chapter, I employ *The Woman on Pier 13* as a privileged example of anticommunist film noir in order to explore the received left critique of the ideological and aesthetic properties of this subgenre—what one might call the unhappy marriage between film noir and anticommunism—as well as to demonstrate how the discourse of anticommunism is intimately related, via the metaphor of marriage, to issues of gender and sexuality.

Section 1, "Production: 'Paint It,'" examines the production history of *The Woman on Pier 13* to highlight the ideological mutability of the film's ostensible right-wing agenda, one actively endorsed by RKO's head of production at the time, Howard Hughes.

Section 2, "Photography: Paint It Black," aims to counter the claim that the anticommunist noir is without aesthetic—that is to say, audiovisual—interest by proffering a close textual analysis of a number of classic noir sequences in *The Woman on Pier 13*. This analysis reveals the structural similarity between the quintessential RKO noir, *Out of the Past* (1947), and *The Woman on Pier 13*, both of which were photographed by Nicholas Musuraca. It suggests, moreover, that the melodramatic aspect of *The Woman on Pier 13*'s dual, hybrid status as a melo-noir—one part thriller, one part "woman's picture"—can be read, not unlike *Out of the Past*, as a masque or allegory of the persecutory character of the anticommunist witch hunt.

Section 3, "Criss Cross," argues that—as the film's original title, *I Married a Communist*, indexes—the political discourse of anticommunism cannot be divorced from contemporary sociocultural notions about marriage, notions that receive their most charged expression in the film's figuration of femininity (the femme fatale) and homosexuality (the queer commie).

Section 4, "Paint It Red," revisits the issue of form—here, mise-en-scène—by exploring the figure of the cargo hook and the role of Diego Rivera's painting *The Flower Carrier* (1935) in *The Woman on Pier 13*. As reiterated in the coda, the mini-narrative of *The Flower Carrier* reflects the larger story of *The Woman on Pier 13*, a motion picture that arguably turns not so much on the men—whether commie boss or "bad boy"—as the women: the "bad blonde" and the "good wife." In fine, just as *The Flower Carrier* illustrates the ideological ambiguity of *The Woman on Pier 13*, so too a stereophonic sense of the film's libidinal economy intimates that the marriage between film noir and anticommunism—like that between film noir and melodrama—is stranger and richer than previously imagined, revealing not simply the changing contours of classic noir in the early 1950s but, among other things, the emergence of the "feminine mystique" in mid-century America.

PRODUCTION: "PAINT IT"

When reexamining the anticommunist noir cycle, there's no better place to start than *I Married a Communist*/*The Woman on Pier 13* (1949/1950). The dual title and release date reflect the complicated history surrounding the film's production.

Melo-Noir: Title card picturing, from left to right, Nan Collins (Laraine Day), Brad Collins (Robert Ryan), and Christine Norman (Janis Carter) in *The Woman on Pier 13*, aka *I Married a Communist*. Note, on the far right, the scenic depiction of the communists' waterfront killing of Ralston (Paul Guilfoyle).

RKO purchased the original title—a sensational one, to be sure—from Eagle Lion Pictures in 1948, but it was changed to *The Woman on Pier 13* after sneak previews in late 1949 in San Francisco and Los Angeles. But perhaps the first thing that needs to be said about *The Woman on Pier 13* is that it was a Howard Hughes production—a pet project, like the infamous *Jet Pilot* (1957).

In May 1948 Hughes bought Floyd Odlum's shares of RKO stock and thereby assumed controlling interest in the studio. Determined to publicize the coup in the Hollywood trade papers but unable to buy the *Hollywood Reporter*, Hughes personally selected William Feeder for an exclusive interview, asking him at the conclusion of their meeting, "I hear Dore Schary is a Communist. Is he?" Not surprisingly, Schary, the famously liberal-minded head of production who had made the acclaimed social problem film *Crossfire* (1947), was gone from RKO by July, and by the end of 1948 "more than half the employees [at RKO] had either left or been laid off, production was down to a handful of projects, and losses were estimated in the millions."[3]

One of the most scandalous stories related to Hughes's tenure at RKO was that, ensconced as usual at the Samuel Goldwyn Studios, he set foot inside his new fiefdom only once: after spending two hours with his entourage inspecting "every sound stage and construction shop," his only comment was "Paint it."[4] Another, rather more notorious story is that the avidly anticommunist Hughes used the screenplay of *The Woman on Pier 13* as a loyalty test for directors. As Joseph Losey, the first but by no means the last director to turn down the project (there were supposedly thirteen in all), recalled, "You offered *I Married a Communist* to anybody you thought was a Communist, and if they turned it down, they were."[5] The same litmus test was allegedly used on screenwriters. Daniel Mainwaring, who had scripted Losey's *The Lawless* (1950) in addition to *Out of the Past*, "stalled" after he was approached by the studio to polish the dialogue of *I Married a Communist*. "That was the end of me," he remembered. "As soon as my option went, I went."[6]

Although the situation at RKO under the erratic Hughes was no doubt grim, it was not quite as black-and-white as Losey's and Mainwaring's remarks suggest. For example, Nicholas Ray refused to direct *I Married a Communist* but managed to survive at RKO as well as the HUAC investigations. "Why did this refusal not cost Ray his career?"[7] Ray's biographer, Bernard Eisenschitz, concludes that "Hughes did indeed protect Ray after his refusal to direct *I Married a Communist*, keeping him at the studio and extending his contract. That protection was tantamount to saving him from the blacklist."[8]

While Hughes's motives vis-à-vis Ray remain something of a mystery, *The Woman on Pier 13* was eventually helmed by Robert Stevenson, who displayed a "Curtiz-like versatility" in Britain in the 1930s and Hollywood in the 1940s before becoming the house director at Disney from the mid-1950s until the 1970s.[9] The remainder of the film's personnel are associated with classic RKO and include Jack Gross (producer), Nicholas Musuraca (cinematography), Leigh Harline (music), Albert S. D'Agostino (art direction), Darrell Silvera (set decoration), and Phil Brigandi and Clem Portman (sound). As for the cast, the film features Robert Ryan, a key figure in classic American noir for over a decade from *Crossfire* to *Odds against Tomorrow* (1959); Laraine Day, most memorable for her performance as Nancy Blair in *The Locket* (1946); Janis Carter, femme fatale Jill Merrill in *Night Editor* (1946) and Paula Craig in *Framed* (1947); Thomas Gomez, an important supporting player in numerous noirs such as *Phantom Lady* (1944), *Ride the Pink Horse* (1947), *Key Largo* (1948), and *Force of Evil* (1949); John Agar, who appeared in *Shield for Murder* (1954) as well as the super-B, Hugo Haas–directed *Bait* (1954) and *Hold Back Tomorrow* (1955); and William Talman, usually a "heavy," as in *Armored Car Robbery* (1950), *City That Never Sleeps* (1953), and *The Hitch-Hiker* (1953).

Robert Ottoson's appraisal of *The Woman on Pier 13* in *American Film Noir* is typical of the "noir" response to the film: "The clear gangster-noir iconography in the depiction of Communist agents—Gomez and his associates wear trench coats, dangle cigarettes from their mouths, and meet in dark, dimly lit waterfront hideouts—is virtually the only thing of value to look at for those interested in the film noir."[10] In "Anti-Communist Film Noir" Peter Lev is even more dismissive: "*I Married a Communist . . .* could be considered a film noir because of its dark images and crime-film plot. It is, however, thoroughly undistinguished in visual style."[11] Lev's estimation of the film earlier in the same chapter insinuates that the issue is not merely aesthetics: "Aside from connecting communists with union corruption, *I Married a Communist* has absolutely nothing to say about Communist ideas or values."[12] Question: is it possible that Lev's categorical judgment of *I Married a Communist* is an alibi for his real criticism—that the film is visually "undistinguished" because it is politically reprehensible?

While such a response might be understandable in the context of the HUAC hearings, what Dalton Trumbo called, invoking Émile Zola, the "Time of the Toad,"[13] a more dialectical perspective—one that attempts to do justice to both the film's textual complexity and cultural-political conditions of possibility—is, I think, available today. A good model here is Philip Kemp's reading of RKO's *Where Danger Lives* (1950) in "From the Nightmare Factory: HUAC and the Politics of Noir." John Farrow's film is "intriguing," according to Kemp, first, "because it can be read, without any strain on the text, as a dramatic exposition of the Marxist dictum ['the bourgeoisie . . . has resolved personal worth into exchange value']" and, second, "because it was almost certainly never intended as any such thing."[14]

Kemp's reading is particularly tonic in part because it foregrounds the issue of intentionality. In other words, Hughes may have intended *I Married a Communist* as the "first volley in [his] personal war on Communism,"[15] but that executive intention was *mediated* by the production process at RKO, which, like that at any major studio, was complex at best and tortured at worst. (In this particular case, the operative word is "tortured.") The evolution of the screenplay is symptomatic of this production process.[16] For example, Art Cohn, who had previously adapted Joseph Moncure March's verse narrative about an African American boxer for the now canonical noir *The Set-Up* (1949),[17] was paired with James Edward Grant, who had scripted a number of minor noirs such as *Johnny Eager* (1941), *Johnny Allegro* (1949), and *Two of a Kind* (1951) before penning one of the most flagrant anticommunist films, *Big Jim McLain*. Herman Mankiewicz—the scenarist, together with Orson Welles, of *Citizen Kane* (1941)—also worked on the screenplay of *I Married a Communist*,[18] having been hired on the recommendation of Nicholas Ray when he was attached to the project.

On a more micro level, in the published version of the screenplay—the "second revised final draft"—the leader of the communist cell is named Nixon. (In the film it's Vanning.) As the director of public relations for the Pacific American Steamship Association (PASA), to whom RKO submitted characters' names for clearance, reported, "If your central character is to bear the name of Nixon and if you are portraying him as a communist, you might be in for a ribbing in view of the identical name of the Congressman from your own district who introduced into the 80th Congress a bill controlling the red brethren."[19] The bill that the director of PASA is referring to is the Internal Security Act, the so-called McCarran Act (1950)—"the most important anti-communist law passed during the cold war"—which was first proposed by Richard M. Nixon in 1948 and "which was designed to eliminate the Communist threat by forcing the Party, its members, and its front groups to register with the government."[20] One can only speculate about the intent behind the use of Nixon's name for the communist boss in *The Woman on Pier 13*, but I think it's safe to say that Richard Nixon would *not* have been amused.

Finally, in light of Kemp's reading, it's noteworthy that "Where Danger Lives" was reportedly one of a hundred titles that Hughes considered in his quixotic quest to remarket *I Married a Communist*. Others that the studio entertained in its attempt to resolve the seemingly intractable issues with the script—"low-budget melodrama vs. communist propaganda"[21]—involved anagrammatic shuffling of the words "midnight," "melodrama," and "San Francisco," as in "Waterfront at Midnight" and "San Francisco Melodrama." While the resemblance between *Where Danger Lives* and *The Woman on Pier 13* is more titular than not, both films share some of the same creative personnel, the most important of whom is Musuraca, whose impact on noir cinematography is arguably second only to that of John Alton. In fact, James Naremore's characterization of Musuraca's photography in *Out of the Past* as a "lyrical or sensuous play of shadow" as well as "low-key, deeply romantic 'painting with light'" (the reference is to Alton's seminal textbook, *Painting with Light*[22])—can be profitably applied to *The Woman on Pier 13*. And, one might add, "without any strain on the text."

PHOTOGRAPHY: PAINT IT BLACK

By way of illustration and to counter Ottoson's and Lev's critiques of *The Woman on Pier 13*, four sequences in the picture demonstrate its very real visual interest. The film opens with Brad Collins (Robert Ryan), an executive vice president at Cornwall Shipping Company, and his new wife, Nan (Laraine Day), registering—with a "honeymoon look" in their eyes—at a luxury resort hotel located somewhere off the coast of California.[23] In the film's second sequence, Brad, preceding his wife, has gone down to the hotel bar. A waiter approaches and cocktail music burbles in the background. As Brad orders drinks ("Two champagne cocktails, use the imported"), a woman sitting in the rear of the frame slips off a bar stool and, starting toward him, says, "It used to be 'Two Ward 8s'—when we could afford them." (A "Ward 8" or "boilermaker"—favored, according to Christine, by the "lower classes of Jersey City"—is a three-ounce glass of whiskey with a beer on the side.)

The woman, Christine Norman (Janis Carter), may not be as "conspicuous as a tarantula on a slice of angel-food cake" (to quote Raymond Chandler),[24] but isolated against the bar—the other customers are at the opposite end—she definitely stands out. Since the lighting is relatively high-key, the visual interest is provided by her costume: not only is she sporting black gloves, black high heels, and a black fur stole over a black dress, her black wide-brimmed hat is almost as obtrusive as Ann Terry's in *Phantom Lady*. When Christine sits down uninvited at Brad's table and continues to talk about the past ("That was back in dear old Jersey City before we learned about the finer things in life"), Brad becomes visibly unhappy, though it's obvious from the way they order drinks—Christine chips in, "Use the *imported* beer"—that they've both moved up in life since the "bad old days."

While the only chromatic similarity between the two—Brad's wearing a light-colored dinner jacket with a white pocket handkerchief—is his dark tie, this detail suggests a hidden, subterranean connection. This connection, which Christine has alluded to in her barbed comments about their impoverished youth in "dear old Jersey City," is photographically documented in a later, daytime scene set at her apartment. A "mild-looking" man named Arnold (Paul E. Burns)—who, according to the script, "might be a bank cashier, an accountant, or private investigator"—is sitting across from a couch where Christine, wearing a black skirt and a white form-fitting top, is flirting on the phone with Nan's brother, Don Lowry (John Agar):

> DON: That voice *has* to have a beautiful face. You sound like a blonde. But I'll settle for a brunette.
> CHRISTINE: But you'd rather have a blonde.

Abruptly concluding the conversation ("*Loved* talking to you"), Christine picks up a package that has just arrived in the mail and starts toward a kitchenette that has been turned into a darkroom. When Arnold wonders why everything has to be on microfilm, Christine, annoyed, responds, "When I have time, I'll explain it to you."

Christine is a successful photographer for a popular magazine (think *Life* or *Look*), and this front—a "valuable" one, as she later reminds Vanning (Thomas Gomez)—is the perfect pretext for Musuraca to introduce a striking high-contrast shot. There's a cut on action as Christine briskly enters the kitchenette, the blinds throwing soft Venetian-blind shadows on her body. After she closes the blinds, the room's momentarily plunged into darkness before she switches on a lamp, the bright white light illuminating her profiled face and breasts as she slips on a sheer plastic apron. Here, the chiaroscuro lighting can be said to carve Christine's body out of the darkness, accenting her sexuality and highlighting the negative, un-American character of her activity: she is not, for instance, cooking a meal for her husband but developing microfilm for the Communist Party.[25]

The third sequence I want to examine is the most elaborate and extended in *The Woman on Pier 13* and occurs on the waterfront. (In its cinematographic recourse to wharfs and waterfronts, stevedores and longshoremen, *The Woman on Pier 13* recollects Paul Schrader's dictum about classic noir's "Freudian attachment to water": "Docks and piers are second only to alleyways as the most popular rendezvous points."[26]) Since Brad was once a union member, he has been tapped by company owner Cornwall (Harry Cheshire)—at a dinner party, no less—to mediate between labor and management: "The union leaders talk your language, and you talk theirs. You came up the hard way, they respect you. Well, so do the owners." There's a catch, though: Vanning has previously visited Brad's office for an interview, claiming to be a reporter writing an article on the "American success story."

Vanning rehearses the life story of a "most unsuccessful young man named Frank Johnson" who once worked for the party—"agitation and propaganda activities, strikes in New Jersey"—before he vanished into thin air. Johnson, according to Vanning, was "typical of that lost generation of the 30s": produced by the Depression and embittered because of the dearth of jobs, he joined the Young Communists League and later became a full-fledged member of the Communist Party. Frank Johnson is, of course, Bradley Collins. After Vanning blithely hands him an updated membership card, Brad makes a beeline for Christine's apartment, where they drink Ward 8s while she tries to rekindle their romance. The seduction, however, doesn't take. Standing up to leave, Brad angrily tells Christine that he "graduated" from her a "long time ago," then, brandishing the party card, adds, "Same time I graduated from this."

Brad appears to have toughed his way out of a potentially disastrous situation, but things take a dark turn, literally, when he's summoned to Communist Party headquarters by Vanning's henchmen, Bailey (William Talman), a "piecework killer," and Grip Wilson (Fred Graham). The sequence opens with a brief but evocative montage: Bailey and Grip hustling Brad into a black sedan outside his apartment building; the car, headlights blazing, traversing a city boulevard at night; and a long pier, where we watch from an elevated angle as the car approaches. The last crane shot is "signed" by Musuraca, the camera panning to the right as the sedan passes underneath before holding for an extra beat on a "painterly" scene, light rippling like mercury on the lapping water.

The initial part of this exterior sequence—the celebrated "dark city" of classic noir—is the obverse of the daytime establishing shot of the waterfront where cranes ferry freight to the holds of ships while cargo-laden trucks pass in full view of the Golden Gate Bridge. The montage of the city at night also contrasts with the opening sequence of the film, in which the newly married Brad and Nan are driving up the coastline in the brilliant California sunshine, a contrast sharpened by a subtle rhyme. Just as this travel montage concludes with a shot of Brad's car swinging around and stopping in front of a luxury hotel (note the uniformed bellhop), so in the waterfront sequence the sedan swings around and comes to rest in front of a metal door. The difference is stark. It's not simply that in the latter sequence we're in the city, not the country, the closed, low-angle composition a counter to the bird's-eye view of the rolling hills and wide-open vistas in the opening montage; rather, Brad's not off honeymooning with his bride—a young, attractive interior decorator who recognizes a reproduction Ming vase when she sees one—but is now "married to the mob."

The interior of the warehouse where the party is headquartered may be the most complexly lighted space in *The Woman on Pier 13*. After a guard raises a roller door, the car drives over a ramp and pulls up to a freight elevator. While the slats of the elevator door throw elongated shadows onto the floor and the hood of the sedan, depth of space is conveyed by an oblong box of light high on the rear wall and by a staircase that creates a diagonal slash from right to left against a large rectangle of light in the background. This garage shot does not appear in the script, but it captures what the screenplay describes as the "maze" of the warehouse and, as such, represents not only the transition from outside to inside—from, that is, the waterfront to the warehouse—but a labyrinth from which Brad will find it increasingly difficult to extricate himself.[27]

The sinister implications of Brad's predicament are made explicit in the penultimate scene of the sequence. After Brad watches Vanning mercilessly interrogate a man named Ralston (Paul Guilfoyle) about being an informant for the FBI, he once again tries to scare off Vanning: "Let me tell you something! I quit taking orders a long time ago. If you crowd me too hard, I'll kick the whole thing over and, if I have to start punching, I'll start at the top." Brad storms off, but Arnold, cued by Vanning, shadows him.

Outside, dwarfed by enormous traveling cranes lit up against the night sky, the two men are walking toward the camera when Arnold asks Brad for a match. Brad gets out a gold lighter—a "symbol" of his lush life, according to Vanning—as the film cuts to Bailey and Grip escorting an agitated Ralston to the brink of the waterfront: "Look, if you'd only give me a chance to explain! This is all a misunderstanding!" A shot from Brad's point of view (POV) of the bridge that Ralston's forced to cross signals, like the flame from Brad's lighter, that the spectacle is expressly for his benefit. As Grip holds Ralston, Bailey loops a belt over his head and tightens it around his body, then ties another belt around his ankles. Cut to a horizontal shot of Ralston as he's carried violently writhing to the edge of the pier (and straight toward the camera), his face distorted in an open-mouthed grimace. Cut again to a high overhead shot of Ralston's body being tossed like garbage into the oil-slick water.

In the following reaction shot Grip looks on straight-faced, and when Ralston's head begins to sink beneath the surface, Bailey smiles. Translation: communists are sadists. Another shot from Brad's POV of the bridge, where Bailey and Grip can be seen exiting screen left, sutures the scene. Although Brad seems resigned to his fate—"Alright, tell Vanning I saw what he wanted me to see. Now I'll find my own way out"—he's determined to blow the lid off Vanning's operation. However, just as he's about to call the police from a telephone box, Vanning materializes in the dark with a photostat of a party report written in Brad's hand about a shop steward that he killed in a street fight in New Jersey.

It's at this dramatic juncture in the film that the "family" resemblance between *The Woman on Pier 13* and *Out of the Past*, the ultimate RKO film noir, becomes apparent.[28] In both films the protagonist appears to be living the good life—Jeff Markham/Bailey (Robert Mitchum) as a gas station owner in Bridgeport, California; Brad Collins as a shipping executive in San Francisco—when the past returns with a vengeance. In both films a killing haunts the protagonist—in *Out of the Past* Kathie Moffat (Jane Greer) has shot and killed Jeff's partner, Fisher (Steve Brodie); in *The Woman on Pier 13* Brad has accidentally killed a man with his own hands. Finally, both films feature a "good girl" and a "bad girl"—Ann Miller (Virginia Huston) and Kathie in *Out of the Past*, Nan and Christine in *The Woman on Pier 13*, respectively.

The other, more oblique relation between the two films pertains to genre. In "Made for Each Other" (1981) Richard Maltby observes that "Hollywood, despite itself, had something in common with [HUAC]. That something was a mode of fictional construction"—melodrama.[29] If the melodramatic aspect of *The Woman on Pier 13* is most obvious in its depiction of "evil" communists versus "good," law-abiding citizens, the film's melodramatic complexion also derives from its particular configuration of the "family romance" in which Christine's incestuous seduction of Don mirrors her original relationship with Brad.

The Woman on Pier 13 is not, of course, simply a melodrama. Franklin Jarlett refers to the picture as a "noir melodrama,"[30] and while the investigative figure of classic noir is, as I elaborate below, a minor, belated one in *The Woman on Pier 13*, the film exhibits many of the themes and character types associated with the genre, such as alienation (Brad's split identity), sexual obsession (Christine with Brad, Don with Christine), the victim/antihero (Brad), the femme fatale (Christine), and the "dark city" (San Francisco, the same metropolitan environs in which *The Maltese Falcon* [1941] is set). Equally importantly, the noir provenance of *The Woman on Pier 13* is a function of the film's syntax or deep structure, "three interlocking sexual triangles" (Vanning/Christine/Brad//Christine/Brad/Nan// Brad/Nan/Jim Travis [Richard Rober]) that's "central to the noir cycle."[31]

The film's generic stereophony or reversibility (noir/melodrama) is reflected, moreover, at the level of subtext. In other words, just as *Out of the Past* can be read as an allegory of the Hollywood witch hunt, so too *The Woman on Pier 13* can be seen as dramatizing the punishing effects of the anticommunist agenda in which—to revise Maltby's reading of *Out of the Past*—the film's plot "might be metaphorically reconstructed as a *sympathetic* portrayal of [Brad Collins] as an ex-communist witness before HUAC."[32] Thus, while on more than one occasion Brad claims that the authorities will understand his past indiscretions if he comes clean, his actions demonstrably contradict this belief and contribute to the film's air of fatalism, a determinism that is itself a prime component of classic noir. In the end, Brad knows full well that it's not enough to recant one's past; one not only has to suffer but also, given the magnitude of the crime (i.e., high treason), die for one's sins.

CRISS CROSS: BAD BOYS AND BLONDES, RED BRIDES AND BENEDICTS

> From the Senate to the FBI, from the anticommunists in Hollywood to Mickey Spillane, moral weakness was associated with sexual degeneracy, which allegedly led to communism. To avoid dire consequences, men as well as women had to contain their sex in marriage, where men would be in control with sexually submissive, competent homemakers at their side.
>
> —Elaine Tyler May, *Homeward Bound: American Families in the Cold War Era*

If the similarity between *Out of the Past* and *The Woman on Pier 13* illustrates just how readily the narrative and audiovisual style of classic noir could be translated into the language of the anticommunist "meller" or thriller, it simultaneously demonstrates the extent to which even a text as ideologically loaded as *The Woman on Pier 13*, which Hughes intended as a showcase for the anticommunist cause, is not without the sort of performative ambiguity that characterizes classic noir.

Consider, for example, the representation of marriage in *The Woman on Pier 13*. In the popular American imagination, the 1950s was the epitome of married domesticity, a state of grace buttressed by television, suburbanization, and conspicuous consumption—all of those glittering, spanking-new, stainless-steel accoutrements. In *The Woman on Pier 13* the discourse of marriage is the magical site where issues of romance and anticommunism intersect. The original title of *The Woman on Pier 13*, *I Married a Communist*, is particularly evocative in this context, recollecting as it does such 1940s features as *I Married a Witch* (1942), *I Married an Angel* (1942), and *I Married a Savage* (1949) as well as presaging late '50s features such as *I Married a Monster from Outer Space* (1958), a title that marries two genres that, like gangster noir, were especially conducive to anticommunist rhetoric: horror and science fiction.[33]

The original, lurid title of *The Woman on Pier 13*—which, it's worth noting, is from Nan's horrified perspective, as if she suddenly woke up one day and realized she was married to a communist—also confers a retroactive, dream-like spell on the film's narrative, endowing its opening with a fairy-tale ambiance. A trailer featuring Nan's voice-over capitalizes on this angle: "Don't say it can't happen to you. It can. It happened to me." Thus, we learn in the very first sequence that Brad and Nan's romance was a whirlwind affair. After hiring her to decorate his offices, Brad fought with her over the "sketches" for a few days, then, out of the "clear blue sky," he proposed and they were married within the week. The twist is that Brad stole her from another man, Jim Travis, a labor leader who later approaches Brad for help in negotiating a new contract for the union.

I will return to Brad and Nan's marriage, a bourgeois one made in heaven, in the conclusion to this chapter, but the opening of *The Woman on Pier 13* suggests that Nan may well have been attracted to Brad's "bad boy" allure (Nan: "You're a very ruthless character"), a characterization that cannot be divorced from the film's figuration of femininity and masculinity. In other words, if the figure of the "Bad Blonde" in Nora Sayre's classic memoir about Cold War films, *Running Time* ("Bad blondes tend to order triple bourbons . . . and they often seduce young 'impressionable' men into joining the Party"), appears to be based on Christine's character—she's the spider-woman at the center of the communist "web of subversion"—party "boss" Vanning is structurally aligned with both the femme fatale and the specter of homosexuality.[34]

I'm thinking here of a peculiar scene set at Christine's apartment that opens on a magazine photo-story about stevedores, "Men Moving Mountains with Their Bare Hands," which features Nan's brother, Don, "stripped to the waist, muscular and smilingly attractive." Christine's talking on the phone with Don about a date—"You'd better make it 8:15. I'm a working gal, and it takes time to get out of my overalls and into something fresh and feminine." However, when the camera pulls back for a wider shot, we realize that it's Vanning, not Christine, who has been studying the layout. To wit, Vanning's character is inverted here: though Christine is dressed in a "smart" black negligee, Vanning's back is turned to her and his gaze is rack-focused instead on the spectacle of Don's muscular body.[35]

The issue of "male trouble" is broached early on in *The Woman on Pier 13* in the form of Nan's brother, Don, whom Brad has paternally taken under his wing. After Brad, looking out a window and seeing a ship from Shanghai that's three days overdue, sends him off to work like a wayward son ("How can you swing a cargo hook from here?"), Nan exclaims, "You've done more to make a man out

of him in two weeks than I was able to do in all my life." Nan's maternal observation, not to mention her brother's cheeky rejoinder to Brad ("And you'll be a
man, my son"), hints that Don—not unlike Brad when he was a member of the
Communist Party—is young or, as Christine notes when talking to him on the
phone, "impressionable." (J. Edgar Hoover refused the studio's request to use
newsreel footage of him in the film, but his fingerprints are all over this scene:
"Of special interest to the Party are young people."[36])

While Brad's seduction of Nan occurs prior to the story (we only hear about
it in retrospect and in passing), Christine's education of Don—which, of course,
is a form of "political seduction"[37]—constitutes a crucial subplot of *The Woman
on Pier 13*. Once Brad has definitively dropped her like a "red-hot poker," to echo
Walter Neff in *Double Indemnity*, she turns her considerable charms on Nan's "kid"
brother. At an after-theater cocktail party at Christine's apartment, the camera
crosscuts between Christine, who has gone to the darkroom with Vanning to
develop more microfilm, and Don, who's discussing politics with a "pretty girl,"
Evelyn, and a character whom the screenplay refers to as "The Professor." Don,
as a working-class stevedore, is no match for either Evelyn ("He's the finest speci-
men of rugged American individualist I ever saw") or the Professor ("the theory
of a scientifically organized state is that . . . man is the state, state is man").

Don feebly protests, "Well, I like it better in a democracy," but Christine (to
quote Jim) already has her "hooks" in him, and in no time Don's a stooge for the
party. The message is transparent as a bug in amber: falling in love is like falling
for communism. Subsequently, in an extended montage of the labor negotiations
that the party wants to sabotage, Don can be seen passionately speaking against
management as a news headline confirms: "UNION SPEAKERS FLAY OWNERS."
Now both Brad and Don are working for the party—Brad, because he's under
duress; Don, because he's been duped by Christine.

Despite the accent on Don's and Brad's character arcs in *The Woman on Pier 13*,
the melodramatic conclusion pivots not so much on the men's actions as on the
women's, a shift that underscores the film's investment in the "woman's picture."
The first twist is that Christine, the femme fatale, falls for Don. Vanning has already warned her about "personal entanglements"—"You have no private life"—so
once the waterfront negotiations have been sabotaged, he promptly sends her off
to Seattle on another magazine assignment, ordering her to stay there until she
gets her "emotions under control." Christine, however, is conflicted: the more she
feels, the less appealing the party appears. Or, in the lingua franca of film noir, the
more femme Christine becomes, the less fatale she is.

Indeed, in a later scene set at the airport, it's as if Christine has become a completely different person. On the verge of hysteria, she throws herself into Don's
arms, and Don, true to the gendered romantic conventions of the period, tells

her to quit her job. Christine replies that she "*can't* quit," but Don, unsurprisingly, doesn't get the double meaning—that, for Christine, there's a "potentially fatal conflict between work and romance."[38] Now, Christine's in the exact same predicament as Brad; the difference is that the only way out for her is to get married. This, then, is the aporia at the dark heart of *The Woman on Pier 13*: marriage is at once the problem (for Nan) and the solution (for Christine).

Don immediately phones Nan from the airport about his engagement to Christine—"I said *married*, like you and Brad and all the best people"—but the restricted composition (he's boxed in by decorative frames) indicates that it's a pipe dream. The bubble bursts when Jim warns him about his fiancée—"This woman you're crazy about has been using you the way she's used plenty of others before you"—an accusation that tars Christine with the sin of, among other things, sexual promiscuity. (Of course, in the 1950s, being branded a prostitute was almost just as bad as being tagged a communist. See, for example, the print advertising for *The Woman on Pier 13*: "Nameless, shameless woman! Trained in an art as old as time!"[39])

Don heads straight to Christine's apartment, like Brad before him, to have it out with her—Don: "I've been told you're a Commie agent"/Christine: "I didn't want to fall in love with you"—although the stereotypical romanticism of the scene is kinked by the film's political-libidinal economy. On one hand, the lighting, as in the initial darkroom sequence, casts soft Venetian-blind shadows on Christine, reiterating her status as a femme fatale. On the other hand, her apologia is strangely moving: "Maybe it is possible to be Communists and still be human beings, too." The extraordinary incongruity of this moment, which performatively enacts the tension in the film between agitprop and melodrama, is indicated by the fact that it can be resolved only via a deus ex machina: the sudden appearance of Vanning, who checks Christine—"You were told to wait in Seattle"—right before Don knocks him down like a bowling pin.

From this dramatic point forward, the film's plot takes a dizzying series of turns like a car on a twisting coastal highway. On Vanning's orders, Don's run down by Bailey outside Brad's apartment building as Nan, alerted by Christine about her brother's situation, races to her bedroom window just in time to see his body crumple up on the street. Christine, distraught over Don's death, is about to commit suicide when Vanning reappears and, reading her suicide note—"before I die I want to tell the truth about the Communist Party"—pushes her out of a window. In a neat reversal of Nan's perspective, Brad's standing outside Christine's apartment when her body sails like a rag doll to the earth, where, according to the script (but masked in the film), it's impaled on the spear-points of an iron fence.

In classical Hollywood fashion, the climax of *The Woman on Pier 13* reprises the initial warehouse sequence, only this time Brad has a revolver and the element of surprise in his favor. In a dynamic passage set in a rising elevator (Arnold has switched off the light), the two men, trapped by towering shadows, grapple like boxers. Once Brad subdues Arnold, Brad and Nan make their escape, chased by gunfire through the maze of the warehouse, briefly taking cover among some boxes and bales, where Brad finally apologizes to his wife—"I thought I quit, but you can't quit, [they] won't let you"—as Vanning, Bailey, and Vanning's bodyguard steadily advance in the dark.

The bloody dénouement of *I Married a Communist* is littered with the bodies of dead Reds. After Brad guns down Bailey and Garth, he sees Vanning standing behind Nan, who's propped up against a bale bathed in a halo of light. In a suicidal act of desperation, he charges Vanning and, despite being mortally wounded, manages to knock the gun out of his hand. As Vanning races after it, Brad sees his chance—a cargo hook stuck in a bale—and hurls the hook, impaling Vanning and sending him over a rail to his death, symbolically avenging Christine's death.

PAINT IT RED: THE RED HOOK AND *THE FLOWER CARRIER*

While the question of whether film noir is a genre or style—a question that I do not pretend to resolve here—has haunted discussions of this movement from its inception, any consideration of the meaning of *The Woman on Pier 13* is inextricably bound up with its form. I've already discussed Musuraca's painterly contribution to *The Woman on Pier 13*, but the film's style is also apparent in its mise-en-scène. In "How Red Was My Valley" (the allusion is to John Ford's film about unionization in a Welsh mining village, *How Green Was My Valley* [1941]), Leab concludes that Cold War anticommunist films such as *The Woman on Pier 13* "figuratively hit audiences over the head with a hammer and sickle."[40] Anticommunist noirs are marked, it's true, by hortatory passages, yet as I have already argued, the moral or message of these films is not nearly as monophonic as Leab's "hammer and sickle" metaphor suggests. In fact, two of the dominant figures in *The Woman on Pier 13*—the cargo hook and Diego Rivera's print, *The Flower Carrier*—are both more *and* less literal.

Consider, to reverse the terms of Leab's argument, how the film's sense or significance is motivated—due in no small part to Musuraca's artful camerawork—by its visual rhetoric, one that's insistently inscribed in the "literal" figure of a cargo hook. This figure first appears when Jim Travis visits the Collinses' apartment to try to talk Brad into reopening labor negotiations and a baling hook can be seen hanging on the wall among stevedore pictures of Brad as a foreman. "You were quite a guy—in those days," Jim exclaims, taking the hook off the wall before replacing it.

Later, Jim visits Don on the waterfront—Don has, in the meantime, become passionately involved with Christine—and as cargo is being hoisted aboard a freighter in the background, Jim interrogates him about his knowledge of un-American activities on the waterfront:

> JIM: Part of my job as I see it is to keep the Commie minority from running the union.
> DON: Why tell me? I'm no Commie and you know it.
> JIM: Well, of course, you know. You think you're a good union man, don't you, Don?
> DON: I know I am.

Cut to a shot of Don poised above a bale signing a manifest, his figure outlined against a wall by a wedge of shadow. In terms of the film's audiovisual economy, this master shot possesses a sculptural, monumental quality not unlike a frieze or tableau, as if it's meant to be read. Hence the iconic image cast on the right-hand side of the screen by a shadow crossed with a cargo hook: a hammer and sickle.

Here, welding the symbolic discourses of communism and trade unionism, the "red hook" recollects the San Francisco waterfront strikes of 1934, 1936, and 1948 as well as the sort of anticommunist rhetoric that marked Hoover's appearance before HUAC on March 26, 1947 ("The communist tactic of infiltrating unions stems from the earliest teachings of Marx, which have been reiterated by Party speakers down the years"[41]). It also anticipates Elia Kazan's *On the Waterfront* (1954), the urtext of which was Arthur Miller's screenplay *The Hook,* based on the Italian American longshoremen of Red Hook, Brooklyn.[42]

Hammer and Sickle: Don Lowry (John Agar) signing shipping manifest in the shadow of the communist specter in *The Woman on Pier 13.*

If the hammer-and-sickle icon in *The Woman on Pier 13* is an ingenious bit of expressionist lighting, not to mention a potent instance of mise-en-scène as agit-prop, the film's employment of Diego Rivera's *The Flower Carrier* presents a rather more ambiguous case. About the painting, which occupies a prominent place in Christine's apartment and which may well have been the result of Nicholas Ray's preproduction input on set design, Frank Krutnik writes:

> The painting presents a striking image of a Mexican peasant laborer who is borne down by the weight of a huge basket of flowers on his back. The woman helps to steady the basket as he begins to lift himself up from the ground. . . . Although each individual flower weighs very little, when collected together as produce for the marketplace they constitute a crushing burden for the peasant worker.[43]

There are any number of ways to interpret *The Flower Carrier* in *The Woman on Pier 13*—say, as a sign indexing Christine's membership in the Communist Party—but the Rivera painting also mobilizes a "more radical set of political associations that create alternative reading possibilities."[44] Krutnik leaves open the issue of *The Flower Carrier*'s "resistant" significance, suggesting that there's an "intense affiliation" between the print and Christine, who, not unlike Laurel Gray (Gloria Grahame) in *In a Lonely Place* (1950), "ultimately lacks agency and authority."[45]

A closer examination of the sequencing of the scenes in which *The Flower Carrier* appears complicates, however, this determination. The first time that the Rivera print is visible, Vanning's studying the photo layout of stevedores while Christine's talking on the phone to Don. After she hangs up, *The Flower Carrier* is isolated on the right-hand side of the screen as Vanning interrogates Christine about her relationship with Don:

VANNING: How did you meet him?
CHRISTINE: Talked to him on the phone by accident. He liked my voice. So I
    talked to him again.
VANNING: Not by accident.
CHRISTINE: I told him I liked his voice.
VANNING: Why?
CHRISTINE: Call it a whim.
VANNING: No, call it what it is. Emotion.

In this scene Vanning embodies one of the most popular stereotypes about communists in the 1950s: that they were unfeeling, remote-controlled intellectuals who, not unlike robots—all head, no heart—would rather die than deviate from the party script. Christine is, by comparison, an anomaly: while her emotionalism is stereotypically feminine, it's also coded as a form of political resistance.

Red Queen or "Human Being": Don Lowry (John Agar) confronts Christine Norman (Janis Carter) in her San Francisco apartment in *The Woman on Pier 13*. Note the Diego Rivera print, *The Flower Carrier*, on the rear wall.

The second time that *The Flower Carrier* appears it's featured in the scene in which Christine has returned—against Vanning's express wishes—from Seattle. Don's standing in the right foreground with his back to us, smoking; Christine, having set down her suitcase, is standing in the left middle ground; and the Rivera painting is located in the charged space between them. Since Christine's commitment to the party has begun to waver, the scene is energized by the tension between the mise-en-scène, which construes Christine as a communist femme fatale, and the aforementioned monologue in which she fervently appeals to Don's sense of humanity.

The third time that the Rivera print appears, it's visible on the left rear wall of Christine's apartment as she sits in the right foreground on the phone, frantically trying to reach Brad. When she can't reach him, she calls Nan, and despite the fact that Christine's offscreen, the reverse shot explains why Nan has phoned her: "Look, Christine, you can't call up and say 'Don's in danger.'" Although Vanning has explicitly ordered Christine not to communicate with anyone, she has disobeyed him by calling Brad and Nan, a signifier of her limited, albeit very real, agency.

The final sequence in which *The Flower Carrier* appears dramatizes Nan's subsequent confrontation with Christine. After Nan discloses Don's death, she threatens to call the police if Christine doesn't divulge what she knows about it. As Nan starts toward the phone, the film cuts to a shot that recalls the earlier one of Don and Christine mediated by the Rivera print, only this time Christine's on the right and Nan's on the left. Suddenly, the phone rings. Since Christine knows that it's Brad, she decides to set a "match to a keg of dynamite," informing Nan that Bailey drove the car that killed Don and that the "great Bradley Collins is really Frank Johnson, a member of the Communist Party." Nan instinctively begins to defend Brad, but Christine pulls out a photograph of Brad and her in swimsuits on the beach in New Jersey—"Young love among the lower classes. Two young communists out to save the world"—the very same photograph that she developed with Arnold in the darkroom sequence and that she later showed Don as proof that communists are human beings.

While a "still" or freeze-frame of the Rivera print suggests that it functions as a mere sign or signal (Christine = communist), such a static interpretation misses the dynamic character of the mise-en-scène in which the succession of contexts, like the motion of the picture itself, yields another, more complex meaning. In this mini-narrative, one that underscores the interpretation of *The Woman on Pier 13* as a masked allegory about the malign influence of HUAC, Christine assumes the role of the woman in *The Flower Carrier*, helping her former comrade unburden himself of his dark, forbidden past.

CODA: THE WOMAN ON PIER 13

The U.S. in the 1950s, in the minds of many people, is characterized by two historical phenomena: McCarthyism and the
resurgence of the idea that women's principal role was that of wife
and mother.

—Kathleen Anne Weigand, *The Red Menace, the Feminine
Mystique, and the Ohio Un-American Activities Committee:
Gender and Anti-Communism in Ohio, 1951–1954*

Beyond the frame of *The Flower Carrier*, Christine is an agent of change for her "sister under the mink," Nan. Christine's occupation as a photojournalist permits her, it's clear, extensive play in the public sphere, a professional mobility that foregrounds the force of Vanning's interdiction, which effectively condemns her to the domestic sphere and, ultimately, death. What happens before Vanning pushes Christine out of that high window is, however, signal. Confined to her apartment, she seizes the only means of communication available to her, the telephone, and manages to connect with the only other person in the film who shares her plight, Nan.

A scene at Bailey's shooting gallery on the midway at night—note the illuminated spokes of a carnival ride turning in the background—marks Nan's medusan transformation. Dressed in a white overcoat offset by black gloves, Nan raises a rifle when she hears a cashier calling out Bailey's name, then cocks and fires the rifle three times in rapid succession. Bailey sidles over—"You need practice, baby"—but after Nan hits the metal targets three straight times—*bing! bing! bing!*—he asks, "Say, who d'ya wanna kill?"

Nan's "bad girl" masquerade continues apace when the two go to a honky-tonk club called the Gay Paree, a dimly lit, garishly decorated burlesque joint frequented by "dockworkers and their women." The Gay Paree, a far cry from the sophisticated hotel bar where Brad and Christine meet at the film's beginning, provides a not so oblique commentary on the debauched pleasures of the working class. Playing the vamp to the hilt, Nan drinks and dances with Bailey—the background music is Harold Arlen's "One for My Baby"—before, referencing a friend's problem, she broaches the idea of murder: "Her husband drinks a lot. He beats her. He's just no good. But he has a lot of insurance." Bailey, who "ain't dumb" (as he himself puts it), puts two and two together: "This guy with the life insurance—he ain't married to no *friend* of yours. Married to you." Until this point in the film Nan has been the very definition of a "good girl," although her character appears at its most illegible here: is she simply trying to find out who murdered her brother, or is she seriously contemplating having her husband knocked off?

At the beginning of *The Woman on Pier 13*, Nan's happily married and the epitome of the '50s supportive spouse. "I want to be a good wife to you," she tells Brad. "I want to be what you want me to be." But as the film progresses, she's relegated to the private sphere by her husband, imprisoned like Rapunzel in her bourgeois castle.[46] It's only after Christine reveals Brad's dark secret that—in an uncharacteristic exchange of characteristics[47]—we see Nan venture outside her home, first to the midway, then to the Gay Paree, where she finally lets down her hair as she transforms into a private detective, playing the femme fatale in order to discover the truth about her brother: "I want to know who killed him and why. And I'm going to find out." In the end it's as if Christine, by dying, momentarily releases Nan from the patriarchal ties that bind her, freeing her to become "the woman on pier 13."

Since the original title of *The Woman on Pier 13* is *I Married a Communist*, it's no surprise that the final scene of the film neatly ties up the narrative threads involving marriage and communism. Having dispatched Vanning and as he lies dying, Brad addresses Jim Travis, the union spokesperson at Cornwall Shipping: "Everything you need to end the tie-up in Vanning's office." With this particular issue resolved, Brad turns to his other "unfinished business," Nan. Still addressing Travis, Brad briefly rallies: "Nan, made a mistake. But that can be—fixed. Take care of her—Jim. . . ."

What's striking about this conclusion is not that Brad dies (which, given his communist past, is inevitable) or that, in a sentimental gesture that masks a classic economy of exchange, he returns Nan to Jim (Nan and Jim had been dating for three years before Brad entered the picture) but that the future marriage between

Nan and Jim represents—in, of course, a condensed, displaced form—a renewed contract between labor and capital in which Nan's realigned with the stevedores associated with her dead brother, Don, rather than with management, a realignment that recollects the capital-labor accords of the late 1940s and 1950s.[48] From another, less class-based perspective, the qualified happy ending of *The Woman on Pier 13* annuls Nan's brief walk on the wild side, reconstituting it as a bad dream from which she'll wake to find herself married not to a communist, "bad boy" Brad, but to Jim Travis, the good anticommunist.

THE RED AND THE BLACK

"BLACK FILM" AND THE RED MENACE

We know the red we want is the red we've got
In the old red, white and blue
It's a brave red, not a slave red
That means liberty to you

—Elton Britt, "The Red We Want Is the Red We
    Got" (Jimmy Kennedy and Bickley Reichner,
    1950)

The Woman on Pier 13 may well be the most symptomatic anticommunist noir, but as I noted at the beginning of the previous chapter, it's by no means the only one. In *Film Noir* Andrew Spicer states that the early "1950s generated a sub-cycle of noirs that was explicit about the Communist threat."[1] And in *Somewhere in the Night* Nicholas Christopher writes that the "films woven of red menace . . . themes are varied and numerous, with a decidedly hyper-urgent, infernal take on urban life."[2] More recently, Wheeler Winston Dixon in *Film Noir and the Cinema of Paranoia* observes that these red scare films were "noir projects is hardly in dispute; their visual and aural structure alone (an extreme use of shadow, constant rain, paranoid voice-over, threatening camera angles, and jarring close-ups . . .) is incontestable proof of the noir origins."[3]

But if such films as *The Woman on Pier 13*, *The Whip Hand*, *I Was a Communist for the F.B.I.*, and *Walk East on Beacon!*—to adduce the most widely cited quartet[4]—are now seen as an integral, if controversial, part of the classical corpus, why did it take so long for this reappraisal?

Reynold Humphries offers three "tendencies" for the general, historical neglect of anticommunist films, reasons that also shed light on the particular relation between film noir and anticommunism. The first was the assumption that the

"Cold War produced anti-communist movies in the same way it produced anti-communism."[5] The problem here was the critical tendency to interpret film *texts* as if their meaning could be simply read off of a specific historical moment. The second reason was the "understandable but misguided desire on the part of Left critics generally to give pride of place to films which they can classify as works of social comment."[6] In this case, the issue was not so much the perceived presence or absence of "social comment"—since anticommunist noirs explicitly, even tendentiously, comment on contemporary society—but whether the commentary is understood to be "conservative" or "progressive." The third reason for the general neglect of anticommunist films was the "systematic downgrading of the films of the '50s,"[7] a tendency that has been especially aggressive in the literature on film noir where the early 1950s has historically been seen as the beginning of the end of the classical period.

The working premise of this chapter is that in the 1950s film noir and anti-communism form a double helix and that even the most notorious of these red menace films is central to our understanding and appreciation of classic noir. More specifically, I argue that a close reading of these films' generic elements, whether thriller, "meller," or semidocumentary, suggests that the anticommunist noir represents a critical moment in the genre's transition from the 1940s to the 1950s—from, say, expressionism to neorealism—and, moreover, that the "red" structure of feeling dramatized in these films is replete with all the attendant performative contradictions one might expect in such a complex social formation. This said, the difference between *The Woman on Pier 13* and the aforementioned anticommunist noirs is that whereas Stevenson's film is about a shipping executive, Brad Collins, who cannot escape his ex-communist past and is condemned to confront it in the form of a CP boss who's intent on extorting him to further the party's nefarious goals, *The Whip Hand*, *I Was a Communist for the F.B.I.*, *Walk East on Beacon!*, and *Big Jim McLain* feature an investigative narrative.

As opposed to the private-eye detective in classic '40s noir, however, the investigative agency in these Cold War noirs is either the FBI, as in *I Was a Communist for the F.B.I.* and *Walk East on Beacon!*, or HUAC, as in *Big Jim McLain*. Thus, even though the primary investigative figure in *The Whip Hand* is a newspaper reporter, in the climactic action of the film the FBI comes, tommy guns ablaze, to his aid. At the same time, while the ideological motivation of these '50s red scare noirs varies from germ warfare (*The Whip Hand*) to union subversion (*I Was a Communist for the F.B.I.*) to a super-secret earth-satellite space program (*Walk East on Beacon!*), this investigative agency is not always portrayed in a unilaterally positive light. For instance, despite its manifest glorification of the new electronic technologies of surveillance, the '50s anticommunist noir is frequently troubled by the implications of these selfsame technologies so that, for instance, the tele-cinematic screen in *Walk East on Beacon!* can be said to become a two-way mirror that reflects the invasive practices of the repressive state apparatus even as this apparatus subjects "un-American" citizens to its panoptical audiovisual regimes.

THE WHIP HAND: THE RED PLAGUE

In February 1954 Howard Hughes announced that he was "willing to purchase every existing share" of RKO stock at "twice the market value."[8] However, before stockholders were able to come to a decision about the offer, Floyd Odlum—from whom Hughes had originally purchased a controlling interest in the studio—entered the fray, buying up all the available stock, at which point a battle royal broke out between the two for control of RKO. (Odlum was offended that Hughes had "not kept his promise to let him have first crack at the purchase of the RKO theatre chain."[9]) It was during this tumultuous time that Hughes was heard to say, "I need RKO like the plague."[10]

Hughes's language is particularly resonant because, having been apprehensive since childhood about germs and diseases, by 1950 he was rapidly "developing an obsessive avoidance of human contact": "He viewed anyone who came near him as a potential germ carrier."[11] His increasingly phobic sensibility was reflected in his vision of a medical institute, eventually outlined in his will, that would undertake the "scientific research necessary to accomplish the discovery or development of methods, substances, or means for the prevention and cure of those diseases or maladies . . . which shall have proven to be the most important and dangerous to the people of the United States."[12]

Hughes's phobia about germs and diseases crystallized around a notion that had engaged his faculties in a way that few issues did: the "red plague." Although on this particular subject critics have tended to focus almost exclusively on such films as *The Woman on Pier 13* and *Jet Pilot*, the picture that arguably best captures Hughes's paranoid personality—and, not so incidentally, the paranoiac "structure of feeling" in the United States in the early 1950s—is William Cameron Menzies's *The Whip Hand*. Like *The Woman on Pier 13*, *The Whip Hand* is a noir-inflected anticommunist thriller; its genesis, though, reflects the transition in the United States from the politics of the Popular Front to that of the red menace. Originally titled *The Man He Found*, *The Whip Hand* was "supposed to be about the discovery of Adolph Hitler, alive and knowingly sheltered by the inhabitants of a small New England village."[13] But after screening the film, Hughes decided that it should be about communists rather than Nazis. Consequently, the main villain is not *der Führer* but an ex-Nazi scientist named Wilhelm Bucholtz (Otto Waldis), who disappeared behind the Iron Curtain in 1946 and who is now working for the communists. (For a similar scenario, see *Red Planet Mars* [1952].)

As with *The Woman on Pier 13*, *The Whip Hand* illustrates the generic and ideological plasticity of the postwar thriller. While it's set in Winnoga, a fictional place in the Upper Midwest rather than in the "naked city," it illustrates, like *Out of the Past*, both Nicholas Musuraca's range as a cinematographer as well as the implicit dialectical relation in classic noir between the city and the country. In fact, *The Whip Hand* offers a tacit critique not simply of what Norman Cameron calls the "pseudo-community"—"What the [paranoiac] takes to be a functional community is only a pseudo-community created by his own unskilled attempts at interpretation"[14]—but of small-town America itself.

The Whip Hand opens with the sort of stentorian voice-over narration associated with the semidocumentary—"At this moment behind the heavily guarded walls of the Kremlin . . ."—but the film's generic identity as a noir also derives, together with Musuraca's typically lustrous photography, from its investigative protagonist, Matt Corbin (Elliott Reid), a magazine reporter for the aptly named *American View*, who's on a fishing excursion when he happens upon "The Town That Ran Out of Fish." (Corbin, no *homme fatal*, is the good, all-American male double of photojournalist Christina in *The Woman on Pier 13*.) Matt finds himself in Winnoga after smacking his head against a rock trying to escape a thunderstorm and then after being rudely turned away in the pouring rain by an armed guard at an estate owned by a Mr. Peterson (Lewis Martin). In Winnoga, Matt's tended to by Janet Keller (Carla Balenda), the sister of the town doctor, Edward Keller (Edgar Barrier), although there's something distinctly fishy about the place— How did all the fish die?—a suspicion fueled for Matt by the townspeople, who, with the exception of the elderly proprietor of the general store, Luther Adams (Frank Darien), are anxious to "bid [him] goodbye."

Matt's investigative juices are whetted by a night out at the movies. The truncated conversation between Matt and the taciturn, blond-haired Chick (Michael Steele) is revealing: Matt: "What's playing?"/Chick: "What's the difference—I ain't seen it yet." After Matt plunks down next to Janet, he sees Dr. Keller and Steve Loomis (Raymond Burr), the owner of the inn he's staying at, leaving right in the middle of the movie. Matt quips, "The life of a doctor. Never gets to see the end of a movie," but the implication is that in a godforsaken ghost town like Winnoga, no one ever walks out of a movie while it's still playing. Later, having dropped Janet off at her house, Matt sees Steve, Dr. Keller, and an anonymous older man pulling up to a pier in a motorboat and overhears the older man's instructions: "Remember, my orders are to be carried out exactly."

While seemingly incidental, this pier passage, bookending as it does the body of the film, is central to the visual economy of *The Whip Hand*. Preceded by a subtly expressionist shot of Matt passing the spiked slats of a wooden fence, the passage itself, which echoes a similar scene in *The Woman on Pier 13* where Brad

Collins watches helplessly as Ralston's hauled away by Vanning's henchmen to be killed, is structured around a high-contrast POV shot from Matt's perspective of a moonlit pier that bridges the abstract black tree trunks in the foreground and the dark lake and forest in the background.

The next day, Matt, equipped with a camera and trailed by the ubiquitous, gum-chewing Chick, sets out to investigate Peterson's fortress-like lodge. Matt's attempt to elude Chick—his investigative instincts aroused, he senses almost immediately that he's being tailed—exhibits Musuraca's flair for low-key lighting and startling camera angles. The first is an unmotivated high-angle shot from inside a pitch-black barn as Matt enters from the brilliant sunshine outside, the crossed black timbers in the foreground reinforcing the frame of the door and, once Matt discovers there's no other exit, his momentary entrapment. After Matt surveys the dark interior of the barn, there's an abrupt straight cut to a low-angle shot of Chick gazing down from the rafters, followed by a high-angle reverse shot of Matt's footprints in the dirt. Cut to Matt slipping under a sign that reads "WARNING / PRIVATE PROPERTY / DO NOT TRESPASS."

As in the darkroom sequence in *The Woman on Pier 13*, the Musuraca touch can be seen in the subsequent passage where Matt traverses a steep wooded landscape, a passage that recollects the fishing sequence in *Out of the Past*, in order to photograph Peterson's secret compound. Matt uses a telescopic lens to scope out the action (a neat visual pun on Musuraca's role as director of photography), after which the film cuts to a telescopic shot of what appears to be a doctor in a white lab coat checking the mouth of a patient who's dressed all in white and using a crutch. When Matt sees a man with a rifle rushing up to confer with the doctor, he decides it's past time to leave, hiding his camera under some brush; what he doesn't know is that he has already been photographed by a surveillance camera hidden in a tree trunk.

Matt never recovers his camera—Chick's easily able to locate it—but he does discover Peterson's secret when he returns to Dr. Keller's house on the pretense that the bandage on his forehead needs to be changed. Matt's musing out loud about the "barbed-wire fences and trigger-happy guards" at Peterson's "armed fort"—"What are these characters trying to do, drop an Iron Curtain around Winnoga?"—when he notices a set of books on "Germs and Diseases" authored by Dr. Wilhelm Bucholtz. Since earlier in his career Matt covered Bucholtz's postwar vanishing act (the "famed Nazi authority on germ warfare" somehow managed to slip through the Allies' fingers), he sends a message via Luther to his editor at *American View* to check out the April 12, 1946, edition, which featured an article by Matt titled "IS WILHELM BUCHOLTZ WORKING FOR THE COMMUNISTS?"

Although Matt is now a prisoner in Winnoga—his car has already been impounded and his phone calls are being monitored by Loomis's wife—he's determined to investigate Peterson's complex one more time. The second investigative

Caught: Lobby card of Matt Corbin (Elliott Reid) captured at gunpoint after investigating Dr. Peterson's fortress in *The Whip Hand*.

sequence conveys, even more so than the first one, Musuraca's mastery of night-for-night shooting. Not only is there an inventive low-angle shot of Matt and Janet—now underneath the pier—sliding a canoe into the water unbeknownst to the armed guard pacing above, but the image of the couple quietly paddling through cattails to the sound of bullfrogs and Paul Sawtell's atmospheric score as they secretively make their way to the other side of the lake, where Peterson's lodge is located, is reminiscent of Bart and Laurie's desperate flight to the mountains in the dramatic conclusion to Joseph Lewis's *Gun Crazy* (1950).

While Janet remains behind with the canoe, Matt re-traverses the hilly, spruce-thick terrain and, after climbing a stone wall, steals up to the compound. What will he see? What's the secret behind Peterson's Dr. No–like mania for privacy? Musuraca ratchets up the tension by cutting not to an exterior shot from Matt's point of view but to a low-angle, interior one—accompanied by a curious, squeaking sound—of a barred, brightly lit window. As Matt's wide-eyed face rises like a moon behind the bars, the film cuts again, this time to a POV shot that pans past cages full of rats and rabbits to a man in a white lab coat sitting at a desk surrounded by all the bric-a-brac—the test tubes, microscopes, and fuming beakers—associated since *Frankenstein* (1931) with the figure of the "mad scientist."

William Cameron Menzies made his mark as an art director in 1924 with *The Thief of Bagdad*, received the first Academy Award for art direction in 1929 for *The Dove* and *The Tempest*, and became the first person to be credited as a production designer for his work on *Gone with the Wind* (1939). His directorial début was the futuristic, H. G. Wells–inspired *Things to Come* (1936),[15] and the above mad scientist scene not only draws on Menzies's experience as a director and production designer but constitutes the audiovisual rebus around which *The Whip Hand* revolves. Befitting its importance, Bucholtz—accompanied by a colleague—makes his first, indelible appearance descending a winding staircase as Matt, mesmerized, continues to watch. Holding a receptacle and lensed in choker close-ups, Bucholtz waxes lyrical about his "master plan": "Hermetically sealed in this little plastic box, it's sufficient to destroy the entire population of Chicago if strategically introduced into that city's water supply on any given day."

Although Bucholtz's grand scheme to loose "germ cultures" such as parrot and bubonic plague on the citizens of the United States is chilling, Menzies's real *coup de théâtre* is the play within the play. After Bucholtz walks over to a drape-darkened interior window that reflects his image, he opens the curtain coincident with a "magical" harp glissando to reveal a mass of milling figures straight out of a horror movie—complete with a man swathed in bandages like the Mummy—who turn their ruined faces toward the camera: these "guinea pigs" are the objects of Bucholtz's Nazi-inspired experiments. (The bandage that Matt sports throughout the movie à la Jake Gittes in *Chinatown* [1974] signifies his allegiance with these patients imprisoned like zoo animals behind glass.) When Bucholtz's colleague becomes squeamish, he chastises him—"You must look at these people through the eyes of a scientist"—explaining that while some of the patients "infected with incurable diseases or infirmities" volunteered for a "last service to the cause," others were traitors who "were turned over to [him] for experimentation."

Matt, having seen enough, beats a hasty retreat back to Janet, but *The Whip Hand* reprises the above spectacular diorama when the two are later captured trying to flee Winnoga by car, then at the end of the film, when the FBI, alerted by Matt's editor, descends en masse on the compound with machine guns blazing. The first reiteration occurs on the heels of another evocative shot of the pier from which Matt and Janet are taken by boat back to Peterson's lodge, where Bucholtz lectures them on the naiveté of the American people:

> You've written your last article, Corbin. From now on you will play a more active part in germ warfare. And so will you, young lady. It's not often that we have such healthy specimens. . . . All you Americans are alike, stupid, guileless. By the time we are finished, *American View* magazine won't even have any readers. There are enough germs here to destroy the United States when the word is given.

As Janet's taken away to be bound and gagged, she makes one final, passionate appeal to her brother: "Edward, you couldn't be involved in all this?"

The third and final appearance of the diorama in *The Whip Hand* is, thematically speaking, the richest. After Matt disarms a guard, Edward refuses to inject his sister with the same drug he used to kill Luther and, instead, exchanges gunfire with Peterson, killing him. Meanwhile, the FBI has stormed the lab and Bucholtz is now among his subjects, standing—detonator in hand—behind the glass. When a machine-gun burst from a G-man only pockmarks the surface, another agent reminds the doctor that the Nobel Prize committee once considered him the "scientist that most benefited mankind." Bucholtz, fanatical to the end, continues to elaborate on his life's work:

> Don't waste your bullets. Before I'm through you might want to use them on yourselves.... No one is leaving here alive.... I shall die willingly knowing that my work has been accomplished. Within the next forty-eight hours America will sink to its knees.... I am benefiting mankind by ridding the world of all the people who stand in the way of Communism.

Even as Bucholtz continues to rhapsodize about the imminent end of the world— "When I turn this handle, the force of the explosion will scatter germs for hundreds of miles. It will spread from one end of the country to the other like wildfire, infecting, corrupting, paralyzing"—Matt retrieves a key from Edward and, sneaking up behind the doctor, disengages the detonator. The sequence concludes on a violent but "poetic" note: Matt punches Bucholtz, knocking him down, after which the patients close in on their oppressor, kicking and hitting him with their crutches.

The happily-ever-after coda to *The Whip Hand* opens on a magazine layout from *American View*—"Communist Germ Center Wiped Out"—the camera zooming in on a photo of a smiling Matt and Janet that dissolves via a live match cut to the two kissing. This vision of the connubial, all-American couple represents a robust, romantic resolution to the body of the film, in which the insidious threat of the red menace is coupled with the "lingering fear of Nazis," a nightmarish scenario that's linked in turn with the fear of biological weapons research.[16] It's therefore no accident that the store owner Luther, the sole original inhabitant of Winnoga, refused to be bought out by the communists in 1945, since this was the year that marked the transition in the United States from the wartime to the postwar period. In other words, *The Whip Hand* appears to be governed by a powerful retroactive fantasy, as if the present red plot were simply a screen for past historical trauma; hence the heroic return of the Warners G-men in the final reel, who harken back to the 1930s and the origins of anti-Nazi sentiment in America.

However, if *The Whip Hand* can be seen as a belated response to the original méconnaissance of Hitlerian fascism, its real fascination derives less from this lurid Nazi constellation than how the film weds its apocalyptic fish story to the dirty allure of germs—communists, as it were, as "germ men"—a metaphor that perfectly captures the contagious rhetoric of the times, as if you could pick up the red virus as easily as the common cold. Of course, for such hysterically hyper-vigilant (i.e., paranoid) institutions as the FBI or HUAC, that was precisely the problem—you could. In the furious two-horse race to the future, in which, it appeared, the winner would take all (the big prize for both the Soviets and Americans was the final frontier of outer space), this, then, was the plague that whipped the masses: the black fear of the red hand.

I WAS A COMMUNIST FOR THE F.B.I.: FEAR OF A RED PLANET

If, as Michael Rogin declares, the "film that introduced cold war demonology into Hollywood was a hot war movie," *Mission to Moscow* (1943), Cold War films "revived and inverted the political popular-front culture of the struggle against Fascism."[17] *I Was a Communist for the F.B.I.* is, according to this logic, the '50s sequel to *Mission to Moscow*. Rogin again:

> Both films used documentary voice-over to give fiction the sound of news; both showed factory sabotage; both glorified a secret, internal police; and both warned against imminent foreign invasion. A contemporary cabal in both films threatened the national defense, played upon divisive social elements, and undermined the nation's will.[18]

In other words, the difference between *Mission to Moscow* and *I Was a Communist for the F.B.I.*, a difference that was a function of the postwar turn against all things "red," was that the "threat was now from Russia, not to it."[19]

If *I Was a Communist for the F.B.I.* mirrors *Mission to Moscow*, it's also inspired by film noir—by, in particular, two other Warner Bros. pictures: *Confessions of a Nazi Spy* (1939) and *Walk a Crooked Mile*. *Confessions of a Nazi Spy* was a "typical Warner picture" in that the film's investigative figure, Inspector Edward Renard, was based on real-life FBI agent Leon Turrou and played, "in the G-man style familiar to American moviegoers," by Edward G. Robinson.[20] Not so incidentally, it also substituted "German-American Bundists for criminals."[21] In fact, John Wexley, who co-scripted *Confessions of a Nazi Spy*, claimed he had seen Martin Dies, the Democratic congressman who founded HUAC with Samuel Dickstein, "exiting from Jack Warner's office and that the executive urged him to include Communist characters along with Nazis as subversives to be curbed."[22] In the end, "hardly a charge made against 'foreign subversion' in *Confessions* would not be turned against Communists during the [German-Soviet] Pact and with more concentrated ferocity during the decade after the war."[23]

While *Confessions of a Nazi Spy* bears a distant inverted relation to *I Was a Communist for the F.B.I.*, the film's immediate precursor is *Walk a Crooked Mile*, which was directed, like the latter feature, by Gordon Douglas, who helmed such gangster noirs as *Kiss Tomorrow Goodbye* (1950) with James Cagney and the early neo-noirs *The Detective* (1968) and *Lady in Cement* (1968) with Frank Sinatra. Douglas also directed the sci-fi-inflected *Them!* (1954), a red scare film that "articulates a fear of atomic radiation" even as it fashions a "fantastic metaphor of the communist menace."[24]

Walk a Crooked Mile tells the story of a joint effort on the part of the FBI and Scotland Yard to discover the origin of top-secret leaks from a nuclear physics laboratory located in Lakeview, California. The atomic secrets are smuggled out of the country via oil paintings, and at one point, searching the San Francisco apartment of Igor Braun—"an urban landscape painter with French sensibilities"[25]—the British agent "Scotty" Grayson (Louis Hayward) comments, "He could be a pretty fair painter." "Yes," colleague Daniel O'Hara (Dennis O'Keefe) responds, "if he didn't have so much red in his work." Wit aside, *Walk a Crooked Mile* is a "pretty fair example" of semidocumentary noir, recording as it does the U.S. government's quest to root out those "who walk their crooked miles along the highways and byways of free America."[26]

As with *Walk a Crooked Mile*, *I Was a Communist for the F.B.I.* is at once a docu-noir and a "melodramatic example of countersubversive anticommunism," "crackling good melodrama," and "tense, violent thriller."[27] Based on a series of *Saturday Evening Post* articles written by Pete Martin under the title "I Posed as a Communist for the F.B.I" that chronicled Matt Cvetic's exploits as an undercover agent,[28] *I Was a Communist for the F.B.I.* was nominated for an Academy Award for Best Documentary in 1951. (The nomination says less about the film's documentary credentials than the academy's abject standards.) Reflecting its sensational title, which flashes up on the screen word by word in sync with Max Steiner's fanfare, Douglas's film sublimates Cvetic's personal sins and pathetic private life into a parable of self-sacrifice: the FBI informant—*not*, mind you, informer—as a paradigm of patriotism, the national hero as saint. (Forget that in real life Cvetic was "retired" by the FBI in 1952 for regularly exercising his demons, among them alcoholism, womanizing, and a violent temper.)

Casting is everything here. Whereas O'Keefe, the American FBI agent in *Walk a Crooked Mile*, made his noir bones in Anthony Mann's *T-Men* (1947) and *Raw Deal* (1948), the role of Matt Cvetic in *I Was a Communist for the F.B.I.* is played by Frank Lovejoy, who had just appeared in Nicholas Ray's *In a Lonely Place* (1950) as an ex-GI cop who is sympathetic to the violently unpredictable Hollywood scribe Dix Steele. Lovejoy also starred as Howard Tyler in Cy Endfield's *The Sound of Fury*, aka *Try and Get Me* (1950), as a family man whose life goes from bad to worse when the petty thief he has inextricably become involved with brutally murders the scion of a wealthy family. (Based on a true-crime story, *Try and Get Me* is justly famous, together with its blacklisted director, for its conclusion, in which the townspeople, enraged by the death of the kidnapping victim, hang the suspects from a tree.)

Lovejoy's "everyman" persona surfaces early on in *I Was a Communist for the F.B.I.* As opposed to *Walk a Crooked Mile* and *The Whip Hand*, both of which resort to third-person voice-over, Douglas's film features first-person narration, a device that accentuates the narrative's subjective, "confessional" character and presents a dramatic contrast to the semidocumentary aspect. (The screenplay for *I Was a Communist for the F.B.I.* is credited to Crane Wilbur, who not only co-authored *He Walked by Night* with John C. Higgins and *The Phenix City Story* with Daniel Mainwaring but scripted and directed such "prison" noirs as *Canon City* [1948] and *The Story of Molly X* [1949].)

After a brief prelude in which we watch the FBI track the movement of Gerhardt Eisler—"Communist agent, spy, convicted perjurer"—boarding a flight from LaGuardia to Pittsburgh (Eisler is played by Konstantin Shayne, the former Nazi concentration camp commandant in Welles's *The Stranger* [1946]),[29] Matt narrates a montage of Pittsburgh's "Golden Triangle," where the "Allegheny and Monongahela Rivers meet to form the mighty Ohio,"[30] as he travels by car to his mother's house:

> So, Gerhardt Eisler . . . was coming to Pittsburgh—Pittsburgh, the heart of America's industrial might, where the Commies had planted themselves to throw their heart off beat. What have I got to do with this? Well, my name is Matt Cvetic. Cvetic is a Slovenian name. Lots of Slovenians in Pittsburgh. . . . My folks are real nice people. They came over to this country forty years ago, became citizens, and raised a family of six kids.

The gist of Cvetic's voice-over narration (note the repetition of the word "heart") is its melodramatic evocation of the "nice" big Slovenian family, which has successfully assimilated into the American way of life.

The documentary-like prologue that precedes Cvetic's voice-over narration is inscribed, however, with a subtle, melodramatic subtext. Thus, when the FBI agent McIntyre (Paul McGuire), having watched Eisler's plane depart from LaGuardia, goes to a telephone booth to call Washington, a mother in the next booth, a baby boy crooked in one arm, can be heard asking her husband, "Do you wanna say goodbye to Gregory?" As in Leo McCarey's *My Son John* (1952), the mother-son relation in *I Was a Communist for the F.B.I.* is an index of Matt's character. In a familiar inversion of the classical-Marxist formulation of the "base" and "superstructure," the economic (here, Pittsburgh's industrial prowess) is predicated on the institutional unit of the family, itself synecdochically figured in the form of the maternal bond.

This melodramatic strain materializes in all its familial hysteria in the extended sequence in which Matt, joining his family for his mother's birthday, interacts with his brother Joe (Paul Picerni) and his son Dick (Ron Hagerthy). The first note of discord is sounded after Matt warmly greets his son, who's sitting off to one side—"Every time I see this guy, he's getting bigger than the last time"—and Joe remarks under his breath, "That's because you don't see him very often." Matt's a bad father, the film suggests, because he spends all of his extracurricular time slaving for the Communist Party, an insinuation that's confirmed when the family is about to sit down for dinner and Matt receives a phone call from the local party boss, Jim Blandon (James Millican): Eisler has arrived and wants to see him, pronto.[31] As Matt's preparing to say good-bye to his mother, Joe, who has overheard the conversation, grabs him by the lapels and shoves him up against the front door, barking, "Get out of the house and don't come back, you slimy Red!"

If Blandon's call, interrupting as it does a sacrosanct family ritual, represents the invasive nature of communism, the only appropriate response to such external threats is violent interdiction. In other words, in order to secure the heart of the home, the hearth (Matt's mother, confined to a wheelchair, is strategically positioned in front of the family fireplace), the "red slime" must be forcibly expelled. But if Joe's behavior is, from one perspective, righteous (since Matt's an unapologetic member of the Communist Party), from another perspective it's patently abusive (since the audience has not only been interpellated via Matt's voice-over but long since divined he's working undercover for the FBI). The birthday sequence therefore has the paradoxical effect of simultaneously "sliming" the nuclear family *and* militant anticommunism.

Not surprisingly, the manifestation of this rhetorical contradiction is the moment when *I Was a Communist for the F.B.I.* assumes a decidedly noir cast. The transition, signified by a neon sign, is visible in the lap dissolve from the foyer of Matt's mother's house to a diner where he stops to phone Ken Crowley (Richard Webb), the head of the FBI's Pittsburgh office and the governmental double of Blandon. Along with its status as an iconic signifier of film noir, the neon sign is symbolically overdetermined, alluding to Matt's "red" destination—the hotel where Eisler's waiting for him—as well as his increasing "lonesomeness" (to remember Matt's observation about his son). In fact, at this particular tumultuous point in his life, Matt is doubly alienated, estranged from both his extended family and its public-sphere surrogate, the Federal Bureau of Investigation.

True to the reversible visual logic of the anticommunist thriller, the FBI appears—like the Communist Party—under the iconographic sign of film noir. After Matt contacts headquarters, there's a straight cut to an office where a female secretary sits alone at a desk as a neon sign blinks behind her in a darkened window. Responding to Matt's request to speak to "Mr. Crowley," she inquires, "Who wants to speak to him?" As she transfers the call, there's another straight cut to a cigarette smoke–wreathed shot of Crowley alone at his desk, positioned between a bust of Lincoln in the foreground and a neon light winking in the Venetian-blinded window behind him. Although Crowley's office is relatively well lit, the neon sign metaphorically links the FBI with the dark metropolitan world outside. The bureau's impersonality is, moreover, evoked when Matt's home office doesn't recognize him. We the audience understand that it's not personal, it's business (the Mafia reference is totally apropos), but given the precariousness of Matt's position, we sense that it can get pretty cold—during a cold war—working for Uncle Sam.

If the institutional representation of the bureau in *I Was a Communist for the F.B.I.* is anomalous, the first mass depiction of the Communist Party is almost equally so. As opposed to *The Woman on Pier 13*, where the party is headquartered in a dark and, one imagines, dank warehouse, the location of Matt and Eisler's special meeting is, in contradistinction to the darkly low-key scene when Matt pulls up in front of the State Hotel, a large, brightly lit, expensively appointed suite. Once Matt makes his entrance (there's enough silver laid out on the buffet table to appease a pirate), Blandon offers him a glass of champagne, and as Matt skeptically eyes the sumptuous spread, Blandon's right-hand man, Harmon (Eddie Norris), chirps, "The way we're all gonna live after we take the country over."

The Bureau: Matt Cvetic's (Frank Lovejoy) FBI contact, Ken Crowley (Richard Webb), in neon-blinking bureau office in *I Was a Communist for the F.B.I.*

Matt's rejoinder—"Workers, too?"—elicits a dismissive snort from Blandon ("The trouble with you, you're too much of a fanatic"), a reaction that flushes out Eisler, a small, bespectacled, intellectual-looking man in a dark suit, who, in heavily accented English, offers a champagne toast to "Comrade Stalin." After informing Matt that he has been named chief organizer of Pittsburgh, Eisler, posed before a fireplace, declares that if the party can "move Pittsburgh an inch," it can "move this country a mile," but first it must "incite riots, discontent, open warfare." Then, while Blandon and the others get ready to leave, Eisler offers another toast—"To the Soviet Union"—before glancing at the buffet table and asking Matt, "Some caviar?"

The caviar-and-champagne reception for the party elite contrasts with the birthday party for Matt's mother, where the men drink beer, as well as with the ensuing meeting at Freedom Hall (the modifier is, of course, satiric), where Blandon practices what Eisler preaches. But whereas in the hotel sequence the communists could be mistaken for fat-cat capitalists, skimming the cream produced by the working class that Matt oversees in his personnel job at North American Steel, in the Freedom Hall scene the party's depicted as positively satanic. Backed by an American flag and portraits of Washington, Stalin, and Lincoln (quite an ideological mash-up, this), Blandon whips up a black audience while Matt interprets

The Red and the Black: African American audience listening to a lecture by local Communist Party honcho Jim Blandon (James Millican) at Freedom Hall in *I Was a Communist for the F.B.I.* See undercover FBI agent Matt Cvetic (Frank Lovejoy), passing as a "red" steelworker, sitting to the right of the black woman with the hat in the center of the screen.

in voice-over: "So they cooked up a hell-brew of hate from a recipe written in the Kremlin. It was the same old line they used for years: divide and conquer."[32]

The real bombshell, though, comes after the meeting when Eisler praises Bland-on's performance and Blandon smugly replies, "Those niggers ate it up." When Matt immediately makes the appropriate liberal response, "You mean 'Negroes,' don't you, Jim?," Blandon mocks his rhetoric of racial solidarity—"Comrades, comrades"—then, citing the Scottsboro case, lays out the party's strategy: "If one of those crowd goes out into the street tonight and picks a fight with a white man and kills him, then gets convicted by a white jury, we can go to bat and raise a defense fund." The profit, according to Blandon, from "defending six niggers": two million dollars (minus the sixty-five grand for expenses). The motivation: "the Pittsburgh branch needs dough," since, as Blandon wags to the amusement of the assembled party members, they're "always in the red." Here, "Hollywood adopted the favorite argument of John Rankin"—the notoriously anti-Semitic, white supremacist Mississippi congressman—"for whom civil rights activists [i.e., communists] were in the South to stir up trouble."[33] The reality, of course, was that communists "were the first to take risks standing up for the rights of blacks."[34] More to the point, if one, prominent anticommunist critique was that communists' employment of racial issues was instrumental—"that is, as a means to a larger political end"—it's also clear that "anti-Communists were no less sus-ceptible to the same charge."[35]

The thriller as opposed to agitprop elements of *I Was a Communist for the F.B.I.* return in the immediate wake of this, our first real glimpse into the nefarious machinations of the Communist Party, as if the issue of blackness had suddenly bled into the narrative. Back on the streets of the naked city at night, Matt stands chatting with Eisler and Blandon as they sit in a parked car outside Freedom Hall. After Matt departs, Blandon, concerned about his "fanaticism," orders Harmon to shadow him. In a classic noir passage, Harmon trails Matt down a dark street in the slanting rain to a diner, where he phones the bureau. ("I'm in a Jam with Baby," recycled from *Race Street* [1948], can be heard playing in the background.) Seeing Harmon, Matt pretends he's talking to his "baby," a bit that demonstrates his ability to think quickly on his feet and, not so incidentally, references the real-life Cvetic's sexual exploits.

This dual sexual and specular thematic receives its most dynamic expression in a form that condenses two of the dominant tropes of the 1950s imaginary—youth and femininity—into a familiar figure: the female high school teacher. The pretext is that Matt's son, Dick, has been getting into trouble at school because he doesn't want to believe what the other kids have been saying about his fa-ther: that he's a commie. In the principal's office, Matt's confirmation of his son's worst fears—"I'm a member of the Communist Party, and I have been for nine years"—produces in Dick the inevitable "better dead than Red" reaction: "I used to tell myself that I wanted to grow up to be like my Dad. Before I'd do that now, I'd drop dead." Although Dick's teacher, Eve Merrick (Dorothy Hart), reassures Matt she'll "keep an eye" on his son, given the film's pervasive atmosphere of paranoia, the audience and Matt can only wonder: who is Eve Merrick, and can she be trusted?

The following three sequences of *I Was a Communist for the F.B.I.* suggest the sort of ideological stakes associated with Eve's character. The first is the highly volatile issue of marriage. In a high-angle, deep-focus shot of the lobby of an apartment building, Matt starts up the stairs as another man quickly descends:

WOMAN: Willie! Willie!
MAN: What's on your mind?
WOMAN: You better be back home by twelve o'clock!
MAN: And if I ain't?
WOMAN: And if you ain't, I won't be here when you do get back.
MAN: That's the best news I've heard all year.

While this repartee is no doubt intended as a commentary on the low-rent lodging that Matt's forced to endure as a double agent, it paints an oddly grim picture of matrimony—odd because the film never explains what happened to his wife. (In his ghosted memoir, Cvetic claims that he and his wife separated after his son received a black eye at school.[36])

The second sequence reintroduces the issue of fatherhood in the guise of America's favorite pastime, baseball, a sport that constitutes one of the main conceits of *Walk a Crooked Mile*. (In Douglas's film, Dr. Townsend, the head of the Lakeview Research Laboratory, refers to Dr. von Stolb as a "mathematical Babe Ruth" and, later, extending the metaphor, remarks that their "team" is only "one inning away" from solving a problem vital to America's national security.[37]) As Matt proceeds down the hall to his apartment, a boy named Jackie appears with a baseball bat—a seeming allusion to Jackie Robinson—and asks him for some tips about bunting. When Matt shows him how to do it, however, the boy's father attacks him as if he were a child molester: "I thought I told you to stay away from my kid. . . . Baseball's an American game!" As in the birthday sequence where Matt's brother Joe berates him for shaming their mother, this scene has a contradictory rhetorical charge: even as it demonstrates that Matt's in fact a good enough father, it documents the extraordinary abuse that he's regularly subjected to as an FBI plant.

The third sequence—marked by voice-over narration, string-laden orchestral music, and images of Dick's bandaged face superimposed over a shot of Matt composing a letter—is the quintessence of melodrama:

I'm helping to fight a dark and dangerous force. And if one word of the truth got out it might mean not only the end of me but perhaps of better men who take the same chances I do every day. . . . If I do go, you'll know the last thought I had on Earth was of you and my mother.

This letter, to be left in the care of the parish priest Father Novac (Roy Roberts) should Matt be killed, conjoins the issue of mother love and fatherhood in the idealized image of the "holy family" in which the battle against communism is waged under the watchful but beneficent eyes of the Almighty. (The figure of Father Novac recollects Bishop Fulton J. Sheen, whose popular DuMont TV show, *Life Is Worth Living* [1952–1957], represented an "unholy alliance" between Catholicism and anticommunism.[38])

When Eve rematerializes, knocking unexpectedly at Matt's door at night (Is this the "RED KNOCK" that special FBI agent Murphy warns Cvetic about in *The Big Decision*?[39]), she invites herself in and then asks if she can sit down. Matt thinks that she there's because of his son, but she quickly sets him straight: "I didn't come here to see you about him. I came to see you about me." Even though, or perhaps because, she's a member of the Communist Party (Eve nonchalantly hands Matt her party card), he's immediately suspicious, asking, "Who sent you?" before proceeding to grill her about her "racket": teaching. Learning there are thirty other women in her branch of the party, he asks, "All of them as attractive as you? That's the idea, isn't it?" "Not in my book," Eve replies, smiling seductively. "If that's heresy, make the most of it."

If these heretical inclinations speak powerfully to Matt's desire to trust her, Eve's forward, not to say aggressive, behavior portrays her as the classic Red temptress. "Look, I came here because I thought you were lonely," she says, moving closer. "I thought you were lonely, too. Remember that if you ever change your mind." And then she picks up her coat and goes, her proposition hanging in the air like the smoke from Matt's still-burning cigarette. Later, we listen along with the FBI (Matt has previously installed a listening device in party headquarters) to a tape recording in which Blandon, discussing Matt's surveillance, refers to Eve as a "tasty little dish."

The FBI, unlike Blandon, isn't salacious, although its view of Eve isn't appreciably different. In a vintage noir scene set at Willard's warehouse near the Allegheny bridge—it's night, a horn sounds in the distance, and lights glimmer in the fog—Crowley warns Matt about Eve: "Smarter guys than you have been tripped up by a dame." Dressed in matching dark coats and fedoras, the two men could be talking about a heist, and when Matt can't strike a match in the fog-heavy air, Crowley hands him his lit cigarette. Translation: unlike Eve (the name is suggestive), men like Crowley can be trusted.

Eve represents a real enigma for both Matt and the FBI—Is she a "bad" or "good girl," earnest schoolteacher or commie vixen?—but before Matt can begin to address this riddle, there's more bad news. Returning to his apartment, he learns from Dick, who's waiting for him on the stairs, that his mother is dying and has asked to see him. By the time he arrives, though, "it's too late," and after his brother Joe gives him a dirty look, Matt leaves without a word. The subsequent post-funeral sequence set outside a Catholic church pits the communists represented by Blandon and Harmon versus Matt's family, with Matt and Eve caught in the crossfire. Father Novac returns Matt's secret letter (the padre has suddenly been called to Rome) and he has to physically intercede when Joe, tossing away the red roses the party has sent, assails Matt, screaming, "Put up your hands, you dirty Red!" before punching him in the head and stomach, knocking him down.

As the plaintive, violin-scored motif swells again on the sound track, Matt returns, alone, to his apartment. Even as the public fight with Joe represents a new low for his character, it threatens to sabotage his undercover work for the FBI since, he belatedly realizes, he's somehow lost the letter Father Novac just returned to him. Matt, like Brad Galt (Mark Stevens) in *The Dark Corner* (1946), is now squarely behind the eight ball: if the "slimy commies" find the letter, they'll "cut his throat and throw him in the river"; if he quits, the FBI will publicly disown him and he'll really be out in the cold. Matt's crisis of faith transpires, ironically enough, in a record shop. After he asks the proprietor for a recording of Beethoven's "Emperor" concerto, he passes a young woman jitterbugging in a booth on his way to the back room to meet up with Crowley and Mason. (Here, the visual force of the "Lend a Hand" Red Cross poster on the rear wall exceeds, like the film itself, its intended patriotic message. How much blood, sweat, and tears must Matt shed before he's allowed to come clean about his real, all-American identity?) While Matt rails against his fate—"Ya gotta get me out of this thing, ya gotta wipe this red smear off of me, I can't take it anymore"—big band music plays in the background like music from another, non-red planet.

Paradoxically enough, the protagonist's salvation is propelled, as in *The Woman on Pier 13*, by a woman's actions. Eve's epiphany, a real eye-opener, occurs during a wildcat strike against North American Steel after a communist-led filibuster has worn down the already work-weary union members. Outside the plant's main gate, party women dressed as union wives scream, "Kill those scabs!" and communist goons imported from New York attack the union leaders with lead pipes wrapped in Jewish newspapers. (The sequence recalls the studio strikes of 1945–1946, the so-called Battle of Burbank, which especially impacted Warner Bros.[40]) As Joe's being taken away in an ambulance, Blandon pronounces, "That's a pretty good day's work." Earlier he had instructed Eve to hand out pamphlets with a "big hello and smile"—lascivious as usual, he added, "If they make any passes at you, don't get sore." Eve's appalled by what she's just seen, telling Matt, "I don't like any part of what happened here today." However, because she blurts this out right in front of another rabid party member—Matt's female secretary, who we've previously seen secretly transcribing his activities in a notebook—he's forced to confront Eve at party headquarters and, as Blandon and company look on, demand her resignation. Eve, who's completely disillusioned, is more than happy to go. Although she once thought "Communism was an intellectual movement," she now knows the truth: that it's only interested in the "complete control of every mind and body in the world," a sentiment spectacularly dramatized in the sci-fi classic *Invasion of the Body Snatchers* (1956).

The following sequences—in which Matt escorts Eve back home to pack and engages Blandon's men on a train and then in a deserted tunnel—are the most visually arresting in the film. (The cinematography, which Robert Porfirio calls the "most visually noir" of all the anticommunist thrillers,[41] was supervised by Edwin DuPar, whose previous noir credits were for his special-effects work on *Danger Signal* [1945] and *Nora Prentiss* [1947].[42]) In the first sequence, Matt, with Blandon's approval, tails Eve after she has threatened to go straight to the school board and "name every teacher who carries a Party card." (Eve—unlike, say, the Hollywood Ten—is not only willing but eager to name names.)

There's a cut on action from a track-in shot of Blandon to a low-angle one of Eve descending a staircase that's half in shadow, half in light, Matt's face a bright spot, like the lightbulb in the high right corner of the frame. Once Matt catches up with Eve at the base of the stairs, he explains that he was forced to turn her in, and she tells him that she should have turned him in, but couldn't, because of the letter. The swing music from the Dreamland dance club next door is a bittersweet reminder, like the big band music in Bryson's record store, of the sort of carefree life that the two might be enjoying if the fates were kinder.

The second sequence is set at Eve's apartment building. As she goes upstairs to pack, Matt checks that the back door is open before pulling the car around to the rear. What he doesn't know is that Blandon's men have been watching them from across the street. Matt and Eve manage to evade them, but as Harmon and Mansanovitch (David McMahon) prepare to enter Eve's apartment, there's a sudden reverse track out to another anonymous man hiding across the hall. Who is he and what is he doing? Illustrating Rogin's observation that it's frequently difficult in anticommunist noirs to "tell the faceless Communists from their counterparts in the F.B.I.,"[43] the man's name, it turns out, is Broderick (Ed Hinton) and he's a federal agent. The other surprise is that after being overpowered by Blandon's men while trying to call headquarters, Broderick dies: in a dynamic low-angle passage worthy of John Alton's work for Anthony Mann, Mansanovitch is trying to strangle the FBI agent when Harmon grabs a butcher knife from the counter and viciously stabs him to death.

In the meantime, Matt and Eve appear to have made a clean escape when we see that yet another man has seen them drive away. The man, tossing a cigarette to the ground, growls to his partner, "Something's gone wrong." At the train station the two men, Brennan (Howard Negley) and Dobbs (John Bradford), furtively watch Eve as she strides toward the departing trains. Continuing the play on "seeing" and "being seen," the film cuts to Matt, who, hiding behind a column watching the men watch Eve, begins to trail Brennan and Dobbs, leaping onto the caboose of the departing train, where, searching for Eve, he works his way through a car crowded with passengers. When he notices that she's trapped, he yanks on the brake, bringing the train to a grinding halt, then punches Brennan, sending him face-first into a pane of glass before knocking down Dobbs with swift, repeated kicks to the body.

Although Matt and Eve manage to escape again, slipping off the train, a canted, low-angle carriage shot of the two making their way deeper into the tunnel, cars flickering past, captures their entrapment. In the cramped, steam-obscured space, Brennan and Dobbs, guns drawn, follow. Once the train pulls away, Matt smashes a lightbulb and—in an echo of the sign to Dreamland, "Climb the Stairs to Heaven"—hides out at the top of a staircase. Brennan, having taken the bait, climbs up after him, but Matt knocks him back down onto the train tracks, the film cutting to a tight close-up of Brennan's horrified face as a rushing locomotive bears down. The death of Dobbs is even more graphic: in a deep-focus shoot-out in which Matt's standing in the left foreground and Brennan's positioned across the tracks in the right background, the two exchange gunfire until there's a sudden reverse-angle shot of Dobbs, his face flashing toward the camera as a bullet creases his forehead.

As if in recompense for this sustained, visceral violence, the dénouement of *I Was a Communist for the F.B.I.* dutifully gets back on message. At a swanky suite at the State Hotel, a homegrown double of Eisler, party bigwig Clyde Garson (Hugh Sanders), warns his comrades about HUAC ("a group of fat-headed politicians whose only aim is to crash the headlines") before announcing that North Korea is about to cross the 38th parallel and invade South Korea. In a revealing sidelight (and in an echo of the earlier, scurrilous fund-raising passage), Matt broaches a defense fund for the eleven committee party members already on trial in New York. Blandon, seizing Matt's initiative, instructs one member to become a "phony Fascist" and start up "another Nazi Bund"—"Call them blackshirts, grayshirts, anything you want"—then orders another to engage the "cultural division" to stage a big rally where "sacred cows," "pinko chumps," and "big-mouth suckers" can "howl their heads off about the rape of the First Amendment."

The news that Brennan and Dobbs have been murdered not only puts an end to the festivities and Matt in the hot seat; it also precipitates a series of reversals that carry the film to its patriotically grandiloquent conclusion. First Blandon, invoking Fritz Kuhn, the head of the German American Bund,[44] threatens Matt: "You know what happens to traitors—Trotsky thought he was safe but they got to him." Then Harmon and Mansanovitch start in on Matt, beating him up for betraying the party when, alerted by the FBI, the police arrive and arrest him for the murder of Broderick, a charge that effectively makes Matt an FBI plant masquerading as a communist agent accused of murdering a G-man. (While imprisoned, Matt narrates a montage featuring the only real documentary footage in the film—significantly, of the Red riots from Harlem to the Battery precipitated by the New York trials.) Blandon eventually springs Matt, who's desperate to testify for the government— "Now I can crawl out of my rat hole and live like a man"—but at the very last minute, Crowley informs him that his hard-won testimony will not be needed, yet.

Matt's laboring again for the party, picketing outside the courthouse, when Blandon tells him what he has been waiting nine long years to hear: that he's been summoned along with the other top men of the Pittsburgh division of the party to appear before HUAC. At the trial, Matt's brother Joe, a scar visible on his face, and his son, Dick, dressed now in a naval uniform, sit apprehensively in the audience. A committee member begins by asking Harmon, "Are you a member, or have you ever been a member, of the Communist Party?" and Harmon, predictably, takes the Fifth. When Matt's called, the chairman of the committee asks him to review his daily FBI reports about the party, and he's finally able to tear off what Cvetic in *The Big Decision* calls the "Red Badge of Treason":

> I learned chiefly that its political activities are nothing more than fronts. It is actually a vast spy system founded in our country by the Soviet. It's composed of American traitors whose only purpose is to deliver the people of the United States into the hands of Russia as a slave colony.[45]

Matt's fervent testimony brings Joe and Dick jubilantly to their feet, relieved at long last to hear that he is not, in fact, a "slimy Red."

True to its tri-form character as a docu-melo-noir, the coda of *I Was a Communist for the F.B.I.* is one part action, one part tearjerker, and one part semi-documentary. In a waiting room to which Matt has repaired after testifying, he encounters Blandon, who, apoplectic at Matt's betrayal of the party, tosses a bird-shaped bookend at his head, shouting, "You dirty stinkin' stool pigeon!" However, not unlike Big Jim McLain at the end of the eponymously titled John Wayne film, Matt gets to kick some commie butt one last time, laying out Blandon like a mackerel. It's only after Matt has turned Blandon over to security—"Your witness, Congressman"—that he sees Joe and Dick. While Dick tearfully apologizes to his father for not believing in him, Matt embraces his son—"I was proud . . . you had the guts to see this slimy thing for just what it is"—as the "Battle Hymn of the Republic" rises on the sound track. The final shot of Lincoln's bust is a parting shot at Stalin and his red minions: America, with the help of the FBI and HUAC, will never be a slave to the Soviet Union.

One of the many ironies of the concluding shot of Lincoln is that it can be said to reference the Abraham Lincoln Brigade, a salient allusion since, as I noted at the outset, *I Was a Communist for the F.B.I.* mirrors *Mission to Moscow* and the antifascism of the 1930s when fighting for the Loyalists against Franco was "considered tantamount to being a communist."[46] The ambiguity of the conclusion is not restricted, however, to this antifascist issue, since the allusion to Lincoln and slavery tellingly reprises the race question that's raised like a red flag in the body of the film.[47] In the aforementioned scene set at Freedom Hall, Blandon, posed before a portrait of Lincoln, addresses an African American audience as Matt observes in voice-over, "It was the same old line they used with racial minorities to create unrest and confusion." Later, after Matt recounts his experience to Crowley and Mason while they're driving at night in the rain, Crowley replies, "That's the way they started the race riots in Detroit in 1943 and the riots in Harlem that same year when five Negroes were killed. Those poor fellas never knew their death warrants were signed in Moscow."

While Crowley's pronouncement may seem fantastical today, it reflects the FBI's considered, albeit deeply paranoid, thinking about the Communist Party circa 1951: that the party was responsible for fomenting black "unrest and confusion." In *Masters of Conceit* Hoover wrote that the "Party's claim that it is working for Negro rights is a deception and fraud. The Party's sole interest . . . is to hoodwink the Negro, to exploit him as a tool to build a Communist America."[48] If, in other words, another one of the ironies of *I Was a Communist for the F.B.I.* is that, in an act of double repression, the "black question" is explicitly raised in the film only to be displaced onto the "red question,"[49] the fact that Blandon addresses an African American audience at a moment when such integrated assemblies were considered verboten in the United States portrays the party, in a curious twist whereby the truth returns "like the repressed to plague those who do not believe it,"[50] as antisegregationist. Such are the film's performative contradictions.

Given the ideological mutability of *I Was a Communist for the F.B.I.*, it's no surprise that the film's logic of repression and overdetermination is operative with respect to the genre of film noir as well. Thus, according to at least one historically dominant reading, Douglas's picture cannot be a film noir because its anticommunist and docu-melodramatic elements are antithetical to the classical tradition, a circumscription reflected in Humphries's concluding assessment of *I Was a Communist for the F.B.I.* On one hand, the film's "entire logic of narration and, especially, representation is difficult to apprehend outside the tradition of film noir"; on the other hand, "neither the documentary nor the much-vaunted 'documentary style' has anything to do with it."[51] Here, in an otherwise penetrating reading of *I Was a Communist for the F.B.I.*, Humphries valorizes its identity as a noir at the direct expense of its semidocumentary elements, as if recognizing this particular aspect somehow meant uncritically accepting the film's truth claims.[52]

The point, of course, is not to suggest that Douglas's film is somehow "progressive." It isn't. The aim, rather, is to propose that partly because of its generic heterogeneity, an ostensibly straightforward "right wing" picture such as a *I Was a Communist for the F.B.I.* not only reflects the changing character of classic noir in the postwar period—from expressionism, via the semidocumentary picture, to neorealism—but offers an unusually complex portrait of the free-floating fears about a red *and* black planet that exercised Americans' imagination in the early 1950s.

WALK EAST ON BEACON! "A RED BEHIND EVERY TREE"

Reprising the style of *The House on 92nd Street* (1945), the original title of which was "Now It Can Be Told," *Walk East on Beacon!* combines the Nazi backstory of *The Whip Hand* with the quasi-documentary melodramatics of *I Was a Communist for the F.B.I.*

The House on 92nd Street was produced by Louis de Rochemont, who in 1935 originated *The March of Time* series, a "monthly magazine . . . that combined authentic footage with dramatizations to produce an innovative and 'in-depth' style of screen journalism."[53] Directed by Henry Hathaway, the film recounts the double life of Bill Dietrich (William Eythe), an agent working for both the FBI and the Nazis, the latter of whom are attempting to steal the secret formula for the A-bomb, so-called Process 97. However, the "most significant factor" in the making of *The House on 92nd Street* was arguably "de Rochemont's ability to convince J. Edgar Hoover and the FBI to allow Twentieth Century-Fox the use of its offices, personnel, and equipment, as well as some of the bureau's files."[54]

As with *The House on 92nd Street*, the FBI's cooperation in the production of *Walk East on Beacon!* appears to be the key element in the film's complex relation to classic noir. In 1942 de Rochemont made *The F.B.I. Front* (Hoover personally thanked him for a "magnificent job" portraying the agency); in 1950, having been "given special access to the bureau's hitherto-unseen training facility at Quantico, Virginia," he made *A Day with the F.B.I.* (which Hoover also endorsed and which the bureau later used for training purposes); and in 1951 de Rochemont was slated to make "The History of Communism," a "teaching film" for the State Department's International Motion Picture Service about "how the Russian people had been enslaved."[55]

Help!: Movie advertisement/public service announcement in the Motion Picture Comics *Walk East on Beacon!* See list of suspicious activities at bottom of page.

If de Rochemont, in close colleague Borden Mace's adroit locution, "saw a Red behind every tree," he was also that not-so-rare breed, a liberal anticommunist, having made *Lost Boundaries* (1949), an "acclaimed racial drama that was banned in some Southern states for showing blacks and whites working and playing together," and *The Whistle at Eaton Falls* (1951), about a "strike at a small-town plastic factory" that depicted the "shared interests between labor and management."[56] Accordingly, de Rochemont's complicated relation to the FBI and Hollywood, liberalism and anticommunism, suggests that *Walk East on Beacon!* was not a top-down affair but, rather, "emerged from above *and* below," demonstrating the "increasingly tight, often consensual relationship that developed on and off screen between filmmakers and governmental agencies during the McCarthy era."[57]

The creative personnel associated with *Walk East on Beacon!* also possess, like de Rochemont, a complicated relation to the discourse of film noir. Before directing *Walk East on Beacon!* Alfred L. Werker had previously helmed the psycho noir *Shock* (1946), starring Vincent Price as a murderous psychiatrist; *Repeat Performance* (1947), in which Broadway actress Sheila Page (Joan Leslie) knocks off her two-timing, alcoholic husband on New Year's Eve and then is magically permitted to relive the past year only to tragically repeat it; and *He Walked by Night* (1948), which chronicles the LAPD's effort to capture a technologically savvy thief who has murdered a police officer. Although Anthony Mann completed *He Walked by Night* (and shot the exteriors with John Alton), the film's procedural, semidocumentary emphasis on modern electronics and new communication technologies (which inspired Jack Webb's radio and television series *Dragnet*) anticipates *Walk East on Beacon!*

Not unlike Webb's TV series, Leo Rosten's script for *Walk East on Beacon!*—based on Hoover's "Crime of the Century" about Klaus Fuchs's courier, Harry Gold, who in 1944–1945 passed top-secret information about the Manhattan Project to the Soviets[58]—was long on procedure and short on the sort of thrills typically associated with film noir. "The days of the dashing Mata Hari," Rosten once opined, "are gone."[59] With the exception of Vincent, aka Malvin, Foss (Jack Manning), the Red taxi driver who mysteriously commits suicide, the featured players in *Walk East on Beacon!* run to type, including and especially leading man Inspector James "Jim" Belden, played by George Murphy. Although Murphy had appeared in various dark crime films such as *The Arnelo Affair* (1947), *Border Incident* (1949), and *No Questions Asked* (1951), in real life he was a die-hard Republican; a former president, like Ronald Reagan, of the Screen Actors Guild (not to mention a future senator from California); and a friendly witness for HUAC.[60]

If the narrative of *Walk East on Beacon!* is not as byzantine as some noirs, it's not without convolution: after an anonymous woman tips off the FBI that "Robert Martin is forcing her husband to work for an espionage ring" (we later learn that the woman on the phone is Vincent's wife, Rita [Vilma Kurer]), the bureau surveils Robert Martin (Ernest Graves) in the Boston Public Garden, then tracks him to a freighter bound for Poland. In Washington, D.C., Belden, a "veteran investigator assigned to domestic intelligence cases," instructs the Boston office of the FBI—on the express orders of Hoover—to pursue this lead. (Hoover himself can be seen, backed by an American flag, in the narrated montage that opens the film.) In Boston, Martin's promptly replaced by Alex Laschenkov (Karel Stepanek), a senior Soviet operative sent by the Kremlin to "speed the penetration of Falcon," a new, hush-hush American project, and to "extract information from Falcon's top mathematician, Professor Albert Kafer" (Finlay Currie).

Alex's first line of business—and he's all business—is to visit a flower shop where, after submitting half of a Russian bill by way of introduction, the owner, Luther Danzig (Bruno Wick), puts him into contact with Millie Zalenko/Teresa Salinka (Virginia Gilmore), the co-proprietor with her husband, Chris/Gino (Peter Capell), of a camera shop. Millie puts the screws to Kafer at a Boston restaurant, using his progeny as bait: since his son Samuel is being held in East Berlin, the professor must either play ball with the Soviets or Samuel will perish like his two other sons, who died in the concentration camps.

In tandem with the stereotypical third-person narration (voiced by Westbrook van Voorhis) and extensive location work ("Shooting on the streets, in offices, at ports and in sight of well-known public buildings"[61]), *Walk East on Beacon!* eschews expressionist lighting in favor of a more naturalistic, semidocumentary look. One exception is the titular sequence that jumpstarts the second part of the film, in which Kafer, responding to a directive, goes to the corner of Beacon and Clarendon in Boston: when the clock strikes eleven, he starts to walk east on Beacon with an umbrella in one hand and an empty cream jar in the other.

It's here that Werker, with the assistance of cinematographer Joseph Brun, who would later photograph Robert Wise's *Odds against Tomorrow*, broaches many of the audiovisual tropes associated with classic noir. The sequence commences with a long shot of Kafer, a small dark figure in the background of the frame, as he walks toward the camera, the sound of his footsteps ricocheting off the houses in the deserted neighborhood streets. After an insert shot of a hatted man in a doorway who partially emerges from the shadows to observe him, the film cuts to a lateral tracking shot of the professor walking east on Beacon. (The hatted man is presumably a federal agent, although his furtive behavior and the low-key lighting—as in a similar sequence in *Pickup on South Street*—render his status ambiguous.)

In a subsequent deep-focus master shot, a siren can be heard wailing in the distance as Kafer, dwarfed by the large, illuminated façade of a building, stops in the middle of an intersection to check his directions when, just as he's about to step into the path of a rushing fire truck, a man carrying a lunchbox grabs him from behind. Another insert shot—this time of a hatted man hiding behind a wrought-iron fence—punctuates Kafer's peregrination. The ambulatory part of the sequence concludes when, offscreen, a male voice inquires, "How do I get to Trinity Church?" The man is Vincent Foss, Kafer's underground contact.

After Vincent informs Kafer that his son Samuel will be released only if Kafer makes his research available to the Soviets, the FBI tracks the cabbie's movements using a push-button camera concealed in a car spotlight. An extended montage accompanied by voice-over narration captures the bureau's intense surveillance of the clandestine red network and, in particular, Vincent: "For four days taxi-man Foss was the subject of continuous scrutiny by a score of FBI cars." On the fifth day, Vincent stops for Kafer in his cab, then, after depositing him in the middle of the West Boston Bridge, picks up Millie, whom he abruptly dumps by the side of the road, telling her, "This is as far as you're going. Get out. Find someone else to do your dirty work."

Vincent's about-face—he's the "only communist shown any sympathy"[62]—is preceded by two shots: a peculiar close-up of the car camera swiveling, as if it has a life of its own, and a rearview-mirror shot of Vincent handing an envelope with Kafer's papers to Millie. (The latter shot anticipates the conclusion of *Walk East on Beacon!* when Laschenkov, his figure doubled in a mirror, threatens to kill Kafer if he doesn't cooperate.) When we next see Vincent, he's back at the cramped apartment that he shares with his wife, sitting with his head in his hands on a stairwell not to heaven but nowhere.

Concerned about his appetite, Rita presses him about a "friend" who keeps calling about "color pictures," and at the mention of Martin's name, Vincent confesses that "it started when [he] was a kid during the Depression": "I wanted to help get the world back on track. . . . When I came to, I had a card in my pocket." Although this anguished confession is a staple of the anticommunist cycle (see, for example, Brad Collins's in *The Woman on Pier 13*), Vincent's indictment of the party is also predicated, like *The Woman on Pier 13*, on a figurative equivalence between marriage and communism: "Being a Party member is like waking up and finding yourself married to a woman you hate."

In fact, Vincent's complaint is part of a larger, subtextual discourse in *Walk East on Beacon!* about women and marriage. Whereas the refugee Kafers are a model of Old World bonhomie, the communists are a motley lot. Thus, when the florist Danzig tells Laschenkov that in his new American guise as Gregory Anders he'll be a "widower," Laschenkov is visibly displeased: "I would have preferred to be a bachelor." Unlike Laschenkov, the film's nominal femmes fatales, Millie and Elaine Wilbon (Louisa Horton), are in committed relationships and reflect the subgenre's popular notion of communist women as either emotionally frigid or blatantly concupiscent like "Venus flytrap" Mollie O'Flaherty (Barbara Fuller) and "red dragon lady" Yvonne Kraus (Betty Lou Gerson) in *The Red Menace*.

We're first introduced to Elaine, whose husband, Nicholas (George Roy Hill), works at the Falcon facility in Virginia, when Danzig sets up a meeting between Laschenkov and her in a private room at a Boston restaurant. (Danzig, utilizing his floral code, schedules the rendezvous by sending Elaine azaleas.) After Laschenkov offers her a cigarette—his manner is seductive, perversely so—he relays that Moscow is "impressed" with her and Nicholas's work:

ELAINE: Together we can do much more than either of us can do alone.
ALEX: Highly practical combination of devotion and service.
ELAINE: The two are inseparable for us.

While the setting is romantic and Laschenkov turns on the charm, Soviet style, giving her a watch for Nicholas that plays "Bells of Moscow," what he really desires is not sex or romance but information—"everything, anything"—about Falcon.

If Elaine and Nicholas's devoted marriage represents, like Laschenkov, the sublimation of sex for "service" (as such, all three embody the ice-cold mentalité of the Cold War), Millie and Chris's relationship is rather more carnal, as becomes evident when Alex goes to the camera shop and asks Millie if she can make a print from half a photographic negative. Cut to a high-contrast shot of Chris lit like a criminal from below and engulfed by shadow, a shot that recollects the darkroom sequence in *The Woman on Pier 13* in which Christine develops microfilm for the party. Next, we watch from above as Chris, hands splayed out on a light box, puts the two halves of the negative together to form a shadowy picture of the Kremlin. Cue Laschenkov, who, joining Chris in the back room of the store, begins to interrogate him about his wife: "Can Millie keep her head?" Shrugging, Chris replies: "Don't worry. We've been together for four years. She's done alright by the Party [pause] and me." The slight pause, punctuated by Chris's knowing smile, intimates that Millie is, unlike Elaine, "hot."

In fact, Millie is not merely the enigma that propels the first part of *Walk East on Beacon!* but the initial object, along with Robert Martin, of the film's cinematic gaze. The narrative proper opens with 16mm footage of Martin and an anonymous woman, her face obscured by a newspaper, sitting on a park bench in the Public Garden. (The famous swan boats can be seen gliding in the background.) Martin places a folded paper on the bench and the woman picks it up. However, when the woman walks away without turning her face to the camera, the only information that the FBI has about her is that she carries a shoulder bag and, as Agent Brown later puts it, walks with a "lope."

Martin, unlike Millie, has already been identified by the FBI. When federal agents visit his wife to inform her that he has suddenly left the country on a "long trip," she breaks down, experiencing—in foreshortened form—Nan Collins's fate in *The Woman on Pier 13*: she insists that she "knows everything [her husband is] doing" only to discover, as in a bad dream, that she has been married to a communist all along. Martin's life also becomes a waking nightmare when Laschenkov, impatient with his progress on Falcon, sends him back against his will to Moscow and, given his reaction—"You can't make me go, I'm an American citizen!"—certain death.

The conclusion of *Walk East on Beacon!* weds scientific to national, international, and even, perhaps, interplanetary security. Having finally completed the "basic computations" for, as the director of Falcon puts it, the "physical laws that govern the development of all weapons," Kafer dictates the formula long-distance from Boston via telephone to the assembled scientists listening in at the facility. As the director turns placards that depict rocket ships and "interstellar space," Kafer triumphantly concludes that "by overcoming the force of gravity, [man] may build mansions or fortresses in space itself": "Heavens can now serve as highways over which man may direct his caravans in peace or in war with unerring accuracy to any point on earth."[63]

Despite the fact that Kafer's breakthrough appears to be compromised when Nicholas manages to smuggle a duplicate of his findings out of Montrose, the FBI arrests Nicholas, along with Millie and Elaine, before they can get the tape recording to Laschenkov. Nicholas, true to type, vehemently denies being a member of the communist spy ring, while Millie, questioned by an FBI agent in an office lined with bar-like shadows (as in the interrogation of Martin's replacement, Michael Dorndoff, at the very beginning of the film), is self-righteously unrepentant: "For every one of us you arrest, there are a lot of others, trained and waiting to take over." Elaine is even more combative. Slapping the papers on the desk before her, she shouts: "Listen and try to understand. I hate everything about you—your double-breasted suits and smooth, arrogant faces. You're nothing but a bunch of pussy-footing, well-paid gangsters."

A commonplace of the anticommunist noir cycle, the association between communism and gangsterism—"underworld crime and underground political subversion"—was a product of the FBI's long-standing war against La Cosa Nostra as well as the 1951 televised congressional hearings on organized crime.[64] Another commonplace of the anticommunist noir is that the "men in blue" are frequently indistinguishable from the "Reds," an ambiguity that's especially pronounced in *Walk East on Beacon!* because of the preponderance of relatively unknown actors and the concomitant emphasis on neorealist as opposed to gangster-noir conventions. (But see the scene early in the film set on the Polish freighter in which Laschenkov—right before he's about to confront Martin and, not so incidentally, as he stands beneath a portrait of Stalin—removes a revolver from a drawer and slips it inside the waistband of his pants.)

In *Hollywood's Cold War* Tony Shaw writes that *Walk East on Beacon!* "charts a new breed of hero," the "quiet security expert who works meticulously and soberly as a member of a professional team."[65] If Shaw's description evokes both the '50s syndicate figure and his corporate double, the "man in the gray flannel suit," Manny Farber's 1951 review in the *Nation* points out how *Walk East on Beacon!* pays "respect to the shrewd, tortoise-like craftsmanship of the spies [who are] seldom seen doing anything except their daily jobs as taxi-driver, florist, or photo-finisher."[66] In other words, if Elaine's attack on the FBI is intended as a preemptive strike against critics of the bureau's methods, it also raises concerns about the state's indiscriminate recourse to surveillance technologies at the expense of Americans' civil liberties. Therefore, what Humphries says about *The Whip Hand* applies equally well to *Walk East on Beacon!*: that despite the lip service, "Werker's film is really about the FBI's surveillance of American citizens."[67]

At the same time, just as the film's recourse to radio and video surveillance performatively contradicts what the narrator calls, over a shot of Laschenkov roaming the streets of Boston, the "freedoms guaranteed by the Bill of Rights to all Americans," its insistent invocation of audiovisual technology introduces a self-reflexive element that's very much at odds with its neorealist, semidocumentary agenda. Consider, for example, the opening 16mm footage of Martin and Millie in the Public Garden, which is later reprised in the body of the film when Belden screens it in Washington for the various agents now working on the case. This footage or, as the narrator refers to it, "movie" is framed in black, Werker's film cutting away to a wide shot of the rapt audience and the projector flickering in the dark.

The meta-cinematic aspect is even more apparent in *Walk East on Beacon!* when the FBI finally identifies Millie. Holding up a strip of panchromatic film that an agent has just developed (the picture is of Millie angrily exiting Vincent's cab), Belden exclaims, "That's our girl!" The subsequent straight cut to the Zalenkos' darkroom, where Chris can be seen hard at work preparing the microfilm for transmission, implicitly equates the secret photographic activities of the FBI with the communist spy ring. As for the microfilm, Chris sends it via a postage stamp to Danzig (see *Walk a Crooked Mile*), the florist transfers it via a box of flowers to Laschenkov, and Laschenkov deposits it in a security box at the airport, where it's retrieved by a Lieutenant Horton, who—in a rhyme of the Public Garden sequence—leaves it on a couch for an anonymous older woman who's about to board an international flight out of Boston. The third-person voice-over narration dramatically caps the montage: "Within thirty-six hours after delivery to the underground, the information was on the way to Moscow."

What Laschenkov and his co-conspirators don't realize is that since Kafer's already working with the FBI, the stolen information—which mathematical computations, in a striking "black" shot, Alex briefly holds up to the light to view—is, practically speaking, useless. Bluntly, the machinations of the Soviet underground are no match for the technological superiority of the FBI. The bureau's secret weapon? Television. With the aid of a patriotic landlord, the Feds have installed a secret video camera in the back room of the Zalenkos' camera shop. Discussing the installation, one agent asks—"Where will you spot the eye?"—and another agent, consulting a model, points to an abandoned flue. Dissolve to a low-angle shot of two agents installing the "eye," "an important new device," in a box located at the top rear wall of the darkroom. When the film cuts away, it's to FBI headquarters, where agents can be seen testing the sound and image on a monitor with speakers. (The fact that this video monitor can be glimpsed in the documentary overview of the FBI's "scientific techniques of crime detection" at the beginning of the film attests to its importance.)

In this insistently self-reflexive, televisual context, the most provocative sequence in *Walk East on Beacon!* revolves around the Zalenkos and begins conventionally enough with Millie greeting Chris in the darkroom with a kiss:

CHRIS: Hey, what's up, baby?
MILLIE: You're gonna miss me for a while. I have to go to Washington on the Federal.

On the word "Washington," the film abruptly cuts away to Belden and his associates watching a live feed of Chris and Millie on the monitor:

MILLIE: I think there's something big at Falcon.
CHRIS: Our professor hit the jackpot?
MILLIE: Search me.

After a shadow-slashed shot of Belden's body and, in the foreground, the silhouette of a technician wearing a headset, the film cuts to a close-up of the television screen:

MILLIE: I need money again, Chris.
CHRIS: That's alright, baby. Hey [looking at his wallet], we're getting down to nothing.
MILLIE: Honestly, I should think for a trip like this they could afford to pay expenses.
CHRIS: Some day, Millie, we won't have to worry about bills. Commisar gets everything for free—*everything*.

Chris then slips his arm around Millie's shoulders, and as the two embrace, Belden and company look on, their disgust as palpable as the couple's kiss.

The tele-cinematic subtext of *Walk East on Beacon!* concludes on a surprising note. Although the bureau has 16mm footage of Danzig in the Public Garden communicating with Michael Dorndoff about Kafer (whom Laschenkov has, in the meantime, kidnapped), there's no audio. Belden's solution: the Plummer School of Lip Reading. While the "silent film" (Belden's words) is being screened, a young Romanian woman excitedly stands up and translates Danzig's orders: "Make sure you are not being followed. Then get an auto. Meet Alex and the others at. . . ." But when the woman is unable to figure out the last, critical part of Danzig's instructions, Belden orders the projectionist to rerun the footage in slow motion, and this time the students collectively enunciate what Danzig is saying: "Mar-vin Fish-ing Vil-lage."

Although the FBI immediately acts on this information, rescuing Kafer before he's transported to a Russian submarine trolling off the coast, this action-packed dénouement is ultimately less suggestive than the meta-cinematic scenario that precedes it. "Between 1950 and 1952," as David Bordwell, Janet Staiger, and Kristin Thompson write in *The Classical Hollywood Cinema*, "film production companies were feeling severe losses in earnings, partly due to the competition of television."[68] Was cinema vis-à-vis television outdated, not unlike silent film après sound, or could it be revivified via new technologies like Eastmancolor? As the Plummer School of Lip Reading sequence demonstrates, the film's response to this dilemma is to dramatically rehearse Hollywood's transition to sound, as if by invoking a prior, "silent" stage in its history, the solution will somehow magically appear.

"Mar-vin Fish-ing Vil-lage": Romanian woman watching 16mm FBI surveillance footage at the Plummer School for the Deaf in *Walk East on Beacon!*

The motion picture industry's hopes and fears are associated in *Walk East on Beacon!* with the ambiguous "red" character Vincent. Explaining his communist past to his wife, Rita, he confesses:

> Once you sign up, they've got you. I tried to run away. Took a job in Rochester with a film outfit. One day a man comes to see me. Says I have to give him the new formula for color emulsion. If I didn't, the company would find out my name was Vincent. So, afterwards, I was listed as an espionage agent. Now if I don't do what they want, they'll turn me in. That's what they mean when they say, "The color pictures are pretty."

This subplot, which involves the industrial formula for "color emulsion," reflects in miniature the central narrative of *Walk East on Beacon!*, which, as we've seen, is about the secret "interstellar space" technologies being developed at Falcon.

Vincent's anecdote about color emulsion in *Walk East on Beacon!* can therefore be said to dramatize in condensed form the internecine war being played out at the time between Technicolor and Eastman Kodak, an issue that posed a special problem for certain genres like film noir or the gangster picture that did not rely, like the musical or biblical epics, on fantasy and spectacle. To wit, would the rise of pretty color pictures mean the death of the thriller and its monochromatic, chiaroscuro vision of the world? The subtext of *Walk East on Beacon!* suggests one answer: that in the not-so-distant future, film noir would be not be in classic black-and-white but in red and black and yellow and blue—in, that is, living color.

BIG JIM MCLAIN: RED HAWAII

Although no one, according to Bosley Crowther in his contemporary review of *Big Jim McLain*, "deserves credit for this film,"[69] the direction is credited to Edward Ludwig, who made *The Fighting Seabees* with John Wayne in 1944, and the script, which was derived from a *Saturday Evening Post* article titled "We Almost Lost Hawaii to the Reds," to Eric Taylor, James Edward Grant, Richard English, and William Wheeler, all of whom were associated at the time—Taylor aside—with either HUAC or the Motion Picture Alliance for the Preservation of American Ideals.[70] Credit aside (the filmmakers "gratefully acknowledged" HUAC's co-operation), *Big Jim McLain* has rightly been viewed as a vehicle for its star, John Wayne, as in "John Wayne is Big Jim McLain."

While *Big Jim McLain* has also been viewed as ideologically simpleminded, it opens with a complex rhetorical address. First, the voice-over narrator reads a dramatic passage from Stephen Vincent Benét's "The Devil and Daniel Webster," a Faust-inspired parable that extols the independent spirit of the American

Kodak Moment: Vincent, aka Malvin Foss (Jack Manning), confesses his "colorful" communist past to his wife, Rita (Vilma Kurer), in *Walk East on Beacon!* Panels from the Motion Picture Comics *Walk East on Beacon!*

people and concludes with a question from Webster: "Neighbor, neighbor, how stands the Union?" We get the answer—a dispiriting one—in the following sequence, in which Dr. Carter (Peter Brocco), a full, "well-paid" professor appearing before a session of HUAC, pleads the Fifth Amendment in response to a series of inquiries posed by Counsel Frank Tavenner (played by himself): "Are you now, or have you ever been, a member of the Communist Party? . . . In the event of armed hostilities between this government and Soviet Russia, would you, if called upon, willingly bear arms on behalf of the government of the United States?"

Cut to a medium close-up of Big Jim McLain, a HUAC special investigator who, in voice-over, draws the conclusion that "any intelligent person" would: "These people were Communists, agents of the Kremlin, and they all walk out free." McLain here echoes the committee's "stated beliefs": "that anyone who continued to be a Communist after 1945 is guilty of high treason." As opposed to the theatrical tenor of the opening, neo-gothic sequence, which features a dark, storm-tossed shot of Daniel Webster's grave, the ensuing sequence, set in full view of the Capitol, is semidocumentary in character and includes footage of actual HUAC members, including Donald L. Jackson, Francis E. Walter, and chairman John Stephens Wood. The sudden shift from expressionism to neorealism sets up a direct, not to say prejudicial, appeal to the emotions: "We, the citizens of the United States of America, owe these, our elected representatives, a great debt. Undaunted by the vicious campaign of slander launched against them as a whole and as individuals, they have staunchly continued their investigation."

As Thomas W. Benson argues in a lucid rhetorical analysis of *Big Jim McLain*, the object of the film's real "suppressed" argument is the American Communist Party, the "subjects of the blacklist and the McCarthy investigations, and, by extension, the bleeding heart liberalism that serves the cause of the Communist enemy."[71] Since we the audience have now learned, if we didn't suspect already, that every member of the Communist Party is "guilty of high treason," the answer is not more debate but action in the fightin' form of Big Jim and his fellow HUAC investigator, Mal Baxter (James Arness), who's even more pugnacious than his partner. Piggybacking on Big Jim's contention that Dr. Carter will continue to "contaminate more kids," Mal's enraged at the thought that this professor of economics "might be delivering a course of lectures to [his] kids one of these days." As Jim loads him up with luggage for their next investigation, Mal snorts: "I shouldn't have handed him that subpoena, I should have stuffed it down his throat with my hands still around it. Just me and him with a subpoena on a dark porch—who would have known the difference if I'd thrown him one left hook?"

Big Jim and Mal's mission is code-named Operation Pineapple and their destination is Hawaii, which circa 1952 was not yet a state and therefore was seen as "particularly susceptible to Communist influence arising from Asian countries" such as North Korea,[72] a communist-controlled country that's previously referenced when Jim, introducing Mal in voice-over, describes him as someone who "hates these people" (communists) because "they had shot at him in Korea."

If, according to Jeff Smith, the ideological thrust of the anticommunist noir is inflected by specific genre conventions,[73] *Big Jim McLain* is a paradigmatic example not simply because it's a hybrid—say, a semidocumentary-inflected detective film—but because of its extraordinary generic heterogeneity. This generic mix, as Benson sagely notes, "seems anomalous today," but it "did not seem incoherent to all of its contemporary viewers."[74] (In fact, *Big Jim McLain* was "by far the most commercial anti-Communist film of 1952, grossing 2.6 million."[75]) For example, *Big Jim McLain* is nominally a detective film, but it's also a travelogue in its general recourse to exoticism and its particular attention to tourist attractions such as Diamond Head and Waikiki as well as "local color" such as leis and hula dancers.

Of course, the touristic, even orientalist slant is not uncommon in '50s classic noir—see *Macao* (1952), *Shanghai Story* (1954), and *World for Ransom* (1954)—nor is the love story that develops between Big Jim and Nancy Vallon (Nancy Olson) that's as obligatory as the romance in Elvis Presley pictures such as *Blue Hawaii* (1961).[76] What is uncommon in both classic noir and the anticommunist thriller is the presence of the sort of "performative, vaudevillian comedy" that threatens to sink not so much the action as the film's ideological agenda. (I'm metaphorically thinking here of the funereal scene early in the film in which Big Jim and Mal visit the memorial site at Pearl Harbor, where Mal's brother's ship, the USS *Arizona*, was sunk on December 7, 1941.) In *Big Jim McLain* this comic strain appears in the scenes between Jim and Madge (Veda Ann Borg), a "loud, comical, sexy, and drunkenly seductive" woman who "makes a play for Wayne [*sic*] despite the jealousy of her comically loutish boyfriend." Madge is the "good bad girl" to Nancy's nice, marriageable widow, and her sexed-up character is indispensable to the political-libidinal economy of *Big Jim McLain*: referring to Big Jim's height, she calls him "76" ("Seventy-six inches? That's a lot of man!"), a risqué sobriquet that cleverly invokes the founding of the United States.

The film's comic absurdism is most apparent, though, in a scene in which a writer of "historical and research treatises" named Robert Henried (Hans Conried) offers to give McLain information about the Communist Party that he has gleaned from his studies. Jim and Nancy initially listen with appropriate seriousness to what Henried has to say; however, when he drops Stalin's name ("as I told Stalin in my last meeting"), then mentions that he flew to the Soviet Union in a "jet plane of [his] own design," they begin to realize that he's not quite right in the head. I'm tempted to say that Henried's jabberwocky defies analysis, but there is, I think, some method to the script's madness, particularly when Henried talks about a new secret weapon that will "make the atomic bomb an obsolete nothing": "it makes everybody look alike," and if "all the men will look alike and all the women will look alike," "how can you possibly fight with someone if he looks exactly as you do?"

This "zany" scene mirrors, as Benson notes, "other, more 'serious' scenes,"[77] as when Big Jim visits the leper colony on Molokai in order to interview Mrs. Nomaka (Madame Soo Yong), the ex-wife of a party member who has begun "jugging it up good," or when Big Jim interviews the Lexiters, an elderly couple who divulge that their son became a communist after a prize study-abroad trip to the Soviet Union. These sequences are true to the tried formula for the anticommunist thriller, invoking as they respectively do the rhetoric of contamination in such films as *Panic in the Streets* (1950) and *The Whip Hand* as well as the spectacle of the alienated "nuclear family" in *My Son John* (1952). The Henried sequence, by contrast, throws a rhetorical wrench into the film's agitprop ambitions, since even as it suggests that the sort of bland egalitarianism promoted by communism is ridiculous on the face of it, it seriously undermines the film's message that the red menace is an urgent threat to the American way of life—a de jure "state of war"[78]—and that direct, aggressive intervention is imperative.

The film's ambivalence about the red scare is reflected in its ambiguous representation of psychoanalysis, a figuration that's tangled up with its ambiguous representation of femininity. As soon as Big Jim and Mal are ensconced at their beachfront bungalow, Mal's checking out some sonic surveillance equipment on a couple honeymooning next door when Big Jim admonishes him, "Who do you think you're working for? Dr. Kinsey?" Later, while attempting to track down Nomaka, Big Jim makes a visit to the office of Dr. Gelster (Gayne Whitman), who has been treating the former party treasurer for a nervous disorder. Since Nancy is studying to become a psychiatrist herself, she tells Big Jim that she's been trying to analyze why Gelster is a communist, theorizing that he has a "neuter of a personality": "He doesn't attract people. . . . He doesn't even have the quality of repelling people." To cite Marge Sherwood on Tom Ripley in *The Talented Mr. Ripley*, he's the queerest sort of person: "He may not be queer. He's just nothing, which is worse. He isn't normal enough to have any kind of sex life."[79] Nancy's analysis of Gelster thus accords with the popular stereotypical notion of communists, which is that they're either hyper- or under-sexualized.

Not surprisingly, as an All-American, red-white-and-blue-blooded man of action, Big Jim has absolutely no use for such fine distinctions: "I've heard all the jive. This one's a commie because his momma won't tuck him in at night, that one because girls wouldn't welcome him with open arms. I don't know the *why*. The *what* I do know. Like when I was wearing a uniform, I shot at the guy on the other side of the perimeter because he was the enemy." Of course, despite the film's critique of "psychological theorizing," *Big Jim McLain* wants to have its cake and eat it too: "to insinuate psychology as a way of stigmatizing the Communist villains [via Nancy's character] and to deny any interest in psychology [via Jim's]."[80] And yet, if "psychological theorizing is a woman's game,"[81] it's also—in the person of Gelster—a communist's. In other words, although communism and psychoanalysis have historically been perceived as intellectually divergent discourses—one primarily concerned with the body politic, the other with the psyche—*Big Jim McLain* conflates the two in order to boost its anti-intellectual brief. From this perspective, doctors are especially suspect. Hence the news that Nomaka, who suffered a nervous breakdown after learning that a boyhood friend was killed in the sabotage of a navy vessel by his Hawaiian communist cell, is under Gelster's "psychic" control.

The anti-psychoanalytic angle is critical, it turns out, to the political-libidinal economy of *Big Jim McLain* when Mal dies after being injected with sodium pentothal. In fact, the scene in which Big Jim mourns his partner's passing at the city morgue, as well as the subsequent montage in which he wanders the fog-shrouded streets of Honolulu at night searching for leads, is one of the few times that Edward Ludwig's film employs the characteristic low-key, shadow-casting lighting associated with film noir. In the former, the camera trains on Jim's face in close-up as, in voice-over, he delivers an impromptu, impassioned obituary on his fallen friend: "Name so and so, age such and such. Does this tell us about a young lawyer who went in the Marine Corps, who lost eight feet of intestine in Korea, gut shot by a grenade made in Czechoslovakia of scrap and by machines that had been shipped from the States to somewhere in Western Europe and then behind the Iron Curtain?" Mal's body is eventually discovered in a lagoon along with a bottle of booze (fabricated evidence that links him with Nomaka), but we later learn from Gelster's superior—the effete, effeminate, i.e., "queer," Sturak (Alan Napier), who has recently arrived on the island to figure out why HUAC has sent another, better financed team of investigators to Hawaii—that the doctor was responsible for Mal's death. In other words, psychoanalysis is not only "jive"; in the wrong communist hands it can be positively dangerous to one's health. (See, for example, the scene near the beginning of the film when Sturak orders Gelster to get rid of Nomaka by, if necessary, overdose.)

With Mal's untimely death, Big Jim goes into hyperdrive. At a private country club where Sturak has assembled all the members of the seventh communist cell, Big Jim decides to make the pinch himself in order to get in Gelster's grill: "I wanted to hit you one punch. Just one full-thrown right hand. But now I find I can't do it because you're too small. That's the difference between you people and us, I guess. We don't hit the little guy, we believe in fair play and all that sort of thing." However, when Poke (Hal Baylor), one of the communist goons, having had a "belly full of this East Texas cotton-choppin' jerk," says, "Choppin' cotton is for white trash and niggers" (this commie hails from the "country club set"), Big Jim throws a haymaker and the good fight is on.

The post-donnybrook conclusion to *Big Jim McLain* is arguably just as rhetorically complex as the film's opening. First, Big Jim and his police contact in Honolulu, Chief Dan Liu (Dan Liu), listen from the rear of the room at a HUAC hearing (note the Venetian-blind lighting) as the party members who haven't already been indicted for Mal's death plead the Fifth. As at the beginning of the film, Big Jim is indignant: "I resent that [the Constitution] can be used and abused by the very people who want to destroy it." Later, he has just joined Nancy on a park bench and been assured of her love—"You just keep looking at me like that for the next hundred years"—when a band strikes up with a spirited rendition of "Anchors Aweigh" and the couple stand to attention as a racially and ethnically diverse platoon of marines, boarding a battleship for Korea, respond one by one to a roll call. It's then that the film's original narrator reprises his voice-over query—"Neighbor, how stands the Union now?"—and as the camera cuts from the departing sailors to the island's security force, Big Jim brightly answers in voice-over: "There stands the Union, Mr. Webster. There stands our Union, sir."

While the rousing conclusion of *Big Jim McLain* "aligns the strength of the Union with America's military might" rather than with the "rich heritage" of the Hawaiian peoples,[82] it implicitly aligns the strength of the United States with the armed services rather than with HUAC or, more pointedly, the constitutional principles it ostensibly embodies and abides by. Still, despite the suggestion that HUAC would be more effective if it weren't constrained by constitutional niceties, the film's potentially downbeat ending is buoyed by the impending marriage of Big Jim and Nancy, in which the former's turbocharged masculinity will not only make good the void produced by the death of her husband while fighting in Saipan but will also temper the "analytical" tendencies associated with femininity and psychoanalysis. Earlier, pondering the "good lightning" that has struck her (an allusion to the auspicious God-sent lightning that opens the film), Nancy queries, "I wonder if it's chemistry that makes two people understand each other without a word being said?" "Stop going to those lectures," Big Jim counsels. "Don't try to analyze it. Just let it be."

PICKUP ON SOUTH STREET

OUT OF THE RED AND INTO THE BLACK

No heart ever yearned the way that mine does
And yet I know too well
Someday you'll say goodbye
Then violins will cry
And so will I, mam'selle.

—"Mam'selle" (Edmund Goulding and Mack
Gordon, 1947)

Released in 1953 at the end of the first cycle of postwar anticommunist films (1947–1954), Samuel Fuller's *Pickup on South Street* is a "canonical Cold War text."[1] It's also one of the "most overdetermined" films made during the blacklist period, "centrally concerned" as it is with the "politics of informing."[2]

Although the police and FBI have a distinct presence in *Pickup on South Street*, Fuller's film, as opposed to *I Was a Communist for the F.B.I.* or *Walk East on Beacon!*, depicts both the cops and Feds as crudely utilitarian, indifferent to the human costs of the national security state apparatus. Moreover, whereas *Big Jim McLain* privileges, via the iconic, militantly anticommunist figure of John Wayne, the "big" exploits of the eponymous, all-American hero, *Pickup on South Street* dramatizes the lives of its small-time hoods and hustlers, for whom the threat of the red menace is less pressing than the day-to-day, dog-eat-dog grind of trying to remain in the black.

With the possible exception of *Kiss Me Deadly* (1955), *Pickup on South Street* is, in addition, the most highly regarded anticommunist noir. Some of the film's cachet has to with Fuller's status as a "maverick" or "primitive" director; some has to do with his contested relation to communism. As for the former epithets, which, like the "anticommunist" moniker, have become part of the received critical wisdom about Fuller, Lisa Dombrowski has persuasively argued that casting the director as a "primitive" obscures his deliberate as opposed to instinctive relation to classical Hollywood cinema. The emphasis on Fuller as an indie or B filmmaker also minimizes the "varied production conditions under which he worked."[3] For example, since the budget for *Pickup on South Street* was $780,000 and the film "premiered at the Roxy in New York—complete with floor show— on June 17, 1953," it was in "no way a B-picture."[4]

Unsurprisingly, the issue of Fuller's anticommunism is tangled up with his reputation as a primitive, maverick auteur. Thus, at the 1953 Venice Film Festival, Georges Sadoul—resident critic of *Les Lettres Françaises* and putative spokesperson for the network of Parisian "left-wing ciné-clubs" under the control of the French Communist Party—called Fuller the "McCarthy of cinema."[5] Following Sadoul's hard-line, Stalinist verdict on *Pickup on South Street*, the French distributor tweaked the film's plot, eliminating any reference to communism and changing the stolen goods from microfilm to heroin, a substitution reflected in the French title for the picture, *Le Port de la drogue* (Port of Drugs).

By the end of the 1950s, however, Fuller's reputation in France had undergone a sea change. In an influential 1959 article in *Cahiers du cinéma* that was a response in part to Sadoul's indictment, Luc Moullet, who characterized the director as an "intelligent primitive," queried, "Could Fuller really be the fascist, right-wing extremist who was denounced not so long ago in the Communist press? I don't think so. He has too much the gift of ambiguity to be able to align himself exclusively with one party."[6] Moullet's position—reflected in a celebrated apothegm later adopted by Jean-Luc Godard, "Morality is a question of tracking shots"[7]—effectively shifted the attention from Fuller's politics to aesthetics. As Peter Stanfield observes in a scrupulously researched chapter on Fuller in *Maximum Movies*, Fuller's canonization in France was replayed in Great Britain, where, writing in *Movie*, V. F. Perkins contended that Fuller's films were "illustrated lectures" (note the Brechtian inflection) in which "ambiguity is such that [it] makes opposites coexist."[8]

This pronounced ambiguity has continued to confound those critics writing on Fuller who are determined to resolve or reconcile the contradictory politics of *Pickup on South Street*. But what Fuller himself has said about the reception of *The Steel Helmet* (1951), which Hedda Hopper termed "strongly anti-red" and the Pentagon a piece of "communist indoctrination," offers not a little insight into his directorial mind-set when shooting *Pickup on South Street*: "I didn't give a goddamn whether lefties or righties liked the picture. I didn't make *The Steel Helmet* to please any constituency."[9] While Fuller supposedly "set the record straight for all time" in his memoir, *A Third Face*—"I'm antitotalitarian, not anticommunist"[10]—

it's perhaps more accurate to say that *Pickup on South Street* is *anti*-anticommunist, except that such a negative construction also fails to capture the film's profoundly antinomian impulse.

Still, one advantage of the above, double-negative locution is that it stresses the anti-McCarthyist thrust of *Pickup on South Street*. Fuller himself, commenting on the film's allusions to Richard Nixon's "phony exposé" of Alger Hiss, commented that with *Pickup on South Street* "he wanted to take a poke at the idiocy of the cold war climate of the fifties,"[11] an observation that recalls his earlier remarks on *The Steel Helmet*: "Soldiers were trained to fight the fascists during the war. Now the bigoted winds of McCarthyism were blowing across democratic America, spreading the seed of another kind of fascism. The only way to fight those people here at home . . . was to poke holes in their fundamentalist bullshit."[12]

The specter of McCarthyism haunts *A Third Face*, surfacing as well in a discussion of Richard Brooks's *Deadline—USA* (1952)—Brooks, like Fuller, was a former newspaperman—where Fuller states that the 1950 McCarran Act "led straight to Hoover's front door, because the infamous senator Joseph R. McCarthy of Wisconsin exploited it to 'uncover' communist influence in the arts."[13] Ruminating about the period in which he was writing *Fixed Bayonets* (1951), Fuller claims, "People constantly try to pigeonhole me as a lefty or righty, and my work as being liberal or conservative, [but] I wanted to transcend the narrow political terms and emblems that imprison a creative person. McCarthyism had spawned a horrible climate of fear and suspicion."[14]

In "Kiss Me Deadly" Michael Rogin concludes that, on one hand, *Pickup on South Street* is a "right-wing anti-liberal B movie" and, on the other, that it's the "only genuine work of art among the films that promote the Cold War."[15] As I've suggested, I'm not at all sure how useful it is to see Fuller's film as "right-wing," a "B movie" or, for that matter, as promoting the Cold War. Rogin's assessment of *Pickup on South Street* as a "genuine work of art," pesky philosophical questions aside (What, exactly, is an *ersatz* work of art?), is, however, trenchant, as is his proposition that *Pickup on South Street* "doubles and inverts pious, anticommunist cinema."[16] Indeed, it might not be too much to say that Fuller's film reverses the inversion that *I Was a Communist for the F.B.I.* performs on *Mission to Moscow*.

If *Pickup on South Street* is neither a straight anticommunist noir nor a "McCarthyite tract," it's nonetheless of particular interest from a film noir perspective thanks to Joseph MacDonald, whose work as a cinematographer spans the genre's classical period from *The Dark Corner*, *The Street with No Name* (1948), and *Call Northside 777* (1948) to *Panic in the Streets*, *Niagara* (1953), *House of Bamboo* (1955), and *The Crimson Kimono* (1959). These films, all of which were made at Twentieth Century-Fox except for the Columbia-produced *Crimson Kimono*, illustrate the range of MacDonald's style and constitute classic examples of expressionist and semidocumentary—not to mention, as in *Niagara* and *House of Bamboo*, color—noir.

MacDonald's cinematography is critical to the look of *Pickup on South Street*. Although Fuller was "stuck on the back lot at Twentieth Century-Fox with make-believe streets," he wanted to emulate the "gritty visuals" of Italian neorealism: "How could you tell a story about petty thieves, informers, and spy rings without a realistic portrayal of their dilapidated, predatory world? The murky bars. The flophouses. The out-of-the-way streets. The tattoo parlors. The subway stations."[17] While art director Lyle Wheeler worked "wonders on a Hollywood soundstage" to make *Pickup on South Street* "look as natural as possible," MacDonald "innovated" to get the shots that Fuller needed to make the scenes look real.[18]

The naturalistic, semidocumentary demeanor of *Pickup on South Street* is indicative of its complicated relation to film noir. Rogin, for example, claims that *Pickup on South Street* is "photographed entirely at night,"[19] but the film is by no means a classic "dark city" picture. In fact, *Pickup on South Street* does not immediately present itself as a film noir. Consider the justly celebrated opening sequence, a wordless fugue set on a subway train during the day that Skip McCoy (Richard Widmark) purloins the purse of Candy (Jean Peters) as FBI agents look on. If it's an unusually intimate portrait of "underworld, U.S.A." circa 1953—Skip is an unabashed pickpocket and Candy is an ex-prostitute courier—there's nothing especially noirish, stylistically speaking, about the sequence except for the brief introductory shot of subway cars flashing through a pitch-black tunnel. The film's darkness derives, rather, from its recourse to signature noir effects such as angular compositions in conjunction with charged physical encounters. As for lighting, the most sustained low-key passage in the first part of the film is set—again, during the day—at the New York Public Library, where Skip views the stolen microfilm on a reading machine.[20]

More characteristic of *Pickup on South Street* is the second, violent encounter between Skip and Candy, which begins with a dynamic, high-contrast shot of the bait-and-tackle shack that he calls home. After the film crosscuts between interior flash-lit shots of someone searching the shack and exterior cut-on-action ones—accented by a fog horn—of Skip approaching the front door, he decks the intruder with a roundhouse right to the jaw. The subsequent shot/counter-shot establishes the initial terms of the couple's relationship: while Skip stands, flashlight in hand, his face halved in shadow, in the medium reverse shot (after he has kicked over the motionless body), Candy lies sprawled on the floor, her arms raised above her head, eyes closed as if in sleep.

There's more than a little irony here not simply because the "burglar" is Candy, whom we've just seen Skip pilfer on the subway, but because he proceeds to rifle through her purse again, extracting a tie and some cash. (Skip, grinning like the bad boy he is, pockets the cash, then tosses the tie, courtesy of neckwear-selling

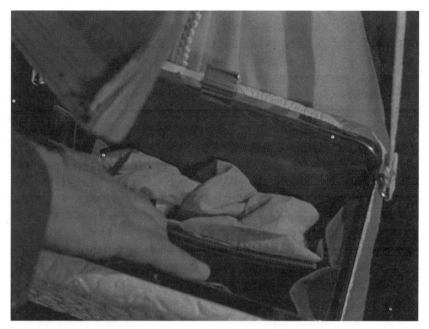

Snatch: Close-up shot of Skip McCoy (Richard Widmark) purloining Candy's (Jean Peters) purse on the New York City subway in *Pickup on South Street*.

stoolie Moe [Thelma Ritter], onto Candy's still unconscious body.) When a kick doesn't revive Candy, Skip uses a rope pulley to raise a wooden crate from the river and takes out a cold bottle of beer, which, having swigged, he pours over her face. (Part of the libidinal kick of Skip's bad-boy behavior derives, like his fingering of Candy's purse on the subway, from its suggestiveness—in this particular case, of a "golden shower.")

Composition and mise-en-scène are crucial to Fuller's commentary on Skip and Candy's evolving relationship. So when Skip asks Candy if she wants a beer and Candy answers, "I want my wallet," the camera pulls back to reveal the hook and pulley in the right foreground. The hook and pulley become even more obtrusive when Candy, holding her chin, groans and Skip, turning her around, massages her face with his hand. The massage appears "more painful" than not; moreover, Skip's hand is located "just inches above Candy's throat," which "leads the viewer to anticipate that at any moment [he] may strangle her."[21]

Still, the most flagrant use of the hook-and-pulley figure occurs when, as an orchestral version of musical director Lionel Newman's "Again" swells on the sound track, Skip kisses Candy and the camera slowly pans to the left so that the image appears superimposed on the couple. Although the pulp, over-the-top

The Bait: Skip McCoy (Richard Widmark) and Candy (Jean Peters) embracing in his bait shack in *Pickup on South Street*. Note hook and rope in the foreground of the frame.

dialogue is classic Fuller—"You look for oil, sometimes you find a gusher"—the flirtation ends and the fighting resumes when Candy explains that the pictures he has discovered on her are of her brother Mickey. "How much is your brother worth?" Skip asks, and it's only then that Candy, caressing his face, realizes that Skip's in possession of the microfilm: "Then you do have it."

In his reading of *Pickup on South Street*, Rogin asserts that in Fuller's film "violence causes sex," but the relation between the two terms is not, I think, causal. Jack Shadoian is closer to the mark (because more attentive to the play of the mise-en-scène) when he writes that the "hook splits the frame down the middle, 'separating' the characters at the moment they 'join,' creating an aura of violence and visualizing the tension."[22] If the hook has been a romantic figure since at least the seventeenth century (see, for example, John Donne's "The Bait"), the intimations of bondage and S&M in the scenes between Skip and Candy speak less to sex per se than to the rough-and-tumble world that the couple inhabits, one in which risk is always part of the mix and trust is a scarce commodity—scarcer, even, than some stolen microfilm.

For example, the second time that Candy goes to Skip's shack (her handler, Joey [Richard Kiley], has offered her five hundred dollars to try her luck again), she initially appears to be in a superior position. It's daytime and there's a low-angle shot of her crossing the rickety bridge from left to right in the middle ground as, in the right foreground, Skip stands watching from the pilings below. Although Skip tells her to take the stairs, the camera, instead of cutting to Candy, pans with Skip as he leans back against a timber. Candy, sitting down on one leg, cuts to the chase: "How many times have you been caught where your hand doesn't belong?" Ignoring the double entendre, Skip truthfully answers that he's been "tapped" three times, adding that they're on the "red side of the ledger."

Fuller's "comic strip" dialogue here is operating on a number of different registers.[23] It's not just that Candy's question points up the transgressive connection between sex and theft; Skip's response also emphasizes the unspoken link between his arrest record and the stolen microfilm. In other words, because Skip has been caught with his hand in the cookie jar again, he's now looking at life in prison. At the same time (and this is his trump card), he's in a position to substantially improve upon the black side of the ledger as long as he remains in possession of the microfilm, which, of course, both the Feds and Reds are desperate to retrieve.

The above sequence, in addition to figuratively broaching the "red" issue (Candy at this particular point doesn't realize that she's acting as a communist courier), introduces another figure familiar from Fuller's pictures: the artist as outsider. So after Skip caresses Candy, continuing their previous "now a punch, now a kiss" routine,[24] she examines his palm and exclaims, "You've got fingers like an artist." For Fuller, Skip is no mere two-bit grifter: in an age of unthinking consensus and conspicuous consumption, his style and vitality, frugality and independence, stand him in good stead as a model for the artist. It's in this iconoclastic sense that Skip's shack, which is without electricity and is an island of sorts, is an exemplary trope of Emersonian individualism.

And yet, if Skip's castle is literally built on water, the film suggests that the only way for him to keep his head above it is to forge some sort of connection with other people. (E. M. Forster's injunction "Only connect" seems particularly apposite here.) In the gospel according to Fuller, social communion, not communism, is indispensable to remaining human as opposed to merely surviving in an increasingly Hobbesian world—that is, nasty, brutish, and short.

However, when Skip discovers that Candy has brought only five hundred dollars, he violently pushes her away, snarling, "You tell that Commie I want a big score for that film." Candy protests that Skip has misread her—"You gotta believe me!" Skip's response brooks no argument—he'll "do business with a Commie," but he doesn't "have to believe one." Although Candy finally gets her licks in, slapping Skip, it doesn't change his mind. If business and belief are separate issues for Skip, for Candy the two are inseparable: she believes in him so much that she can't believe he'd do business with a Red.

Later, in a scene set in a drab office where Candy paces nervously while Joey and two of his superiors look on, she suddenly realizes that Joey's working for the Reds and, furthermore (when the man behind the desk pulls a revolver from a drawer), that they mean business. The fact that the man behind the desk uses a cigarette holder is a clue that the commies in *Pickup on South Street* are, not unlike the police or Feds, stereotypes. In fact, only Joey and Tiger (Murvyn Vye) have any real personality, and if Joey is weak-willed (the man behind the desk chastises him for letting Candy do his dirty work for him), Tiger is—as his name hints—a one-note nemesis. In *Pickup on South Street* it's the small-time cannons and stoolies and ex-hookers—Skip and Moe and Candy—who register as full-blooded if not all-American figures.

Thus, when Joey, his hand forced by his party superiors, confronts Candy, she lies to him about Skip's address and gives him Moe's instead. At Moe's apartment, as Candy paces again—"Who'd believe I didn't know what I was passing? ... Would you believe me?"—the camera pans back and forth across the ties that hang like black bars in the foreground of the frame. Candy pleads with Moe not to divulge Skip's address—"You wouldn't sell him to a Commie?"—to which question Moe indignantly replies, "What do you think I am, an informer?"[25]

In the following scene, set at a diner, Moe and Skip are sitting at the counter—Moe: "What's the matter with you, playin' footsies with the Commies?"/ Skip: "You wavin' the flag, too?"—and on the back wall between them there's a model of a ship. The prop suggests something important about Skip: he's a "skipper," captain of his own soul, and the "real McCoy."[26] In other words, Skip may be "playin' footsies with the Commies," but he'll eventually come to his senses.

Just as Moe's parting advice to Skip—"Stop using your hands and start using your head"—recalls Candy's earlier, sexually fraught comment, so Skip's rebuke to Moe—"You wavin' the flag, too?"—echoes his response to Tiger and FBI agent Zara (Willis Bouchey) at the beginning of the film after he's been brought in, thanks to Moe, for questioning. When Skip originally purloined Candy's purse, she was about to pass the microfilm secreted with classified government information to a "top Red agent." Now the Feds are willing to make the charge go away if Skip cooperates. Zara, the "big thumb," raises the ideological stakes: "If you refuse to cooperate, you'll be as guilty as the traitors that gave Stalin the A-bomb." Skip, though, isn't buying: "Are you gonna wave the flag at me?"

Skip's rejoinder to Zara's second question—"Do you know what treason means?"/"Who cares?"—recalls the iconic exchange in *The Wild One* (1953) where Mildred (Peggy Maley) asks Johnny (Marlon Brando), "Hey, Johnny, what are you rebelling against?" and Johnny replies, "Whadya got?" Since Skip's response is, given the hyper-conformist climate of the Cold War era, tantamount to treason, it's no surprise that the character's "political apathy"—Skip, as Fuller says, is a "guy who doesn't give a shit about the cold war"—"infuriated Hoover."[27] It's also no surprise that Fuller's reaction to Hoover—"I didn't give a damn whether Hoover approved or not"—recollects Skip's rejoinder to Zara.[28] In fact, Fuller's use of the word "damn" recalls the line as it was originally scripted, which read, "Don't wave your *goddamn* flag at me." Although Fox executive/producer Darryl Zanuck agreed in the end to delete the word, he steadfastly objected to Hoover's efforts to soft-pedal Skip's lack of patriotism, and the line consequently remained in the film.[29]

Moe's subsequent death at the hands of Joey, "propped up in bed and surrounded by a litter of male ties,"[30] simultaneously mimes and critiques Skip's apathy. On one hand, Moe's life is so hard and she's so tired that Joey would be doing her a "big favor" if he blew her head off. On the other hand, Moe, unlike Skip, won't do business with a commie "crumb" like Joey. Moe's grand refusal crowns a series of sellouts that structure the film: "Moe sells information to Tiger. . . . Lightning Louie [Vic Perry] sells Moe to Candy, [and] Moe sells Skip to Candy."[31] More importantly, Moe's sacrificial act not only negates Candy's sellout—the buck stops with Moe—but anticipates Skip's own grand refusal at the very end of the film.

Meanwhile, once the police find out about Moe's death, they round up the usual suspects, including Skip. The sequence is especially fascinating in the context of anticommunist noir because of its ambiguous representation of the FBI. The film cuts from a close-up of the needle skipping on Moe's record player, punctuated by a gunshot, to a low-angle nighttime shot of two men crossing the bridge to Skip's shack. When they surprise Skip, who's been lying in the hammock that he uses for a bed, he asks, "What is this, a stickup?" The men are from Homicide, but Skip's reaction—"Oh, cops, sure. For a moment there, I thought it was a stickup"—evinces just how difficult it is in the all-cows-are-gray world of *Pickup on South Street* to distinguish between the good and bad guys.

If Tiger's continual animosity toward Skip portrays him as a rogue cop in the making, the ensuing action also sheds darkness, as it were, on the representation of the Feds in Fuller's film. After Lieutenant Campion (John Gallaudet) ushers Skip outside and informs him of Moe's death, he's interrupted by a man who comes up and whispers into his ear. Then, while Campion's partner, Eddie (Clancy Cooper), watches Skip, the camera tracks in reverse as the man leads Campion back across the bridge. The silhouette of a slouch-hatted figure suddenly appears on a brick wall; when the man emerges into the shadow-fractured light, he pulls out a badge. His name is Enyart (Jerry O'Sullivan), he's a Fed, and he immediately countermands Campion's order.

Although the Reds are clearly bad news (we've just seen Joey kill an old woman in cold blood), Enyart's association with the shadow world and iconography of the gangster film casts the Feds in a darkly ambiguous light. By contrast, the understated sequence set on the water at night where Skip picks up Moe's coffin as it's in the process of being ferried by skip boat to Potter's Field (Moe's life was devoted, paradoxically enough, to having a proper burial) highlights Skip's very real humanity. The maritime imagery, as in the diner, is revelatory: Skip, who has a sailor's sense of the elemental mutability of water, typically goes with the flow, but Moe's death is a reminder that no man is an island. One person's actions—in this case, Skip's insistence on hitting it big without absolutely any regard for others—can have dramatic, unexpected consequences. Indeed, if, in terms of the film's "family romance," Moe's a surrogate maternal figure for both Skip and Candy, the two are now effectively orphans in the storm.

The most startling reversal in *Pickup on South Street* occurs in the wake of Moe's burial. After an establishing shot of Skip traversing the bridge to his shack, a high overhead view that emphasizes his solitary nature, he closes the door and the shadow of a cross falls across him. A marked man, he's registering, perhaps for the very first time, the double bind that he's in. Indexing his stormy relationship with Candy as well as the microfilm hidden in the river below, the mise-en-scène speaks volumes when Skip goes over to the window that looks out onto the river and rests his head on the ledge, the rope from the pulley plainly visible in the near foreground. Then, as if on cue, Skip glances to the right and the camera travels down the rope to the hammock where Candy lies fast asleep.

As in their initial physical encounter, Skip picks up Candy's purse and checks its contents before knocking the hammock to wake her: "What are you doing here without the dough?" If for a moment it appears that Skip has been changed by Moe's death—that, say, he's had a change of heart about Candy—we now know better. *Plus ça change. . . .* Once Skip and Candy have kissed, he breaks the clinch—"[Joey] better have that twenty-five grand ready"—in order to hoist the refrigerator box and remove the microfilm from the container. (In a self-reflexive twist, the metal canister is "precisely the sort used to store Hollywood 16mm and 35mm prints."[32]) However, before Skip can leave—note the shadow of a cross again on his back—Candy picks up an empty beer bottle, conks him over the head, and steals away with the microfilm. Love, for Fuller, "is a battleground," and everything is fair in love and war.

Unlike Skip, Candy goes straight to the authorities and turns in the microfilm, claiming that he sent her: "He's been fightin' something inside him, something decent that's trying to crawl out." Also very much unlike Skip, Candy agrees to help "fight Communism," despite the fact that, as Zara tells her, "it might be dangerous." Candy is game; she's also brave, unlike Joey, who's downright skittish without a gun in his hand. Still, it's clear from Fuller's framing—Zara and Tiger loom over a seated Candy—that the Feds don't care what happens to her as long as they get what they want.

In her book on Fuller, Dombrowski details how sound and staging work together in the sequence where Joey shows up at Candy's apartment looking for the microfilm that the FBI has just returned to her as bait. This action sequence, which produces an effect that's "intensely brutal" and "disturbingly immediate,"[33] also illustrates the film's scrupulous attention to costuming. When Joey first ar-rives at Candy's apartment, she's in the bathroom behind locked doors taking a bubble bath, a scenario that plays up her femininity and vulnerability. (The cigarette dangling from her mouth suggests, though, that she's not all sugar and spice.) The crucial passage occurs right before Candy goes out to confront Joey and do the FBI's bidding when, having donned a white bathrobe, she slips the hood over her head. The meaning, especially if we remember the boxing photos on the walls of Skip's shack, is obvious: Candy's dressed like a boxer because she knows she's in for the fight of her life. Given the film's insistent rhyming here and elsewhere, Joey's attack therefore invites comparison with Skip's initial encoun-ter with her. When Skip initially coldcocks Candy, he doesn't realize that she's a woman and never hits her again; Joey, however, knocks her around the room like a rag doll, then—after shooting her—leaves her for dead. The fact that the police whistle sounds only after Candy has been shot and Joey has managed to escape points to both the police and FBI's complicity in the assault (as well as, not so incidentally, their utter ineptitude).

The following high-contrast, highly constricted shots of Joey, gun in hand, hiding from the authorities in the dumbwaiter together with the black "under-head" ones of the slowly descending "coffin" exhibit Fuller's penchant for fusing action and expressionism, or what J. Hoberman calls "abstract sensationalism."[34] Similarly, the concluding image of the sequence provides a compact expression of Fuller's philosophy of life. One of the "good guys," Gibbs, lies on the floor among some garbage cans, having been beaten to death by Joey, but as soon as Joey leaves, a cat leaps back into the frame and into a square of light to feed on some scraps. Life goes on. "Gotta eat."

The climax of *Pickup on South Street* reprises even as it revises the film's vari-ous motifs. In the hospital, the black-and-blue bruise on Candy's face stands out against the white sheets and pillow, the white headboard and white bandage wrapped around her head. While the shot of "Skip's face divided by the bars of the headboard" is diegetically impossible (since the bed is pushed up against the wall),[35] the bars vanish coincident with Skip's realization that Candy endured the beating in order to protect him. The last shot of the hospital scene—of Skip cradling Candy's face in his palm as he kisses her—finds its verso in the following sequence set at his shack in which a dark close-up of Skip's face, lost in thought, is framed by the pulley ropes.

Once the camera pulls back, we see that Skip's holding the missing frame of microfilm. Should he go after Joey or cash in his chips? The sound of a car outside decides the matter. After Skip slips down the stairs to the pilings below, his par-tially lit face recalls Joey's in the dumbwaiter, only now it's Skip who's in the cat-bird seat, since Joey has come with one of his commie associates. When the latter men separate—the superior orders Joey to make the delivery as planned—Skip makes his play: he grabs a buoy that's hooked on a long rope and, as the camera rapidly tracks in reverse, swings like Tarzan from the pilings to the dock. Here Fuller marries the film's marine imagery to the hook-and-pulley figure associated with Skip and Candy's "bad romance." Buoyed by her love, Skip finally does the right thing for Candy, if not—and this is critical—for his country.

Pickup on South Street ends where it begins: in a subway station. Since Joey doesn't know what Skip looks like, Skip trails him onto a train where, using what Moe calls his "trademark" method, he pretends to be reading a newspaper while he steals Joey's gun. The key element of the mise-en-scène, though, is the flap on the uniform of a serviceman standing next to Skip on which the bars and stripes are visible, a motif that appears in the first subway sequence in the film (note the soldier standing next to Candy, whose place Skip eventually assumes) and that's later reprised when Joey exits the train (see, as the camera tracks across the station, a sailor talking to a girl).

After Skip shadows Joey to a bathroom where the delivery is supposed to take place, he interrupts the exchange, knocking down the anonymous communist agent—"There's a frame missing, buster!"—before turning his attention to Joey, who suddenly realizes that he has been stripped of his weapon. Although Joey momentarily manages to escape the confines of the bathroom, the police whistle doesn't stop the fight. Skip, relentlessly pursuing Joey, pins him against the bars of a fence, drags him face-first down a flight of stairs, then, after flipping him over a turnstile, sends him flying onto the tracks below. In a poetic reversal of his fight with Candy, this time it's Joey who's the punching bag.

Unlike the first part of the sequence, which is set in the high-key, fluorescent-bright lighting of the subway station and is marked by aggressively mobile camerawork, the last part plunges us into the noir world. We watch in the dark, from across the tracks, as Skip chases Joey deeper and deeper into the tunnel: "In a final cut to a medium shot, Skip stands in front of a niche in the wall delivering an unending series of blows, each punch propelling Joey's face into the light and back again into the darkness."[36] In fact, right before the final medium shot, there's a lightning-fast cut to the fixed master shot where we watch through the flashing windows of a passing train as Skip continues to administer his beating to Joey, a shot that's repeated when the film reverts to the aforementioned medium shot, the rushing train adding a stroboscopic flourish that performatively mimics the action of a motion picture.

CODA: *MADE IN U.S.A.*

The coda to *Pickup on South Street*—set at the police station—is not without a certain astringency. Skip dogs Tiger ("How's the whip?") and Tiger responds in kind: "You'll always be a two-bit purse snatcher." Candy, however, has the

last word: "You wanna bet?" While this dénouement strikes an eminently in-
terrogative note, a number of critics have complained that Fuller's film doesn't
offer a satisfactory alternative to the cutthroat practices of communism *and*
capitalism. The conjunction is appropriate, since if it's true that Joey and his
red friends are engaged, as he tells Candy at the beginning of the film, in industrial, not political espionage—"How may times do I have to tell you we're
not criminals. This is big business"—Skip, Candy, and Moe are working the
black market on the fringes of the official economy and, as such, are members
of the *Lumpenproletariat*.

At the same time, if Fuller reposits individualism versus both capitalism and
communism, albeit an individualism that's as "subtle as the structure of Jeffer-
sonian democracy,"[37] the conclusion to *Pickup on South Street* tenders what one
might call the inextricable intimacies of the social contract. This qualified happy
ending doesn't sound especially noirish, but then American noir has always been
a queer thing. For instance, the French arguably "found" it just as they later "discovered" Fuller. In both instances, the act involved a certain productive misrecognition.

Consider Fuller's complaint about Jean-Luc Godard in *A Third Face*: "Let's
face it, Godard had stolen a bunch of ideas from *Pickup on South Street* and *Underworld U.S.A.* (1961) for his early pictures. I don't mind, but why not call it what
it was?"[38] Fuller's gripe with Godard, of course, didn't stop him from appearing
in Godard's *Pierrot le fou* (1965) as himself. The fact is, as Godard's dedication
to Fuller and Nick Ray at the beginning of *Made in U.S.A.* (1966) makes clear—
"Whose pupil I am in terms of sight and sound"—what looks like one thing can
sometimes be another. In other words, just as a theft can sometimes function as
a gift or homage, misrecognition is at the very heart of identity.

In *A Third Face* Fuller records how he went to see Al "Pappy" Newman, the
"legendary composer at Fox," to find out if he could get the rights to the popular
French ballad "Mam'selle," which plays on the Victrola in Moe's death scene.[39]
Newman's response to Fuller's question about who owned the rights to this ballad
elucidates the complex, nonidentical nature of things: "The song's not French!
Edmund Goulding wrote the song for *The Razor's Edge*. We already own it!"[40] One
can only guess what cinéastes made of "Mam'selle"—a simulacrum of a French
ballad made in the U.S.A.—when *Pickup on South Street* finally played in France.

One thing is certain: the song not only underscores Moe's long good-bye but
gestures beyond her death to Skip and Candy's alliance, one that begins with a
pickup and ends not, as in a classic noir like *Double Indemnity* (1944) or *Out of
the Past*, with their deaths but a true-blue romance, one that "abrogates the twin
economics of communism *and* capitalism."[41]

PART TWO

'50S NOIR IN THE ATOMIC AGE

A lot of it had fallen into place, piece by piece. Things I didn't see before were suddenly clear. It was a gigantic puzzle that only started here in Manhattan. . . . The rest of it reached to Washington, across to San Francisco, then on across the ocean. And onward still until it encompassed the world. . . .

They were photostats, ten in all, both negatives and positives, on extra thin paper. They were photos of a maze of symbols, diagrams and meaningless words. . . . A serious-voiced commentator . . . told the nation of the calamity that had befallen it. The secret of our newest, most powerful weapon was now, most likely, in the hands of agents of an unfriendly power. He told of the destruction that could be wrought, hinted at the continuance of the cold war with an aftermath of a hotter one. . . . The guardians of our government were jumping through hoops because the people demanded to know why the most heavily guarded secret we ever had could be swiped so easily. There were shakeups from the top to bottom and the rats were scurrying for cover, pleading for mercy. Investigators were turning up reds in the damnedest spots imaginable. . . .

I took all the parts and let them drop, watching to see how they fit in place. They were all there now, every one. I could go out any time and show that picture around and anybody could tell that it was a big red flag with a star and a hammer and sickle.

—Mickey Spillane, *One Lonely Night* (1951)

4

D.O.A.

FATALITY, SEXUALITY, RADIOACTIVITY

It's the drink that you don't pour
Now when you take one sip you won't need any more
You're small as a beetle or big as a whale—BOOM!—
atomic cocktail

—"Atomic Cocktail," Slim Gaillard Quartette
(Gaillard, 1946)

Pickup on South Street is both an atomic espionage and anti-anticommunist noir, since the top-secret microfilm that Skip McCoy purloins from Candy's purse, which is related to the production of the A-bomb, has itself been purloined by the Reds. Yet if it's true that the stolen microfilm in Fuller's film is something of a MacGuffin, the nuclear subtext of Rudolph Maté's *D.O.A.* (1950), at least from an atomic perspective, is even more oblique and overdetermined so that from another, generic perspective (say, the classic investigative narrative of film noir) it's virtually nonexistent, an anamorphic trick or hallucinatory figment of the film's paranoid imagination. In this, *D.O.A.* foreshadows *Kiss Me Deadly*, in which the latter film's motivating device, the "Great Whatsit," is a riddle-like rebus. While the stolen iridium in *D.O.A.* is more immaterial than the microfilm canister in *Pickup on South Street* and less apocalyptic than the Pandora's box in *Kiss Me Deadly*, it nevertheless evokes, as in Fuller's and Aldrich's films, a determinate structure of feeling, a postwar world defined not simply by the lingering fear of radioactivity and the lure of unfettered sexuality but by the mushrooming dread of instant annihilation: "Boom!"

*   *   *

In *American Bomb Cinema* Jerome F. Shapiro records that *D.O.A.* was "completed about two months after Joe 1," the United States' code name for the first successful Soviet atomic test, on August 20, 1949.[1] Like the first post-Hiroshima "nuclear noir," *The House on 92nd Street*, which was released a little over a month after the bombing of Hiroshima and which was "revised at the last minute" to make the "secret ingredient of the atomic bomb" the object of the Nazi secret agents' quest,[2] *D.O.A.* capitalizes on the conventions of the semidocumentary film—"actual locations" and "natural light"[3]—that were ascendant in film noir at the time.

The neorealist look produced by Ernest Lazlo's "hard-edged, documentary photography" is fused in Maté's film with a Germanic sensibility that echoes the origins of classic noir.[4] In fact, *D.O.A.* was loosely based on Robert Siodmak's 1931 *Der Mann, der seinen Mörder sucht* (*The Man Who Searched for His Murderer*), which was co-written by Billy Wilder, the narrators of whose *Double Indemnity* and *Sunset Blvd.* (1950) are, respectively, dying or dead. (Maté himself began his career as a cameraman in Weimar cinema, photographing, among other things, Carl Dryer's *La Passion de Jeanne d'Arc* [1928] and *Vampyr* [1932].)

"Nuclear angst made itself felt in films of all genres after Hiroshima," according to Nicholas Christopher, "with a notable infusion of hysteria after the 1949 Soviet test."[5] However, the difference between, say, sci-fi and film noir is that in the latter genre the "same nuclear angst is repressed, introverted, rechanneled, and not nearly so containable, much less resolvable, in the physical world."[6] In other words, in '50s noir the discourse of the bomb becomes internalized, subjectivized; the consequence is a collective "atomic" neurosis in which the symptoms are dread, anxiety, and, in particular, paranoia.

One of the causes of this free-floating formation was what Austin M. Brues, a "member of the advisory committee of the Atomic Bomb Casualty Commission, a Hiroshima research center set up by the Atomic Energy Commission in 1946 to study bomb survivors," called the "mystery" of radiation.[7] While Frank Bigelow (Edmond O'Brien) in *D.O.A.* does not feel the physical effects of the radioactive toxin that he accidentally imbibes at the Fisherman nightclub, except for a mysterious "belly ache," not only does the toxin kill him sooner rather than later, but the film becomes more expressive the closer it comes to its grim conclusion ("Dead on Arrival"). Hence the surprise of the postscript, which abruptly reverts to the veridical language of the semidocumentary: "The medical facts in this motion picture are authentic. Luminous toxin is a descriptive term for an actual poison. Technical Adviser. Edward F. Dunne, M.D."

Given the picture we have just watched—full of sound and fury, signifying nothing—this postmortem reads like a sick joke or gallows humor. "*D.O.A.* is funny," as Jack Shadoian says, "like Kafka."[8] At the same time, if in retrospect the whole notion of a "luminous toxin" seems improbable, not to say fantastic, what appears to be a purely expressionist device actually has a basis in reality, since the toxin in *D.O.A.* is linked to iridium, and the isotope of iridium is radioactive.

The origins of Bigelow's involvement with the iridium are appropriately random and fateful. Once upon a time, in the small, sleepy town of Banning, in one of those benighted but irrevocable acts that are the very essence of the noir ethos—"one little paper, one little paper among hundreds"—Bigelow notarized a shipment of iridium for a certain Eugene Phillips. The owner of an import-export company in Los Angeles, Phillips purchased the iridium—"a very rare metal, very costly"—from George Reynolds, aka Raymond Rakubian, before selling it in turn to a self-described dealer named Majak (Luther Adler). Unbeknownst to Phillips, however, Reynolds was working with Majak and the iridium was stolen. Phillips, facing a "pretty stiff prison term" but unable, according to his wife, to produce "evidence of the [iridium] transaction" because the bill of sale went "mysteriously missing," committed suicide—or so Phillips's brother, Stanley (Henry Hart), believes.

LOS ANGELES/BANNING: DEATH IN LIFE

The iridium subplot of *D.O.A.* is as convoluted as anything in *The Big Sleep* (1946) or *The Lady from Shanghai* (1948). The film's deep atomic structure of feeling, though, is not limited to the mystery of radioactivity or the secrecy associated with iridium; it's also reflected in the fact that everyone in *D.O.A.*, including Bigelow, appears to be harboring some sort of secret. Consider, for example, the film's main body or corpus, which assumes the form of an extended flashback.

D.O.A. begins at night with a tilt-down shot from the top of Los Angeles City Hall to a man, his back to us, walking into the frame. As the steeply slanted letters of the title flash up onto the screen, the man starts across the street, the camera tracking behind him as he walks down a long corridor, at the end of which a policeman engaged in conversation with another man jerks his finger to the right, pointing down yet another corridor. The camera continues to track behind the man until he comes to a door that reads "HOMICIDE DIVISION."

Any number of things might be said about this opening sequence, but three will suffice. First, the sequence would not be nearly so dramatic without Dmitri Tiomkin's music, which is "cleverly synchronized in mickey-mouse fashion with each move [Bigelow] makes."[9] Even though the underscore introduces what we will later recognize as the film's ultraromantic motif, the martial air and ascending movement propel the film forward and upward, as if we're on a musical escalator. Second, although we do not see the man's face nor know his name, the forward tracking shots, as in Hitchcock's *Vertigo*, facilitate our identification with his character. Third, since the sign on the door says "Homicide," we suspect that the man has come to the police station to report a murder, and the ensuing laconic exchange between the police captain and the man appears to confirm our expectations:

MAN: I wanna report a murder.
CAPTAIN: Sit down. Where was this murder committed?
MAN: San Francisco last night.
CAPTAIN: Who was murdered?

It's only after the last question that we finally get a reverse shot, the camera cutting to a close-up of the man's face before he declares—after a long pause—"I was." The captain rifles through some papers, then, glancing at a mimeographed sheet, turns back to the man, "Your name Bigelow? Frank Bigelow?" The man replies, "That's right," at which point the captain hands the sheet to an officer who's standing offscreen: "Answer the San Francisco APB. Send it direct to Inspector Bannon in Homicide. Tell him we've found Frank Bigelow."

While we now know the man's name and that he's been "murdered," the opening sequence of *D.O.A.*, as in the noir or crime film more generally, poses as many questions as it answers, producing enigmas that it will be the work of the flashback to answer. To wit, if Bigelow has been murdered, how can he still be alive? He doesn't look like Walter Neff at the beginning of *Double Indemnity*, who, even as he's bleeding to death, has to muster all of his rapidly dwindling resources to light a cigarette. Bigelow's rumpled, dirt-stained suit aside, he looks surprisingly hale—for a dead man. The other, more obvious questions are, Who murdered him and why?

The captain prompts Bigelow, and almost as soon as he begins to tell his story— "I live in a little town called Banning out on the desert. It's on the way to Palm Springs. I have a small business . . ."—a whirlpool suddenly appears, signaling the onset of the flashback. The flashback itself effects a change both with respect to time (present to past) and setting (Los Angeles to Banning); it also precipitates a change in lighting (from low- to high-key) and on the sound track (from the absence of music to a lilting underscore). But perhaps the most dramatic contrast between Los Angeles and Banning is that in the LAPD police station Bigelow is literally surrounded by men while in his accountant's office in Banning he's compositionally dominated by women.

Thus, in the very first part of the Banning sequence, a flirtatious young brunette named Kitty (Carol Hughes) is perched on Bigelow's desk to the right while his blonde secretary, Paula (Pamela Britton), stands above and to the left of him. In this particular scenario Bigelow's trapped between two women: if Paula, in white, is the "good girl," then Kitty, in a busy print, is the "bad girl." Kitty, true to type, simultaneously manages to insult Paula and convey her sexual attraction to Bigelow: "Paula, why don't you come down to the place and let me give you another permanent. It makes your hair so much easier to manage [Kitty glances at Bigelow] in all this heat." Paula is no doormat, however. She may have to put up with overly familiar clients like Kitty, but when she discovers that Bigelow's going to San Francisco to "get away from town for a few days" (he "forgot" to tell her), she reads him like an X-ray: "Get away from town or get away from me?"

Although Paula and Bigelow quickly kiss and make up, later at Eddie's bar, which is completely deserted except for a beat cop reading the newspaper (a scene that speaks to just how uneventful Banning is), she assumes a less direct, more solicitous approach: "I know what's going on inside of you, Frank. You're just like any other man only a little more so. You have a feeling of being trapped, hemmed in." When Bigelow gets up and goes over to the jukebox to play a song, Paula switches their beers (she's barely touched hers while Bigelow has almost finished his); when he returns, she confesses, "I thought that by now we'd be married."

Here, *D.O.A.* broaches one of the definitive topics of '50s noir (see, par excellence, *The Bigamist* [1953]): marriage. If, as Beverley Carter argues in "The War of the Sexes," Paula is a "working girl" and her voice is equal to Bigelow's in the "work environment,"[10] the issue of marriage in Maté's film is posed, as in *The Bigamist*, from a male perspective: will Bigelow continue to play the field (say, Kitty) or commit to his present girlfriend (Paula)? This said, Paula's character does not represent simply romance or marriage but a whole way of life, the sort of stereotypical little town and small business associated in the early 1950s with the American dream. Therefore, the fact that the scene at Eddie's ends with another kiss between the two suggests that Bigelow will eventually see the light and reconcile himself to marriage, monogamy, and his safe, if unexciting life, in Banning, California.

SAN FRANCISCO: ATOMIC COCKTAIL

Things change dramatically the moment that Bigelow arrives at the St. Francis Hotel in San Francisco (it's "Market Week") where women appear here, there, and everywhere. It's as if the world, in a flush of wish fulfillment, has become Bigelow's oyster, a transformation marked on the sound track by a series of slide-flute wolf whistles. Bigelow's id continues to be stoked when he gets to his room, where he checks out a woman dancing in the hallway at the same time that he's talking to Paula on the telephone. Paula's answer to Bigelow's question about whether they've done any business with Phillips—"Not unless you've been keeping it a secret from me"—inaugurates what will become one of the film's dominant themes: the intimate connection between business and adultery. This theme is accented when a traveling salesman named Sam (Jess Kirkpatrick) invites Bigelow to a post-convention party already raucously in progress (the music is loud, Latin, and up-tempo) and Sam's "dutiful wife," Sue (Cay Forrester)—the woman in the black cobra-plumed hat and dress whom we've just seen dancing in the hallway—starts to rumba with Bigelow: "Hey, you're good!"

Still, it's not until the party shifts to the Fisherman, the site of one of the most expressive—and, for some, notorious—musical sequences in classic noir, that *D.O.A.* really shifts into overdrive. First, an iris opens like an eye onto an image of a black saxophonist, below which caricature is written—like the sign outside the nightclub—"Fisherman." As smoke wafts upward, the shadow of a tenor saxophonist appears superimposed over the image, then the saxophonist (James van Streeter) juts into the frame as the camera pulls back for a wide shot of a quintet: bass (Shifty Henry) and drums (Al "Cake" Wichard) to the left, trumpet (Teddy Buckner) and piano (Ray LaRue) to the right, the saxophonist front and center. On the bamboo-matted wall behind the saxophonist, a buoy reads "Jive" and, inside the buoy, there's the open skeletal mouth of a fish. "Although the style of jazz is not bebop," David Butler notes, "the drummer, in black shades and sporting a crew cut, is clearly fashioned after the popular image of the bop musician" à la Dizzy Gillespie or Thelonious Monk.[11]

But if the black jazz band and the white bop audience with their finger clicking and jive exhortations are stereotypical, they're also, unlike the canned, big band music playing on the jukebox at Eddie's, alive. To paraphrase another film, we're not in Banning anymore: instead of a small town with its dry desert heat and scorching sunlight (at Eddie's, Bigelow gulps down his beer like there's no tomorrow), the Fisherman is a white-hot club on the Embarcadero at night. And true to the Hollywood conventions of the time, as the jazz number progresses to its feverish, drum solo–propelled climax (see *Phantom Lady*),[12] a feverish montage of the drummer's and saxophonist's sweating faces is followed by a garish close-up of the hopped-up, bug-eyed pianist, whose gaping mouth and teeth-baring grin echo the fish head tacked to the wall.

While the "sexual, rhythmic, impulsive aspects of jazz," "the very aspects upon which the white culture industry mythologized jazz as dark, exotic forbidden music,"[13] are highlighted in the first part of the Fisherman sequence, the second part has a decidedly different tenor. Hence, when the film finally cuts away to Bigelow, Sue's leaning against him, one hand on his shoulder, as her husband looks on unhappily. The next time that the camera cuts away to Bigelow, he's being repeatedly bumped by a man writhing in ecstasy behind him. (In *D.O.A.*, at least, jive is gender-indiscriminate.)

These cutaways complicate the reflexive association between jazz and sexuality in *D.O.A.* and speak to what Robert Porfirio calls the "complex ambivalence invoked by jazz."[14] First, Sue has already come on to Bigelow at the St. Francis Hotel (married women stray too, the film implies), and Bigelow loses interest in her not so much because of her increasingly agitated husband but because she's a displaced double of Paula. Second, like the bartender (who prefers Guy Lombardo) and opposed to the male hipster (who's "enlightened" by the music), Bigelow's emphatically *not* enamored with the Fisherman.

The film's ambivalence about jazz is recapitulated in the second part of the sequence when Bigelow retreats to the bar, where he meets a society blonde named Jeanie (Virginia Lee)—her code word is "easy"—whom he's immediately attracted to despite her overt and vocal enthusiasm for the Fisherman: "Listen to that piano! Feel those vibrations!" The shift in tone from the first to the second part of the sequence, a subtle but marked one, is registered on the sound track by a change in musical cue, a bluesy torch song reminiscent of Billie Holiday.

In fact, it's while Bigelow's chatting up Jeanie that an enigmatic man in a slouch hat, crisscross scarf, and houndstooth coat (his back is to us, like Bigelow's at the beginning of the film) switches out his bourbon and water with another one spiked with a "tasteless and odorless" toxin. This drink, like the one invented right after the bombing of Hiroshima, is an "atomic cocktail,"[15] and hints that the Fisherman sequence is not only about jazz and sexuality but "atomic energy," the "mix of desire *and* dread that marked attitudes toward two dangerously intoxicating entities: blackness and the Bomb."[16]

PANTOMIME: LIFE IN DEATH

D.O.A.'s pervasive, determinate ambiguity about sexuality or, more properly, infidelity is reiterated when Bigelow returns to his hotel room with Jeanie's phone number only to rip it up once he reads Paula's note—"I'll keep a light burning in the window"—and notices the flowers she has sent. At this point in the film Bigelow appears to have survived his "dark night of the soul," although it turns out to be a faux happy ending when he wakes up the next morning with a massive hangover.[17] (The blues song in the background is a haunting reminder of his big night out on the town.) Bigelow promptly orders a Bloody Mary from room service, then thinks better of it: "Take it away—I don't even want to look at it!"

When next we see Bigelow, he's exiting the St. Francis Hotel, where he stops to lean against a post. Sweating profusely (not unlike the musicians at the Fisherman), he starts to walk, repeatedly taking off his hat to wipe his brow before pulling up short in front of a medical building. (The canted hospital sign is an "objective correlative" of Bigelow's disorientation.) Cut to a doctor peering at an X-ray of his vital organs: "Well, it's a good thing everybody's isn't like you, Mr. Bigelow—put us doctors out of business!" Linked, however, as it is with radiation, the X-ray foreshadows the real diagnosis. According to the specialist, Dr.

Schaefer (Lawrence Dobkin), the tests reveal the presence in Bigelow's body of a poison "for which there is no antidote." The prognosis: "a day, two days, a week at the most."

Cut to the Southern Pacific Hospital and one of the most ingenious shots in all of classic noir.[18] In order to demonstrate to Bigelow that he has absorbed the radioactive poison, Dr. MacDonald (Frank Gerstle) turns off the light, and the vial—one critic has wagged it's filled with urine[19]—glows in the dark. As Bigelow, dazed, repeats the prognosis to himself—"A day, two days . . ."—the doctor, who's about to dial the police, gives him the ultimate bad news: "You've been murdered." Bigelow's first, instinctive reaction—to the utter astonishment of the attending doctor and nurses—is to run. In an exhilarating sequence composed of wipes and impelled by a swiftly tracking camera, Bigelow races like a madman down Market Street, knocking down pedestrians and, at one point, haphazardly crossing a busy thoroughfare right in front of a honking car. Bigelow, it's clear, is a man possessed, yet if we know what he's running from, it's not at all clear what he's running to.

The camera set-up changes from a mobile to a fixed one as Bigelow, turning a corner and dwarfed by the bridge above him, runs breathlessly toward a newsstand. To his left is an advertisement decorated with a bird on a clothesline for the *San Francisco Chronicle* ("Brighten your morning . . . with the *San Francisco*

"I am become Death": Dr. MacDonald (Frank Gerstle) holding up an iridium-illuminated vial as Frank Bigelow (Edmond O'Brien) looks on in *D.O.A.*

Chronicle"), to his right a staggered stack of *Life* magazines. The obviousness of the mise-en-scène does not diminish its force: Bigelow has been murdered all right, but, for the moment at least, he's alive.

While this scene has extraordinary existential resonance if only in the sense that we're all "sick unto" or "beings toward death," the nuclear subtext is an oblique, period-specific one given that the "most important print medium through which the American people formed their initial impressions of the atomic bomb was Henry Luce's photo magazine *Life*."[20] The atomic-age mentality of "life one moment, death the next" is brilliantly captured when Bigelow, having briefly closed his eyes, looks up to see the overexposed sun hanging low in the sky like a giant orb, a shot that recalls J. Robert Oppenheimer's *Bhagavad Gita*–inspired description of the first nuclear explosion as possessing the "radiance of a thousand suns."[21] On the sound track the doctor's voice repeats like a broken record—"A day, two days, a week at the most."

The subsequent pantomime is totally hallucinatory and, like the serial *Life* magazines and the *San Francisco Chronicle* advert, mocks both Bigelow's dreams and the "sunny" optimism of post-boom America. A rubber ball rolls out of the shadows toward Bigelow's feet. Bigelow picks the ball up and hands it to a little girl, who's whisked away by her mother. A woman in a suit then appears, and after hailing her male lover the two passionately embrace to Strauss's "Blue Danube"

Life: Frank Bigelow (Edmond O'Brien) catching his breath, post–terminal diagnosis, in front of a San Francisco newspaper stand in *D.O.A.*

as Bigelow stands off to one side, watching. If the first scenario represents the children that Bigelow will never have and the second the romantic relationship that might have developed with Paula if he had never left Banning,[22] these things are now lost to him forever. What, to accent the existential thrust of the film, will or can he *do*?

Although the doctor's voice on the sound track intones, "There's nothing anyone can do now," these cruel admonishments appear, paradoxically enough, to catalyze Bigelow, who, backed by the march-like score, starts to walk again with renewed determination. His life has suddenly acquired a new purpose or meaning; instead of being a victim, he will discover who poisoned him. At this liminal moment, *D.O.A.* does an abrupt about-face, changing from a melodrama about the fate of romance and the romance of fate to a revenge-inflected investigative film (see the seminal neo-noir *Point Blank* [1967]) in which Bigelow becomes both detective and victim, pursuer and pursued.

LOS ANGELES REDUX: DEAD END

The third and final section of *D.O.A.* is set in Los Angeles (Lee's Drugstore, Wilshire Boulevard, Hollywood and Highland) and is structured around a series of baleful encounters between Bigelow and a cast of characters, all of whom, at least initially, thwart his desire for knowledge: Halliday (William Ching), the comptroller of Phillips's import-export company; Stanley Phillips, Eugene's brother; Mrs. Phillips (Lynne Baggett), Eugene's widow, whom we first see, like Bertha Duncan in *The Big Heat* (1953), mourning the death of her husband; Marla Rakubian (Laurette Luez), a model/femme fatale ("If I was a man, I'd punch your dirty face in") with whom Phillips was having an affair; Raymond Rakubian, Marla's brother and the only other person besides Bigelow whom Eugene Phillips attempted to contact before he died; Miss Foster (Beverly Campbell), the secretary at Phillips's company; Chester (Neville Brand), a sadistic henchman; and Majak, the super-suave criminal mastermind behind the iridium deal.

In *San Francisco Noir* Nathaniel Rich claims that it's "best not to try to sort out the Byzantine plot turns that result in [Bigelow's] murder," an opinion seconded by Alexander Ballinger and Danny Graydon in *The Rough Guide to Film Noir*, who maintain: "It's best not to try to disentangle *D.O.A.*'s absurd plotline."[23] *D.O.A.*'s plot might be described as a "*reductio ad absurdum* of *Oedipus Rex*,"[24] but it repays, like a lot of classic noirs, sustained attention. Consider, for example, the narrative thread involving Raymond Rakubian. When Bigelow discovers that George Reynolds, the man who sold Phillips the iridium, was an alias of Raymond Rakubian (he learns this from a picture that he has forcibly taken from Marla Rakubian and brought to a photographic studio), he thinks that he has finally solved the case. However, no sooner has he exited the studio than he's shot at by a sniper.

The Maze: Frank Bigelow (Edmond O'Brien) lost in the intestinal labyrinth of the abandoned warehouse in *D.O.A.*

Bigelow tracks the perpetrator down to an abandoned warehouse that's a maze of "intestinal complexity,"[25] although the only thing he finds, as the blues song fades up on the sound track, is a matchbox with the Fisherman logo on the cover.

Later, Chester and another henchman take Bigelow to Majak's house, where Bigelow confronts the dealer with his recent, hard-won knowledge that Raymond Rakubian poisoned him. Majak sends Chester away like a spoiled child—"He's unhappy unless he gives pain. He likes to see blood"—before opening a curtain off his living room and we espy, atop a tapestry-backed cabinet, a gold burial urn with a candle burning on either side. "Raymond Rakubian was my nephew," Majak solemnly explains. "He could not possibly have tried to kill you. He's been dead for five months." Then, while Tiomkin's score segues into an orientalist passage capped by clashing cymbals, the camera cuts to a close-up of the urn, upon which is inscribed, "Here Lie the Beloved Remains of Raymond Rakubian," and below which inscription is a passage written in Armenian.

This scene in *D.O.A.* represents a rather different sort of maze than the abandoned warehouse—it's more metaphysical than not—and constitutes the navel of the film. There's no escape from this maze, because it's a dead end in more ways than one. In other words, it's not a "living" room but a place or space dedicated to death, where the urn represents what Bigelow will soon be—ashes—and the Armenian script is an orientalist figure for the absolute Other: what cannot be known in this life, what lies beyond the curtain or veil.[26] Hence the futility of Bigelow's attempt to escape via a door that Majak, blithely waving his hand, observes is a closet.

Bigelow is dead wrong about Raymond Rakubian, but since he now knows too much about Majak's business, he has to be summarily disposed of. (Majak reasons that at this stage of his life—he's an older man—"ten years in jail is his entire life.") The rear projection shots of Chester driving Bigelow in Los Angeles—"I'm going to enjoy this, Bigelow"—are, like the newsstand sequence, completely surreal, not least because of Neville Brand's inspired, lunatic performance (his début as an actor); they also epitomize the film's oscillation between realism and expressionism. Indeed, because Bigelow refuses to respond to Chester's threats—"I think I'll give it to you in the belly"—the henchman's monologue about what he's going to do to Bigelow and just how much he's going to enjoy it betrays a certain homosocial charge. The net effect is to point out the intimate resemblance between the hired killer and the post-diagnosis Bigelow, who, in his all-consuming quest to find his murderer, starts to resemble what he's ostensibly opposed to.

Bigelow's increasingly violent nature is manifest in the film's penultimate sequence, where he returns to the Bradbury Building in search of his nemesis. However, before doing so, he briefly reunites with Paula, who has come to Los Angeles after having been contacted by the San Francisco police and is nervously pacing outside the Allison Hotel. "You don't even act like yourself," she exclaims, looking at a wild-eyed, disheveled Bigelow. "You frighten me." Bigelow professes his undying love for her—"I was never more certain of anything in my life"—although he still doesn't let her in on his radioactive secret. Rather, he asks her to wait in the hotel lobby until he returns. Then they wave good-bye to each other and we're reminded of the lovers joyously rendezvousing at the newsstand.

Bigelow is off and running again—this time to Stanley Phillips's apartment, where he roughly interrogates Miss Foster about the whereabouts of Eugene's brother, whom he now passionately believes to be the culprit. However, when Stanley, shades of Bigelow, limps out of a room clutching a letter to his stomach, it becomes just another dead end. (The letter, which Stanley found after his brother's death, proves that Halliday was having an affair with Eugene's wife; Eugene then confronted the lovers and Halliday pushed him off a balcony to make it look like a suicide.) The doubling motif continues apace when Bigelow à la Halliday confronts Mrs. Phillips at the Sunset Arms and threatens to throw her off the balcony of her apartment unless she reveals why he was poisoned. The motive, according to Mrs. Phillips: Bigelow was the only person alive who could testify that there was a bill of sale for the iridium shipment, which would have definitively proved that her husband, Eugene, had no reason to commit suicide. As Bigelow himself previously explained to Miss Foster, "Innocent men don't have to jump out of windows."

Despite the fact that Majak and his goons arrive just in time to see Bigelow threatening Mrs. Phillips, Bigelow uses his wits (he boards a bus) and the police (as a screen) to escape them and make his way back to the Bradbury Building. The mise-en-scène couldn't be richer: a neon sign reading "Million Dollar" illuminates a long shot of Bigelow running toward the building, where two windows burn like eyes in the night. (The sign is for the producer Harry Popkin's "Million Dollar Theatre"; it can also, of course, be read as a sly critique of the "cash nexus": What good is money, even a million dollars, if you're no longer alive to enjoy it?) A shot of Bigelow exiting a wrought-iron elevator, shadows crisscrossing his face, precedes the materialization of his heart's desire: Halliday, sporting the same exotic ensemble—hat, scarf, and coat—he was wearing at the Fisherman. The blues song echoes again on the sound track, and after Bigelow stumbles like a drunk, Halliday, a cigarette dangling from his mouth, turns around to look.

The subsequent deep-focus long shot of Bigelow lost among the shadows and serpentine ironwork of the Bradbury Building recalls the labyrinth of the abandoned warehouse, only this time the roles are reversed and the pursued has the pursuer squarely in his sights. Gun in hand, Bigelow starts toward Halliday—another rhyme, this time of the newsstand sequence and his momentous decision to search for his murderer—when his assailant ducks down a staircase. The low-angle shot of Bigelow staggering like Frankenstein's monster, his face contorted into a death mask as he empties his gun into Halliday's body, provides an emphatic coda to the distended body of the film. If Bigelow's aggressivity can be seen as a deferred form of sexual discharge, the telos of D.O.A.—as it's been ever since the Fisherman club—is not sex but death, and one is reminded again of Oppenheimer: "Now I am become death."

Suddenly the whirlpool reappears and we're back at the beginning, back to Bigelow sitting at the Homicide desk in Los Angeles surrounded by policemen. It could be a bad dream, as in Lang's *The Woman in the Window* (1944), although it's all too real. After Bigelow explains why Halliday poisoned him, he hands over Marla Rakubian's gun before, wracked with pain, he makes one final request: "Would you . . . Paula . . . ?" As Tiomkin's romantic motif rises for the final time on the sound track, the captain's reaction, as in the film's opening sequence, is as curt as a nail in a coffin: "Call the morgue." The final shot, a hand stamping "D.O.A." on a missing person's report, is simultaneously exclamatory and unsentimental. The dying Bigelow's story has been for naught.

EPILOGUE: "TELL HER NO"

One of the many surprises of *D.O.A.* is that, in the end, the iridium subplot appears to be a smokescreen for the film's real donnée: sexuality or, more precisely, infidelity. So, in addition to learning that Halliday killed Bigelow because he was having an affair with Eugene Phillips's wife, we learn from Miss Foster that Phillips himself was having an affair with Marla Rakubian. (Although we can only speculate about Marla's motivations, it would appear that, given her cozy relationship with Majak, she was setting up Eugene for her brother Raymond's iridium scheme.)

Consequently, Phillips is not only betrayed by his lover, Marla, and his partner, Halliday; despite his relative innocence, he's also punished for his affair. The fact that Bigelow is symbolically disciplined for merely fantasizing about rather than actually committing infidelity suggests the exorbitant nature of sexuality as well as the super-repressive character of American society in the early 1950s. As Elaine Tyler May observes in *Homeward Bound*, "It was not just nuclear energy that had to be contained but the social and sexual fallout of the atomic age."[27] With this "containment" model in mind, it's clear that the iridium angle of *D.O.A.* is not so much peripheral as central to its sociosexual dialectic in which, to recollect Michel Foucault, the discourse of the bomb produces desire. At the same time, if fantasmatic sex in Maté's film is the flip side of the era's free-floating fears and anxieties about nuclear apocalypse, the prohibitive message of *D.O.A.* is as old and axiomatic as one of the Ten Commandments: just say no.

5

"BLACK FILM" AND THE BOMB

SPIES AND "COWBOYS," RED PROFESSORS AND THIEVES

> Some men with brains in their cranium
> Took a piece of uranium
> They did what other men couldn't do
> They split the atom right in two
>
> —Sir Lancelot, "Atomic Energy" (Raymond
> Glazer and L. V. Pinard, 1947)

In *D.O.A.* the atomic subtext is obliquely articulated to the sexual psychopathology of everyday life and the fatalism associated with the investigative narrative of classic noir—with the twist, of course, that the "detective" is also the victim and the scene of the crime his human, all-too-human body. However, in the prototypical '50s nuclear noir, the protagonist is not an everyman like Frank Bigelow in *D.O.A.* but an elite scientist—a nuclear physicist, to be precise—who's either overtly opposed to or intimately aligned with the nation-state and its institutional agencies such as One-Worlder "Wicked Wizards" like Robert Oppenheimer and anti-internationalist "Master Mechanics" like Edward Teller, respectively.[1] Although the FBI, as in the anticommunist noir, is the dominant investigative figure in these films, it's also oddly superfluous (as in *The Thief* [1952]), more concerned with national security than individual human lives (as in *The Atomic City* [1952]), or risibly incompetent (as in *Shack Out on 101* [1955]). *City of Fear* (1959) is not, unlike *The Thief*, *The Atomic City*, and *Shack Out on 101*, an atomic espionage noir. However, if Lerner's film is another hybrid subgenre—say, a nuclear-epidemiological noir—the representation of the LAPD in *City of Fear* reiterates the ambivalent figuration of the FBI in the prototypical atomic noir as well as the distinctly unsympathetic view of the police and federal authorities in both *Pickup on South Street* and *Kiss Me Deadly*.

* * *

The Atomic Energy Commission (AEC) was established in 1946 after the bombing of Hiroshima and Nagasaki but before Operation Crossroads, the atomic bomb tests at Bikini. A civilian institution, the AEC sought to "oversee atomic energy research and development."[2] The turning point in the early history of the commission occurred in April 1949 and involved the AEC Fellowship Program. An American citizen discovered that Hans Freistadt, a graduate student in physics at the University of North Carolina at Chapel Hill, had "received an AEC fellowship to do research on general relativity."[3] The problem was that Freistadt—in the words of contemporary, right-wing radio commentator Fulton Lewis Jr.—was a "professed communist."[4]

On July 7, 1949, the Senate Appropriations Committee approved a rider that "required FBI investigations for all AEC fellowship recipients."[5] The arrest of Klaus Fuchs in London in February 1950—one month before the release of *D.O.A.*—transformed the subject of atomic espionage from an academic to a national security issue. In *American Society in an Age of Anxiety*, Jessica Wang summarizes the swiftly unfolding events: "The identification of Harry Gold, a Philadelphia industrial chemist, as Fuchs's American contact subsequently led to the arrest of David Greenglass, an army machinist who had relayed limited information about the design of the plutonium bomb to Gold and to his brother-in-law, Julius Rosenberg. Rosenberg and his wife, Ethel, were arrested in the summer of 1950, convicted of conspiracy to commit espionage in March 1951, and executed in June 1953."[6]

Fuchs's act of espionage—to cite the second volume of the massive history of the AEC, *Atomic Shield*—"was not an isolated instance of betrayal but part of an organized Soviet intelligence operation against the US atomic energy project."[7] In other words, the arrest of Fuchs confirmed the existence of an internal domestic threat in the United States and raised the specter of Soviet-sponsored subversion. Since "all the known instances of wartime atomic espionage" (Harry Gold, Morris and "Lona" Cohen, David and Ruth Greenglass, Julius and Ethel Rosenberg) were, with the exception of Gold, "members of the Communist Party or other communist organizations at some time in their lives," atomic espionage became irrevocably linked with the red menace, despite the fact that the vast majority of Americans who joined the Communist Party did so "in good faith and never engaged in illegal clandestine acts."[8]

THE THIEF: ALIEN NATION

The above moment is the charged historical context in which *The Thief* was made. Starring Ray Milland as a nuclear physicist, *The Thief*—"one of the most influential 1950s noirs"[9]—was made by a number of the same people who made

Silenced: Title card featuring Dr. Allan Fields (Ray Milland) and the "dark lady" (Rita Gam) in *The Thief*.

D.O.A. It was executive-produced, as was *D.O.A.*, by Harry Popkin and directed by Russell Rouse, who co-scripted Rudolph Maté's film. *The Thief* also reflects, like *D.O.A.*, the characteristic look of '50s noir in which the film's "dark visual style" (furnished by Sam Leavitt) "works against the documentary nature of the location photography."[10] At the same time, unlike *D.O.A.* and "almost unique in motion picture history," *The Thief* was "shot entirely without dialogue," albeit not without sound.[11] (The film's ambient properties are central to its design, including and especially Herschel Burke Gilbert's riveting, Academy Award–nominated score.)

The absence of dialogue in *The Thief* is the switch point between the varying descriptions of the film as "experimental" and "propaganda." Robert Porfirio, for instance, writes that although *The Thief* "was the most publicized of the anti-Red films produced as a political ploy in the early 1950s," the lack of dialogue is an "asset in toning down didacticism."[12] And in "The Big Secret" Mark Osteen argues that *The Thief* is an "intriguing experimental film" that "uses silence as a metaphor for the blanket of secrecy that surrounds atomic silence."[13] In other words, in addition to being, like a lot of '50s noirs, a docu-noir, *The Thief* is that rare thing, part agitprop, part experimental feature film, where the latter construction—at least in the context of classical Hollywood—is something of a contradiction in terms.

The tension between experimental and feature film is reflected in the opening sequence of *The Thief*. The unusually mobile camera tracks from a ringing telephone around and through an apartment to a bedroom where Allan Fields (Ray Milland) lies wide awake and dressed in his street clothes. Milland would have been familiar to '50s audiences from such noirs as *The Big Clock* (1948) and *So Evil My Love* (1948) as well as, more generally, *The Lost Weekend* (1945). While the ringing phone anticipates Hitchcock's *Dial M for Murder* (1954), the most relevant precursor is Fritz Lang's *Ministry of Fear* (1944), in which Milland plays Stephen Neale, an ex-con who becomes enmeshed in a Nazi espionage plot.

In *The Thief* the espionage scenario surfaces when Fields finally gets out of bed, dons his hat and coat, and leaves his apartment. It's night and as he walks down a leafy, shop-lined street toward the camera, a man wearing glasses lights a cigarette, then drops a crumpled piece of paper to the ground. Back at his apartment Fields drops the paper on a desk before gazing at a plaque:

International Physicists Academy
Awarded To
Dr. Allan Fields
Of The United States
For His Contributions
In The Field Of Nuclear Physics
Geneva, Switzerland
1950

Not a single word of dialogue has been spoken, but it's clear from the preceding silent action that Fields is involved, whether for good or ill, in the spy business.

Two of the dominant visual motifs of *The Thief*—fire and eyes—are reiterated in the next sequence. After putting on a pair of glasses and reading the message, Fields sets fire to the tinfoil-backed paper, the camera steadily tracking in to his eyeglass-framed face. This ocular shot not only associates Fields with the eyeglass-wearing Mr. Bleek (Martin Gabel) at the drop point but provides a specular segue to the subsequent scene set at the Washington, D.C., offices of the Atomic Energy Commission. Against a background of slanting Venetian-blind shadows, Fields, now dressed in a white laboratory coat, takes out a Minox camera and begins photographing a set of documents marked "SECRET" that he has just removed from a safe. Especially striking is an extreme close-up insert shot of Fields peering through the eye of the miniature camera, a shot that's later matched with an extreme close-up of a phone receiver pressed against Fields's ear. The phone buzzes three times, a signal that it's time for another rendezvous with Bleek.

The drop point this time is the Library of Congress. After Fields transfers the microfilm to Bleek by hiding it in a row of books, it's transported via anonymous

foreign agents to New York City, where, at a counter in Macy's hosiery department, a passing male agent drops the microfilm into a woman's purse, a scene
that foreshadows the suggestive use of purse imagery in Fuller's *Pickup on South
Street*. The mise-en-scène, framed as it is by a pair of mannequin legs, insinuates
that foreign agents are somehow sexually deviant or, more precisely, that foreign
female agents are promiscuous. The stereotypical character of the subtext is reflected by the fact that the tenor of the metaphor, sexuality, is not commensurate
with the vehicle, espionage. Given this cluster of stereotypical associations, it's no
surprise that, as we see in the concluding scene of the sequence, the microfilm is
bound for the "Orient": Cairo, Egypt.

The Thief returns to more familiar, less exotic terrain when it circles back to
Fields, who, in an echo of *The Lost Weekend*, is hitting the bottle, hard. As in Fritz
Lang's films, a lap dissolve is symptomatic: as Fields sits down, drink in hand, in a
living room chair next to a radio and telephone, a shot of the dark-hatted, spectacle-
wearing Mr. Bleek fleetingly appears superimposed over the former "domestic" image. The effect is startling and hints that Mr. Bleek and, by implication, his Soviet
sponsors are surveilling Fields and that, rather more insidiously, Bleek has gotten
into Fields's head. The latter suggestion is reinforced when the phone rings and
rings and, in response, an agitated Fields turns on the radio. However, since he can
still hear the phone ringing in the background, he clamps his hands over his ears.

One of the cardinal tropes of both the crime and anticommunist film is that
once the criminals/commies have someone on the hook, they won't let him or her
off; instead, they raise the ante and thereby the "wages of sin." In *The Thief* Fields
steals into the office of a colleague, Dr. Hans Linstrum (John McKutcheon), in order to microfilm more secret and—in this case, equation-scribbled—documents.
In '50s nuclear noirs, the occult, mysterious character of scientific knowledge is
frequently figured by mathematical equations, which are either reproduced in
miniaturized form on microfilm or scribbled on a blackboard à la Einstein at the
Institute for Advanced Study at Princeton. In other words, the mathematical
equations are material signifiers of the sort of abstruse knowledge necessary for
atomic-bomb research: such knowledge is not only secret but arcane as well.

Before Fields can escape with the microfilm, though, Linstrum comes back to
the office looking for his glasses. There's a rapid zoom-in from Fields's POV—he's
hiding behind a wingback chair—to the microfilm camera he has inadvertently
left on top of the desk. Linstrum starts to leave, then returns to his desk for a book;
the fact that he fails to see the microfilm camera sitting on the desk suggests he's as
blind as a bat to the un-American activities happening literally right under his eyes.

However, in *The Thief* the enemy is also blind or, at least, subject to blind
chance. In the process of transporting the new microfilm, a male, vaguely British-
looking agent nonchalantly puffing on a cigarette strolls off a sidewalk and into

the path of an incoming car. The action is captured in an Eisensteinian "montage of collisions" and the consequence is that the FBI is now acutely aware that the security of the AEC has been breached. A shot of Fields dropping the microfilm camera into a canal is followed by a shot of an FBI agent using a projector to view the microfilm that's been retrieved from the dead courier, the image gradually coming into focus as in a photographic bath.

Back at his office, Fields opens the blinds and watches as Linstrum's driven away by the Feds. In the reverse shot, a dark shadow image of the Capitol is reflected on the glass behind which Fields stands. The glass imagery is not accidental: each time an AEC scientist who's suspected of being a spy exits the AEC building—McNaughton, a female colleague of Fields—one of the FBI agents watching from inside leaves to trail him or her. Later, in a sequence that anticipates *The Conversation* (1974), Fields returns to his apartment, where he searches first calmly, then frantically, every nook and cranny—closet, dresser, desk, bookcase— for any sign that his apartment has been bugged. His gaze finally lights on the telephone, at which point he dials a number and the camera cuts to a headphoned FBI agent in another location tape-recording the call.

The fact that Fields is being actively surveilled by the FBI does not go unnoticed by his superiors. But when Fields returns to the Library of Congress looking for his contact, a high-angle shot of Mr. Bleek furtively watching from above indicates that the Soviets still retain the upper hand. Thus, when FBI agents appear outside Fields's apartment, he's able to flee in the dark via a fire escape because Bleek has, in the meantime, been able to get a telegram to him. Fields's evasive actions—climbing a telephone pole, running across a roof—mime the behavior of a conventional cat burglar and play up the demotic connotations of the film's title—Fields, that is, as a "common thief."

Despite the fact that the FBI manages to intercept Bleek's telegram—"Unless payment is made on Acc't #2374 immediately quick legal action will be taken. Stadium Installment Co."—they're unable to decode it. Fields, however, can: the number refers to a license plate and "Stadium" to the home of the Washington Senators. Cut to a night-for-night shot of Fields searching for a car outside Griffith Stadium, where a baseball game is in progress. (The hyper-bright stadium lighting and ambient sound of the cheering crowd are extraordinarily atmospheric.) If baseball is America's favorite pastime, the nation—the license plate reads "19 D.C. 52"—has become utterly alien to Fields.

Although Fields locates the car, a key, and another crumpled message in the glove compartment, the headlights in the rear window and the brightly lit dome of the Capitol in the distance as he drives away from the city are reminders of his fugitive status in the eyes of the U.S. government. The subsequent daytime, high-key shots of New York City therefore represent a welcome relief from the habitual gloom of the first, D.C. part of the film, unlike the dark, dilapidated safe house that is Fields's destination. (Note the overflowing garbage on the sidewalk outside the brownstone.)

The diegetic jazz music playing in the background signifies, though, that Fields is not alone, and when he opens the door to his apartment, a raven-haired woman in a tight, cream-colored nightdress appears in the hallway. (The woman with no name—"The Girl"—is played by the curiously but appropriately named Rita Gam in her début film.) While Fields only glances at the woman, she continues to stare at him until he enters his apartment, the camera cutting away when she places a coin in a wall phone. If the "dark lady" is a vision of loveliness, Fields's studio apartment is the epitome of urban squalor: small, dingy, spare. Dismayed, Fields reads the note he previously retrieved together with a suitcase from a locker at Grand Central Station: "86th floor of Empire State. Woman will carry 3 books tied with string. When preparations are completed you will receive signal."

Suddenly the phone rings, but when Fields opens the door to see if the call is for him, the woman's look indicates that it's for her. Fields paces his room (at one point he looks out the only window in the room at the brick wall directly opposite), a neon light blinking on and off like a metronome as he sits smoking on his bed in the dark. Later, Fields goes out for groceries and returns just as the woman—now in a black dress—is descending a staircase. Once he arrives at his apartment, he turns around and looks at the woman, who, taking a deep drag on a cigarette, walks down the hall and stands outside his door as Fields, his arm full of groceries, stands on the other side, listening intently. As the camera dollies in for a close-up of the woman, she takes another drag on her cigarette before exhaling and turning on her heel.

Cut to Fields dressed in a white shirt and tie in his apartment, pouring a drink, newspapers scattered everywhere on the floor around him. There's the sudden sound of music and, opening the door, he sees the woman—at the end of the hallway and framed by the door jamb—sitting on a bed, the camera panning up her tensed legs to a medium shot of her buffing her nails. After standing up to brush her hair in the mirror (Fields's dwarfed image is reflected in the bottom corner of the glass), she turns around and, directly meeting his gaze, strolls over to the door and slowly closes it.

Claustrophobia is a preeminent motif of classic noir, and there's no better example of it than the scene in which Fields anxiously paces his room, the light from the window casting bar-like shadows on the wall. Three times the camera rapidly zooms toward the wall, vividly expressing Fields's incipient madness and sense of entrapment. Finally, in a sequence reminiscent of Bigelow's post-diagnosis dash through the streets of downtown San Francisco, Fields bolts from his apartment and runs and runs until he's too tired to run anymore. The screen ripples like a wave (see *D.O.A.*) and suddenly he's back at his apartment, still breathing heavily, when the phone rings again.

A woman in a dark suit carrying three books—the same woman that we earlier saw checking out stockings at Macy's—gets off a bus in midtown Manhattan, closely followed by a man in a dark suit and hat. At the Empire State Building the woman takes an elevator to the observation deck, "1050 feet above New York City." Cut to a vertiginous, extreme low-angle shot of the Empire State Building from Fields's point of view. On the 86th floor the camera cuts from a medium exterior shot of Fields standing in front of coin-operated binoculars—he's looking at the woman, who's sitting on a bench—to an interior, slightly elevated shot of an FBI agent watching her through a window, the city laid out in all its nakedness beyond the lozenge-wired fencing.

In the diner, Fields reads a slip of newspaper with the "Shipping News" for April 19:

Tonight's Departures		
Vessel	Destination	Time
Eugene C	Norfolk	1:00 p.m.
Stolzbergen	Cairo	3:30 a.m.
Crescent G	Alaska	1:30 p.m.
Golden Crest	Keelung	1:00 a.m.
Martin P.	San Jose	3:45 a.m.
Oil Queen	Callao	4:00 a.m.
Master Drake	London	4:30 a.m.

Looking up, Fields accidentally meets the gaze of the FBI agent, and in a heart-stopping sequence, the agent chases him—staircase by staircase, landing by landing—from the 87th to the glassed-in observatory on the 102nd floor, the city now ghost-like behind the safety glass.

When Fields discovers that the elevator door on the 102nd floor is closed, he climbs a ladder, then another, the space becoming darker and more constricted until, opening a grate, he emerges into the open air at the very top of the building. Fields is turning in circles, hat in hand, in the cramped space when the FBI agent grabs his foot; without thinking, he stomps on the man's face and hands again and again—a low-angle insert shot captures the savagery of his action—until the FBI agent falls. A choker shot of the man's bruised and bloodied face, eyes staring blankly into space, reveals what Fields has done. The subsequent tight two-shot of Fields passing the dead man on his way back down the ladder—with the man's death-gnarled hand in the foreground and Fields's anguished face above—encapsulates noir's bleak existential ethos.

Returning to his shadow-barred apartment, Fields sits down on his bed, the camera tracking into his face as he registers the full weight of his actions and begins to weep. The nightmare sequence that follows, one of the most expressive set-pieces in '50s noir, reflects Fields's tortured psyche. First, superimposed over his sweating face as he fitfully sleeps is the dial of a rotary telephone, and peering out from its center is the face of the fedora-hatted, bespectacled Mr. Bleek. While the dial turns crazily first clockwise, then counter-clockwise, the telephone rings and rings. There's a series of disparate images—Fields looking through the finder of a microfilm camera, Linstrum's equation-filled documents, Bleek sans hat at the Library of Congress, a flame consuming a scrap of paper against the backdrop of the Capitol Building—when the plaque awarded to Fields, which he previously smashed in disgust after his second rendezvous with Bleek, zooms toward the camera, wavering like a mirage before dissolving to a shot of a file being opened ("F") and the bloodied, wide-eyed face of the dead FBI agent.

After the phone begins to ring again in the background, Lincoln's sculpted, iconic face materializes in the upper left-hand part of the frame before it metamorphoses into a head shot of Bleek and then the dead FBI agent, who, bloodied

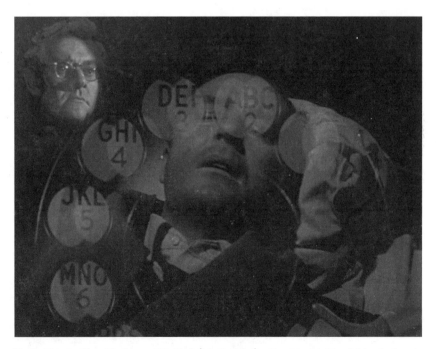

Bleek → Lincoln: Face of Soviet agent Mr. Bleek (Martin Gabel) as it mutates into Lincoln's iconic visage in Allan Fields's nightmare in *The Thief*.

but still alive, gazes down like Bleek on the sleeping Fields. In the climax to the sequence, a lightning shot of a microfilm camera is succeeded by a zoom-in to the plaque succeeded in turn by a choker shot of the maniacally laughing FBI agent, his contorted face completely blotting out Fields's.

Waking abruptly to the neon light blinking on and off like an alarm, Fields glances at his watch and realizes with a start that it's time to change into the maritime outfit that his contacts packed for him in the suitcase. As he makes his way to the dock, he walks alone through the bustling streets of New York City at night, his hands deep in his overcoat pockets, the neon signs flashing up like fragments from a flâneur's dream:

Playland   Astor Bar   Automat   Roseland   Chop Suey   Sardi's
Amusement Centre (Ladies Invited   Flea Circus   Ladies Invited)
Baseball Tickets   Ham n Eggs   Tango Palace   Billiards   Lindy's
Steaks   Schraffts   Frankfurters

A compendium of New York City in all its blaring vibrancy, the montage signifies what Fields has forfeited for his traitorous behavior.

The dénouement of *The Thief*, given the poignancy of the above sequence, is unsurprising. When Fields arrives at the dock, he pauses at the base of a gangway, the ship laying at rest like a colossus. After studying the documents in his hands—his passport, a seaman's certificate—he rips them up and they flutter to the ground, the camera steadily tracking in reverse as he slowly walks away. Dissolve to Fields walking at dawn down a dark, cavernous street in lower Manhattan toward an imposing Greek-columned building: the New York City offices of the FBI. In the final shot—one, ironically enough, that's even darker than the preceding shots—Fields ascends the steps of the building as a light burns brightly in the transom.

In *Celluloid Mushroom Clouds*, Joyce A. Evans observes that film noir was "adapted by Hollywood producers to portray themes of subversive communist activity and communist attempts to infiltrate American cities and steal atomic secrets."[14] Evans also observes that "scientists are depicted either as renegades who want to sell their secrets to the communists for their own personal gain (*Tangier Incident*, 1954, *The Thief*, 1952) or as mere vessels of information vulnerable to kidnapping and extortion" (*The Atomic City*, *World for Ransom*).[15]

To take up only *The Thief* here, Evans's attribution of the motive of "personal gain" to Fields is moot, since one of the most pronounced aspects of both the film and his character is that it's not at all obvious or even perhaps explicable why he's doing what he does.[16] The notion of personal gain intimates that Fields's motivation is, to adduce the classic ones in film noir, sex or money. (I'm thinking of Walter

Neff's Dictaphone confession in *Double Indemnity*: "I didn't get the girl and I didn't get the money.") Money, however, never appears or changes hands in *The Thief*.

As for sex, Fields never reciprocates the raven-haired woman's interest. In fact, it's not at all clear what she, like Fields, wants or represents. Is she a random stranger, alone like Fields and looking for love, or a prostitute set up by his Soviet contacts to keep him distracted while he waits for his ship to depart? If the answer is the former, then Fields's renunciation of her testifies to his inability to break out of his self-imposed state of isolation; if it's the latter, the implication is that Fields is ethically superior to his morally challenged superiors who, in the interests of the state, would stoop to such depraved behavior. (But see, in this context, Hitchcock's *Notorious* [1946] and *North by Northwest* [1959], in which the West is depicted as not above using such stratagems.)

Since Fields's espionage does not appear to be motivated by either sex or money, another possibility is that he's a closeted homosexual and that the Soviets are using his sexual orientation to blackmail him. Such a scenario recalls how '50s national security discourses exploited Americans' fear that it was impossible to "tell homosexuals from heterosexuals."[17] The "red" analogy is tacit: "The possibility that gay men could escape detection . . . linked them in the Cold War imaginary to the Communists who were allegedly conspiring to overthrow the government."[18]

Finally, Fields's motivation for engaging in espionage could be ideological—belief in, say, the communist cause—an interpretation that gains some credence if one reconsiders the conclusion to *The Thief*. When Fields inadvertently kills the FBI agent at the top of the Empire State Building, he suddenly comprehends that he has not only crossed some sort of line but has done so in the service of an "alien" ideal. (The suggestion here is that such craven, murderous behavior is commonplace in communism: communists do not have super-egos; therefore, they do not think twice about killing people.)

Whatever Fields's motivation may be, the notion of belief is central to *The Thief* because, despite the conventional wisdom about the representation of the "repressive state apparatuses" in '50s noir, the FBI, for all its bureaucratic ingenuity, ultimately fails to apprehend him. In other words, the accent in Rouse's film is not on "law enforcement and government agencies."[19] (In fact, the FBI plays a surprisingly small part—in every sense of the word—in the film's action.) Instead, the rhetorical emphasis in *The Thief* is on Fields's recognition, in the agonizing aftermath of the FBI agent's death, of the superiority of the American way of life; his belated acknowledgment that the United States, however meretricious it may sometimes appear to be (personified here by the peopled, neon-lit streets of New York City), is preferable to the Soviet state; that the exigencies of the collective are no substitution for the inextricable intimacies of the social contract; that America and its declared principles—life, liberty, and the pursuit of happiness—cannot, in the final analysis, be gainsaid.

THE ATOMIC CITY: ATOMIC COWBOYS AND UN-AMERICAN INDIANS

Whereas *The Thief* is set in New York City and Washington, D.C., and is, as such, an Eastern noir, *The Atomic City*, which is set in Los Alamos, Los Angeles, and the Puye ruins of New Mexico, is a Southwestern one. Moreover, although both films are about atomic scientists, *The Atomic City* is not concerned with the plight of a single individual, as in *The Thief*, but is instead about a (nuclear) family and community. As the "nucleus of the nation's atomic defense complex," Los Alamos was composed of a federal laboratory or reservation under the jurisdiction of the AEC and a model community that, "like an oyster surrounding a pearl, supplied support for the staff at the laboratory."[20]

In *Inventing Los Alamos* Jon Hunner utilizes the notion of "code-switching" to describe the negotiations that occurred between the American Indians, Nuevo Mexicano, and European cultures at Los Alamos, a notion that simultaneously captures the way that *The Atomic City* puts various genres and subgenres into conversation. Thus, if *The Atomic City* is, like *The Thief* and *Shack Out on 101*, an atomic espionage noir, it's unique in that it features a kidnapped child. (Classic noirs, apart from a picture such as *The Window* [1949], are notoriously childless.) In addition to this super-melodramatic subplot, *The Atomic City* rack-focuses on the counter-espionage practices of the FBI and therefore reads like a docu-melo-noir.

As in the classic semidocumentary film noir, *The Atomic City* begins with a third-person voice-over narration—in this particular instance, with a synopsis of the history of the atomic bomb from the first successful test in, as the text reads, Alamogordo, New Mexico, on July 16, 1945, at 5:30 A.M. to the Japanese bombing of Pearl Harbor that precipitated the U.S. bombing of Hiroshima. After showing the devastation of the latter city, the prologue circles back to Los Alamos, where "American and allied scientists and technicians had worked and struggled for four years" to produce the first A-bomb:

> Since then, those same people and others like them have continued to work, to invent, to improvise, to improve the old weapons and develop new ones because the spirit of aggression is not yet dead in the world. But the atom is not all death and destruction. . . . Isotopes and other atomic techniques are saving lives all over the world.

While this section of the prologue limns the positive, nonmilitaristic benefits of atomic research, the recourse to masking in the security section in order to protect the identities of Los Alamos personnel has the paradoxical effect of miming the visual codes of pornography.

In the conclusion to the prologue, the narrator rehearses the omnipresent hazards associated with atomic research before reiterating both the importance of security measures and the rationale for the nuclear imperative:

> And the people, the men and women who man the laboratories and factories at Los Alamos, what of them? Their work is almost unbelievably dangerous, every move carefully checked and double-checked. The slightest misstep is serious; anything more, disaster. Outside the laboratories the same checking goes on, their daily comings and goings scrutinized minutely. . . . But they know it is necessary. Absolute secrecy is vital if the free world is to survive and if the atomic age is to, at last, free man from his long bondage to power.

Given the emphasis on security in the introductory voice-over narration ("Everywhere the barbed wire, the gates, the signs, the guards"), it's no surprise that *The Atomic City* commences with a TV serviceman negotiating the various checkpoints at Los Alamos.

What is surprising is that the initial sequence—set, true to melodrama, in the living room of the Addison home—revolves around the installation of a new television set. After Tommy (Lee Aaker) asks the deliveryman about the electrical connections, the man asks him, "Is your father an electrician?" Tommy answers that his father is a nuclear physicist, but when the deliveryman follows up with a question about whether Dr. Addison is "one of them bomb-makers," Tommy replies, "That's classified information," at which point his mother, Martha (Lydia Clarke), calls to him from the kitchen that it's time for lunch. (Tommy and his mother have thoroughly internalized the interdictions of the national security apparatus.)

That the TV is alien technology also becomes clear when Dr. Frank Addison (Gene Barry) returns home and Martha, in the midst of vacuuming, observes, "I didn't know where you wanted to put it." The television set will eventually assume its rightful place in the American home as the "electronic hearth," but at this early, transitional moment in its history, it's an uncanny object—both homely and unhomely—an uncanniness that, not unlike the bomb, is registered twice in the initial domestic sequence.

In the first instance, Tommy's seriously contemplating the deliveryman's throwaway suggestion that he should build his own bicycle. The implicit analogy is that if Dr. Addison can build an atomic bomb, then Tommy should be able to build the sort of two-wheel bike he hopes to win that day at the Santa Fe fiesta. The bomb/bike analogy here can be said to domesticate the issue of nuclear arms development, implying not only that Tommy's father is a bomb-maker in the same sense that his mother is a homemaker but that the bomb is ultimately safe, like a bike, because it's built by human hands.

The uncanniness of the television set is remarked upon a second time when Tommy's friend Peggy Marston (Bonnie Kay Eddy) announces as she joins him in the kitchen, "My mother says we're gonna wait to see if your television set works before we buy one." If Peggy's remark reflects television's status as a luxury commodity for middle-class American families circa 1952, it also reflects the nation's anxiety about the technology of the H-bomb: to wit, will it work?[21] We get the answer to this question when an explosion suddenly rocks the Addison house. Tommy, like his mother and Peggy, is completely unfazed, continuing to talk about how he's going to build "millions and millions" of bicycles. But the deliveryman, shocked by the force of the blast, rushes into the kitchen only to be told by Mrs. Addison that it's "just a routine morning test."[22]

The deliveryman's sotto voce response—"What a way to live"—is the transition to the ensuing sequence in which Tommy and Peggy walk to school past ten-foot-high, barbed-wire fences with signs that read "RESTRICTED AREA / WEAR YOUR PHOTOGRAPH & PASS." The very real danger is dramatized when the film cuts to Dr. Addison, who, upon entering the grounds of the atomic energy plant, must pass through security checks and comply with various safety measures (radioactive testing, "contaminated" versus "uncontaminated" lab coats, etc.). While we listen in as, offscreen, Dr. Addison checks the "neutron monitors" and prepares to "ease the control rods," we do not learn what happens to one of his colleagues until he returns home later that day.

As soon as he walks in the door, Dr. Addison notices the television set and, after he absentmindedly turns it on, his wife reminds him, "There's nothing on until five o'clock." The mise-en-scène is salient: although the TV set occupies the center of the screen, Dr. Addison informs his wife that Gus Schwambach was "burned" when he was "overexposed to radiation," then exits the room, leaving Martha alone with the TV set, her arm resting on top of the cabinet as if it were already a familiar piece of furniture. In this, the second domestic sequence, television is associated—unlike the bomb—with the feminine sphere and promises an escape from the travails of the outside world: the TV may be strange but, unlike the H-bomb, it won't burn or blow up anyone.

The television set in fact becomes the medium for the searching questions that Mrs. Addison directs at her husband about living in "the atomic city." Even as she continues to do her domestic duties, checking the oven, she wonders, "Don't you ever get tired of the barbed wire, Frank, having an FBI man on your heels every time you step out of the main gate?" Frank's sarcastic response—"You make it sound like Siberia"—is no doubt intended to mollify her, although Martha insists, accessing the language of developmental psychology becoming popular at the time, that it isn't "normal" to say, as Tommy has just done, "*If* I grow up. . . ."

Nuclear (Family) TV: Martha Addison (Lydia Clarke) and Dr. Frank Addison (Gene Barry) discussing the burning of Gus Schwambach in the living room and kitchen of their home in Los Alamos, New Mexico, in *The Atomic City*. Note the TV-mediated three-shot. Panels from Ciné-Périodiques' *Le Vol du secret de l'atome*.

For the moment, the Addisons resolve to go to the square dance that night, but as in a nightmare, Martha's worst fears come true when a telegram arrives with the news that Tommy has been kidnapped: "TOMMY IS OUR GUEST. YOU WILL GET DETAILS ABOUT IT AT THE DANCE." Earlier we've seen Tommy's teacher, Ellen Haskell (Nancy Gates), becoming increasingly agitated when she cannot find him at the fiesta; however, when she calls the Addison home to inquire about Tommy's whereabouts, Frank lies to her in order to buy time.

At the square dance (in real life a biweekly event at Los Alamos[23]), Frank and Martha apprehensively wait to hear from the kidnappers. The mise-en-scène is again salient: everyone appears to be dressed in cowboy clothes except for two Native Americans wearing full headdresses. When a man named Gregson (Houseley Stevenson) approaches Dr. Addison and Frank snaps at him, "I'm just getting some air—alone!" Gregson reminds the doctor that they're "outside Los Alamos." Frank's dark shirt and tie code him, as in the Western, as an ambiguous figure and raise the question: who's the bad guy here, Frank or Gregson, the atomic scientist or the FBI agent?

Martha's answering a phone call at the bar when a letter is surreptitiously left for the Addisons at their table, which they rush home to read:

If you talk to POLICE boy DIES
PLACE: Santa Fe Cathedral
TIME: 9 A.M. Tomorrow
Only MOTHER to come
he will be SAFE if you don't TALK

Despite the explicit warning, Frank's immediate impulse is to call the police, but Martha literally won't let him, taking the phone out of his hand. Frank doesn't think that the kidnappers, as Martha hopes, want money—"You know what they want"—he agrees, however, to wait until she talks to them.

Cut to a deep-focus long shot of the Santa Fe Cathedral in the background and a phone booth in the foreground. The phone rings and Martha races to answer it. The man on the phone, Emil Jablons (Bert Freed), says: "You know why I'm calling. Then tell your husband to play ball with us. Tell him he doesn't have to worry that we'll ever tell what he did." Jablons then puts Tommy on the line: "I can come home after Daddy does what they want." Martha is jubilant, although in the reverse shot we see that Tommy's voice was tape-recorded.

The subsequent conversation between Frank and Martha in their living room puts the issue in the starkest, most nuclear-familial terms:

MARTHA: Frank, the man promised that no one will ever know.
FRANK: No. No one would. Not until they wrecked half the world.
MARTHA: I only know that Tommy is our world, Frank, our whole world.

In this pivotal scene, Frank is the voice of reason, albeit a reluctant one, while Martha, the stay-at-home mother, is the embodiment of family and domesticity.

The dissolve first to a sign—"DANGER/CONTAMINATED AREA / DO NOT ENTER"—and then to Frank's Venetian-blind-shadowed office portends what he's about to do. After he enters the security code into the knob of a safe-like door, the shadow of a hatted man appears. As in the anticommunist noir, the iconography is ambiguous: the man, who's accompanied by a friend of the Addisons, Russ Farley (Michael Moore), introduces himself as Inspector Mann (Milburn Stone) of the FBI. Mann immediately takes the file out of Frank's hand, but Dr. Addison insists it's a "blind alley experiment" involving "useless," "intricate equations" that will "take a very competent mathematician several days to check." Although Mann agrees to Frank's plan, he remains skeptical, echoing the disturbing way Tommy previously talked about the future with his mother: "Well, if you're telling the truth, and that's a big 'if.'"

Up until this point *The Atomic City* has been a melodrama with noir overtones. The remainder of the film focuses, however, on the institutional investigative work and surveillance techniques associated with the semidocumentary noir. The '50s wrinkle here is the figure of Dr. Addison, who, as the narrative develops, begins to resemble the classic American antihero, the upholder of a "justice outside the traditional channels of authority."[24] He becomes, in a word, a cowboy. Thus, just as "Philip Marlowe indicates the weaknesses of the LAPD that must be answered by a knight detective who polices the mean streets," so the atomic scientist Dr. Addison "serves as a savior-detective figure."[25]

The bureaucratic prowess of the FBI is represented first, and the stakes couldn't be higher: if, according to Inspector Mann, Frank were to hand over "everything we have on the H-bomb" to the kidnappers (the "we" presumably refers to both the Los Alamos community and the United States as in "We the People"), the enemy would not only "turn [Frank] into a traitor" but possess a "pipeline into Los Alamos." Unlike Martha, for whom Tommy "counts more than the millions" of American lives in the balance—"They're just numbers"—Frank understands that he has become a "calculated risk" and offers to be placed into custody. Mann gruffly declines, laying out the bureau's reasoning: "Our job is to keep the bomb at home, apprehend the kidnappers, and bring your son back home safely."

The fact that Mann's later shown repeating the FBI's position at a meeting of federal agents—"Is getting Tommy back more important [than the United States retaining nuclear supremacy]? No"—suggests just how callous the agency's logic would have appeared to the average American citizen at the time. (For a similar predicament, see *Walk East on Beacon!*, in which Professor Kafer's son's freedom in West Germany is dependent upon the scientist's cooperation with communist agents.) In *The Atomic City* the melodramatic "real" of the nuclear family ("for

Martha," as Frank puts it, "Tommy is real") is pitted against the abstract law and institutional imperatives of the nation-state. A child's life comes in a poor third after keeping the "bomb at home" and capturing the criminals. Tommy, as Frank glumly concedes, "is number three."

Although the ideology of *The Atomic City* is driven by the secrecy surrounding the production of the H-bomb, another industrial logic emerges in the Hollywood sequence set at the Hotel Belford, where the kidnappers have instructed Frank to deliver the "phony formula." A. Costandina Titus notes that the director, Jerry Hopper, "had previously worked only on Army training films" and that *The Atomic City*, shot in black-and-white film stock, resembles the "official reels being distributed by the government during the same period."[26] In fact, the Belford sequence is a brilliant example of super- or meta-semidocumentary noir, since it publicizes the FBI's surveillance practices (Feds positioned around the lobby reading magazines, agent-packed cars outside the hotel on Melrose and Sunset) even as it stages the play of cinematic production via the figure of the "man with a movie camera."

The Hollywood sequence begins with a tight three-shot in which Ellen Haskell and Russ Farley are sitting in the front seat of a police car while another agent with a movie camera is positioned between them in the backseat. (Since Russ has been "outed" earlier as a Fed, the law can literally be seen coming between the couple, whose blossoming romance is broached at the beginning of the film.) The reverse is a cinema verité POV shot—viewed through the restricted frame of the car's front window—of William Masters, aka David Rogers (Norman Budd), exiting the hotel with the phony formula.

The following sequence set at Gilmore Field is even more symptomatic, depicting the fluid relations that obtained in the early 1950s between the cinematic and televisual modes of production. A FBI agent films Masters as he walks, pillow and program in hand, toward his seat, but the real action occurs when Mann commandeers the television booth. (The inspector stands to the left of the headphoned man "in charge," both of whom are dwarfed by an enormous television camera.) After asking the man whether the footage can be "kinescoped," Mann tells him that it's an emergency and shows him his badge: since it's only a "local show" (KTLA),[27] Mann wants to film Masters without the feed "going out to the public." A low-angle, deep-focus shot shows Masters's head in the foreground and the television booth high in the background, an angle at once realistic and symbolic that illustrates the dominance of the national over the local, the institutional over the individual.

The above ballpark sequence invites comparison with the stadium sequence in *The Thief*. However, whereas in the latter we sympathize with Allan Fields's alienation from the quotidian pleasures of baseball, in *The Atomic City* we are distanced from Masters, who is the object of both the governmental and televisual gaze. The subsequent wide shot of fans happily exiting the stadium (note the African American men and women) contrasts with the tense crosscutting between Masters, the television booth, and the action happening on the field in the previous sequence; it also sets up the dramatic moment when Masters starts his car and it explodes. This scene, which demonstrates the communists' brutally utilitarian view of human life, not only recalls the atomic blast that opens the film and the "routine test" explosion that rocks the Addison house but anticipates the fiery car explosion that kills Dave Bannion's wife, Katie, in *The Big Heat*: not every life, *The Atomic City* intimates, is equal. If the death of Bannion's wife is the emotional pivot on which Lang's exposé turns (Bannion is a "good" rogue cop), Masters's death is just a number, another statistic in the Cold War between the United States and the Soviet Union for nuclear supremacy.

While the dissolve to a shot of the Capitol Building at night recollects *The Thief*, the projection room sequence that follows is reminiscent of the scene set at the School for the Deaf in *Walk East on Beacon!*, in which the FBI enlists the help of the students there to decode silent surveillance footage. The difference between *Walk East on Beacon!* and *The Atomic City* is that in the latter film the projection space is located at FBI headquarters and features special enclosed cubicles to shield "undercover [Communist] Party members" sitting in along with Mann and Farley. Unlike the scene in *Walk East on Beacon!*, it's also more noirish in accord with the presence of undercover agents. Thus, when the projectionist turns on the machine, the light splits the screen along a diagonal axis with the bottom half bathed in low-key light and the top hazed with drifting cigarette smoke.

Although an offscreen voice, which sounds suspiciously like the film's voice-over narrator, gives out instructions—"Don't hesitate to stop the machine or run it backwards"—the assembled agents diligently watch the black-and-white surveillance footage of the Hotel Belford and Gilmore Field. When two undercover agents identify the hot-dog vendor to whom Masters slipped the phony formula during the baseball game, the camera cuts to a wide shot of the screen—American flags are prominently placed on either side—before the camera zooms in for a close-up of the vendor's badge.

As in *Walk East on Beacon!* this passage suggests that the FBI has actively appropriated the technologies of film and television and that these technologies have been mobilized in the interests of national security. Moreover, as in the semidocumentary noir, the fact that "Paramount was the first Hollywood studio to receive permission from the Atomic Energy Commission to film inside the plant" at Los Alamos attests to the close working relationship, not to say collusion, between the motion picture industry and the "state's atomic program."[28]

Ultimately, both the AEC and the FBI are depicted in a positive light in *The Atomic City*, though there are any number of ideologically odd moments in the

"Foreign" Movie: Unidentified FBI agent, Inspector Harold Mann (Milburn Stone), Russ Farley (Michael Moore), and, in the rear, undercover agents in cubicles screening KTLA footage of Soviet spy David Rogers, aka William Masters, interacting with a hot-dog vendor in *The Atomic City*. Panels from Ciné-Périodiques' *Le Vol du secret de l'atome*.

film, one of which occurs when Mann and Farley are unable to extract any information from the hot-dog vendor, Donald Clark (Leonard Strong). In fact, after Farley threatens to slap Clark "into the middle of next Monday," the suspect lectures *him* on the FBI's "book of regulations": "Yeah, that's not very democratic. Remember what they taught you in Washington? . . . 'No prisoner should be subject to physical punishment by any member of the bureau or in the presence of any member of the bureau.'" Of course, Dr. Addison is not bound by these rules, so when Mann and Farley leave, he takes the matter into his own hands. (Frank's beating of Clark is discreetly elided.) When Inspector Mann returns, though, and sees what Dr. Addison has done, he tells the doctor he had no right to do what he did, and Frank snaps, "Any more right than they had to take my son. I'd have beaten him to death if I had to." Sometimes, *The Atomic City* suggests, the individual citizen, unencumbered by regulations, can accomplish what the FBI cannot; sometimes, especially in the Cold War against communism, it's not only necessary to break the rules, it's the right thing to do.

While the information that Frank has beaten out of the suspect leads Martha, Frank, and the FBI to a house on 19 Elevado Street in Los Angeles (*The Atomic City* opened in Los Angeles area theaters as *19 Elevado Street*), the equations on the blackboard there reveal that the kidnappers—including Dr. Peter Rassett (John Damler), a nuclear physicist who is "well-known abroad"—have already proved that the calculations are false. However, the tense conclusion of *The Atomic City*—the clock is ticking—takes place not in Los Angeles, the "dark city," nor the "atomic" one, Los Alamos, but at the Frijoles Canyon in the New Mexican desert, home of the Puye Indian ruins. There, Jablons and another man, Arnie Molter (Anthony Warde), have used their disguises as park rangers to keep Tommy hidden in an ancient cave dwelling at the top of the cliffs.

In *Inventing Los Alamos* Hunner writes: "Building on the frontier myth, nuclear weapons replaced six-shooters, and atomic cowboys rode to the rescue of the country, defending the nation and the free world from Stalin's gang of villains in black hats."[29] In the "New West" of *The Atomic City*, Dr. Frank Addison is figured as both an "atomic cowboy" and a "savior-detective." More complexly, domestic communists, the ultimate bearers of sociocultural contradiction in the 1950s, are figured as black-hatted villains, Indians, *and* Feds, a metaphorical overdetermination that, as in the anticommunist noir, undercuts the classic stereotypical opposition between the "white hats" and "black hats."[30]

Still, about one thing there's no doubt: the communist ringleaders are murderous. Once Dr. Rassett and Robert Kalnick (George M. Lynn) arrive at the site, Kalnick orders Jablons and Molter—over Rasset's "theoretical" objections—to dispose of Tommy. (Lesson: scientists, even communist ones, are not as cold-blooded as their political masters.) Yet even as the kidnappers are conversing, Tommy—in a series of extremely restricted shots that echo the Empire State Building sequence in *The Thief*—manages to escape the dwelling, running across the mesa and hiding behind some brick ruins until he's forced to clamber down the face of a cliff and hide in a cave. Writing about the Pueblo Indians, Mark Osteen observes that just as "these early American civilizations came to ruin, so might our own."[31] The fact that Tommy's able to evade his captors when they catch up with him by squeezing through a crevice and retreating deeper into the cave also suggests that the natural landscape—as opposed to the man-made ruins—"protects and saves him."[32] The cave imagery is particularly resonant since it's historically associated with the maternal womb and therefore with Tommy's mother, who's waiting anxiously along with Tommy's teacher at the bottom of the cliff.

The climax of *The Atomic City* is the epitome of Griffith-style melodrama. After a police helicopter corners Dr. Rassett as he's trying to flee, the FBI confronts the remaining kidnappers, who are now trapped inside the same cave as Tommy. Jablons and Molter decide to turn themselves in (they opt for life at the hands of the Feds rather than death), though Kalnick executes them before they can do so. In the meantime, Tommy has climbed out onto the face of the cliff and, after slipping, dangles from a rock. Dr. Addison's tying a rope around his waist when Mann stops him mid-act: "Sorry, doctor, we can't risk losing you. I can't let you, even if I have to use force."

Instead, Farley is gradually lowered down the steep face of the cliff, where he pulls Tommy to safety. While this dramatic rescue makes for a classically happy ending capped by a triumphant three-shot of Tommy in his parents' arms, Inspector Mann's earlier contravention of Dr. Addison—backed by the threat of force—retroactively reconfigures the doctor's "cowboy" status. In the final analysis, Dr. Addison's character is defined not by his detective or action-hero exploits but by his scientific expertise. Just as Tommy's kidnapping "becomes a metaphor for all the children of the nuclear age"—"born in the shadow of the bomb, they are all hostages"[33]—so too Dr. Addison is a hostage of the nation-state. In other words, if the doctor's post-kidnapping assumption of the "private detective" mantle promises to counter the negative image of the nuclear scientist whose love of family makes him "vulnerable to espionage,"[34] the conclusion of *The Atomic City* radically circumscribes this cowboy aspect by forcefully underlining the very real limits of his freedom: even after the communists are dead or have been captured and the secrets of the atomic bomb secured, Dr. Addison's life is not his to risk—at least for anything unrelated to atomic research. In sum, it's this particular cowboy's fate, like the historical one of the American Indian, to be *reserved*—to be sent, in other words, back to the reservation.

SHACK OUT ON 101: BIKINIS, BOMBSHELLS, AND THE (RED) PLANET OF THE APES

The fact that *Shack Out on 101* was released by Allied Artists, which was formerly Monogram, the infamous Poverty Row studio, says a lot about the film. Like the film's title, it says that *Shack Out on 101* is a B movie. It says that it's an exploitation movie as well. The twist is that what's being exploited in *Shack Out on 101* is not simply sex but the rhetoric of anticommunism and atomic espionage.

The studio is significant because the film's director, Edward Dein, is probably best remembered today—if he's remembered at all—for *The Leech Woman* (1960). Dein did, however, write the screenplay for *Shack Out on 101* with his wife, Mildred (he had been a working screenwriter for ten years before he helmed his first feature, *Manchas de sangre en la luna,* in 1952), and if *Shack Out on 101* is, according to Leonard Maltin, a "trash classic" (and it indubitably is), it's because of the screenplay and the ensemble cast.[35]

The top-billed star is Terry Moore, who had been loaned out to RKO for *Mighty Joe Young* (1949) and in later life claimed to have been married to Howard Hughes. The opening of *Shack Out on 101* capitalizes on her sex appeal even as it shamelessly exploits the celebrated "love in the surf" sequence in *From Here to Eternity* (1953). Referring to the "single-set diner" in which most of the film's action is set, an online critic has opined that *Shack Out on 101* is "filmed in a stark, '50s television 'playhouse' style."[36] This said, *Shack Out on 101* is not without flashes of visual panache. Although the film's director of photography, Floyd Crosby, won an Academy Award in 1931 for *Tabu* and lensed the classic Cold War Western *High Noon* (1952) as well as the 3-D noir *Man in the Dark,* his work became associated in the late 1950s and early '60s with various B genres, such as JD (*Hot Rod Gang* [1958]), "monster" (*Attack of the Crab Monsters* [1957]), "bad girl" (*Reform School Girls* [1957]), and "bikini" (*Beach Blanket Bingo* [1965]).

Consider, for example, the introductory frames of *Shack Out on 101*: the camera opens on a long shot of the Pacific surf, then pans across the bikini-clad body of a woman lying out on the beach before tilting up to a deep-focus long shot of Kotty (Moore) in the foreground—eyes closed, breasts jutting out—and a male figure standing erect in the background. The man is the diner's cook, Leo, aka Slob (Lee Marvin), and after listening to a seashell, he walks up to Kotty and starts kissing her. For a moment, she appears to be responding positively to him, but then she starts to violently resist, eventually fighting him off. In its prurient conflation of sex and violence, it's a classic '50s exploitation scene.

It's not until the action moves up to the shack to which Slob has retreated that we realize that the man Kotty momentarily thought she was kissing is Sam Bastion,

"Good Exploitation Bet": Cover of Showmanship Campaign Book for *Shack Out on 101*. From top to bottom on the left: Leo, aka "Slob," aka Mr. Gregory (Lee Marvin); George Bater (Keenan Wynn); Eddie Miller (Whit Bissell); and Professor Sam Bastion (Frank Lovejoy). Erratum: Contrary to this advertisement, Eddie never kisses Kotty; Leo is the "brute."

aka the Professor (Frank Lovejoy). The Professor has come to her bedroom, and as the jazzy score fades up and the camera tracks in for an intimate two-shot, the couple engages in badinage not about, say, speeding, as in *Double Indemnity*, but political science. (The narrative pretext is that Kotty's studying for a civil service exam.)

> THE PROFESSOR (caressing Kotty's cheek): Tell me something else. You know what branches does the Constitution divide governmental powers?
> KOTTY: Judicial. (The Professor kisses her) Legislative. (The Professor kisses her again) Executive. (The Professor kisses her once more) Oh, I wish there were more branches.

Later, after Kotty has walked Sam out of the diner, two Acme Poultry salesmen who have just entered stand at the window and watch them kiss: "Va-voom!" At the counter, the salesmen, Artie (Jess Barker) and Pepe (Donald Murphy), wonder out loud about what's so special about Sam, and Kotty explains that he's a "nuclear physicist": "he's a *big, big* man!"

Previously, we've seen Slob in the kitchen exchanging cash with Perch (Len Lesser) for a microfilm canister, then stealing off to his room to check out the microfilm on a viewfinder. As in *The Thief*, the microfilm contains mathematical equations (sample: "$E = S + 2$"), and once Slob has examined them, he burns the evidence. Now, having retrieved a book secreted with money from the kitchen, he confers after hours with Sam in the diner, ostensibly about the seashells that he's collected for the Professor's "hobby." In reality, Slob gives the Professor the money that's hidden in the book's hollowed spine and, in return, the Professor relays information about the top-secret project he's working on at the university down the road. While Slob claims that the Professor is only interested in money—"Money, money, money, that's all you think about"—Sam insists that he's interested in meeting the big man behind the operation, the mysterious Mr. Gregory, since, as he tells Slob, "there are a lot of things that can't be written down on paper" such as the "secret of a new element" or the "power of the hydrogen force."

After punching out Slob for bragging about his plan to get even with Kotty for treating him "like dirt" (the low-swinging single-source light is a classic noir touch), the Professor's about to leave when a drunk confederate, Professor Claude Dillon (Frank de Kova), appears at the door, babbling about the disappearance of a scientist who allegedly committed suicide by jumping off a boat while fishing. Dillon doesn't think it's a coincidence, since another scientist working on the same top-secret project disappeared before him. Dillon never utters the "C" word, but he swears that "they" won't "stop at anything": "they preach liberty and practice slavery."

Dillon's begging the Professor to "open his eyes"—"We're traitors! We're traitors!"—when Kotty (dressed, naturally, in a negligee) opens the door to her bedroom and overhears the conversation. Although she slips back into her room (to get sick, as she later tells Sam) just as Slob plunges a knife into Dillon's back, the next day she metaphorically throws the book at the Professor, informing him that she's added a new word to her vocabulary: "traitor," meaning "one who violates his allegiance or betrays his country, one who delivers his country to an enemy, one who aids an enemy to conquer his country."

The film's first reversal occurs when we see Artie and Pepe communicating with an FBI agent who's positioned outside the shack surveilling the short-order cook's actions as the two chicken salesmen are about to search Slob's room for the "point of contact" between Mr. Gregory and him. Meanwhile, Slob and Kotty are inside watching the diner's owner, George (Keenan Wynn), and his ex-serviceman buddy Eddie (Whit Bissell) trying out the new deep-sea fishing gear that they've just purchased for a trip to Acapulco. (When they put on the snorkels and flippers, Kotty comments, "All you two need is a flying saucer.") In one of the film's many outrageously absurd conceits, Eddie has taken up deep-sea fishing as therapy for the trauma that he suffered during the invasion of Normandy: after wading through all the blood running on Omaha Beach on D-Day to save George's life, Eddie still can't forget "how choppy the channel looked through [George's] chest."

The film's second reversal occurs when Kotty inadvertently betrays Artie and Pepe when she tells Slob that she saw them sneaking out of his room. Correctly deducing that the Acme salesmen must be Feds, Slob telephones Perch and orders him to prepare the boat for a quick getaway; Perch, confirming Slob's suspicion, reports back that he just saw the Professor talking to Artie and Pepe. Armed with this knowledge, Slob not only threatens to kill Kotty if she doesn't come clean about the Professor but is in the process of strangling her when Sam appears at the door bearing more microfilm.

Baiting the Professor, Slob asks Sam if he's ready to meet Mr. Gregory that night off the coast of Ensenada. When the Professor tries to buy time by claiming he has to call his houseboy to cancel a faculty meeting, Slob screams, "What kind of a uniform does your houseboy wear? I bet he carries a gold-plated watch!" In the meantime, Kotty, still dazed from Slob's attack, stumbles out of her bedroom to discover that the Professor is not in fact in league with Slob.

Although Kotty's epiphany prompts Sam to utter the classic anticommunist line, "I'd rather be dead," the real rhetorical climax of *Shack Out on 101* does not happen until George returns to the diner and Slob shoots him in the arm. Since George can't figure out why Slob's acting the way he is ("Slob, have you lost all your buttons?"), the Professor sets him straight about "Mr. Gregory":

"He's got all four feet on the ground. Can't you see what's happened? The apes have taken over. When we were busy watching television and filling our freezers, they've come out of the jungle and moved in. And, what's worse, they've begun to dress like us and pretend to think like us."

Unlike his previous, "better dead than red" declaration, the Professor's reference to apes paints communism not as the final phase of human history, as in Marx, but an earlier, atavistic one.

Somewhat surprisingly, Slob concedes that the communist minions are apes but not the leaders. No ape, he plans to kidnap the trio and take them—in Kotty's words—"on a one-way cruise to Mexican waters." However, when Eddie manages to sneak in through the back door, the Professor, addressing George, obliquely encourages the ex-serviceman to act:

PROFESSOR: Eddie can even an old score for you. All he would have to do is get
   a hold of himself, put his hand on the harpoon and shoot . . . someday.
SLOB: Not that physical coward. No, your harpoon would have no use. That's a
   man's weapon.

Despite the Professor's prompting, Eddie still doesn't act. It's only after Slob, exchanging fire with the Feds, tries to escape through the front door that Eddie finally finds the courage to pull the trigger on the harpoon, spearing not Pancho—the mythical Mexican fish that he and George have dreamed of catching—but a man.

In *Out of the Past: Adventures in Film Noir*, Barry Gifford writes that *Shack Out on 101* is a "silly little Red spy drama from the smack-dab middle of the 1950s" and, as a "dead-on minimalist portrait of America at its most paranoid," the "one to show the history class."[37] These observations would appear to contradict each other, but they're both true. While most historians wouldn't be caught dead watching *Shack Out on 101*, let alone screening it for a history class, it projects the ideological zaniness of the zeitgeist more than other, more serious-minded films. Among other things, *Shack Out on 101* demonstrates just how deeply the public discourse about the bomb penetrated the practices of everyday life. Thus, when George reveals to Eddie (like everyone else, it seems) that he's carrying a torch for Kotty, Eddie replies that it's all about "chemistry": "she's A, the Professor's B, and you don't fit into the formula."

The most provocative scenes in *The Shack Out on 101*, though, showcase Terry Moore's "bombshell" persona and the bikini that Kotty's character wears in the film. Although the bikini was "invented" by Louis Réard in 1946, "only four days after the first American nuclear test in the Bikini Atoll,"[38] it did not become popular until the 1950s. (Brigitte Bardot was the first to wear a bikini onscreen, in 1952 in *Manina, la fille sans voiles*.) In other words, the significance of the bikini that Kotty models twice in *Shack Out on 101* is not just a function of its novelty but the adjacent notion of the "bombshell," a word that entered the American lexicon during the Depression as "slang for a dangerous woman" à la Bonnie Parker and that subsequently acquired new meaning in the aftermath of the testing and detonation of the atomic bomb.

As for Moore, she was just one of many sex symbols who flourished in the bright afterglow of *the* '50s bombshell, Marilyn Monroe, a platinum-blonde rebus for the "Cold War, atomic-bomb generation" whose impact on film was "likened to the radiance and sublime luminosity . . . of the first Trinity tests."[39] Moore's status as a bombshell is sonically evoked in *Shack Out on 101* when Kotty, describing the Professor's occupation, throws her hands in the air and says, "Boom!" Moore has—to understate the matter—considerably less charisma than Monroe or her bombshell predecessor Rita Hayworth, yet in *Shack Out on 101* Kotty's sexual magnetism is the sun around which all the other men in the film—with the notable exception of Eddie—revolve like so many satellites. Even the federal agents Artie and Pepe are not immune to her charms, so much so that their aggressive lasciviousness is not mitigated when it's revealed that their Acme Poultry persona is a masquerade. In fact, the hypersexualization of the FBI agents in Dein's film represents an unusually subversive portrait of Hoover's purportedly abstemious G-men.

As in *Split Second* (1953), *Shack Out on 101* also revisits the legacy of World War II in the changed circumstances of the Cold War, a legacy that's most apparent in the film's conflicting notions about masculinity. Unlike Sam Hurley (Steven McNally) in *Split Second*, who can't stop killing for the life of him, Eddie remains so traumatized by the blood and violence he witnessed in the European theater that he's afraid to hook a fish. (George in fact has to remind him that fish are cold-blooded.) Even the Professor, who has been graciously acting as Eddie's psychiatrist, thinks he should get professional help for his phobia—hence the deep-sea fishing. Thus, when in the film's dénouement Eddie spears Slob, this "manly" act promises to effect, as in the classic Hollywood happy ending, a therapeutic catharsis, although Eddie, alas, can only excuse himself, like Kotty, to be "sick," lamenting that his "first fish was a man."

As the film's reversible human/animal metaphors intimate, what it means to be a (hu)man is a vexed issue in *Shack Out on 101*. Fish are men, and men are apes. If the Professor's soliloquy about apes anticipates *Planet of the Apes* (1968) even as it recycles the usual period criticism of communists—that, like aliens, they merely ape the behavior of real, red-blooded Americans—it also communicates a genuine anxiety about the natural order of things. Maybe, as Marx, if not Darwin, theorized, it's a godless world after all. In this topsy-turvy, fish-eat-man world, the wealth of nations may not be just a matter of "money, money, money"; the easy-come, easy-go affluence of post-boom consumer capitalism may itself be a lure. Accordingly, unlike *The Atomic City*, which demonstrates the political use value of television, *Shack Out on 101* targets it as one of the commodities, like freezers, that's turning Americans into zombies or aliens—that is, communists—rather than the sort of vigilant citizens inspired by the Constitution and the Bill of Rights that the Professor quizzes Kotty about at the beginning of the film.

Of course, Sam himself personifies the country's ambivalence about professors and scientists. Are professors vessels of civic education or dupes of foreign intrigue? Are scientists working to secure the safety of the nation-state or, like Allan Fields in *The Thief*, abetting the enemy? In *Shack Out on 101* Frank Lovejoy's character is only pretending to be a Red, as in *I Was a Communist for the F.B.I.*, in order to flush out Mr. Gregory. Ultimately Sam Bastion, as his surname suggests, is not merely a "good psychiatrist" but a good professor who's working on "our," Uncle Sam's, side.

But how to tell the difference between a short-order cook like Slob and a communist bigwig like Mr. Gregory? The fact that Slob, as he complains at one point to his boss, George, does all the "cookin' and cleanin'" at the diner is one clue. It's also no accident that Slob complains at one point that George treats him like an appliance: "It's a good thing I'm not wired; you'd be shoving me around like a vacuum cleaner." Eddie's masculinity may have been compromised by his combat experiences in the war, but at least he's not doing women's work. Although Lee Marvin, coming off his bravura performance in *The Big Heat*, is able to inject the stock commie character of Slob with his usual, irrepressible ferocity, in the end we know that big-picture, rule-the-world communists like Mr. Gregory are just wannabes with low self-esteem, she-men: not monstrous fish like Pancho or Moby Dick who reign over the "kingdom of sea creatures," but small fry or, in a word (as Kotty memorably puts it), "garbage."

CITY OF FEAR: COBALT-60

City of Fear was directed by Irving Lerner and released in 1959. In *The Film Encyclopedia* Ephraim Katz writes that Lerner helmed "several starvation-budget feature films on near-impossible shooting schedules," the two most striking of which were made with Vince Edwards: *Murder by Contract* (1958) and *City of Fear*. About the former, Andrew Sarris in *American Cinema* notes that "*Murder by Contract* is a minor classic of murderous understatement."[40] The same could be said of *City of Fear*, a classic late '50s B noir.

Part of the cachet of *City of Fear* is a direct function of its audiovisual properties. The sharply lensed, docu-verité cinematography is by Lucien Ballard, who had photographed a number of noirs such as *Berlin Express* (1948), *The House on Telegraph Hill* (1951), *The Killer Is Loose* (1956), and, most notably, *The Killing* (1956). The contemporary, jazz-spiked score is by Jerry Goldsmith, who had studied with Miklós Rózsa and would go on to compose the inimitable score for *Chinatown*. While Ballard and Goldsmith's contributions invest *City of Fear*, despite its bargain-basement budget (the film was produced for under one hundred thousand dollars), with an eye- and ear-catching "audio-vision," Lerner's involvement as an editor and second-unit director with the American documentary movement of the 1930s—in particular, the Workers Film and Photo League—are reflected in the film's neorealist aesthetic and seedy LA locations.

In fact, it's worth noting that during World War II Lerner also worked in the Motion Picture Division of the Office of War Information (OWI) and was allegedly engaged in espionage for the Soviet Union. In the winter of 1944 a counterintelligence officer caught Lerner "attempting to photograph the cyclotron at the University of California at Berkeley without authorization."[41] (The cyclotron was integral to the Manhattan Project and the production of the plutonium used to fuel the first detonated nuclear device.) Consequently, if *City of Fear* is not, strictly speaking, an "atomic espionage" noir, it's nevertheless informed by the atmospheric paranoia and subversive spirit of other '50s nuclear noirs such as *Pickup on South Street*, *The Thief*, and *Shack Out on 101*.

The beginning of *City of Fear* recalls the opening of *Split Second*: two convicts have just escaped from San Quentin. The difference is that, in addition to having hijacked an ambulance, Vince Ryker (Vince Edwards) and his prison buddy are in possession of what Vince believes is a "pound of 100 percent pure snow," or heroin. Unlike Sam Hurley, Vince also doesn't care that his partner is gravely wounded. In fact, after Vince eludes a police roadblock by disguising himself as a cosmetics salesman (having earlier forced the salesman's car off the road and stolen both his car and identity), we learn from a report on the car radio that inside the "charred wreckage" of the ambulance are two bodies, the prison buddy's and the salesman's.

Cut to the LAPD, where Chief Jensen (Lyle Talbot) is explaining to Lt. Mark Richards (John Archer) that Vince is "one man holding the lives of three million people in his hands" and that the canister he has just carried into a hotel, hidden in his salesman's suitcase, is a "cylinder of death." Waiting inside the hotel for Vince is June Marlowe (Patricia Blair), and although she claims she would have waited eight years for him to serve out his sentence, Vince insists that he knows "what's good in life and what's bad"—that, in short, he's "not an animal."

The last exclamation, which is something of a non sequitur, appears to refer to Vince's recent stint in the penitentiary, but it assumes additional significance when, back at LAPD headquarters, Dr. John Wallace (Steven Ritch), "radiological coordinator" at the Air Pollution Control District, informs Jensen and Richards that maximum-security inmates at San Quentin were volunteers in controlled experiments at the prison hospital (see *The Whip Hand*), what Vince later refers to as "secret junkie tests." However, what the inmates thought was heroin was in fact Cobalt-60, which in "granular form," according to Wallace (and in an echo of *D.O.A.*), "is the most deadly thing in existence. Contamination begins almost immediately. Within forty-eight hours you're dead."[42]

When Wallace asks how big the canister is, Richards holds his hands apart eight inches. Cut to the hotel room where June, stripped down to a slip and rummaging through the cosmetics in Vince's suitcase, picks up and briefly considers the canister, which is wrapped in brightly colored paper like a birthday gift. Vince, wearing a "wife-beater"—Edwards appears, with his dark matinee looks, to be reprising his role as Sherry Peatty's (Marie Windsor) stud lover, Val Cannon, in *The Killing*—comes over to June and takes her in his arms, whispering that he's "gonna make this night last." As in *Kiss Me Deadly*, the proximity of the radioactive canister heats up the characters as if it's a veritable aphrodisiac. (See also the scene where Vince, lying on the bed in his hotel room—and not, I might add, with June but the canister—gazes fondly at the deadly cylinder before kissing it.)

Unlike the sexy scene with Vince and June, the subsequent semidocumentary montage shows Wallace's radiological unit fanning out across the city of Los Angeles in patrol cars equipped with Motorola Geiger counters, an image that, according to Edward Dimendberg, "secures the significance of *City of Fear* in any history of postwar cinematic and spatial surveillance."[43] If Jensen, Richards, and Wallace can't locate the cylinder sooner rather than later, they'll have to inform the public ("The people should know," Jensen maintains), although Wallace protests that the results would be catastrophic:

> You could tell them it won't wipe out the whole city—there's not enough of it, it's not a bomb. However, it will contaminate entire farms, milk, butter, eggs; get carried into markets, on meat, produce, into theaters and restaurants; get carried around by people on their clothes and their shoes, on insects and birds, and on children. Then you'll have to describe the symptoms to watch out for—hoarse coughing, heavy sweating, horrible retching—and then the blood begins to break down, then the cells. If you merely touch your skin, the watered blood just oozes out of pores. Finally, you hemorrhage internally, blood fills the lungs.

Wallace's verdict: "I doubt anyone could explain that calmly to millions of people without touching off the worst panic in history."

Vince is obviously bad news—he has already knifed a guard and torched two bodies before the credit sequence—but the authorities, especially Jensen, are so harshly lit that it's as if they're engaged in a criminal conspiracy. In fact, there's a distinct discrepancy between what Jensen, Richards, and Wallace say and the way they're photographed:

> The establishment representatives . . . are repeatedly triangulated through overhead shots and camera movements into one monolithic force. That they are institutional symbols, not idiosyncratic individuals, is reinforced by their constant depersonalization through visual strategies that cut them off at the waist, shooting them linked from behind or from below in expressive displays not unlike those deployed for Nazis in pre-war Hollywood.[44]

Like *Panic in the Streets* and *The Killer That Stalked New York* (1950), *City of Fear* is a species of "epidemic" noir and, like the former '50s films, draws liberally on the police procedural.

So even as Wallace is using all the technological means at his disposal to vivisect the city (see the deep-focus exterior shot where, standing before a blackboard, he's obstructed by a mobile telephone in the foreground), the police bring in and interrogate three of Vince's acquaintances: June, shoe salesman/drug dealer Eddie Crown (Joseph Mell), and gum-chewing peddler Pete Hallon (Sherwood Price). Pete has previously shown up at Eddie's shoe store looking to worm his way into whatever Vince is peddling—like Mike Hammer in *Kiss Me Deadly*, he doesn't know what it is, but he knows it's big—although Eddie's momentarily able to buy him off by offering him a pair of alligator shoes on the house. June, like Vince, is an object of the institutional gaze, "seen first by the bureaucrats"—in an unmarked POV shot—"from the ankles up," like Phyllis Dietrichson in *Double Indemnity* and Cora Smith in *The Postman Always Rings Twice* (1946).[45] Then, once the interrogation is over, Richards tells June, "Keep yourself available," to which June smartly replies, "Would you like a key to my apartment?"

As the dragnet tightens across the city (the authorities have staked out Ryker's haunts), Ryker starts to move again, and so does Lerner's film, cutting from a panoramic view of Los Angeles to a lateral tracking shot of Vince walking down an alley at night, his "irradiated" shadow blown up like a balloon on the side of a building.[46] Next, there's a shot of a flashing stop sign, followed by a whiplash pan to a billboard with the upper left quadrant of a face exposed, one eye wide open.

With one hand firmly on the cylinder in his sports coat, Vince strides over to a bus stop, where he sits down on a bench with an advertisement for milk, nervously fondling the canister as he waits. By the time he makes it to Eddie's warehouse, lit by a single overhead light, he's sweating like Bigelow in *D.O.A.*

However, unlike Bigelow, he desperately wants a drink. (It's no accident, I think, that Vince's symptoms are similar to someone who's going "cold turkey."[47]) Vince figures that since the heroin in the canister contains "440 grains to the ounce," it's worth a million dollars on the street. Eddie thinks that he should go to Miami, then Cuba—"sun, ocean, casinos"—until things calm down, but Vince wants the score, now. Therefore, when "Rabbit Ears" Pete, still looking to horn his way into the action, shows up, Vince welcomes him by mangling his arm in the door. The next day Pete's body is found in an unidentified car on Palm Drive. As a policeman disperses the gawkers on the sidewalk, children's voices and the sound of an ice cream truck can be heard in the background.

Back at the warehouse, Vince is hard at work, desperately trying to open the canister with a hammer and chisel, when Eddie threatens to cut him off. (He's just brought him an altered suit and a ticket to Miami.) Vince promptly shuts him up with a knife. (The police, having discovered Pete's body, eventually trace his new alligator shoes to the shoe store where they discover Eddie's body.) The irony is that although Vince is leaving a trail of corpses in his wake, he's dying himself. He's also dying of thirst, almost losing the canister when he stops at a Texaco gas station to use the fountain, and the canister, which he has tossed into the backseat, rolls out of the convertible. The mise-en-scène at the gas station subtly comments on Vince's condition: a sign reads GET A TEXACO SAFE-T CHECK UP and a deep-focus wide shot features a garbage bin filled with empty Quaker oil cans. Gloss: Vince is rapidly running out of gas.

After returning to his hotel room, where he tries again in vain to break the steel casing off the canister (at one point he throws it at a mirror, shattering the glass), Vince is eventually flushed out by the police, who, in the meantime, have talked June into revealing his whereabouts. (Richards submits that "even prison is better than death," but given the sort of experiments going on there, the lieutenant's claim is patently absurd.) As Vince runs, not unlike Bigelow in *D.O.A.*, the editing, mise-en-scène, and camerawork coalesce to produce a stunning example of late classic '50s noir, the originality of which sequence derives from the fact that it's shot during the day, with natural light, and on location. The highlight occurs when Vince, hugging the canister to his sweat-stained shirt like a baby, pauses beneath a decrepit billboard that reads TERMITES RATS ROACHES. At the conclusion of *Panic in the Streets*, Blackie (Jack Palance), a down-on-his-heels criminal who doesn't realize that he's carrying a "deadly communicable disease," is cornered on a New Orleans dock by the authorities and tries to escape by crawling up a ship's "hawser designed to prevent rats from climbing aboard"; he slips and falls into the water.[48]

At the end of *City of Fear*, Vince, like Blackie, is a rat in a maze. Having staggered to a seedy bar, where he coughs uncontrollably and perspires like there's no

Radioactive Man: Cobalt-60-contaminated Vince Ryker (Vince Edwards) passing under a Los Angeles billboard as he flees the authorities in *City of Fear*.

tomorrow, he orders a coffee while, on the radio, the mayor interrupts the jazzy, up-tempo music to directly address him: "I beg him not only to save his own life but the thousands of other lives that can become fatally contaminated if the canister is opened and the cobalt allowed to escape. Now, listen to me: the container does not contain heroin. It is certain death unless you give it up right now." Vince, thinking it's a con—"It's a lie! It's worth a million!"—lurches for the front door, and as he does so, the camera cuts outside to a kneecap-high shot of three men—one holding a gun, another a Geiger counter—then to police sharpshooters positioned on balconies and roofs. (The sign on one building—an allusion to Oscar Wilde's *Picture of Dorian Gray*—reads: DORIAN LTD. WESTERN MENSWEAR.)

After Vince hurtles himself through the front door, he falls face-first to the ground, the canister still pressed to his chest. Although Richards tries to reason with him—"You're finished, Ryker"—Vince just can't give up on his dream of the big score: "No, they said it was worth a million!" Richards's response, like the film's message, is double-edged: "It's not even worth your life." The dénouement of *City of Fear* is as abrupt and unsentimental as the conclusion to *D.O.A.* and shorn, as well, of the redeeming social significance of *Odds against Tomorrow:* Vince convulses a few times, then dies. While Richards and Wallace look on poker-faced, a man wearing alligator shoes (appropriated, it appears, from Pete's remains) puts a blanket over Vince's body and another man leans a card up against the dark clump of matter: CAUTION HIGH CONTAMINATION AREA.

Richards mumbles to Wallace, "C'mon, I wanna go home," at which point the shot of the card-draped body begins to dissolve to a panoramic view of the city at night, now momentarily cleansed of fear. For a fleeting moment, though (and

"Your money or your life!": Lobby card of a dying Vince Ryker (Vince Edwards) holding on to the Cobalt-60 canister for dear life in *City of Fear*.

anticipating the death's-head shot superimposed over Norman Bates's face at the end of *Psycho* [1960]), the three triangles on the civil-defense sign resemble two eyes and a mouth, as if a skull were pasted over the twinkling lights of Los Angeles. The lap dissolve is an apt epitaph for the end of the classical period of film noir and a grimly evocative metaphor of the "City of Angels": the "dream city that turned into a nightmare."[49]

6

KISS ME DEADLY

THE X FACTOR, OR THE "GREAT WHATSIT"

Reading the Mike Hammer of the early '50s today is still a
powerful experience: the violence . . . still shocks, and the
sexual content remains potent. . . . It is not hard to imagine
the furor Spillane caused in those days of Howdy Doody and
Ike. Spillane was to mystery writing what Elvis Presley was to
popular music.

—Max Allan Collins, "I, The Intro," *Mickey Spillane's Mike
    Hammer: The Comic Strip* (1982)

The first man-made nuclear explosion would be a historic
event and its designation therefore a name that history might
remember. Oppenheimer coded the test and the test site
Trinity. "Why I chose that name is not clear, but I know what
thoughts were in my mind. There is a poem of John Donne,
written just before his death, which I know and love. From it
a quotation:
> *As West and East*
> *In all flatt Maps—and I am one—are one,*
> *So death doth touch the Resurrection."*

—Richard Rhodes, *The Making of the Atomic Bomb* (1986)

TEASER

In part because of its notorious, Mickey Spillane provenance, *Kiss Me Deadly* has
been interpreted as an anticommunist film, yet it's arguably better interpreted as
an atomic or apocalyptic noir with the proviso that in the 1950s, as I remarked
in the preface, the discourse about the red menace is frequently imbricated with

the discourse about "the bomb." While there may be some ambiguity about the film's exact subgeneric status (Is enigmatic mastermind Dr. Soberin a free agent or a fellow traveler?), there's little doubt that Robert Aldrich's picture is a film noir since, unlike *The Thief, The Atomic City, Shack Out on 101*, and *City of Fear*, it features a hard-boiled investigative narrative as well as a private detective whose moral sense and relationship to the law are even more compromised than Sam Spade's in *The Maltese Falcon*. At the same time, the police and FBI are even less efficacious than the members of law enforcement in the above nuclear noirs because in the final analysis they're unable to prevent an atomic detonation that, paradoxically enough, can itself be interpreted as both destructive and orgasmic, cataclysmic and regenerative.

* * *

Poetry/pulp fiction. Bezzerides/Spillane. Aldrich/PCA. Anti-bomb/anticommunism. Sex/violence. Death/resurrection.

If the above dyads are some of the binary oppositions that *Kiss Me Deadly* generates, the film itself stages and self-consciously thematizes the process of interpretation. This is the X factor, where "X" refers to the object or mystery of the quest, the "Great Whatsit," and the "cross" or chiasmus that marks the hermeneutic act as action in which form is crossed with content, aesthetics with cultural politics, style with "structure of feeling." One consequence of this crisscross is that *Kiss Me Deadly* represents a highly allusive, savagely satiric take on Spillane's crypto-McCarthyite novel *Kiss Me, Deadly*. Thus, while Aldrich's film mobilizes the conventions of classic noir such as the "private dick" (Mike Hammer) and the femme fatale (Lily Carver), it also subjects these very same "pulp" elements to a poetic critique that is one part John Donne, one part Howdy Doody, one part Christina Rossetti, one part Elvis Presley. Another consequence of the authorial and institutional preconditions of *Kiss Me Deadly*—for instance, screenwriter A. I. Bezzerides and the Production Code Administration, respectively—is that even as Aldrich's picture raises the specter of thermonuclear destruction, it gesticulates, via the trope of resurrection, to another, better world beyond the complacent narcissism and materialism of 1950s Eisenhower-era America.

SPILLANE: IKE'S LAUREATE, OR "I LIKE MIKE"

Mickey Spillane began with the "slicks" and "pulps," then became a "story-writer for comic books."[1] When he was unable to place a private-eye hero named Mike Danger with a publisher, he renamed the character Mike Hammer and the laureate of the Eisenhower era was born.[2] The first Hammer novel, *I, the Jury*, appeared in 1947—not so coincidentally, at the advent of the HUAC investigations—and by

1952, when *Kiss Me, Deadly*, the seventh Hammer novel was published, Spillane had secured his reputation as, in his own self-deprecatory words, "the chewing gum of American literature."[3]

In *Hardboiled Hollywood* Max Décharné writes that "critics absolutely despised Spillane and his creation, but with hindsight it seems clear that at the time of the McCarthy witch-hunts, an All-American, gun-toting, Commie-hating, one-man attack force like Mike Hammer . . . was tailor-made to sell books by the millions."[4] And sell books Spillane did. In 1953 New American Library boasted that "over 15,000,000 copies of [Spillane's] books have been published in Signet editions."[5] The Hammer phenomenon was not limited, however, to books. Eventually, there was a radio series, *The Mickey Spillane Mystery: That Hammer Guy* (1953); a comic strip, *From the Files of . . . Mike Hammer* (1953–1954); an LP, *Mickey Spillane's Mike Hammer Story* (1954); and a television series, *Mickey Spillane's Mike Hammer* (CBS, 1958–1959). Describing the Spillane brand, the author himself averred that "sex and violence are punctuation marks in a story."[6]

Surprisingly, there is no sex per se in Spillane's *Kiss Me, Deadly*. Hammer does, as the title promises, kiss a number of lovely femmes, and even though not all of them turn out to be *fatale*, he often seems content just to gaze—and from a distance. The following passage—in which the author indulges, damn the reader, in classical allusions—is illustrative:

> I said, "Velda . . ." and she turned around, knowing damn well what I was going to say. "Show me your legs."
> She grinned impishly, her eyes dancing, standing in a pose no calendar artist could duplicate. She was Circe, a lusty temptress, a piece of living statuary on display, that only one guy would be able to see. The hem of the dress came up quickly, letting the roundness under the nylon evolve into a magical symmetry, then the nylon ended in the quick whiteness of her thigh and I said, "Enough, kitten. Quit it."
> Before I could say anything else she laughed down deep, threw me a kiss and grinned. "Now we know how Ulysses felt."
> Now I knew. The guy was a sucker. He should have jumped ship.[7]

Velda, Hammer's secretary/associate, is a pin-up calendar girl come to life and he can barely stand to look. The last brave line aside, he's a "sucker" like Ulysses and would never jump ship.

In fact, all the real exclamation points in *Kiss Me, Deadly*—the sex scenes are soft-boiled—involve violence, as in the scene set at a bar called Long John's ("The bartender had a patch over one eye and a peg leg. No parrot"), where a hood named Charlie Max pulls a "rod" on Hammer: "The gun was there in his fist, coming up and around as I brought my foot up and the things that were in

Charlie's face splashed all over the floor."[8] This is pulp fiction with a vengeance, where what is pulped is not paper but human flesh. In *Kiss Me, Deadly*, even and especially the Mafia—"the stinking, slimy Mafia"—are the stuff of pulp: "Just soft, pulpy people . . . filthy and twisted who gorged themselves on flesh and puffed up with the power they had so that when they got stuck they popped like ripe melons and splashed all over the ground."[9]

While violence, not sex, propels the plot of *Kiss Me, Deadly*, the story, such as it is, is about a missing cache of narcotics worth "two million bucks after conversion"—"Tax free"—hidden in "two metal containers the size of lunch pails."[10] I say "about" because the narcotics are a pretext or, to invoke the Russian Formalists, a device to justify the "manic movement from scene to scene, action to action, seduction to seduction, beating to beating, cigarette to cigarette, and killing to killing."[11]

SAVILLE, BEZZERIDES, ALDRICH: "THE MEAT HOOK"

In his unpublished memoirs Victor Saville observed that "nothing could be further removed from [his] previous work" than Spillane's novels (Saville as a director and producer had been previously associated with "prestige" pictures both at Gaumont-British and M-G-M),[12] but he nevertheless purchased the rights to Spillane's books and approached Robert Aldrich to direct. (Saville's Park Lane Productions had already made *I, the Jury* [1953] and *The Long Wait* [1954].) Aldrich, coming off the Superscope widescreen blockbuster *Vera Cruz* (1954), agreed, "provided [Saville] would let [him] make the kind of movie [he] wanted and provided [he] could produce."[13]

However, in September 1954 the Production Code Administration (PCA) informed Aldrich that the story for *Kiss Me Deadly* was "basically unacceptable" and therefore could not be approved by the office.[14] There were two main reasons: first, the "basic prop" of the "murder melodrama" was narcotics, which in 1954 was still considered taboo by the PCA (this restriction would change in 1956 in the wake of the Kefauver Committee hearings on juvenile delinquency), and, second, the portrayal of Hammer as a "cold-blooded murderer whose numerous killings are completely unjustified" was also forbidden.[15]

While Aldrich and Bezzerides's subversive conception of Hammer is crucial to their adaptation of *Kiss Me, Deadly*, the radioactive box is the central plot device of both the novel and film.[16] In an interview Bezzerides remarked that the "atomic MacGuffin" in the film was a "substitute for the dope."[17] More specifically, when asked about the A-bomb and McCarthyism, he said that "these things were in the air": "There was a lot of talk about nuclear war at the time, and it was the foremost fear in people's minds. Nuclear arms race."[18]

Taking a rather different tack, Aldrich in a 1968 interview with *Sight and Sound* claimed, not unlike Hitchcock with respect to *Psycho*, that the "book had nothing": "We took the title and threw the book away."[19] (In fact, the plot of *Kiss Me Deadly* owes quite a lot to Spillane's novel.[20]) In 1971 Aldrich also claimed that the character of Mike Hammer was a "fascistic private eye" for whom he had "utter contempt and loathing."[21] But as Richard Maltby demonstrates, Aldrich's, if not Bezzerides's, remarks belie the complexity of the authorial and institutional circumstances in which the film was made. On one hand, Aldrich had to satisfy the censors; on the other hand, he was not unaware, like the savvy Saville, of the economic imperatives of what Maltby calls "serially produced industrial culture."[22]

Thus, in a February 1955 letter to Geoffrey Shurlock at the PCA, Aldrich wrote that the filmmakers had tried to "successfully marry the commercial value of the Spillane properties with a morality that states that justice is not to be found in a self-appointed one-man vigilante."[23] Since both Aldrich and Bezzerides were associated at the time with the cultural left in the United States (Aldrich was "'grey-listed' by HUAC" and Bezzerides was "temporarily blacklisted after the film's release"[24]), Aldrich's later statement that "*Kiss Me Deadly*, at its depth, had to do with the McCarthy era" is consonant with what in an April 1955 telegram to Shurlock he called the film's "voice of moral righteousness."[25] And yet, in an article titled "You Can't Hang Up the Meat Hook," which appeared in the *New York Herald Tribune* in February 1955, Aldrich also made clear that he was committed to keeping "faith with 60 million Spillane readers"—that is to say, milking the novel's "blood, action, and sex" for, to quote *Variety*, "exploitable b[ox] o[ffice]."[26]

"You Can't Hang Up the Meat Hook" was plainly intended as a "promotional exercise." Still, given the New York daily newspaper venue, it's an extraordinary document in its detailed attention to the audiovisual elements of the medium:

> The camera focuses first on the helpless girl and her antagonists. . . . Hands are then laid on the victim, and from that moment suspense is maintained, the violence high-keyed and the horror spotlighted through the sound effects, focusing the camera in a series of close shots, on her feet, her hands, shadows on the wall and similar devices.[27]

This passage in "You Can't Hang Up the Meat Hook" is the spot where the cultural politics or authorial and institutional axes of *Kiss Me Deadly* (Spillane, PCA) are crossed with its aesthetics or formal attributes (lighting, camerawork, sound design). In other words, just as Aldrich's endeavor to marry commerce and "morality," Spillane and anti-McCarthyism, points to the film's contradictory, ideological conditions of possibility, so too *Kiss Me Deadly*'s X factor betokens the play or tension in the film between sex and violence, death and resurrection.

X MARKS THE SPOT: "DIAMONDS, RUBIES, GOLD"

In "Evidence of a Style" Alain Silver points out the "X-shaped pose which Christina Bailey [Cloris Leachman] assumes as she flags down Hammer's [Ralph Meeker] car" at the very beginning of *Kiss Me Deadly*, a shape that's also "recalled in the painted figure on the wall of her room" and in the "image of Hammer tied to [a] bed in Soberin's beach house."[28] Similarly, in *Dreams and Dead Ends* Jack Shadoian notes the "recurrent 'x' patterns—outside [Hammer's] apartment, at Nick's garage, [and] in the repeated shot of the beach from under the house."[29]

Although the X figure recurs throughout *Kiss Me Deadly*,[30] its structural or architectural function is evidenced not so much by the long shot of the beach house when the "torpedoes" Sugar Smallhouse (Jack Lambert) and Charlie Max (Jack Elam) chase Hammer down to the surf and then drag his unconscious body back up to the house as by the abstract shots—the pitch-black timbers forming an X in the foreground against the sunlit surf in the background—that bookend the sequence in which Hammer is tied to a bed. In fact, after Max and Smallhouse drag Hammer back to the beach house, the film fades to black before fading in to the opening exterior foundation shot, followed by a straight cut to Hammer's right hand bound to the posts of a headboard, followed in turn by the aforementioned wide shot of the detective spread-eagled on the bed.

Va-Va-Boom: Mike Hammer and car mechanic Sammy (Jerry Zinneman) in Nick's automobile repair shop in *Kiss Me Deadly*. Note crossed beams in the ceiling above Hammer.

It's at this point that Dr. Soberin (Albert Dekker) appears, addressing Mike as he prepares a shot of sodium Pentothal:

"Why torment yourself? Who would you seek? Someone you do not know, a stranger? What is it we are seeking? Diamonds, rubies, gold, perhaps narcotics? How civilized this Earth used to be. But as the world becomes more primitive, its treasures become more fabulous. Perhaps sentiment will succeed where greed failed. You will die, Mr. Hammer. . . . The young lady you picked up on the highway, she wrote you a letter. In it were two words: 'Remember me.' She asked you to remember. What is it you must remember?"

Here, portentously referencing precious stones and metals as well as narcotics (the last an allusion to the novel's original banned material), Soberin makes the connection between Christina and Mike that the film has already introduced via the figure of the X: the "big secret" that has been surreptitiously passed from her to Hammer. That is to say, Soberin knows *what* the Great Whatsit is; he just doesn't know *where* it is.

Soberin thinks that the secret to its location is in Hammer's subconscious, but it's not there. While Mike mumbles incoherently under the influence of the "truth serum," Carl Evello (Paul Stewart), a mob boss in cahoots with Soberin, prompts him with questions: "'Remember me'—what did she mean?" Later, after Hammer has ingeniously disposed of Evello and Sugar (the latter via some "mysterious, off-camera, martial arts action"),[31] Charlie Max enters, sees the dead bodies, and looks out the open window. There's the sound of a car ignition turning over and tires on gravel. Cut to the abstract exterior X shot of the pitch-black timbers.

When the camera cuts again, it's to Hammer standing outside the door to his apartment. Still dopey from the Pentothal, he slips his hand inside the chain-locked door and turns the light on and off to signal Lily Carver (Gaby Rodgers), Christina's gamine, pixie-coiffed former roommate, whom he's momentarily taken under his wing, that he's there. When the light's off, a cross-shaped shadow appears on the brick façade of the fireplace. Mike, remembering Soberin's question, makes a drink—"What did she mean, 'Remember me'?"—then, after sitting down on the couch, hands Lily the Rossetti book that he lifted from Christina's apartment and says, "Read this." Lily reads:

Remember me when no more day by day
You tell me of a future that you'd planned.
Only remember me; you'll understand,
But if the darkness and corruption leave
A vestige of the thoughts that once we had.

The passage that Lily reads from Christina Rossetti's "Remember" is a corruption of the original,[32] but since Mike—as Christina surmised when she first met him—is not a devotee of poetry, the words are not so much symbolic, like the X, as literal. Consequently, "he takes them at face value": "to him, they mean he should go to Christina's corpse (or her 'members')."[33]

Cut, via a close-up of a body tag, to a morgue, where Mike, gazing at Christina's corpse, recites a couplet from the Rossetti poem out loud to himself—"if the darkness and corruption leave / A vestige of the thoughts that once we had"—while Lily and Doc Kennedy (Percy Helton) look on. Hammer reflects that "it's got to be a thing"—"something small, something she could hide"—then concludes that Christina swallowed it. When Doc Kennedy smiles, Mike and Lily follow him to his office, where a large cross-shaped shadow is tattooed to the wall. Standing behind his desk, Doc Kennedy takes a key from a drawer and puts out his hand; Mike takes out some money and peels off some bills. Doc Kennedy puts out his hand again and Mike peels off some more bills. However, when Doc Kennedy refuses to turn over the key, Hammer crushes his hand in a desk drawer. Doc Kennedy begins to squeal with pain, and Lily covers her ears with her hands; now it's Mike who's smiling. (This is perhaps the most obvious example in the film of the pronounced and oft-commented-upon sadism of Hammer's character in Spillane's novels.)

At the Hollywood Athletic Club (a play on "H[U]AC"?), Mike presents the key to the clerk behind the counter, who inquires, "Are you a member, sir?" When the clerk sniffs at Hammer's bribe ("My dear sir"), Mike slaps him around until he

X: Henchmen parked outside Mike Hammer's (Ralph Meeker) apartment in *Kiss Me Deadly*.

agrees to show him Nicholas Raymondo's locker, inside of which is a box covered by a leather strap. Hammer undoes the strap and, after removing the top—inside, there's a box, a box within a box—he's about to open it when he feels something hot. Undeterred and right before his hand instinctively recoils in pain, he pries it open just enough to see a blinding white light accompanied by a strange guttural noise, as if the box were alive. Mike now knows where the box is.

Since Lily has, in the meantime, vanished, Mike returns to his apartment, where Captain Pat Murphy (Wesley Addy) and a number of uniformed policemen are waiting for him. Pat wants the key; Hammer, however, first wants to make sure that Velda (Maxine Cooper), who has been kidnapped, is safe. (In the short time that the authorities have been on the case, there's been a steady trail of bodies— Christina's, Raymondo's, Lee Kawolsky's, Nick's.[34]) When Mike mentions Lily's name, Pat tells him that they "fished Carver's body out of the harbor a week ago," then starts to berate him: "You're so bright working on your own. You penny-ante gumshoe. You thought you saw something big and you tried to horn in." In response, Hammer reaches for the pack of cigarettes in the breast pocket of Pat's jacket, and Pat grabs his wrist. Cut to a close-up of a fresh burn scar.

Pat—who, like Soberin, knows what the Great Whatsit is—decides that it's time to level with Hammer:

> "Now listen, Mike, listen carefully. I'm going to pronounce a few words. They're harmless words. Just a bunch of letters scrambled together. But their meaning is very important. Try to understand what they mean. Manhattan Project. Los Alamos. Trinity."

Hammer glances at his wrist, then hands the key to Pat. As the captain's leaving, Mike admits, "I didn't know," and Pat contemptuously replies, "You didn't know. Do you think you'd have done any different if you had known?"

Since Mike must now find the box in order to find Velda, he picks up the phone. Cut to the Hollywood Athletic Club, the camera tilting down—the locker's empty—before panning to the right, where the clerk is splayed out on the linoleum floor, mouth open, glasses off, his left arm thrown out so that his corpse forms a cross. Time for Hammer to retrace his steps.

When Mike previously visited Ray Diker's (Mort Marshall) apartment, the science editor/newspaper columnist gave him Christina's last name and address. This time he extracts the name of William Mist. (As in Mike's first visit, the marks on Diker's face suggest that he's been worked over by "them" or that, as with Hammer, the marks are radioactive burns.) At Mist's address—a plaque outside reads "Mist's Gallery of Modern Art"—Mike breaks a windowpane and lets himself in. After winding his way past contemporary Italian paintings,[35] he tries to knock down a bathroom door behind which Mist is hiding, although the art dealer, having heard the sound of a breaking window, has already swallowed a bottle of sleeping pills. Mike slaps Mist silly—"Where is she? Where is she?"—but the only clue is the name on a bottle of sleeping pills: "Dr. G. E. Soberin." Velda's voice in the form of a sonic flashback resonates on the sound track: "Does that do anything for you?"

EXCURSUS: BLUE SUEDE SHOES

Cut to a pair of shoes, the same wing-tipped, white-stitched ones visible at the beginning of the film when Mike picks up Christina and helps her negotiate a police roadblock before another car forces them off the road. The very same shoes that appear in the ensuing torture sequence when the camera cuts, via a match shot, to a high-angle shot of Christina's legs cut off at the knees and Mike unconscious on a bed. Christina's still screaming when the man with the wing-tipped, white-stitched shoes kicks Mike's body off an exposed-spring bed. After someone offscreen says, "She's passed out," and another person replies, "I'll bring her to," the man in the distinctive shoes responds: "If you revive her, do you know what that will be? Resurrection. That's what it will be. And you know what resurrection means? It means raise the dead. And just who do you think you are that you think you can raise the dead?"[36]

Mike raises his head. He's not dead. He sees two pairs of shoes, Christina's trench coat crumpled up on the floor, and her now motionless white legs dangling from

The Cross: Low-angle shot from Hammer's POV of Soberin (Albert Dekker) on the right and one of his henchmen on the left, and, in the background of the frame, the legs of Christina Bailey (Cloris Leachman) dangling from a cross-legged high chair.

the table. Like Hammer, we cannot see her torso or her face, but she's perched on a table, the two bottom legs forming an X.

CLIMAX: LE GRAND MORT

As the man in the wing-tipped, white-stitched shoes reflects about traveling—"There is something sad and melancholy about trips"—the camera pans up from his shoes past the revolver in his hands to his face: it's Dr. Soberin, the Man Who Knew Too Much. Cut to a close-up of Lily, who, caressing the box, asks, "What's in the box?" "Curiosity killed a cat," Soberin answers, busying himself packing his papers, "and it certainly would have if you followed your impulse to open it."

Whereas Lily is stereotypically impulsive, Soberin is sober, a learned man of science. Indeed, from his condescending tone, it's obvious that he doesn't think of Lily as his intellectual equal; moreover, he's not remotely afraid of her. (About the latter, of course, he's fatally mistaken.)

> LILY (ignoring Soberin): But what's in it?
> SOBERIN: You have been misnamed, Gabrielle. You should have been called Pandora. She had a curiosity about a box and opened it and let loose all the evil in the world.

Although the allusion here is to Pandora, whose jar "full of ills" is associated in Hesiod with a "thing of evil for mankind,"[37] the fact that Soberin addresses Lily as "Gabrielle" points to her feminine masquerade and highly mutable, allusive self. In fact, if Lily's name is associated via funerals with death and via Easter with the resurrection, Gabrielle's name alludes to the archangel Gabriel and Christina Rossetti's "pre-Raphaelite" brother, Dante Gabriel Rossetti, as well as to Christina Bailey, who represents the "redemptive power" of poetry.[38]

"Never mind about the evil," Gabrielle retorts, sniffing the box. "What's in it?" Soberin, still packing his papers, issues another warning:

> SOBERIN: Did you ever hear of Lot's wife?
> GABRIELLE: No.
> SOBERIN: No. Well, she was told not to look back, but she disobeyed and she was changed into a pillar of salt.

Critics have understandably trained their attention, as in the Pandora passage, on the dialogue—in this case, Soberin's allusion to Lot's wife—yet the above passage also exhibits one of the celebrated deep-focus long takes in *Kiss Me Deadly*. As Soberin moves in the left background between a valise and an open suitcase on the couch, Gabrielle stands in the right foreground directly in front of the box. More importantly, right after Soberin mentions Lot's wife, Gabrielle moves to the side of the box, in the process revealing—in the background, in the dead center

Atomic Apéritif: Dr. Soberin (Albert Dekker) prepares a cocktail, pre-sojourn, as Gabrielle, aka Lily Carver (Gaby Rodgers), contemplates Pandora's Box in *Kiss Me Deadly*.

of the frame—a cocktail cart, the legs of which, as in the torture scene, form an X, so that the cocktail cart is visually aligned with the box, as if to equate the two.

In the torture scene, Christina refused to tell her captors where the box was located, choosing instead to go to her death with the secret. The situation is reversed here. Despite the fact that Gabrielle has been instrumental in acquiring the Great Whatsit, Soberin continues to employ circumlocution rather than share the big secret with her:

SOBERIN: Would you believe me if I told you? Would you be satisfied?
GABRIELLE: Maybe.
SOBERIN (facing Gabrielle and, drink in hand, moving toward the camera): The head of the Medusa. That's what's in the box. And whoever looks on her will be changed not into stone but into brimstone and ashes. But, of course, you wouldn't believe me. You'd have to see for yourself, wouldn't you?

The irony here—a dramatic one—is that Gabrielle, unlike Hammer (and the audience), has no idea what's in the box. Accordingly, although Soberin's invocation of the Medusa is no doubt intended to dissuade Gabrielle from opening the box, it has the exact opposite effect, accelerating her desire.

But once Gabrielle realizes that Soberin will not be divulging what's in the box, she asks him where they're going, and the doctor, recalling Christ addressing his "disciples before the crucifixion" (John 13:36),[39] tells her, "Where I am going it is not possible for you to go." Gabrielle, spurned, returns her attention to the box, speculating about its contents—"Whatever is in that box must be very precious. So many people have died for it"—before announcing that she wants half. Soberin explains that the "object in this box cannot be divided," after which Gabrielle casually picks up his gun and says, "Then I'll take it all." Bang.

Even though he has been shot at point-blank range, Soberin continues to warn Gabrielle about the box, this time invoking the three-headed hounds who guard Hades: "Listen to me, as if I were Cerberus barking with all his heads at the gates of hell. I will tell you where to take it. But don't . . . don't open . . . the box." However, despite or perhaps because of Soberin's warning, Gabrielle goes straight to the box, the crisscross legs of the table abruptly swimming back into view, and is about to unwrap it when Hammer throws open the door: "Where's Velda?" As the box continues to hiss in the background like a serpent, Gabrielle, the gun again in her hand, tells Mike: "Kiss me. The liar's kiss that says 'I love you' that means something else. You're good at giving such kisses. Kiss me." Then, without warning, she pulls the trigger and Hammer, like Soberin, goes down like a tree.

That the box is growling even louder now does not deter Christina, who removes the outer leather casing and tentatively touches the top. Like Hammer earlier in the film, she feels the heat, but, unlike him, she lifts the lid and the box emits a howling sound, the light demonically illuminating her face from below. She screams. Cut to a high overhead shot of the contents of the box: a smoking rectangle of blinding white light.

When Mike eventually comes to, Gabrielle's holding on to the box as if her life depended on it, her screams indistinguishable from its deafening roar. As the flames engulf her body, turning her not into a pillar of salt but fire, Hammer, crawling toward the door, looks back one last time, not unlike Lot's wife, then turns away, a hand shielding his face from the conflagration.

Mike's stumbling around in the hallway trying to find Velda when he finally hears her voice and breaks down a door. Cut to an exterior long shot of the beach house as flames begin to consume the second story, where Mike and Velda, holding on to each other, make their way down a hallway, then down an exterior staircase past the pitch-black timbers that form the house's foundation. Dragging themselves toward the surf, they cross the path that Mike's body previously traced in the sand. Cut to an extreme low angle as they collapse to the ground. Velda helps Mike up, and they stagger into the surf, looking back just in time to see the house detonate in a series of sky-high explosions.

The End.

POSTMORTEM: REVELATIONS

The explosive ending of *Kiss Me Deadly* recollects both the sci-fi-inspired conclusion of *White Heat* (J. Hoberman has described *Kiss Me Deadly* as "Mickey

Spillane on Mars"[40]) and the cataclysmic dénouement of *Odds against Tomorrow*. But unlike these films, the ending of Aldrich's picture has a specifically nuclear dimension.

Another salient difference between *Kiss Me Deadly* and the two film noirs mentioned above is that it features a private detective. As opposed to, say, Raymond Chandler's not-so-tarnished knight, Philip Marlowe, behind whose tough-guy persona and world-weary cynicism "lies the *chevalier sans peur et sans reproche*,"[41] Mike Hammer is a "bedroom dick" who's perpetually on the lookout for number one: a "private eye-for-an-eye," illicit sexuality is his métier and vengeance is his alone. If Hammer represents a perversion of the classic detective archetype, the mystery that he's chasing is equally perverse. The Great Whatsit is an exorbitant object of desire, and this exorbitance is signified in *Kiss Me Deadly* by all the X's. These X's underline both the enigmatic character of the Great Whatsit—its utter mysteriousness—and its seductive tenor, a suggestion encapsulated by the film's title, *Kiss Me Deadly*, in which desire as death is figured as so many kisses (XXX).

X, of course, also marks the spot where treasure can be found. In this sense the Great Whatsit is reminiscent of the *rara avis* in *The Maltese Falcon*. The Maltese falcon is a sublime object of desire, treasure incarnate, and any number of people die—as Gabrielle observes about the Great Whatsit—pursuing it. However, the Maltese falcon is not in itself dangerous, and in Huston's film the object that Sam Spade (Humphrey Bogart) and, eventually, Kasper Gutman (Sidney Greenstreet) get their hands on is a simulacrum, a fake. Equally importantly, despite Hammer's narcissistic "What's in it for me?" character, he renounces his quest for the box when Pat Murphy elliptically describes its contents. Therefore, while it's true that this "sudden acquiescence to governmental authority at the invocation of nuclear warfare privileges national security over the material concerns of a greedy private eye,"[42] Murphy's warning is itself a response to Mike's belated, albeit genuine, concern about Velda's life. In an inversion that mirrors the film's modus operandi (see, for example, the reverse crawl of the title sequence), Mike now knows *what* the box is but not *where* it is.

The only question that therefore remains at the end of *Kiss Me Deadly* is: who has the box and what do "they," what Velda calls the "nameless ones," plan to do with it? The culmination of Mike's search for the Great Whatsit, now driven by his desire to save Velda's life, takes him to Soberin's beach house, which, like Chinatown in the conclusion to Roman Polanski's neo-noir, is the site of a traumatic repetition. The first time that Hammer's forcibly taken there, he's tied to the bed and the X figure his body makes points to the film's beginning (Christina's Christlike hailing of Mike) and its ending (nuclear annihilation as apocalypse).

In the end, of course, we never do learn what Soberin plans to do with the Great Whatsit. (The implication is that he intends to sell it.[43]) In a displacement typical of the period, Hammer's narcissism is transferred to Lily, aka Gabrielle, the "bad girl" to Christina and Velda's "good-bad girls," in which sexual desire is connected to both death (kiss = death) and femininity. (It's no accident, I think, that Gabrielle's screams after she opens the box recall Christina's in the torture scene and that the latter, in turn, recall her heavy panting in the film's opening sequence.) Gabrielle may not be a bombshell like Rita Hayworth in *Gilda* (1946), but just as Pandora's jar is an extension of her body, so too the secretive "hot box" in *Kiss Me Deadly* is connected with the mystery of femininity. As Carol Flinn explains in her article on the Great Whatsit, Aldrich's film "fuses the widespread fear of atomic destruction in the Fifties with the . . . widespread fear of women, effectively mapping the former onto the latter."[44]

The twist (and *Kiss Me Deadly* is nothing if not twisted in terms of its tropes) is that Gabrielle's character also exceeds her stereotypical determination as a femme fatale, since in addition to disobeying Soberin, she actively gazes at the Great Whatsit.[45] In other words, Gabrielle exhibits the same obsessional desire for the box as Hammer does before he relinquishes his quest. And in appropriating the investigative prerogatives of the private detective, she speaks to the audience's own burning desire to plumb the mystery of the "big secret" no matter how catastrophic the consequences, a desire "central to the nuclear era."[46]

While the strategic use of offscreen space in *Kiss Me Deadly* can be said to elicit, as Aldrich's "You Can't Hang Up the Meat Hook" intimates, "a desire to see and to know what kinds of violence and spectacle lie outside the frame,"[47] the hermeneutic impulse that precipitates the film's plot is already graphically present in the form of the letter "X," which appears within the frame even as it gestures, as a material signifier of the boxed mystery, to what is inside *and* outside the screen. At the same time, it's apparent that, however one figures the contents of the box, the radioactive fallout from the atomic explosion that climaxes Aldrich's film will kill Mike and Velda as well as, depending on how one construes the climax (for instance, a thermonuclear chain reaction), destroy the planet.[48] As Raymond Borde and Étienne Chaumeton put in the "Postface" to *A Panorama of American Film Noir*, *Kiss Me Deadly* offers the "most radical of solutions: nuclear apocalypse."[49]

And yet, as with the ambiguous, overdetermined representation of femininity in Aldrich's picture, the X figure does not refer simply to death or devastation. That is to say, the biblical allusions (e.g., Lazarus), not to mention the cross or Christian imagery (Christina as a "crucified," "female Christ figure"),[50] simultaneously foreground *Kiss Me Deadly*'s status as an "apocalyptic noir."[51] Put yet another way, if Aldrich's film can be said to constitute a satiric critique of both the private detective picture and the fallen, materialistic world—Hammer as the smug, stuporous face of '50s mid-century America—it also promises, through the critical negation of this world, its rebirth or resurrection.

And here one would do well to remember the film's authorial and institutional preconditions, both Spillane's "profane" novel and the censorial ministrations of the PCA, which ultimately temper any transcendental interpretation of Aldrich's film. The director—the first, according to Claude Chabrol, of the atomic age—famously claimed that the film is "anti-Spillane," "anti-McCarthy," and "anti-bomb."[52] In a nutshell, to quote Aldrich himself again, the "ends do not justify the means."[53] The irony—an irreducible one—is that, at least in the very particular case of *Kiss Me Deadly*, sometimes the ends do justify the means. No PCA, no bomb. No Spillane, no movie. No pulp fiction, no poetry.

PART THREE

NEW MEDIA AND TECHNOLOGIES

More and more . . . than the *coup d'état* of sound, it seems to me that the history of cinema has its turning point in the irresistible infiltration of color.

—Jacques Rivette, "The Age of *Metteurs en scène*" (1954)

The difference between CinemaScope and the routine talking picture of the past is comparable in impact to the difference between a crystal radio and a high fidelity FM receiver. . . . More and more we are thinking in terms of width rather than height. We live wide nowadays, preferring the ranch house to the two-flight.

—Charles Einfield, "CinemaScope and the Public" (1953)

Now three-dimension, complemented by directional sound and color, literally enables us to give the spectator the thrilling experience of actually being a participant in the dramatic action.

—Jack L. Warner, "1927, Sound—1953, 3-D" (1953)

NOIR EN COULEUR

COLOR AND WIDESCREEN

> Today to get the public to attend a picture show
> It's not enough to advertise a famous star they know.
> If you want to get the crowd to come around
> You've got to have glorious Technicolor, breathtaking
> CinemaScope and Stereophonic Sound.
>
> —Fred Astaire, "Stereophonic Sound," *Silk Stockings*
> (Cole Porter, 1955)

It has been argued that the decline of film noir is coincident not simply with the advent of the red menace and the blacklist but with the transformation of the motion picture industry occasioned by new media and technologies such as TV, 3-D, Eastmancolor, and CinemaScope. If, for example, color film stock necessitated higher, brighter key lighting and CinemaScope was premised upon opening up or elongating the standard screen (from, that is, the academy ratio of 1.33:1 to the new, anamorphic one of 2.55:1 or 2.35:1), these developments appeared to militate against the sort of expressionist devices such as low, Venetian-blind lighting and skewed, claustrophobic compositions associated with classic noir. However, a close examination of, among other things, color and widescreen in select feature films of the period suggests that film noir in the 1950s, crossing location shooting with studio-bound theatrics, canted angles with CinemaScopic effects, Technicolor hues with black-and-white "mystery" lighting, adapted to the rapidly changing industrial and technological landscape of Hollywood, in the process laying down the audiovisual tracks for the renascence that is neo-noir.

More specifically, the stereotypical critique of '50s noir is that, in conjunction with the exaltation of the police officer, the genre embraced the retrograde politics of American neorealism at the expense of the insurgent, expressionist aesthetic that had previously defined the genre. Late, "baroque" film noirs like *Touch of Evil* (1958) were therefore an exception to the rule. Is it possible, though, that this interpretation is a technologically determinist one, where '50s noir, in a perverse *après coup*, is retrospectively View-Mastered through the narrow, black-and-white lens of TV? In other words, if it's true that color, widescreen, and directional sound were understood to promote greater realism, the new technologies were also understood to produce a "kind of excess, which in turn was packaged as spectacle."[1] Thus, if the restrained pastel palette of *Black Widow* (1954) can be seen as subjecting the prismatic glories of Technicolor to the exigencies of the "classic realist text," the super-saturated colors of *Slightly Scarlet* (1956) can, by contrast, be said to signify excess and spectacle—in a word, expressionism. Similarly, if the relatively static blocking and immobile, mid-angled camerawork of *Black Widow* appear to revert to a certain theatrical tendency in American cinema, the dynamic choreography as well as axial, vertical, and lateral compositions of *House of Bamboo* and *A Kiss before Dying* (1956) disclose the expressive, spectacular possibilities of CinemaScope.

NOIR EN COULEUR

In "Noir in Color?" (the question mark is illustrative), Alex Ballinger and Danny Graydon claim that "dramatic contrasts of light and shade are such a defining feature of film noir, especially of those films made in the 1940s and 1950s, that the idea of noir filmed in color . . . sounds like an oxymoron."[2] This sentiment is most eloquently expressed by John Alton, who once quipped that he "could see more in the dark than [he] could in color."[3]

The grand exception in the classical period has always been *Leave Her to Heaven* (1945). About John Stahl's picture and its desert landscape the "color of dried blood," Raymond Borde and Étienne Chaumeton in *A Panorama of American Film Noir* write that this was "the first time Technicolor [had] been used in a crime film."[4] *Leave Her to Heaven*'s exceptionalism can be gauged by comparing it to "another 'limit' work," Alfred Hitchcock's *Rope* (1948), which, according to the Warner Bros. press book, was the first film to utilize color "for a suspenseful story of murder and detection."[5] (We can attribute the difference of opinion about which film, *Leave Her to Heaven* or *Rope*, has priority to the Warner Bros. publicity department.)

Unlike Leon Shamroy, who seems intent in *Leave Her to Heaven* on maximizing the play of the color orange, Hitchcock in *Rope* was determined, in his own words, "to reduce the color to a minimum," going so far as to fire his director of photography because the orange in the New York City skyline set was "too strong"—"like a lurid postcard."[6] In fact, the film "maintains a polite, drawing-room atmosphere until the climactic moment, when repressed color breaks free in almost garish form," shading Rupert Cadell's (James Stewart) face with a "sickly green and then with a bloody red."[7] In other words, whereas Shamroy pushes "pictorialism to the point where it dominates all other functions" (see his riposte to Darryl Zanuck during the production of *The Black Swan*: "When you're shooting a sunset, use yellow light . . . and ignore realism"), Hitchcock uses color as dramatic punctuation.[8]

If the limit or exceptional status of color noir tends to hold true for the 1940s (but see, in addition to *Leave Her to Heaven* and *Rope*, *Desert Fury* [1947]), this becomes categorically less so in the 1950s, as the wide release of color crime films demonstrates; for example, *Hell on Frisco Bay* (Warnercolor, CinemaScope [1955]), *Hell's Island* (Technicolor, VistaVision [1955]), *I Died a Thousand Times* (Warnercolor, CinemaScope [1955]), *Violent Saturday* (DeLuxe, CinemaScope [1955]), *Accused of Murder* (Trucolor, Naturama [1956]), *The Unholy Wife* (Technicolor, Superscope [1957]), *Party Girl* (Metrocolor, CinemaScope [1958]), and *The Trap* (Technicolor, VistaVision [1959]), not to mention *Rear Window* (Technicolor [1954]) and *Vertigo* (Technicolor, VistaVision [1958]). The reasons for this new production trend are at once cultural and historical, political and technological, and include the "1948 consent decree that separated distribution from exhibition; an antitrust suit against Technicolor that accused them of monopolizing the color field; the introduction of Eastmancolor negative; and competition from a new medium, television."[9]

The contradictory nature of color during its decades-long diffusion throughout the motion picture industry—between, that is, "color as an index of realism and color as a mark of fantasy"[10]—has additional significance in the context of '50s noir given the increasing recourse to realist aesthetics in the postwar era. In brief, color complicates the trend toward neorealism in '50s noir: on one hand, like widescreen, magnetic sound, and 3-D, it can be seen to enhance verisimilitude; on the other hand, as in *Leave Her to Heaven*, it can generate the sort of "fantastic," expressionist effects that were achieved in the classic, pre-realist period via black-and-white chiaroscuro and high-contrast, low-key lighting. In other words, color in the 1950s, supplemented as it is by widescreen and four-track stereo, acts as value-added spectacle in the post-decree age of TV.

More specifically, '50s noirs use color to dramatize the genre's formal and thematic components. Thus, in "Under the Color Rainbow" Katherine Glitre proposes that color in classic noir tends to enhance the characterization of the femme fatale, to accentuate the "tonal contrast of chiaroscuro," or to emphasize a "morally dangerous situation through garish mise-en-scène."[11] Fifties noirs also employ color via, among other things, costuming and temperature ("warm" versus "cool") not only to "paint" the lighting and mise-en-scène but to tincture other, prototypical noir character types such as the femme detective and homme fatal, the gangster and the "good-bad girl."

BLACK WIDOW: RED HERRING

Black Widow—scripted, directed, and produced by Nunnally Johnson, who produced and wrote the screenplay for *How to Marry a Millionaire* (1953)—immediately announces itself as a film noir. Unlike *Leave Her to Heaven*, which is arguably a film noir masquerading as a melodrama, *Black Widow*, based on Patrick Quentin's 1952 novel of the same name, might be said to be a melodrama disguised as a film noir, or a Manhattan murder mystery.

After the requisite shot of the Fox production logo and Leigh Harline's fanfare, followed in turn by the CinemaScope "card," *Black Widow* opens with the image of a fat black spider trembling in a sticky web of white filaments against a sky-blue background. Although this opening shot recollects *The Glass Web* (1953), the widescreen format and DeLuxe saturated colors of *Black Widow* make the three-dimensional spectacle of the credit sequence of the former picture pale in comparison. The voice-over narration glosses the DeLuxe image: "The black widow, deadliest of all spiders, earned its dark title from its deplorable practice of devouring its mate."

The mystery that the film will tease out as it unspools like a spidery thread is, of course, who among the female characters is the black widow? (While the recourse to the pronoun "it" in the voice-over narration is ambiguous, the fact that the narrator is male leaves little doubt "it" will be a female.) Could it be Iris (Gene Tierney), the wife of Broadway producer Peter Denver (Van Heflin), whose flashback opens the film: "And so I went to Lottie's party"? Or is it Broadway diva Carlotta "Lottie" Marin (Ginger Rogers), to whose party Peter reluctantly goes? Or is it Nancy "Nanny" Ordway (Peggy Ann Garner), the ingénue who Peter, slipping out of the party, meets on the balcony of Lottie's apartment, an apartment that, not so incidentally, mirrors the Denvers'?

According to Darryl Zanuck, CinemaScope was ideal for "large-scale spectacles" such as Fox's début CinemaScope feature, the biblical epic *The Robe* (1953), and "big outdoor films" such as *Beneath the 12-Mile Reef* (1953), though he also believed that it would, in time, be suitable for more "intimate stories."[12] One of the ironies of Zanuck's pronouncements about CinemaScope is that even as he claimed that "small," "domestic" dramas "would mean nothing on this system" (Zanuck did not change his mind until the successful release of *Three Coins in a Fountain* [1954]), Fox advertisements for the new "Miracle Mirror Screen" promised "audiences that they would be drawn into the space of the picture much as if they were attending a play in the theater," and the *Hollywood Reporter* trumpeted that "CinemaScope is the new theater."[13] In other words, despite the initial emphasis on the spectacular, monumental aspect of CinemaScope, the technology was also consonant, as Charles G. Clarke outlined in "The Techniques of CinemaScope Pictures," with the intimacy and choreography of the stage.[14] *Black Widow*—"the first crime-of-passion story in CinemaScope," as the Australian day bill heralds—is one such intimate drama, a DeLuxe *All About Eve* (1950) featuring not so much "snakes and funerals" as wasps and black widows.

In addition to waxing poetic about the "pictorial values" of CinemaScope,[15] Zanuck fervently believed that color and CinemaScope went hand in hand. It's a truism of classical Hollywood cinema that the most vibrant colors tend to be carried by the principals, in particular the female stars, and *Black Widow* bears this out. In the first, post-title sequence, set at an airport, Peter's saying good-bye to his wife, who's flying off to see her ailing mother. Attired in ivory-white, Iris looks like the solicitous nurse she's about to become. Even more striking, if one happens to have *Leave Her to Heaven* in mind, is Gene Tierney's appearance. Is this the same woman in white who ravished the gaze of Richard Harland (Cornel Wilde) at the beginning of John Stahl's film? Iris does not appear to be a black widow, but, then again, as in Bob Rafelson's 1987 neo-noir of the same name starring Theresa Russell and Debra Winger, masquerade is the name of the game.

Clothes are inseparable from female masquerade, and Travilla, whose costuming is relatively subdued in such noirs as *Nora Prentiss, Panic in the Streets*, and *Pickup on South Street* but who's most famous for designing Marilyn Monroe's "simple halter-front, écru-colored summer dress with the sunburst pleats" in *The Seven Year Itch* (1955),[16] is decidedly more extravagant in *Black Widow*. Thus, when we first meet Nancy on the balcony of Lottie's apartment, she's dressed demurely in blue and seems every bit the schoolgirl in pigtails from Savannah, Georgia, that her uncle, Gordon Ling (Otto Kruger), fondly remembers her as. Even after the film flashes back to when she first arrives at her actor uncle's flat in Greenwich Village (three months before the party at Lottie's, as Peter relates in voice-over), she appears—with her white gloves, tightly curled blonde hair, and plain, white-collar, slate-blue dress—less like a black widow than an understudy for a production of Peter Pan. The only unusual thing about her outfit, coloristically speaking, is her black hat, topped as it is by a red ball.

The red and black combination dramatically reappears after Nancy has moved up in the world (she's now living on Tenth Avenue and West Twenty-Fourth Street). Exiting an afternoon performance of Peter's production "Star Rising," she goes around to the stage entrance to ask after her uncle. When she learns he's not there, she's joined on the street by Lottie's husband, Brian Mullen (Reginald Gardiner). Although Nancy's ensemble—pearls, white gloves, and a black print dress with a wide white collar—is slightly more sophisticated than when we're first introduced to her, the key to her character is her red hat, which is trimmed in snow white and harmonizes with the red print on the white poster prominently displayed in the reverse two-shot:

Peter Denver
Presents
CARLOTTA MARIN
"STAR RISING"

If it's clear that Lottie is the star, the mise-en-scène suggests that Nancy's star is rising and that the two women are sisters, *blood* sisters.

The film's subsequent transition to the present tense—"Let me now pick up the story of my friendship with Nancy," Peter confides in voice-over—punctuates our next spectacular vision of Nancy, who has called him (he has since become her patron) with the news that she has sold her first short story, which is not so much like Maugham or Capote, as he guesses, as "pure Damon Runyon." With the receiver in one hand and a cigarette in the other, her head resting against a blood-red pillow, Nancy's laid out like an odalisque on a green, floral-patterned divan. The real "killer," though, is her ensemble: if the candy-striped top hints that she's no nightingale like Iris, her baby-pink short shorts display her shapely,

Odalisque: Nancy "Nanny" Ordway (Peggy Ann Garner) lolling like Lolita in her Greenwich Village apartment in *Black Widow*.

widescreen-elongated legs and sandaled feet. A DeLuxe confection, she's a clothed *maja*. The orientalist motif is mirrored in the décor of the principals' apartments, most notably the hieratic female Asian figure in Lottie's living room. (The meticulous sets were designed by Lyle Wheeler and Maurice Ransford and decorated by Dorcy Howard and Walter M. Scott.)

A panoramic shot of New York City—note the blinking red Essex sign atop the tallest building—is prelude to a match shot of Nancy in a white-starred black gown propped up in the powder-blue-pillowed corner of the Denvers' couch, the city majestically framed in the enormous picture window behind her, a match shot that captures Nancy's sudden ascent from the Village to the Upper East Side. Not so incidentally, her recumbent position on the Denvers' couch, whose horizontality underlines both the picture window and the CinemaScope screen, signifies that she has symbolically displaced Iris as the mistress of the house.

As a tuxedoed Peter sits off to one side, the "Dance of the Seven Veils" from Richard Strauss's *Salome* plays on the phonograph. "The secret of love is greater than the secret of death," Nancy declaims, hastening to add that with such mood music—together with, of course, the sort of magnificent view Peter's room affords—she might one day reach the stars. (Virginia Woolf is spinning in her grave.) An "oriental princess" (in Strauss's words) and "everyone's favorite fin de siècle dragon lady" à la Carmen and Lulu, the figure of Salome links Nancy with neurosis—in particular, hysteria—and nymphomania.[17] In the world of classical Hollywood cinema, her "deadlier than the male" persona ranges from Theda Bara, the "Vamp of Vamps," who played the title role in Fox's 1918 *Salome*, to Rita Hayworth in Columbia's 1953 version of the biblical story.[18] As for classic noir, there's also Norma Desmond (Gloria Swanson) in *Sunset Blvd.* (1950), who, with the assistance of her young male amanuensis, Joe Gillis (William Holden), seeks to resurrect her career on the Big Screen by rewriting Salome's tale, with herself, however ludicrously, in the title role.[19]

Strauss's *Salome* is in fact the musical bridge to the film noir nested within the drawing-room mystery of *Black Widow*. Like the wealthy social-register sister and brother, the Amberlys, before him (who graciously invite Nancy to live with them), Peter allows her to use his apartment. However, when the Denvers return from the airport, they enter their darkened apartment to the ominous strains of Strauss. While Peter turns off the record player, muttering under his breath, "She's a nut about that piece," Iris proceeds to the master bedroom, where she discovers Nancy hanging from a rope, her body silhouetted against the blue window light and bisected by vertical and horizontal bars of shadow.

Nancy appears to have committed suicide, but when the police rule the death a homicide (it turns out that she was pregnant), it initiates a dual investigation—led separately by Peter and the detective assigned to the case, Lieutenant Bruce (George Raft)—that retroactively motivates the opening voice-over flashbacks.

Since Peter is also the main suspect, he's determined to the point of violence to clear his name. After putting Claire Amberly (Virginia Leith) in a stranglehold in a vain attempt to wring the truth out of her, he checks out a joint named Sylvia's, where Nancy previously worked as a waitress, and then, once he discovers it's closed, the bar and grill where Sylvia's former hat-check girl, Anne (Hilda Simms), is now employed. It's midday outside, but inside, except for the violet and aquamarine ceiling light, the bar is dark as night, as is Peter's demeanor: "The girl's got me in a box, and apparently no one's gonna help me out of it but myself."

There's down-tempo jazz on the jukebox and, as in a Hopper painting, people sit isolated at the bar and at the red-and-white banquettes. Anne, a pretty, light-skinned black woman, is Peter's Virgil, helping him escape his infernal Houdini box and setting him straight about Nancy, whom she calls a "purpose girl": "Girls like that don't kill themselves; they're too busy for that." Anne recalls that when Humphrey Bogart visited Sylvia's, Nancy gave her "two bucks" so that she could be the one to help him put on his coat. Unlike Mildred Atkinson (Martha Stewart) in *In a Lonely Place* (1950), who ends up dead after a brief flirtation with Bogart's character, Dix Steele, Nancy is wise beyond her years.

Anne also recalls that Nancy was living at the time with her uncle, so Peter makes a call on Gordon Ling, and after interrogating him, becomes convinced that Lottie's husband, Brian, was involved with Nancy and may even have murdered her. Though Peter thinks he has solved the mystery of Nancy's death, color, costuming, and CinemaScope—at least in this particular melodrama—ultimately provide the best clues. For example, the last time that we see Nancy alive—at the Denvers' apartment—she's dressed in a blouse and poodle skirt, and despite the fact that she has just moved in, already looks as if she lived there. When, in the following sequence, Peter and Iris return home, a sheer white curtain adorns the picture window and Nancy's hanging body is, as it were, offscreen. More to the point, in the postmortem sequence set in the Denvers' spacious living room, which is the size of a Broadway stage (and which makes good on Fox's pledge—to cite a trade ad for *How to Marry a Millionaire*—that the "Anamorphic Lens engulfs you in the gay world of Manhattan penthouses and skyscrapers!"), Iris is curled up on the far left side of the couch, Peter and Sergeant Welch (Harry Carter) are standing to her left, and Detective Bruce is standing to the right. While Iris has returned to her rightful place as the mistress of the house, the fact that she's sitting (vertical) rather than recumbent (horizontal) draws the viewer's attention to the empty space at the center of the screen. In other words, Nancy's death can be said to have emptied out or decentered the composition. The implication is that there's something amiss with the Denvers' marriage, a situation that's borne out when Iris, wearing a turquoise housedress and sitting on the couch perpendicular

Widescreen "Whodunit": "Clothesline" composition in *Black Widow* with, from left to right, Det. Lt. C. A. Bruce (George Raft), Peter Denver (Van Heflin), Iris Denver (Gene Tierney), and Sergeant Welch (Harry Carter).

to the picture window, reads a letter from Nancy in which "Little Miss Muffet" names Peter as her lover. In other words, Nancy, in death, has literally displaced Iris, so much so that the marital scene ends with Iris telling Peter, "I can't stay here any longer" as she's leaving for the bedroom to pack.

Color and costuming are equally revelatory. When Lottie interrupts Lieutenant Bruce's postmortem interrogation of Peter, a policeman bars her entrance, but Lottie, wearing long black gloves and a matching black hat with half veil, dismisses the officer as if he were one of her black servants: "Will you please stop this silly imitation of *Dragnet* and let me in." The fact that Peter later sardonically refers to his own investigative efforts as "slumming around town like a TV detective" suggests just how déclassé TV was considered in the mid-1950s vis-à-vis "the Theatre" (as it's referred to in Quentin's novel) or, for that matter, "the cinema." The irony, of course, is that the mystery mechanics of *Black Widow* predate the hard-boiled American detective fiction of Cain, Hammett, and Chandler that inspired classic noir and that put a dagger though the heart of the drawing-room whodunit.

The penultimate sequence of *Black Widow* revives the latter genre, assembling all the major players—Peter, Iris, Lottie, Brian, Lieutenant Bruce, and Sergeant Welch—in Lottie's apartment, where the lieutenant plays his trump card: a tape recording in which Brian explains to Peter how there was no way he could have killed Nancy. (Sergeant Welch bugged the place.) As Lottie rushes to her husband's defense, the film flashes back to her listening outside the door to the Denvers' apartment, where Peter can be heard inside murdering Nancy: "Let me go, Peter! . . . Help, police!" Color and costuming, however, point directly to Lottie as the culprit. Unable to bear seeing her husband taking the brunt of Lieutenant Bruce's interrogation, Lottie stands defenseless, the long black gloves that she's wringing in her hands a perfect match for the white kerchief that Nancy wears around her neck like a noose in the final, true flashback.

The mise-en-scène and widescreen format also point to Lottie. Although chinoiserie can be glimpsed in Peter's office and the Denvers' apartment, the female Asian figure in Lottie's living room is the most conspicuous objet d'art and tropes not only the discourse of femininity but oriental inscrutability, where it's not so much about what women want (love, money, social status) as which one wants it desperately enough to kill. In the flashback sequence in which Lottie overhears Nancy's conversation with Brian (Nancy tells Brian that she plans to use her pregnancy to blackmail Peter to the tune of fifty thousand dollars), Lottie's standing to the right of the hieratic female figure. This Asiatic totem can also be seen in the background of the frame right before Lieutenant Bruce traverses the space between Lottie and him to hand her a drawing of a hanging body with the inscription "The Secret of Love Is Greater Than the Secret of Death," a drawing that Lottie previously forged to implicate Nancy. *Touché.*

If in the penultimate scene of *Black Widow,* set in Lottie's apartment, the grand dame assumes—true to her big Broadway persona—center stage, in the final scene of the film Iris and Peter are sitting together on the main couch in their living room while Lieutenant Bruce stands, Manhattan in hand, to the right. Despite the fact that the spider-woman has been exorcized and the real perpetrator arrested, Peter wryly observes that he can't wait to see Lottie, "one of the greatest dramatic actresses in this country," on the witness stand. As the principals silently contemplate this scenario, the camera rises and the picture window, sans curtain, fills the screen, the Manhattan skyline visible in all of its CinemaScopic magnificence.

In Quentin's novel, Peter Denver describes Nanny as "an unobtrusive little spider, spinning delicate, devious webs, crouching in dark corners . . . only to spring down the threads at her victims."[20] Nancy is what the narrator calls the "Nanny-spider" because she threatens to destroy the real father of her baby, Brian, "the helpless male spider, destined, in true arachnid fashion, to be devoured by its mate."[21] However, since Nancy does not "devour" either Peter or Brian, the title of *Black Widow* is, in the final analysis, something of a red herring. The real vamp of the film is not the *jeune première* but the prima donna Lottie, who is not so much a black widow as Nancy's arch-enemy, the wasp, who kills because love for her is a form of violent possession.

While classic noir is full of violently possessive men such as Alan Garroway (Robert Taylor) in *Undercurrent* (1946), in *Black Widow* Lottie—played against type by Ginger Rogers, reprising her role as the aging diva Beatrice Page in *Forever Female* (1953) and anticipating her turn as the hard-bitten moll Sherry Conley in *Tight Spot* (1955)—recalls noir's great scorned women such as Ellen Berent in *Leave Her to Heaven* and Louise Howell Graham (Joan Crawford) in *Possessed* (1947). Right before Lottie's taken away by the police, she rushes out to the terrace to make one final, desperate plea for her husband's love. Her once starry career in ruins, Carlotta Marin is sister here to Norma Desmond in *Sunset Blvd.*, just as the neurotic, Salome-obsessed Nancy echoes Madeleine's alter ego, "mad" Carlotta, in Hitchcock's *Vertigo*, another color noir about the twin secrets of romance and death.

HOUSE OF BAMBOO: "KIMONO GIRL" (RED), GAIJIN GANGSTER-DETECTIVE (BLACK)

Although the screenplay for *House of Bamboo* is credited to Harry Kleiner, the scenarist of the neorealist Fox noir *The Street with No Name* on which the former film is based, Samuel Fuller transformed the story by transposing it to postwar Japan. Fuller himself has talked about the "exploitation" elements of his script,[22] which become particularly pointed in the case of *House of Bamboo,* since the American occupation of Japan "had never before been presented" as a form of criminal exploitation.[23]

This subversive presentation is perspicuous in the opening pre-credit sequence of *House of Bamboo* when a gang of American ex-servicemen led by Sandy Dawson (Robert Ryan) raids a munitions train. Ironically, while this sequence maximizes the CinemaScope format (the train moving from right to left reaccentuates the horizontality of the screen) and gestures, via the iconic image of Mt. Fuji in the distance, to the depth of field associated with post-Wellesian classical Hollywood cinema,[24] it does not exploit the bright, primary-hued DeLuxe palette that's brilliantly in evidence throughout the remainder of the film. Instead, Fuller and director of cinematography Joe MacDonald (who also photographed *The Street with No Name*) index the monochromatic tonality of classic '40s noir, juxtaposing a "*black* train" with "white against white against white."[25]

Since an American soldier has been killed in the raid, the U.S. Army sends Eddie Kenner, aka Eddie Spanier (Robert Stack), to investigate Dawson's operation and to ingratiate himself with Mariko (Shirley Yamaguchi), a "kimono girl" who was formerly married to a member of Sandy's outfit before he was wounded in a heist and executed by another member of the crew. Arriving in Tokyo dressed like a prototypical private detective in fedora and trench coat (Dawson later sarcastically asks him, "What museum did you crawl out of?"), Eddie tracks down Mariko to a bathhouse and then to her domicile in the "ant city" located on the Sumida River—a search milked, as in the opening sequence, for all its CinemaScopic value—where he tells her that he's an old friend of her deceased husband, Webber (Biff Elliot of *I, the Jury*).

As with the play of the picture window in *Black Widow*, *House of Bamboo* mobilizes bamboo screens to double the CinemaScope frame. Fuller in fact plays on the supposed flatness of the widescreen format in a sequence early in the film where Eddie is trying to get Sandy's attention. Eddie's in the process of hitting up another pachinko parlor for "protection money"—the parlors are a front, we later learn from Detective Hanson (Brad Dexter), for Dawson's gambling interests—when Griff (Cameron Mitchell) knocks him through the rear bamboo-screen wall of the parlor into a back room where Sandy and his men are waiting.

The above, self-reflexive flourish is typical of Fuller's style in *House of Bamboo*. In an interview, Fuller recounted about making the film: "Personally, the thrill I got out of making *House of Bamboo* was shooting in Japan . . . and working counter to stereotypes. In terms of style I wanted the wide-screen and the color. I loathe this cliché vision of the underworld. Dark alleys *and* wet streets. I've done it. Everybody's done it."[26] Although Fuller's interest in color and widescreen is obvious in the exterior location sequences, the most expressive, sustained deployment of DeLuxe color in *House of Bamboo* is reserved for the interior, studio-shot scenes in the titular "house of bamboo" where Eddie's staying and where he and Mariko negotiate the terms of their relationship. In these scenes, Fuller marries widescreen and tatami shots, CinemaScope and interior design, classical Hollywood cinema and traditional Japanese architecture. It's nighttime, and as Eddie lies smoking reflectively on top of a blue *kakebuton*, his face half in light, half in shadow, Mariko appears in the same white kimono and multicolored obi that she was wearing in the previous scene when, in Eddie's presence, Sandy brutally interrogated her about her relationship with him. Eddie asks Mariko to be his kimono girl as a cover—"Stay here with me"—but she's fearful, as Sandy has already intuited, about losing "face playing around with a foreigner," or gaijin. After Eddie says, "Forget it," and lies down, turning away from her, Mariko starts to leave, then closes the blue shoji screen door and, taking out a matching blue futon, lowers a bamboo screen between them.

The next morning, Mariko, dressed now in a black-accented, pink-and-white kimono, brings Eddie tea while he readies himself for a bath in the steaming-hot tub that she has prepared for him. Self-conscious about his nakedness (and echo-

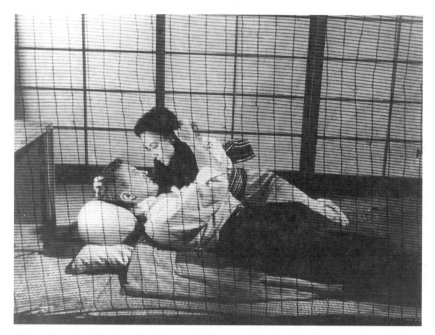

Gangster/Kimono Girl: Kenner aka Eddie Spanier (Robert Stack) and Mariko (Shirley Yamaguchi) beyond the bamboo curtain in *House of Bamboo*.

ing Mariko's actions of the previous night), Eddie sets up a screen and closes a shoji door. In this scene, Eddie's body rather than Mariko's is the object of the gaze, a reversal of the gendered specular conventions of classical Hollywood cinema that foreshadows Sandy's later execution of Griff later as his *ichiban* is bathing.[27]

That night, Mariko, having been shamed while shopping on the waterfront, sits before Eddie separated by a bamboo screen and confesses that she "can't go through with it" ("Living with you here, like this, brings dishonor"), the curve of her red kimono—the same color as the scarlet one she wore earlier in the day—in "sharp contrast against the blue squares of the room's rear wall."[28] When the camera pulls back for a wider shot, Eddie's staring into space, lying as before on a blue futon, the top part of his body dressed in black, the remainder, like the rear shoji screen, in blue. The camera holds on this painterly tableau until Mariko, throwing open the screen door and rapidly raising the *sudare* screen, orders Eddie, "Hold me, hold me, quick!" The abrupt change in her behavior is explained when Griff suddenly appears in the doorway with the message that Sandy wants to see him, then leers, "I'm in no hurry—go ahead, kiss her again," a remark that emphasizes the shameful nature of Eddie and Mariko's interracial relationship as well as our complicity in Griff's blatant voyeurism.

In the ensuing robbery of the cashier's office at a gravel-and-cement works, the set decoration in the form of red tanks, trucks, oil cans, and Japanese characters dynamically counters the muted, black-and-white visual scheme. Pictorially speaking, the most dynamic passage (one referenced in, among other films, Quentin Tarantino's *Reservoir Dogs* [1992]) is a rapidly tracking lateral shot of Sandy's crew, dressed in identical dark suits and fedoras, running from left to right past a series of white warehouses marked with black numerals and red Japanese characters. (The sound of the running men is audibly marked on the sound track.) Narratively speaking, the pivotal moment occurs when a guard fires and Eddie, outfitted in a black hat and Navy peacoat, is hit in the leg and stumbles to the ground. Although Dawson's code of conduct—in direct opposition to that of the U.S. armed services—is to execute the wounded (we've just seen Griff finish off yet another member of the crew), Sandy, countermanding his own order, stops him from shooting Eddie.

The color scheme of the cement-works heist is carried over to the later scenes at Dawson's house. In the first sequence, Sandy wonders out loud to the assembled members of his crew, "Somebody tell me why I saved Eddie. . . . You're not my brother." While Sandy's dressed in a brown suit and tie and Eddie's in a white shirt and black *montsuki* with a white *mon* or crest, Mariko's costumed in a matching black kimono with a red and gold obi. The striking sartorial difference between the two men suggests that whereas Sandy's Japanese trappings—like his house—are a façade, Eddie, as a result of Mariko's influence, is becoming genuinely attuned to Japanese culture. This transformation is borne out when Eddie and Mariko retreat to an expansive, brightly lit room in Sandy's house where, realizing that it's time to reveal his true identity, Eddie sits down on an elevated cot next to a rose-colored screen and confesses, "I'm not Eddie Spanier. . . . I'm a sergeant in the U.S. Army."

Band à part: Sandy Dawson's (Robert Ryan) band on the run in the gravel-and-cement-works heist sequence in *House of Bamboo*.

If Eddie's use of Mariko has turned into something other than "sexual exploitation,"[29] his increasingly intimate relationship with Sandy begins to assume a more complicated, volatile cast. The fractious relations that have developed between Griff and Sandy come to a head at a celebratory, post-heist party in which Eddie, dressed like Sandy in a blue kimono, is seated next to him, while Griff's relegated to a position beside Mariko. The fireworks begin when the traditionally dressed Japanese women performing a traditional fan dance to traditional Japanese music strip off their clothes to reveal contemporary Western clothes, then begin wildly jitterbugging, complete with aerials, to hot swing music. An obviously drunk Griff asks Mariko to dance, but after scuffling with Eddie and being scolded by Sandy, exclaims, "I don't like being shoved out of my number one position!"

Eddie and Mariko retreat again, this time to a gazebo with a view of Mt. Fuji in the background, where Sandy previously explained to Eddie how he organized his outfit—"all ex-cons before they were drafted, all stockade hounds in the Army dishonorably discharged"—and where Eddie now asks Mariko to explain why one of the kimono girls at the party, mirroring Griff's breach of protocol, bared her neck with a pair of chopsticks. (In the old days, according to Mariko, "it was traditional for a refined Japanese woman to keep the back of her neck covered because it was the first thing that a man found attractive.") The key to the scene is a visual pun, Eddie's neckwear, a red tie that connects him to both Mariko and Sandy. In other words, Eddie is an American military "detective" pretending to be a Tokyo gangster living with a kimono girl; at the same time, he's simultaneously in love with Mariko and the object of Sandy's growing affections, what Fuller, talking about the relationship between Sandy and Eddie, calls the "love between men."[30]

Eddie's red tie also supplies the chromatic segue to the next scene, which is set in the same room where Eddie revealed his double identity to Mariko, although the intimate ambience and Mariko's bright crimson kimono recontextualize the relations between Eddie and her established in his bamboo shack. In the foreground, Eddie lies face down on the bedding, his naked neck and shoulders set off by his black and white kimono; in the middle ground and slightly off center, Mariko massages his neck, her jet-black hair and brilliant red lipstick echoing his kimono and the knotted red drawstring to her right; in the rear, a shoji screen casts its midnight-blue light.

A straight cut to the same shoji screen, now light blue, marks the sudden passage of time—it's dawn and the day of the next big heist. Eddie asks Mariko how to say good-bye in Japanese, and after he parrots her sayonara, she lowers the sudare blind as the camera pulls back and to the left for an elevated master shot. The concluding shot/reverse shot—in matching, medium close-ups—reflects the reciprocity of their gaze and all but renders the screen invisible,[31] preserving a certain sexual propriety even as it promises the eventual consummation of the couple's still forbidden romance.

In the final interior scene between Eddie and Mariko, the lighting is high-key and the bamboo screen is behind rather than between them. Dressed in a charcoal-black suit brightened by a red tie, Eddie's penning a note for Mariko to deliver to Captain Hanson, warning him about Sandy's plan to hold up a Bank of Tokyo bus. Eddie's plans go awry, though, when Sandy's mole in the police department, Ceram (Sandro Giglio), interrupts the progress of the red bus that Sandy's using as a control center and informs him that the Tokyo police have been tipped off.

Since we've previously seen Sandy dressing down Griff and publicly excluding him from the bank job because he's been "pitching too hard" and suffering from "battle fatigue," he instinctively suspects that his former ichiban is the snitch and, bursting through the front door of Griff's shack while he's bathing, empties his 9mm revolver into the tub. As the water shoots out of the bullet holes like blood, Sandy tenderly lifts Griff's slumped head and cradles it in his right hand like a baby's: "And I knew, Griff, I knew [it was you], when you started blowing your buttons for no reason whatsoever." In this scene, which intimates, via the logic of displacement, that the real object of Sandy's rage is not Griff but Eddie, the blanched color scheme throws Sandy's gray suit and black-banded fedora into sharp relief.

Later, after Ceram disabuses Sandy about who the "enemy agent behind enemy lines" really is (the latter's response—"I screened him"—is, given the extensive presence of screens in the film, richly suggestive), Sandy decides to get revenge by literally setting up Eddie to be killed by the police during the robbery of a pearl dealer. After Sandy warns the police about the heist and saps Eddie, he and Charlie (DeForest "Bones" Kelley) prop up Eddie's body in front of a screen. However, when the police arrive before Sandy and Charlie can escape, Charlie's shot as he's standing in front of the screen, and Eddie chases Sandy onto the roof of the Matsuma department store where, in an echo of the film's pre-credit sequence and accompanied by canned, amusement-park music, brightly clad children ride a toy train amid multicolored banners and balloons. (In one of the most inventive passages in the film, the camera dollies behind Sandy as he jogs down the tracks in front of the moving train.) Eventually, Sandy's forced onto the roof, where he shoots wildly into the crowd below until Eddie orders a Tokyo policeman to set a Saturn-shaped whirligig in motion. In an ironic echo of Sandy's execute-the-wounded policy, Eddie shoots and kills Sandy, then walks away from the scene as Sandy's lifeless body hangs over the rail of the slowly revolving globe.

House of Bamboo concludes with Eddie and Mariko walking hand in hand in an ornamental garden through which he originally shadowed her to her house on the Sumida River. Reflecting his true identity as Kenner, not Spanier, Eddie is decked out in his army dress uniform, while Mariko is wearing a blue kimono that recollects Eddie's costuming in the first part of the film as a "man in blue." But if Eddie's uniform represents the positive, lawful aspect of the American occupation of Japan, his character remains haunted by the black kimono and suit that's associated with his gangster persona. This noir-inflected color coding complicates the film's happy ending, as Ceram's retrospectively ironic remark suggests: "That's the kind of story I like to follow, where the Japanese police and the American Army co-operate." In a postwar, post-imperial world in which military cops masquerade as mobsters and criminal gangs are modeled on the U.S. military, the color black points to Eddie's status as a Judas figure. This is Fuller's final, perverse twist on the widescreen, DeLuxe gangster noir that is *House of Bamboo*: the success of Eddie and Mariko's romance and, by extension, American and Japanese law enforcement are predicated on the double cross of sexual exploitation—of, in a word, betrayal, *intimate* betrayal.

SLIGHTLY SCARLET: COLOR ME BAD

Although Nicholas Christopher in *Somewhere in the Night*, making reference to Sherlock Holmes, calls *Slightly Scarlet* a "study in scarlet," the film bears almost no relation to the classic private investigative narrative associated with Holmes.[32] What it does have, in addition to its ambiguous gangster-noir plot, is a particolored palette and enough sexual subtext to fuel a fire engine.

The plot is lifted from James M. Cain's *Love's Lovely Counterfeit* (1942), a novel that's almost as odd—compared to *The Postman Always Rings Twice* (1934) or *Double Indemnity* (1943)—as *Slightly Scarlet*: whereas the former novels are taut thrillers, *Love's Lovely Counterfeit* is positively dilatory, revolving around a chauffeur named Ben Grace who's conspiring to overthrow his big-op boss, Salvatore Gasparro, aka Sol Caspar. The agent of Ben's machinations is June Lyons, a personal assistant to mayoral reform candidate Frank Jansen, who has promised to smash the corrupt hookup in Lake City between the mob, law enforcement, and the current mayor.

At the beginning of *Love's Lovely Counterfeit*, Ben goes to the local RKO theater to kill time, taking in a "pleasant little item with Ginger Rogers." (This is not the Ginger Rogers of *Black Widow*, who's anything but "pleasant.") After Ben contrives with June to elect Jansen and flush Caspar to Mexico City, he sees her in a new light:

> The neat, school-teacherish blue silk had given way to a small black polka dot, with belt, bag, and shoes of coral alligator skin, hat of red straw, and stockings of powdery sheer that set off an exciting pair of legs. It all combined beautifully

with her dark, creamy good looks, and it seemed perhaps that she knew it. She came in with liquid hauteur, or at least the imitation of liquid hauteur; it might be recent, but it was not innocent.[33]

June appears to be the prototypical good-bad girl, but she's just an imitation. The real thing is her sister Dorothy.

In fact, June has agreed to collaborate with Ben only because she needs to make restitution to the "college authorities" from whom her little sister has stolen a not inconsiderable sum of money. When Ben and Dorothy first lay eyes on each other, they skirmish—Ben: "You're bad"/Dorothy: "I didn't speak to you"/Ben: "I said you're bad"—before he invites her up to his apartment: "Her eyes opened. She stared straight ahead of her, and for a long time she said nothing. Then she licked her lips. 'You're bad, too.'" Ben's riposte: "We're both bad."

In *Slightly Scarlet* June and Dorothy are played by Rhonda Fleming and Arlene Dahl, respectively. While Dahl's only other substantial noir role is as the supportive cop's wife in *Scene of the Crime* (1949), Fleming's most memorable performances in the genre are bad girls Meta Carson in *Out of the Past* and Nancy Morgan in *Cry Danger* (1951). In Cain's novel Dorothy makes a belated, if dramatic, entrance; in *Slightly Scarlet* she's introduced along with her sister at the very beginning of the film, perhaps—as Blake Lucas speculates—"as complementary redheaded visual objects."[34]

Lucas attributes the casting and matching hair color to the director Alan Dwan's "passion for symmetry," although the most singular aspect of *Slightly Scarlet* from a noir perspective is the film's director of photography, John Alton. It's worth comparing Alton's delirious cinematography in *Slightly Scarlet* with Clarke's classically tempered approach in *Black Widow*. Whereas Clarke was president of the American Society of Cinematographers (ASC) from 1948 to 1950 and from 1951 to 1953, Alton's Hollywood career might be characterized as a running battle with John Arnold, the cinematographic "policeman" at Metro and the first president of the ASC. Here, for example, is Clarke in *Professional Cinematography* on the employment of "cool tints" to convey unhappiness or loneliness: "Please observe that I have said *subtle tints*, for we would certainly not wish it apparent that we were using projected colored lighting casting colored shadows that would be theatrical, unreal, and artificial."[35] Compare this prescription with Alton's Academy Award–winning work on the ballet sequence in Vincente Minnelli's *An American in Paris* (1951) or, even more theatrically, Richard Brooks's *The Brothers Karamazov* (1958), in which "numerous scenes are lit in utterly unrealistic ways, with lighting sources remaining unjustified and odd colors . . . bouncing off ceilings or bathing the characters in back light."[36]

Slightly Scarlet is one of a series of RKO films—*Silver Lode* (1954), *Passion* (1954), *Cattle Queen of Montana* (1954), *Escape to Burma* (1955), *Pearl of the South*

Pacific (1955), and *Tennessee's Partner* (1955)—directed by Dwan, photographed by Alton, and designed by Van Nest Polglase that, despite having been made on extremely modest budgets, "are among the most richly colored and decorated of the period."[37] *Slightly Scarlet's* Technicolor title sequence makes good on these claims; it also punctuates—with, as it were, an exclamation point—the differ- ence between the gritty, black-and-white pictures that Alton made with Anthony Mann at Eagle Lion and the sort of Superscope, Technicolor features that RKO was producing by the mid-1950s.

Three shots. In the first, relatively monochromatic opening shot of *Slightly Scarlet*, a sign for the State Prison for Women is accompanied by a clanking sound. The camera dips as a guard opens a gate ("Good luck, sister") and a woman in a black suit saunters out, a black beret rakishly angled over her clipped red hair, her high heels clicking on the pavement like dice. After she pauses, she inhales the fresh air, then turns her head as the producer's name—Benedict Bogeaus—is splashed across the wide Superscope screen in vermilion-lipstick script. In the second, deep-focus shot, the woman in black stands waiting in the left back- ground, a hand on one hip, while in the right foreground, a redheaded woman in a cream-white vest and marigold blouse sits across the street in a parked con- vertible. In the third, wide-angle shot ("Starring John Payne"), a dark-haired man pulls up in a blue sedan. The sedan is pointed to the left as if the man's gazing at the second red-haired woman ("Rhonda Fleming"), but despite the fact that her car is pointed to the right, she's not looking at him nor is she aware of the woman standing in the distance behind her ("Arlene Dahl").

The final shot of the credit sequence concludes on a self-reflexive, cinemato- graphic note ("Directed by Alan Dwan"): the man opens his car door and, toss- ing a cigarette to the street, pulls out a camera with a telephoto lens. Every pic- ture here—carefully composed, of course, by Alton—tells a story: that the first woman, Dorothy Lyons (Arlene Dahl), is an ex-con; that the second woman, June (Rhonda Fleming), is so caught up in her own life that she remains oblivi- ous of her sister; and that the man, Ben Grace (John Payne), will somehow be intimately involved in the fortunes of these twin redheaded women. (One of the studio's racy taglines for the film was "rackets and red heads.")

In his entry on *Slightly Scarlet* in *Film Noir*, Lucas observes that Dwan's film con- firms that "Alton's imagination is as distinctive in color as it is in black and white."[38] Another "generic" way of putting this would be to say that Alton's black-and-white cinematography in *Slightly Scarlet* is as distinctive as his color photography. For instance, unlike the high-key, super-saturated exterior sequence that opens the film, the interior of Sol Caspar's (Ted de Corsia) house is lit like a funeral home, only darker. Although it's a brilliantly sunny day outside (we know this because we've just seen Ben cruise up the long, curved driveway to his house), the only

"Rifle Camera": Lobby card with Ben Grace (John Payne) scoping out June (Rhonda Fleming) and Dorothy Lyons (Arlene Dahl) in *Slightly Scarlet*.

light, it appears, is coming from the TV set that Sol and his associates are watching in the parlor. On the small screen, Norman B. Marlowe (Roy Gordon), the publisher of the *Bay City Journal*, is posed next to a campaign sign for Jansen; the word "ELECT" in red and the metallic frame of the TV in blue gleam in the general gloom of Caspar's house.

One could argue that the low-key lighting here is motivated by the fact that Caspar and his men are watching TV (the wide shots can also be said to mock the smallness of the "narrow screen"), but when Ben and his boss retire to Caspar's study, the light is almost equally sepulchral and Sol, unlike Ben, is lit like a "Valentine"—Jimmy Valentine, that is.[39] Alton frequently "photographs silhouetted or half-lit faces" and makes extensive use of backlighting and indirect light to create a sense of depth in darkened rooms,"[40] although in *Slightly Scarlet* he also revels in the "painterly," hyperrealistic compositions made possible by Technicolor and Superscope. Consider an early scene in *Slightly Scarlet* in which Ben makes a surprise visit to June's home in the suburbs. June opens the door and the camera cuts to Dorothy sunbathing on the veranda. Dwan would later complain that the Production Code prevented him from making the sort of adult-oriented film that he originally intended to make; still, Dwan and Alton are able to capture Dorothy's sexual perversity through a combination of color, costuming, and body language.

In the cutaway Dorothy's dolled up in a black low-cut jumpsuit and laid out on a chaise lounge like Nancy Ordway in *Black Widow*, and when she hears Ben's voice, she lightly touches the nape of her neck. June's dressed even more flamboyantly in a milk-white halter over lavender short shorts. Once Ben and June are ensconced in the living room (with Dorothy relegated to the background between Ben and June in the foreground), the Superscope composition, which belies the supposed incompatibility of widescreen and staging in depth, suggests both sibling rivalry and sexual triangulation. (The fact that Dorothy never stops moving in the wide shots—nervously rocking her leg, caressing the lounge's fabric—only contributes to the impression that she's trouble.)

In addition to the glories of Technicolor, chiaroscuro is invoked via audio flashback when Ben plays a tape recording for June. Right before the camera cuts to a tight shot of a white portable tape recorder encased in brown leather (novel technology circa 1956), Dorothy, intrigued, sits up in the background to listen. On the tape recording, Caspar's threatening Marlowe, who's crusading against the syndicate by supporting the mayoral candidacy of June's boss and paramour, Frank Jansen (Kent Taylor). Marlowe's about to leave the *Bay City Journal* building for the night when he's met at the elevator by Caspar's goons and dragged into an empty office where larger-than-life shadows dwarf the publisher as, slumped in a chair, he complains about feeling sick. June hears Marlowe being intimidated— "You're gonna stop backing Jansen, you're gonna stop printing all that stuff about me." However, she doesn't see, as we do, Caspar hitting the old man so hard that he expires. (In a viciously witty bit, Caspar gestures to the window and orders his men to give the publisher some air—"plenty of air.")

Since June doesn't know how Marlowe died and therefore isn't interested in what Ben's selling—"I don't like your brand, it's too cheap"—Ben, after being slapped for his temerity, produces the black-and-white photo of her and Dorothy embracing outside the state prison. The insinuation is that even if June won't use Ben's inside dope about Caspar to help Jansen, she has no choice when it comes to protecting her sister. When Dorothy appears at her side, June starts to show Ben to the door, but her sister takes his hand—"Please call me Dor, the frank and open Dor"—then fingers his jacket: "Hey, I love that material. I love the feel of it." "Your sister's a nice girl," Ben says, bidding adieu. Nice and naughty.

Despite June's initial reservations about Ben, she eventually agrees to his scheme and things go like clockwork: Caspar's forced to take a powder, Jansen's elected mayor, and Ben becomes the big operator in town. (In *Slightly Scarlet* the first event is conveyed via a striking silhouette shot of a public relations man informing Caspar, who's facing a grand-jury indictment, that his days in Bay City are numbered.) In no time at all, June's swooning in Ben's arms on the threshold to her house, while Dorothy is cooped up inside, imprisoned by triangular planes of gray and black shadow, drinking all by her lonesome self: she wants out and she wants Ben.

While the world of *Slightly Scarlet* is candy-colored, Dorothy is no wide-eyed innocent from Kansas; rather, she's a cross between Carmen Sternwood, the bad little sister to Vivian's good one in *The Big Sleep*, and classic noir kleptomaniacs like Nancy Blair in *The Locket* and Ann Sutton (Gene Tierney) in *Whirlpool* (1950). Ben first becomes acquainted with Dorothy's nymphomaniac side after he agrees to take her to her psychiatric appointment. Sitting curbside, he lights her cigarette, but when he asks for his lighter back (Dorothy has momentarily palmed it), she tries to burn one of his digits. "You crazy _____!" Ben ejaculates, leaving the audience to fill in the blank. Since Dorothy refuses to see her "head shrinker" (she wants to go "shopping," i.e., shoplifting, instead), Ben drives her out to Caspar's beach house, where he hopes to find the big man's cache. Dorothy's eyes light up when she sees the former roadhouse, the inside of which—amplified by the Superscope ratio—is as cavernous as the picture-puzzle room in Charles Foster Kane's Xanadu and decorated in every color under the rainbow. Ben tosses a demure bathing suit at Dorothy and sends her upstairs to change as he checks out the safe hidden behind a modern, Miró-like painting.

Although the safe turns out to be empty, Dorothy waltzes down the stairs carrying a spear gun and clad in a leopard-print bathing suit under her white terry-cloth robe. "Put that thing down," Ben orders her. Previously, Ben, presenting the evidence of Marlowe's murder to June, told her, "All I can do is to give you a gun. If you haven't got the guts to pull the trigger, I can't help you." Dorothy has guts to spare—"This little ole thing!"—pulling the trigger and almost spearing Ben in the heart. "You play rough," Ben says, alluding to Dorothy's earlier appraisal of him in the car. Dor: "I told you we were the same."

As in *Shack Out on 101*, which also features a spear gun, the Chekhovian principle is realized in the conclusion to *Slightly Scarlet* when Dorothy's caught shoplifting a pearl necklace from Hathaway's Department Store. However, before Ben can intercede on June's behalf with the chief of police, Dietz (Frank Gerstle), she arrives home to learn that Dorothy has already fled—"Goodbye Sister" is written not on the wind but in pink lipstick on the bedroom mirror—and Ben discovers from a teletype in Dietz's office that Caspar's already on his way back to Bay City.

Meanwhile, Dorothy has escaped to the big op's beach house, where Sol, fresh from Mexico, finds her lolling on the couch, one bare leg in the air, playing with a back-scratcher like Dixie Evans in *The Big Knife* (1955). Captivated by her bad-girl vibe (Dorothy has got the itch and he's just the man to scratch it), Caspar, having emptied out his war chest, tosses wads of bills on the oriental-carpeted floor, where she massages them with her bare feet. The magic really happens, though, when he catches Dorothy trying to snatch some of the money and, rather than chastising her—"If you want more, just ask for it. I don't mind"—invites her to fly down to Mexico with him: "upside down like bats and every which way."

Treating her like the spoiled child that she is, Caspar enlists Dorothy in a little game to pay back Ben for his betrayal, positioning her in front of the door as, gun drawn, he lies in wait. When June shows up instead and tries to take Dorothy home, Sol aims the gun at her: "Back up, smart girl." While June's forced into the shadows, Dorothy's sexually excited by the prospect of seeing her overbearing sister gunned down: "Are you really gonna give it to her?" Caspar slowly backs June out to the terrace and onto a chaise lounge, sneering, "Too bad you won't be around for the floor show," right before she spears him in the chest, then shoots him twice in the gut with his own gun for good measure.

Caspar appears to be good and dead, but when Ben finally shows up, he comes back blazing from the grave, exchanging fire with his former lieutenant, who, after being wounded, retreats to the second floor with the two women—June immediately puts her little sister, like a child, to bed—as Sol and his men commandeer the first floor. The deal that Ben strikes with his former boss is a raw one: Caspar will let June and Dorothy go if he gives himself up. Since Ben knows that the police are on the way (he has just called Dietz), he staggers out to the second-floor landing, where, his shadow towering behind him, he eggs Sol on: "Got me zeroed in and still can't do it yourself. Big man!" Although Caspar blasts away, Ben manages to stay on his feet long enough for the law to hear the last, ricocheting shot.

Slightly Scarlet completely reshuffles the psychosexual dynamics of *Love's Lovely Counterfeit*. In Cain's novel Dorothy shoots Caspar just as he's about to shoot Ben in his bathroom, and Ben himself is later shot by a policeman when he and Dorothy stop for a pack of cigarettes on their way to Canada. The finale, in which Ben and June are married by a buddy before he expires from the gunshot wound as Dorothy looks on, is also marked by a grave romanticism: "One of them [June], small and dark, sobbed jerkily. The other [Dorothy] staring unhearing into the night. For once her eyes did not dance, and for once she attained a great somber beauty."[41]

By contrast, *Slightly Scarlet* concludes when Ben, in an unexpected act of grace, sacrifices himself in order to save June and Dorothy. In the final shot of the film, "equal distances separate the three as they exit, with June presented as a figure caught in space between the man whom she loves and the sister whom she obsessively protects."[42] In fact, the final widescreen shot is slightly more complex. As Ben's body is wheeled away stage right, June looks back at Dorothy and Jansen huddled together on the landing before she pivots on her heel and walks toward the exit. Since June has previously mentioned their father's death in the context of her sister's waywardness—"I tried to look after you after Dad died"—the two-shot of Dorothy and Jansen suggests that both women have been returned to the patriarchal fold: June as Jansen's soon-to-be "good wife" and Dorothy safely settled in a rest home.

While this ending is obviously pat, it should not obscure the picture's visceral appeal, a retinal address that we're forcibly reminded of when the scarlet-lettered title flashes up on the screen for the last, lurid time. Here as elsewhere, Alton's cinematography has the same effect as Shamroy's in *Leave Her to Heaven*, "rendering the film less realistic so as to direct the audience's attention toward sexual and psychological aspects."[43] From this melo-noir angle, the film is not so much about Ben and Caspar (this is the gangster plot) as June and Dorothy. In other words, the two sisters are, like Ellen and Ruth Berent in *Leave Her to Heaven*, the film's real focal point, and the titular hero played by John Payne is a mere pawn or foil—a grace note.

Is it any surprise, then, that Arlene Dahl—"Dahl-face" or "Hollywood Dahl-ling"—was called the "girl for whom Technicolor was invented" or that Rhonda Fleming, the she-devil with the "lustrous auburn hair" and "gray-green eyes," was a "natural for color films"?[44] In Allen Dwan's over-the-top picture, June and Dorothy are camped-up, Russ Meyeresque "dolls" (the costuming is credited to Norma Koch and Arlene Dahl Creations) who exude sex as if they're constantly in heat:

> Both wear stunning outfits that highlight their busts, hips and long legs. They are in a constant state of décolletage, with slinky robes slit up to the hips, lacy bustiers, tight slacks or even tighter pepper-red short shorts over halter tops, gold pumps, and swishy silk pajamas. They have green eyes, almond shaped. The high planes of their cheeks are rouged. Bright crimson glistens on their mouths.[45]

Indeed, in *Slightly Scarlet* Fleming and Dahl resemble each other so much that it's almost impossible to tell them apart, as if they're cut from the same motley cloth—not unlike the twin sisters, one innocent, one murderous, in Robert Siodmak's study in black-and-white, *The Dark Mirror* (1946).

The difference between these two classic film noirs is that June and Dorothy, appearing as they do at the "dead center of the Eisenhower fifties" (rather than, as in *The Dark Mirror*, at the end of the Second World War[46]), embody—in hyperbolic, coloring-book form—the dominant culture's ambivalence about women. Despite being quartered in the suburbs, June and Dorothy—sexy, single, and childless—are anything but happy little homemakers. In this they're akin to the Red temptresses in anticommunist noirs who appear to be one thing, good like June, but turn out to be another, mad and bad and totally scarlet like Dorothy.

A KISS BEFORE DYING: PINK IS THE NEW BLACK

Like *Black Widow* and *Slightly Scarlet*, *A Kiss before Dying* is based on a literary property—Ira Levin's novel, which received a "certain kind of tabloid notoriety" when it first appeared in 1953: "a murdered young woman was found with a copy of the book in her hand, and a little while later Levin won the Edgar Allan Poe Award from the Mystery Writers of America."[47]

The title card for *A Kiss before Dying* is both mimetic and evocative: a pair of red lips floats to the right of the title, all of the letters of which are aquamarine except for the letter "K," which is orange or, more precisely, copper. Although Robert Ottoson contends that the "film's use of color and CinemaScope negates some of the sordidness of the story,"[48] the film actually represents a synthesis of '40s and '50s noir, one that anticipates neo-noir. Color as opposed to black-and-white film stock is one element of this new, synthetic look.

A Kiss before Dying, like *Leave Her to Heaven* and *Slightly Scarlet*, "is awash in oranges and reds."[49] The color red, the color of the lipsticked lips in the title sequence, is a key component of *Black Widow*, *House of Bamboo*, *Slightly Scarlet*, and *A Kiss before Dying*. As for orange, the classical noir precedent is *Leave Her to Heaven*. "The warm amber glow of *Leave Her to Heaven*," Lee Sanders and Meredith Brody write in their entry on the film for *Film Noir*, "occurs in many of the most prominent photographers of this pre-1954 Technicolor period," producing a "distinctive tone" that "can be as ominous as the grays and blacks of standard film noir."[50] Similarly, in *The Rough Guide to Film Noir* Ballinger and Graydon note that Shamroy's cinematography "saturates the frame with a sickly, amber patina which lends it the same degree of foreboding that is found in the black-and-white noirs of the period."[51] In other words, the orange or amber hue of *Leave Her to Heaven* not only chromatically reflects femme fatale Ellen Berent's (Gene Tierney) "sickness," her unhealthy romantic possessiveness, but insinuates that the natural beauty of Arizona and its red-desert landscapes is only a veneer. One thinks immediately of Tierney's classically beautiful face: "not content with restricting the application of an orange gel light to the backlight, Shamroy emblazons Tierney's face with an orange cross light, flagging off the top to keep her forehead in shadow."[52] One consequence of this "mannerist" lighting is that there are "two color temperatures on Tierney's face."[53]

The issue of temperature is critical to the chromatic economy of *A Kiss before Dying*. For instance, in the film's title sequence, the "cool" aquamarine letters—again, with the exception of the copper letter "K"—contrast with the red "hot" lips. The beginning of the narrative proper offers additional chromatic clues, the film cutting from the title sequence to a "cool," blue-tinted, diffuse-shadowed shot of a framed newspaper article that features a black-and-white photograph of Bud Corliss (Robert Wagner).

As a subdued version of Lionel Newman's bluesy theme plays on the sound track, the camera pans across a red-and-white "STODDARD" pennant imprinted with Venetian-blind shadows and then down past a typewriter and pack of cigarettes to a bed. Offscreen, a woman is softly crying. Dressed in a pink shirt and red skirt, Dorothy "Dorrie" Kingship (Joanne Woodward) is crying because she's pregnant and unmarried. With her "poodle" blonde hair and fair complexion, she could be a twin sister of femme fatale Nancy Ordway in *Black Widow*.

When Dorrie asks Bud, the young man in the white shirt sitting next to her on the bed, "What are we gonna do?" he offers her a drag of his cigarette before pledging his undying love: "I wanna marry you more than anything else in the world only...." Dorrie replies, "It doesn't matter." Bud, however, is quietly adamant: "He's your father.... What he thinks is important." While it's not clear why Bud cares so much about what Dorrie's father thinks, it's obvious from the framed high school article—the headline reads "Taft HS's Triple Threat/Best Dancer/Most Ambitious/Most Likely to Succeed"—that, unlike the red-jacketed Jim Stark (James Dean) in *Rebel without a Cause* (1955), Bud is no rebel, he's a go-getter.

Later, when Bud returns home, he tells his mother, who's busy ironing his shirts, that he doesn't want any dinner before he picks up a piece of mail and goes straight to his room. Mrs. Corliss—played by Mary Astor, the treacherous femme fatale to Bogart's private detective Sam Spade in *The Maltese Falcon*—is a redhead like June and Dorothy Lyons in *Slightly Scarlet*, and her skirt is copper, the same color as the convertible that Dorrie drove off in at the end of the previous sequence. (Bud and Dorrie stopped by a drugstore to purchase some pills for her upset stomach). Mrs. Corliss's skirt is also the same color as the pamphlet that Bud, once inside the sanctuary of his bedroom, eagerly slips from an envelope. In the novel Levin writes:

> [He] was reading *Rebecca* and pretending to love it because it was Dorothy's book [when] the pamphlets arrived. They proved wonderful—*Technical Information on Kingship Copper and Copper Alloys* and *Kingship Copper, Pioneer in Peace and War* ... and they were crammed with photographs: mines and furnaces, reversing mills, rolling mills, concentrators and converters, rod mills and tube mills. He read them a hundred times and knew every caption by heart. ... He returned to them at odd moments, a musing smile on his lips, like a woman with a love letter.[54]

When, in the film, Bud's mother brings him dinner as he's "musing," he hides the pamphlets, "whose supple covers gleamed with a copper finish,"[55] behind his back before blurting out, "Where am I? No place. I don't want to wind up like Dad with holes in my shoes." Mrs. Corliss, whose faith in her son knows no bounds, bucks him up: "You're not like him. Not at all. Anything you decide to do, you'll do it, I know."

What Bud decides to do, after unsuccessfully trying to induce a miscarriage by "accidentally" bumping into Dorrie and sending her tumbling down the bleachers at Stoddard Stadium, is poison her. First, sporting a dark-blue checked jacket (blue being Bud's default color in the first part of the film), he goes to the library and takes out a gold-embossed book bound in red leather—it's not *Rebecca*—then to the School of Pharmacy, where a brightly painted red sprinkler marks the entrance to the chemistry supply room. He's about to trail a female student into the room when the mise-en-scène pops again: two fire-engine-red valves to Bud's right and in the rear of the frame reflect the red book in his hand, *Toxicology: Poisons and Their Antidotes*. Levin provides the chromatic link: "Each bottle had a white label with black lettering. A few bore an additional label that glared POISON in red."[56] Here, the color red, which is initially associated with Dorrie, is transferred to Bud.

At the conclusion of the second bedroom scene, Bud's mother refers to her son as a "genius," and although Bud may not be Einstein, his plan is ingenious, as is director Gerd Oswald's staging of the first part of his scheme. The setting is a classroom and the professor is lecturing—there'll be a test!—about the philosophical antipodes of nineteenth-century American literature:

Theological	
Pessimism	Rationalism
Predestination	Free Will
Mather	Franklin

As the professor drones on about Jonathan Edwards ("a man trying to reconcile predestination with free will and not succeeding"), Bud, who's wearing a dark cardigan over a white shirt, passes a red-covered book to Dorothy, who's wearing, true to her patrimony, a copper-colored skirt. Bud may be predestined to become a failure like his father, but he's determined to make something of himself, even if it means killing off his pregnant girlfriend in order to ingratiate himself with his future father-in-law, Leo Kingship (George Macready).

Inside the book is a sheet of paper with a passage in Spanish that Bud wants Dorothy to translate: *Querido, Espero que me perdonares por la infelicidad que causaré. No hay ninguna otra cosa que puedo hacer.* After Dorothy unthinkingly translates the passage ("Darling, I hope you will forgive me for the unhappiness that I will cause. There is nothing else that I can do"), Bud deposits the enveloped note into a mailbox that stands next to a bright-red fire box. By the time Dorrie's sister Ellen receives the letter, Bud reasons, Dorrie will be dead from the poisoned "high-potency" vitamins that, thanks to a pharmacy friend, he has procured and that he'll have persuaded Dorrie to take for the health of their unborn baby.

In the meantime, Bud happily goes about the business of life. A meticulous dresser, he's in his bedroom getting ready for class when his mother brings him a glass of orange juice. He asks her to pick out a tie for him: "Hey, you know, I've got an idea. Why don't you quit work early tonight and we'll go out to dinner and catch an early show." Although his mother begs off—"Oh, you don't want to go out with me"—Bud gallantly insists: "You tell Mr. Muller that you want to leave early tonight, that you've got a date . . . with your son." (The oedipal subtext is plain as day.) Then Bud leaves for school, but not before looking in the mirror one more time and changing the tie that his mother just picked out for him.

Bud gets the shock of his life—the camera zooming in on his startled face—when Dorrie strolls into English class not only alive but lovely as ever in a lavender dress, an unusually cool color for her character, one that intimates that she may not be quite as passive or pliable as Bud thinks. Now it's Bud's fate that appears to be sealed, since it's too late to retrieve the suicide letter that he sent to Ellen. However, after he walks out of the post office and past the poster of a service-man and young woman walking happily arm in arm ("There's something about a soldier"), his eyes gravitate to the top of the Municipal Building, located kitty-corner across the street in downtown Lupton. Framed against a cloud-scalloped blue sky, it houses the marriage license bureau, and as the camera pans swiftly to the ground, Bud's prayers are answered. (This POV shot and the succeeding rooftop sequence eerily foreshadow both *Niagara* and *Vertigo*.)

Since the marriage bureau is conveniently closed when Bud brings Dorrie there at noon, he suggests they go up to the roof to kill some time before it opens again. While both Bud and Dorrie are wearing light-colored suits, Dorrie's also wearing an "old" green blouse, "new" white gloves, and a "borrowed" brown belt. "Look at that sky!" Bud exclaims, looking down at the wide expanse of red tile. Calculating that a body might get lodged there, he proceeds to maneuver Dor-rie to another part of the roof, ostensibly for a better view of the campus in the distance as the film cuts to a steep, vertiginously angled overhead shot. Bud: "Are you gonna write your sister or phone her?" Dorrie: "Oh, phone. Who can wait for letters? You'll like Ellen, you'll see." Bud: "I'm sure I will."

Standing with his back against the waist-high parapet, Bud shares a cigarette with Dorrie (this is his signature move), pressing her body close to him. When she confesses that she never actually took the "vitamin" pills that he gave her for the baby, Bud turns her around and sits her down on the parapet—"Don't look down"—their bodies silhouetted against a sky that's as limpid-blue as the background in the title sequence. "The thing is, you'll never really know how much I love you. No one can really understand the way the other loves," Bud

Push Comes to Shove: Italian *fotobusta* of Bud Corliss (Robert Wagner) pushing Dorothy Kingship (Joanne Woodward) off the roof of the Lupton Municipal Building in *A Kiss before Dying.*

reflects, then, after kissing her, pushes her off the ledge. Dorrie's purse sits on the suddenly empty parapet, a handkerchief—"something blue"—fluttering in the breeze.

Cut to Ellen lying facedown in the sun in a black, one-piece bathing suit next to an aquamarine-blue pool at her father's house in Tucson. Cut again to a long shot. In the background, framed by a red-brick wall, Ellen dives into the pool; in the foreground, Bill (Bill Walker), a black servant in a brilliant white jacket, is carrying a phone: "Miss Ellen, a Mr. Corliss is calling!" Birds chirp in the crystalline, sun-stunned air as Ellen, drying herself off with a citron-yellow towel, takes the receiver of the copper-colored phone from Bill: "Hello, Bud, you're coming here for Thanksgiving."

In this critical scene, the expressive use of DeLuxe color demonstrates the way '50s noirs like *A Kiss before Dying* subtly evince the genre in the process of reinventing it. For example, if the cool blue sky and pool in the first part of the scene recall the preceding murder sequence, Ellen's black bathing suit implies that she's still mourning her sister's death even as it recalls, since she's wearing a white bathing cap when she drives into the pool, the dominant black-and-white palette of classic noir. The second part of the scene has a slightly different tonality: while the warm yellow towel mirrors, like the sunshine, her happiness, the copper-colored telephone highlights her privileged status as a Kingship heiress and, more ominously, the trophy that she represents for Bud.

In Levin's novel, Bud refers to Ellen as the "girl detective," taunting her right before he shoots her: "No, you had to be the girl detective! Well, this is what happens to girl detectives!"[57] In Oswald's film the dive symbolically links the two Kingship sisters, although Ellen, unlike Dorrie, ultimately refuses to take the dive when push comes to shove. Instead, she actively pursues her sister's case, which has been ruled a suicide, when both the police and her father have long since given up. The turning point occurs when, after talking to Bud about a ballet date that night, she opens a package that Bill has just brought her. The camera slowly tracks in to a medium shot of Ellen as she sits in the right foreground in her black bathing suit, her back against a sunflower-yellow robe. In the left background, there's a red-and-white umbrella (an echo of Dorrie in the first sequence); in the left foreground, a phone sits on the table. Inside the package is a box that contains a brown leather belt and a note:

> Dear Ellen, you may recognize this as the belt of the suit that Dorothy wore last. We were sorority sisters and, on her last day just before she went out, she borrowed one of my belts. It was a cheap leather belt and we both knew it didn't go with her suit at all. Still, she wanted it and left this one in its place. I hope I was right waiting these many months before sending it. Sincerely, Annabel Koch

Having read the letter, Ellen immediately calls Bud and breaks her date with him in order to enlist the help of Dorrie's former tutor, Gordon Grant (Jeffrey Hunter), the nephew of the police chief entrusted with investigating her sister's death. The cotton dress that she decides to wear is pink, a "warm" color associated in the film with Dorrie and, more generally, conventional femininity. While Gordon's initially skeptical (he writes off Ellen's investigative impulse to an overactive imagination), he eventually accedes to her wishes and Ellen sets out on her own to meet one of Dorrie's former boyfriends, a DJ who works at KBRI, which happens to be located at the top of the Municipal Building.

The sequence, a remarkable demonstration of the electric affinity between DeLuxe CinemaScope and noir-affiliated techniques, begins with a straight cut from Ellen talking on the phone to a canted high-angle shot of her approaching the Esquire Club. It's late in the evening (the hands on a clock are clearly visible) and a burlesque number is playing in the background as light spills out of the club's open door onto the sidewalk. A red neon sign spelling "COCKTAIL LOUNGE" flashes on and off like a semaphore. In the ensuing high-angle shot, Ellen strides into a dark alley—she's dressed all in white except for her black purse—as the camera cranes up and out to the indigo-blue street, where a sedan pulls up, the film cutting on action to Ellen as she turns to listen. Footsteps ring out on the pavement. As she backs deeper into the alley, a woman bangs open a blind: "What are you doing out there, it's too late for you!" When a man suddenly appears at the other end of the alley, Ellen starts to run, but the man, who looks just like Bud in his dark-blue checked jacket, starts to run after her. Ellen, her face slashed with shadow, violently struggles with the man: "Don't touch me, let me go!"

Surprisingly, the man lets her go. His name is Dwight Powell (Robert Quarry), and as Ellen later discovers at a tiki bar called Pago Pago, he briefly dated Dorrie after meeting her in an English lit class. Since he also has the address of Dorrie's last boyfriend, Ellen agrees to return with him to his apartment building. There, as she patiently waits in the lobby, Bud—dressed to kill in a dark, blood-red sports jacket—makes short work of him, shooting the DJ point-blank in the head as he sits in front of a typewriter on which Bud has just typed another suicide note: "I've lived with Dorrie's killing on my conscience for far too long. Now that her sister suspects, I know there's no other way. Please forgive me for everything."

When the police later discover the note, the chief solemnly pronounces, "Case opened again, case closed again," then pays Ellen a backhanded compliment for her "police work": "You did it all, and if I had known you were doing it, I'd have stopped you." The chief's not-so-subtle message is that girls shouldn't try to be detectives, that—to quote James Brown—"it's a man's world," a sentiment that aligns the law not only with Ellen's callous father, whom the film indicates was responsible for his wife's death, but with the psychopathic Bud, whose masculinity is murderously utilitarian.

Although Ellen returns safely home in a chauffeured black limousine, the long cypress shadows on the gravel driveway outside her father's house suggest that the case is not quite closed yet. And sure enough, as soon as Ellen walks in the door, her father tells her that someone's waiting for her in the den and—cue the stinger on the sound track—it's Bud, dressed in an oyster-white sports jacket and sulfur-yellow shirt, smiling as if he just swallowed a canary. Although the character's costuming here may seem a little anomalous (the film's wardrobe is credited to Henry Helfman and Evelyn Carruth), it's entirely appropriate given Bud's deceptive, chameleon-like nature: just as the yellow shirt recalls Ellen's towel and bathrobe in the diving sequence (as well as, later, her lemon-yellow, off-the-shoulder engagement dress), so the light-colored sports jacket recollects the summer suit that he was wearing when he murdered Dorrie.

The following sequence, in which Bud and Ellen ride in long shot across a desert trail—one that underlines the scenic, lateral properties of the CinemaScope screen—directly quotes *Leave Her to Heaven* and, in particular, the celebrated passage in which another Ellen on horseback wildly strews her father's ashes across a landscape the color of dried blood. In *A Kiss before Dying*, though, it's not Ellen but Bud who's in love with her father or, at least, her father's money. In the muted ocher and umber landscape, it's also Bud, turned out in tight matching denim-blue pants and jacket, not Ellen, wearing a powder-blue checked shirt over khaki riding pants, who stands out. In this scene Bud's character exhibits the sort of arresting, color-accented costuming typically reserved for the female star. In fact, Bud reverts to form here, wearing the cool color that he's most associated with in the film: blue.

However, in the intervening time since the discovery of Dwight's body, Ellen has also changed perceptibly. She has not only finally reconciled herself to her sister's death but reached a rapprochement with her father. Bud inquires whether he had something to do with it—her happiness, that is—and she says "everything," attributing it to his "diabolic spell." Bud, whose mind never strays far from her father's mines, attributes it to something else: "Our relationship is a simple matter of chemistry. Like attracts like. It happens with minerals, it happens with people."

Prompting her assent, Bud offers Ellen a drag from his cigarette, but when she politely declines, he tosses it to the ground, reflecting, "No good if you really don't know what the other's thinking." The audience, remembering Bud's final words to Dorrie before he pushed her off the roof of the Municipal Building, has a pretty good idea what he's thinking. After Ellen jokingly alludes to Bud's dark past, he reluctantly admits to a "shameful, sinister secret": "I've never really been in love before." In the reverse shot, a tall cactus plant stands silent as a totem. Kiss, kiss. Fade to black.

In the concluding, climactic sequence of *A Kiss before Dying*, Ellen drives Bud out to her father's smelter in a white convertible whose red-trim interior is the same color as the lipstick in the film's title card. In this scene Bud's sporting his usual post-Dorrie look, a light-colored shirt and jacket, although in a sartorial twist that speaks volumes (since it's the first time in the film that Ellen reprises an outfit), she's dressed in the same pink cotton dress she donned when she decided to act on her suspicion that her sister's death was not in fact a suicide.

Admiring a fleet of trucks, Bud caresses a lamp guard, absolutely entranced by what he sees—"Two million dollars on wheels!"—then gazes longingly into an enormous pit, which he describes as the "center of creation," and it's as if he has been reborn. This is the moment he has dreamed about all his life—about to marry into the Kingship fortune, about to meet his fate like, as Levin writes, "a lover going to a long-awaited tryst."[58] However, when Bud reflexively corrects Ellen about how long her father's company has been mining the pit and she responds, "Darling, you sound like you knew the Kingship mine long before the Kingship girl," his masquerade begins to crumble. Leading him on (Bud claims that he never met Dorrie), Ellen mentions her sister's favorite composer, Debussy—"How were the concerts in Lupton?"—and Bud swallows the lure hook, line, and sinker: "Not bad for a town. . . ." Outed yet unapologetic—"Your father and I, we'll grieve"—Bud is trying to shove Ellen over the edge of the pit when a truck appears out of the blue, slamming into him and sending his body hurtling into the abyss.

In Levin's *A Kiss before Dying* Bud is even more avariciously cold-blooded than he is in the film. After he manages to knock off Dorrie and Ellen, he's working on the third sister, Marion (he thinks to himself, "Faith, Hope . . . and Charity") when Leo Kingship corners him high on a catwalk, from which he falls to his death into a vat of smoking copper:

> The scream, which had knifed through the sudden stillness of the smelter, ended in a vicious splash. From the other side of the vat, a sheet of green leaped up. Arcing, it sheared down to the floor where it splattered into a million pools of droplets. They hissed softly on the cement and slowly dawned from green to copper.[59]

Bud's spectacular dive recollects Dorrie's fall to her death from the top of the Municipal Building; it also comments on his obsession with wealth in the form of copper, the color of the penny, the color of money.

In both the novel and the film, Bud Corliss is a young man on the make and waspish women are his prey. Indeed, in his own perverse fashion, he's the optimistic, Franklinian embodiment of the Protestant work ethic, using his boyish, Prince Valiant good looks and the Puritans' whipping boy, sex, to push back against his humble, lower-class station in life, what the professor in the American lit class calls the "pain" of predestination. With his relentless social climbing, he's reminiscent of the multitalented, surreally self-composed protagonist of Patricia Highsmith's 1955 novel, *The Talented Mr. Ripley*.

But whereas Tom Ripley is a genuinely queer character, ambivalent about both men and women ("I can't make up my mind whether I like men or women, so I'm thinking of giving *both* up"), Bud's catnip for the opposite sex: a double or mirror image of the black widow, he's that rare noir type, a homme fatal.[60] Like the reborn Ripley (Matt Damon) in Anthony Minghella's 1999 adaptation of Highsmith's novel, he's also something of a clothes horse.[61] In *A Kiss before Dying* clothes make the man, and Bud's costuming—dark in the first part of the film, lighter after he kills Dorrie and begins to court Ellen—is a kind of disguise.

Woe to the woman who's the object of Bud's heart's desire, unless, of course, she's that equally rare type in '50s noir, a woman with a real nose for detection. Though pink has traditionally been associated with femininity—with the accent on the word *femme*—it's also a mixture of red and white, danger and purity. Ellen's pink cotton dress therefore marks the moment in *A Kiss before Dying* when she transitions from being a potential victim to a private eye.[62] In Levin's novel Ellen Kingship falls prey to the kiss of the spider-man and pays for it, like Dorrie, with her life. However, in Gerd Oswald's *noir en couleur*, it's the "girl detective" Ellen—pretty in pink, not black—who masters the man who would be king.

8

NIAGARA

COLORED MARILYNS

I've planned everything,
The church and the ring,
The one who doesn't know it yet
Is Marilyn.

She hasn't said "Yes"
I have to confess;
I haven't kissed, or even met
My Marilyn.

—Ray Anthony and His Orchestra, "Marilyn" (Jimmy Shirl
and Ervin M. Drake, 1952)

It's a wonderful world within these cinema walls
Where a shower of affection becomes Niagara Falls
And you wish she could step down from the screen to your
seat in the stalls.

—Elvis Costello and the Attractions, "The Invisible Man,"
Punch the Clock (Costello, 1983)

Although *Niagara* was released in 1953 and therefore appeared before *Black Widow*, *House of Bamboo*, *Slightly Scarlet*, and *A Kiss before Dying*, it is in many ways the definitive '50s color noir. One reason is that it was directed by Henry Hathaway, who had previously helmed *The House on 92nd Street*, *The Dark Corner*, *13 Rue Madeleine* (1947), *Kiss of Death* (1947), and *Call Northside 777*. Frequently described as a "company man" or "house director," the "consummate Hollywood professional" who "handled his material straightforwardly with few complications or pretensions,"[1] Hathaway is one of the most underrated figures in classic noir, and *Niagara*—his only '50s entry in the genre—is the key to a renewed appreciation of his work and its unique synthesis of "mystery narration" and "documentary realism."[2]

The other reason that *Niagara* may be the definitive '50s color noir is the photography of Joe MacDonald, who filmed *The Dark Corner* and *Call Northside 777* for Hathaway and *Pickup on South Street* and *House of Bamboo* for Samuel Fuller. MacDonald's Technicolor cinematography in *Niagara* is more rigorously expressive than John Alton's in *Slightly Scarlet* and presages his extraordinary widescreen location work in *House of Bamboo*. More generally, MacDonald's camera activates color, lighting, and composition to plumb the mysteries of the film's donnée: a marriage on the brink of destruction.

In his contemporary review of *Niagara* in *L'Observateur*, "Chutes de reins et autres Niagara," André Bazin observed that the film's dual cinematic attractions were the "famous Falls and Marilyn Monroe."[3] While the American and Canadian Falls, like Technicolor and CinemaScope, possess an undeniable retinal charge, Monroe introduces, as Bazin remarks, a "whole system" of "complex allusions and metaphors."[4] Bazin himself alludes to this system in the title of his review, which couples the falls and Monroe's character, Rose Loomis, in the punning figure of the "small of her back" (*chutes de reins*).

Bazin's anatomical figure alludes to the second sequence in *Niagara,* in which Rose's husband, George Loomis (Joseph Cotten), has returned from an early-morning sojourn to the American Falls. Rose, hearing him at the door to the cabin they've rented, crushes a cigarette in an ashtray and turns her back to the camera, pretending to be asleep. In "Curving into a Straight Line," Ann Reynolds remarks that in the subsequent reverse shot, Rose faces the camera, "her body extending almost the full width of the lower portion of the frame. The white bedsheets wrap and fall around her apparently naked body, accentuating her curvaceous horizontality."[5] A poster for *Niagara* exploits this figuration—"woman as landscape"—"representing Monroe's reclining body as a horizontal supplement to the lip of the Falls, its curves simultaneously sheathed and shaped by the rushing water that folds over and around them, mimicking the way in which the sheets wrap around her body in the film."[6]

The "curvaceous horizontality" of *Niagara*'s second sequence derives its visual force from the vertical thrust of the film's opening, which commences with a wide, deep-focus view of the American Falls in the left foreground and the Canadian Horseshoe Falls in the right background before the camera descends to a long shot of a man traversing the rocky, mist-obscured base. If the rainbow that arcs across the screen conjures a primeval, Edenic scenario even as it nods to the prismatic glories of Technicolor overseen by color consultant Leonard Doss (a key Technicolor advisor during the late 1940s and early 1950s), Loomis's gloomy voice-over dispels any such paradisal notions:

> Why should the Falls drag me down here at five o'clock in the morning—to show me how big they are and how small I am, to remind me they can get along without any help? Alright, so they've proved it. But why not? They've had ten thousand years to get independent. What's so wonderful about that? I suppose I could too, only it might take a little more time.

Loomis's voice-over is accompanied by an extremely low angle shot that underscores the immensity of the falls ("how big they are") compared to the speaker's smallness ("how small I am"). Although the sexual subtext is too obvious to require commentary, it's not readily apparent why the narrator desires to be as "independent" as the falls. What is apparent is that the narrator's reflections spring from some recess or deep place in his mind, as if he's not fully conscious of their import, as if—as in another of the insert shots—they're tumbling out of his psyche like the headlong, plunging waters of the falls themselves. Here, the landscape's "traumatic past" and "mentally destabilizing character"—death, suicide, and mental derangement—are sublimely invoked.[7]

The dissolve to a long shot of George walking aboveground, a rainbow refracted in a sprinkler's spray, suggests that he has finally cleared his mind, exorcized his demons. But the minor-key score and the debris on the deserted streets (George kicks some trash at one point) also suggest that what's troubling him will not evaporate like mist in the morning light. While it's not literally humid in *Niagara* as it is in, say, Lawrence Kasdan's *Body Heat* (1981), the whirring sound of the sprinklers gestures to the film's "all-pervasive humidity,"[8] epitomized for Bazin by the moisture of Rose's skin.

In fact, we see very little of Rose's body in our first, extended view of her, since the sheets of the twin bed she's lolling in cover her chest. ("She actually *was* naked," Maurice Zolotow recounts. "She told Hathaway that she couldn't project the mood unless she played [the scene] without any clothes."[9]) Instead, we see a stunning tableau of light and shadow, a painterly composition emblazoned by explosive accents of color: sunlight streaming through a window, Rose's milk-white skin, cherry-red lips, and platinum-blonde curls. This tableau, however, is no still life. When Rose glances at the lit cigarette in her outstretched hand, her legs are visibly moving under the sheets and her lips are moving as well, as if she's talking to herself, although it's impossible to know what she, as opposed to George, is thinking.

Still, you'd have to be blind not to be able to read the signs writ large in the Venetian-blind shadows slanting across the wood-paneled wall. This woman's another clothed *maja* like Nancy Ordway (Peggy Ann Garner) in *Black Widow*, but unlike her, she's the "incarnation of every male fantasy of available sex."[10]

Between the Sheets: Venetian-blind shot of Rose Loomis (Marilyn Monroe) alone and smoking in bed in Rainbow Cabin B in *Niagara*.

And there's the rub for George: what's a dream for every other man has become, for him, a nightmare. Accordingly, after he enters the cabin and sees Rose sound asleep, he lies down on his bed, rubbing his face and head with his hands. When Rose opens her eyes and sees her husband, she sniffs contemptuously and turns her back to him. Till death do us part.

COLORED MARILYN

The dissolve to a panoramic, bird's-eye view of the American and Canadian Falls as the camera pans to the Rainbow Bridge is the scenic segue to the arrival of Ray (Casey Adams) and Polly Cutler (Jean Peters) at Canadian customs. (Reviewers were quick to point out the travelogue aspects of *Niagara*; however, the carillon tower not only evokes the sound of wedding bells but initiates what will become a major sonic conceit.) The Cutlers have come to the falls for a "delayed honeymoon"—like the Loomises, this is the second time around for them—but when the customs officer at the bridge asks Ray what's in the trunk in the car's backseat, he answers "books" (he's reading "Winnie" Churchill), a response that puzzles the officer and embarrasses Polly.

The Cutlers are ostensibly the happily married, middle-class antithesis to low-brow, "trashy" tourists like George and Rose,[11] but Ray's gaffe is the first sign that their marriage is not without its own undercurrents. Another is when the Cutlers discover to their dismay that the cabin they've booked overlooking the falls is still occupied by the Loomises. (The lodgings are named, appropriately enough, the Rainbow Cabins.) The manager knocks repeatedly on the door of Cabin B (Rose is in the midst of pulling up a stocking), and when she appears—wrapped in a knee-length, rabbit fur-trimmed negligee cinched around her waist that emphasizes her hourglass figure—she explains that her husband just fell asleep after wandering around the falls in the middle of the night. She also mentions a hospital, and once the Cutlers are out of earshot, Ray whispers to Polly that it's an "army hospital—mostly psycho."

The issue of marital discord—comically broached with respect to the Cutlers, seriously with respect to the Loomises—is developed when Ray and Polly take a tunnel trip under the Horseshoe Falls. The men and women are color-coded—the men in black hats and raincoats, the women in bright crayon-yellow. Ray's standing on a balcony positioning his wife for a photo when she spies Rose passionately kissing a stranger. Since Polly is the only character in the film who witnesses Rose's infidelity, it's not insignificant that when we're first introduced to her, she's wearing a rose-colored sweater that visually allies her with Mrs. Loomis.

Unlike Polly, whose point of view is privileged, her husband's almost completely oblivious to the Loomises' problems, although he does gape when Rose, swiveling her hips, strolls past them in a light blue dress so form-fitting that she seems to have been born in it. (The costume designer is Dorothy Jeakins.) As performed by Monroe and accompanied by a comically sexy musical cue, Rose's wiggle is the epitome of cinematic spectacle, so much so that "on the surface *Niagara* may seem less like a film noir than a . . . showcase designed by 20th Century-Fox to exploit its contract star, Marilyn Monroe."[12] (The studio had signed her to a seven-year contract in 1950.) But if Rose's character is initially treated "as little more than a sexual object" in the first part of the film,[13] one of the twists is that, as in the above scene, she's the object of both the male *and* female gaze.

Monroe's status as sexual spectacle is supersized in the most famous sequence in *Niagara*, which is set at a *plein air* party outside the Rainbow Cabins and which capitalizes on the cinematographic surplus value of Technicolor. Framed statuesquely in the doorway of Cabin B, Rose first appears in a hot-pink dress. (This off-the-shoulder number, which is decorated with a bow as well as a below-the-breast cutout and zippered bodice, was supposed to read red—wardrobe test shots indicate—but in fact appears pink.[14])

Ray's sitting off to one side with Polly on the steps of the manager's office, but when he sees Rose he exclaims, "Get out the fire hose!" before asking his wife, who's wearing a white tea-length cotton dress and a white ribbon in her pulled-back hair, "Why don't you ever get a dress like that?" "Listen," Polly replies, "for a dress like that you gotta start laying plans when you're about thirteen." Rose then sashays across the width of the courtyard, a record in her hands, a white scarf across her shoulders. The view of Rose is from the Cutlers' perspective and differentiates Ray and Polly from both the "kids" dancing to the swing music and George, who is watching secretively from behind the partially closed blinds of Cabin B.

A phonograph table has been set up, and after Rose asks a young man to play the record, she begins to sing along: "This is the moment / Thrill me, thrill me / Take me in your arms / And make my life perfection / Take me, and don't forsake me / Kiss me, hold me tight." In this celebrated sequence (which inspired Andy Warhol's iconic series of "Colored Marilyns"), Rose, singing in a "smoky vibrato,"[15] is the classic noir temptress whose siren song is fatal, a woman who, according to the trailer, "sang of love just as she had lived for love, like Lorelei flaunting her charms as she lured men on and on to their eternal destruction. When a man took her loveliness in his arms, he took his life in his hands." (Lorelei Lee is the name of the "dumb blonde," "gold digger" character that Monroe would go on to play in Howard Hawks's *Gentlemen Prefer Blondes* [1953].)

Watching Rose croon her siren song, George storms out of the cabin and smashes the record with his hands. In the deafening silence that follows (the only, albeit distinct, sound on the stereo sound track is the distant roar of the falls), Rose is sitting on a stoop next to and positioned beneath the Cutlers, a composition that complicates our reading of her: if Rose is playing the record to antagonize George in front of, as it were, the whole world, the blocking also allies her with the Cutlers. This ambiguity raises the issue of the audience's identification with her character. On one hand, in his review of *Niagara* Bazin addresses what he calls the "femme fatale story" in which the "woman's sexuality provokes the man's destiny."[16] On the other hand, in their entry in *Film Noir*, Alain Silver and Meredith Brody assert that "there is no invocation in Monroe's performance of the stereotypical femme fatale."[17]

Any number of issues are at play in these differing, not to say contradictory, readings of Rose. Setting aside for the moment Monroe's persona and performance, it's significant that when Ray mentions to Rose that George doesn't appear to like music, she sarcastically replies that he'll "get right down if you give him a rocking chair and a corny old tune like 'In the Gloaming.'"[18] Rose's insult about George's musical tastes is the first explicit reference in the film to the substantial age difference between the two, and in *Niagara*, as in Billy Wilder's *Double Indemnity* and Orson Welles's *The Lady from Shanghai*, this difference is translated into sexual terms, the implication being that George is unable to physically satisfy his much younger wife.

This motif is repeated when Polly, not Rose, goes to Cabin B with Mercurochrome to treat George's hand—it's bleeding, as if Rose's provocation has in fact drawn blood—and the first thing he says is, "I suppose she sent you to find out if I cut it off. Well, tell her I didn't." The passage is rife with castratory imagery, as is the following passage:

> GEORGE: Parading around, showing herself off in that dress, cut down so low in front you can see her kneecaps.
> POLLY: It's a stunning dress.
> GEORGE: Would you wear it?
> POLLY: Well, I'm not the kneecap type. She's a pretty girl. Why hide it?
> GEORGE: Don't worry about that. She'd like to wear that dress where everybody can see her—right in the middle of Yankee Stadium. She's a tramp.

In *Niagara* Monroe plays a character "entirely at odds with the safe, sexy beauty with whom Fox and American audiences felt comfortable" and, in so doing, "confirmed the fears of a puritanical America that sex was perilous."[19] In other words, Rose functions in many ways as a screen onto which '50s audiences could project their fears and anxieties about (female) sexuality: you were either a virgin or a "tramp," good or a "kneecap" girl.

In retrospect, George's derogatory remarks about Rose have also acquired a specific, extra-diegetic resonance, since it's common knowledge that Monroe was involved at the time with Joe DiMaggio, the "Yankee Clipper." Despite being devoted to her, "Joltin' Joe," not unlike George Loomis vis-à-vis Rose, could not countenance Monroe's exhibitionistic tendencies. Perhaps the most notorious example of this exhibitionism was the publicity stunt that Monroe participated in for Billy Wilder's *The Seven Year Itch*, in which she posed for photographers over an open subway grate, her white dress billowing in the updraft and exposing her panties. (For a parodic instance, see, for example, the simulation in Jack Rabbit Slim's in Quentin Tarantino's *Pulp Fiction* [1994].) A classically conservative Italian American male, DiMaggio wanted Marilyn to stop being sexy, but, as one commentator has quipped, "one might as well have asked the waters of Niagara to stop falling."[20]

THE FALLS OF NO RETURN

The above history, however anecdotal, illustrates just how difficult it is to separate Monroe's star image from Rose's character, a slippage that's particularly apparent in *Niagara* not simply because Hathaway's film established Monroe as a star but because her persona assumes a different, emphatically more comic inflection in her next film, *Gentlemen Prefer Blondes*.[21] Unsurprisingly, the tone of *Niagara* in the wake of George's outburst is anything but comic, the film reverting to its noir impulses, but with a color twist. George and Polly are standing in front of a window when the colored lights come on—what Ray calls the "big show"—and the falls light up like a tinted postcard.

Although the rainbow-colored American Falls seems to augur a more positive mood (Ray, as usual, is the embodiment of unbridled enthusiasm: "a couple of colors I never heard of!"), George's rambling, unsolicited recitation of his past—his post-Korean "battle fatigue," his bad luck at sheep ranching after he met Rose when she was the most popular waitress at a "big beer hall" in Duluth—only seems to fuel his barely suppressed resentment. Working himself into a rage, he smashes the 1907 toy-model Maxwell we earlier saw him studiously building. (The model, which, according to George, "belongs on a mantle—if you own a mantle," is associated with adolescent masculinity and "occupational therapy," associations that code him as hopelessly regressive.[22]) Stunned by the violence of this spectacle, Polly admonishes George: "Didn't do any good to fix that hand. You like to suffer."

While George, it's clear, is a masochist, the succeeding two sequences suggest that his madness is being methodically provoked by Rose—"She'd like everybody to believe I'm crazy." In the first one, we watch as Rose, still sheathed in her hot-pink dress, phones a boardinghouse—"It's got to be tomorrow, do you hear me? . . . it's made to order"—where a well-built young man wearing a white T-shirt listens to her instructions, then, whistling "Kiss," lies down on a bed, revealing two-toned shoes. (The young man is never named in the film but is identified in the credits as Ted Patrick [Richard Allan].) The second sequence reprises our initial view of Rose, only this time George has joined her in Cabin B, where she's lying in bed, laughingly holding her hands in the air, her pink dress rumpled on the floor next to her. The fact that George is still wearing pajamas conveys the postcoital mood of the scene, as does his ebullient promise to Rose: "We're gonna go straight to Marshall Fields. I'm gonna buy you the slinkiest, meanest, laciest evening gown they've got."

As in the introductory bedroom sequence of Niagara, the chiaroscuro lighting is classically low-key and high-contrast. The difference again is George, who goes over to the window and starts playing with the blinds, modulating the amount of light and shadow that falls on Rose as if he's an artist and she's the model. While this passage self-reflexively reframes the opening view of Rose, explicitly reinscribing the active male viewer, there's not a little irony inasmuch as Rose is plainly putting on a big show for George. The concluding shot of the sequence—a restricted two-shot of George and Rose passionately embracing in bed—is therefore, despite the buoyant atmosphere, ominous. The slightly canted, horizontal bars of shadow imprisoning the couple in fact foreshadow a sudden change of tone.

Consequently, when George notices Rose putting on perfume and humming "Kiss" (she claims that she's getting dressed to pick up their bus tickets to Chicago), his suspicions are immediately aroused: "Why? Where you going?" The sound of Rose's bracelet jingling every time that she moves her hand pricks George's sexual paranoia, as do the carillon bells chiming in the background as he shadows her to the Table Rock souvenir shop. Although the bells cannot be heard inside the shop, a man offscreen begins to whistle "Kiss" until George enters and the whistling stops. The message the man leaves for Rose on a postcard carousel punctuates the musical conceit on a mute but eloquent note: "If everything [is] OK you'll hear the Bell Tower play our song—see you in Chicago."

The following sequence features the Cutlers and offers some momentary comic respite. Polly's lying out in a plaid, red-and-blue two-piece bathing suit when Ray, grabbing a camera, begins to instruct her about how to pose: "Now, swing around and get a profile. [Ray turns and pushes out his chest] C'mon, Polly, profile! That's it. Now, inhale! You've got nothing to hide. Inhale!" (Ray's behavior here can be said to mimic George's desire to aesthetically master his wife's sexuality.) The photo session is abruptly interrupted, however, when a shadow literally falls over Polly—it's Rose, who is seriously concerned about her husband's whereabouts.

Acting on her behalf, the Cutlers contact Inspector Starkey (Dennis O'Dea) of the Canadian police, who agrees to meet up with them at the souvenir shop. Whereas Rose was previously dressed in a plain white top and gray skirt, she's now outfitted in a blood-red jacket over a white blouse and black skirt. (These colors—red, white, and black—reflect the film's chromatic revision of classic noir, in which red signifies danger or desire, white purity or innocence, and black aggressivity or death.) As Inspector Starkey escorts the group downstairs, Rose's bracelet can be heard faintly ringing like a bell. An attendant there points out that a black raincoat is missing and a pair of brown shoes has been left behind, after which Rose, distraught, identifies the shoes as her husband's. Moments later, though, she's outside again in the sunlight, where, having been escorted by the Cutlers, she leaves them standing at the curb as she starts toward the bell tower in the distance—it's playing "Kiss"—a smile dawning on her face. (This is "The Walk," a "horizontal" one over cobblestones and in long shot from a fixed camera that has since become the stuff of legend.[23])

If the sharp contrast between Rose's bright red jacket and jet-black skirt in the souvenir shop reflects the opposition between her libidinal and murderous desires, she's appropriately garbed in black when Inspector Starkey ushers her into the city morgue to identify her husband's remains. (A lifeless body, signaled by a man waving a red flag, has been discovered in the rapids below the falls.) While Rose is the very image of a grieving widow, the silhouette shot as she approaches the sheeted body in the back room, the sound of her footsteps reverberating in the stillness, suggests that she's the one in the dark. When Inspector Starkey turns on the overhead light, pulling back a sheet so that Rose can see the face, she faints dead away: Niagara, to paraphrase Bazin, has not returned the body she had hoped it would. The sound of Rose's bracelet as her body slumps to the floor is a sonic coup de grâce.

DEAD MAN WALKING

Cut to a hospital room where Rose lies semiconscious in a pillowless bed, her hospital gown pulled up around her neck—in a baleful echo of the initial cabin scene—like a shroud. The angle is slightly elevated, and as a nurse attends to her (Rose is moaning, "I wanna get away"), a doctor prepares a sedative. Rose, not George, is now the shell-shocked, hospitalized one. Comic relief is again introduced, this time in the form of J. C. Kettering (Don Wilson) and his wife, who have belatedly arrived at the Rainbow Cabins. Ray works at the Toledo branch of Shredded Wheat and has been dying to meet the "King of the VPs" ever since he won the cash prize for the "most imaginative sales campaign": stuffing a turkey with Shredded Wheat.

Kettering is a hyperbolic, even more buffoonish version of Ray. (Ray and Kettering, gray-flannel businessmen wed to the aspirational ethos of mid-century American corporate culture, both yammer at some point about "getting organized.") But Kettering, at least from Polly's point of view, is something of a terror. She has just returned from the hospital after seeing Rose when he thrusts a bouquet of flowers into her hands. The dark red roses have a funereal cast, not unlike the flowers in the alley sequence in *Vertigo*, indirectly summoning Rose's "illness" and, by implication, George's death. (Both the police and the Cutlers believe that he committed suicide.)

The manager, who's hosing down the flower beds (water in various forms is ubiquitous in *Niagara*), informs Polly that he has belatedly moved the couple's things to Cabin B. Inside the cabin, Polly's lying down on the bed formerly occupied by George when she becomes so blinded by the afternoon light that she has to close the blinds. The camera suddenly pans out to the window—the movement's oddly unmotivated and the focus slightly distorted—where, in the background, a slouch-hatted man's hiding behind some hedges. A medium shot of the man's feet as he swiftly crosses the yard reveals that he's wearing the same two-toned shoes that Patrick wore in the rooming house. When, however, he opens the Venetian-blinded door, we see that it's George, not Patrick.

It's now obvious that Rose's lover is dead and that George is not only alive but masquerading as the dead man (see Walter Neff in *Double Indemnity*). Therefore, when Polly subsequently sees George coming through the kitchen door armed with a knife, she screams. Although Ray's reaction—"It's probably just a nightmare. Calm yourself down"—paints Polly as the prototypical hysterical woman, "neurotic" like George, Ray himself is not immune to the Loomis curse, muttering under his breath as he goes to the kitchen to get her a glass of water, "Mr. Loomis! If I hear that name once more, I'll start yelling myself," adding, "We wait three years for a honeymoon and spend it with a couple of spooks." (Both the cabins and the Cutlers are, I think it's safe to say, haunted by the Loomises.)

Ray's about to kiss off the falls for good when Polly relays the news that Mr. Kettering has arrived and Ray has an abrupt change of heart, ordering her to lie down while he shaves. Disobeying her husband (and, not so incidentally, mirroring Rose's willful behavior), Polly steals out of the cabin to call Inspector Starkey: in the mirror above the pay phone (the same one in which we previously saw Rose applying makeup while calling Patrick), George's face, his forehead scored by a dark-blue bruise, is clearly visible through the slatted blinds of a window.

The ensuing sequence, in which the Cutlers and Ketterings visit the Cave of the Winds, recalls the earlier scene in which Polly saw Rose kissing Patrick. This time, though, Polly has decided to hold back from the group (she's had enough adventure for one day) when she spies George. While her isolation emphasizes her privileged point of view, the unspoken connection between George and her is underscored when he chases her up the mist-drenched stairs, then, when another couple materializes, muffles her scream with a hand and pretends to embrace her. George, shielded from the other sightseers in a shallow cave, confesses that he killed Rose's lover in self-defense—"he came at me with a wrench"—pleading, "You're the only one that knows I'm alive. . . . Let me stay dead."

Two cuts—the first to George depositing a note in the bell tower's "musical requests" box, the second to a high, foreshortened shot of Rose immobile in her hospital bed, the drapes billowing in the open window—reveal George's intent and Rose's vulnerability. As the carillon plays "Kiss," Rose's hands begin to twitch, the camera rapidly panning out to a long exterior shot of the bell tower framed in the window. When the camera, after a startling montage composed of dark, low-angle shots of the tongue-linked bells, cuts back to Rose, it's to a choker shot: her eyes are closed and she's tearing at her hair. In a close rhyme of the film's second sequence, Rose opens her eyes and there's a brief moment between sleeping and waking when she thinks it's Patrick signaling her—"If everything [is] OK you'll hear the Bell Tower play our song"—until she remembers, horrified, that he's dead.

VERTIGO

If *Niagara*'s conclusion, set on the rapids, proffers the sort of exciting action for which classical Hollywood had primed '50s audiences, the penultimate bell tower sequence is the film's real audiovisual climax. In this sequence Rose's costume captures her character's desperation: just as her chartreuse handkerchief visually sets her off from the background, so her jingling bracelet audibly marks her changing location.

The mise-en-scène mirrors her imprisonment as well. After unsuccessfully trying to call an elevator, she's enframed by shadow, momentarily fixed between a forest-green chair in the right foreground and, in the middle ground, the closed red door of the elevator, the black diagonal staircase to the right her only exit. (Note the picture of the falls on the left rear wall of the elevator.) When the elevator doesn't appear, Rose races up the stairs to the second floor, where she frantically searches her purse for change to make a phone call as, below, George enters the building. In this scene the screen is effectively split in two: while Rose is located on the left-hand side, barred by strong vertical and diagonal shadows (the camera angle is high), George, silhouetted against the late afternoon light spilling into the doorway through which he has just entered, looks up when he hears the sound of her bracelet.

The pace of the editing quickens as Rose, abandoning her suitcase and purse, climbs the stairs to the next floor. Viewed through the black steps of the stairwell—yet another, horizontal compositional variation—she's knocking on the

Split Screen: In the upper left hand of the frame, Rose Loomis (Marilyn Monroe) desperately tries to use the phone; in the lower right hand, George Loomis (Joseph Cotten) enters the ground floor of the carillon bell tower in *Niagara*.

red elevator door with her kerchiefed hand when she hears George. The cutaway to the interior of the elevator, where the black janitor holds a folded American flag in his hands, is both prosaic and pregnant: it's not only the end of another day at Niagara Falls but the beginning of the end for Rose. Having reached the top floor of the bell tower, Rose finally locates an open door, but George is already there and forces his way in, his Venetian blind–shadowed figure momentarily masked by the door frame. "Too bad they can't play it for you now," he says, indicating the bells, and, as if in response, the camera slowly rises, ascending to a dark, slatted-window shot of the carillon, now silent.

The straight cut to a wide shot of the bells precipitates a stunning montage. As George approaches Rose, their elongated shadows moving on a canted, chiaroscuro-lit floor, a red light burns in the right-hand corner of the screen. Cut to a medium shot of Rose frozen in the blood-red light, a louvered window to her right, her face set off by the bright white cowl of her blouse as George, hands raised, embraces her for the very last time.

With its braying trumpets and pounding timpani, Sol Kaplan's score has been building inexorably to this moment. However, when George puts his hands around Rose's throat, the music suddenly dies down, the camera cutting to a

La Belle Dame sans merci: Abstract high-angle shot of stilled bells and, below, George Loomis (Joseph Cotten), scarf in hand, standing over the motionless body of Rose Loomis (Marilyn Monroe) on the carillon-shadowed floor of the bell chamber in *Niagara*.

multi-angled montage of the bells, their tongues stilled.[24] It's a profoundly disturbing sound-image: where once the carillon, like the song "Kiss" and the ringing bracelet, signified Rose in all her vitality, it now marks the moment of her death and the end of the Loomises' marriage.

A reprise of the overhead shot from the perspective of the silenced bells shows George again in silhouette, unraveling the white scarf from around Rose's neck with a flourish as her body slumps soundlessly to the floor. The conclusion to the sequence—an overhead master shot of Rose's body gashed by vertical bars of shadow, her hand still grasping the chartreuse handkerchief—prefigures *Vertigo* and the dream-haunting shot of Madeleine Elster's (Kim Novak) fallen body splayed out on the bell tower roof like a silhouette.

FEMME VITAL

The dénouement of *Niagara* provides a final, perverse twist to the troubling questions about identification provoked by the body of the film. For instance, despite the fact that George is fated to die, the narrative labors strenuously to exonerate his character. When, after having strangled Rose, he finds himself locked inside the bell tower, he returns to the scene of the crime, where, picking up Rose's lipstick case, he kneels beside her and whispers, "I loved you, Rose, you know that." George also saves Polly's life. Slipping out of the bell tower the morning after murdering his wife, he steals a fishing boat that the Ketterings have docked above the rapids. But unbeknownst to him, Polly's aboard and as he tries to make his escape the launch runs out of gas. Although George makes a heroic effort to scuttle the boat, the two are swept together toward the precipice. However, just as it's about to go over the falls, he helps Polly onto a rock, where she holds on until a police helicopter comes to her rescue.

This dramatic conclusion literalizes a speech about love that George made to Polly when she went to his cabin to nurse his hand:

> "You're young, you're in love. . . . Don't let it get out of hand like those Falls out there. Ever see the river above the Falls—it's calm and easy? You throw in a log and it floats around. Let it move a little farther down and it gets going, hits some rocks and, in a minute, it's in the lower rapids and nothing can keep it from going over the edge."

This cautionary discourse on desire, which bookends George's pessimistic voice-over reflections at the beginning of the film, offers a proleptic *apologia pro vita sua*. Still, if desire is "as perilous as proximity to the torrent" and the torrent is Rose,[25] the real question is not so much how we're meant to understand George as how we're meant to construe his spouse.

Drawing on Klaus Theweleit's distinction in *Male Fantasies* between the "red" and "white woman,"[26] Clara Juncker argues that Monroe in *Niagara* appears as a "'Red Woman' in the character of Rose, who gets killed off in the end for her sexuality and adultery."[27] Similarly, in *Marilyn Monroe* Graham McCann writes that while the "'White Woman' serves man's needs and withdraws into the home, the 'Red Woman' disturbs the man's composure, unsettling his 'masculine' image of self-control and moral strength."[28] McCann, like Juncker, rehearses the classic opposition between the femme fatale and "redeemer" figure that Janey Place first articulated in "Women in Film Noir": "Socially the war had brought women into the labor market. . . . 'White women' suddenly seemed 'red': the old order was disturbed. Sex offered men short-term pleasure but long-term pain. Women were desirable but destructive, dangerous to men."[29]

The only problem with the above "bad girl" script is that, not unlike Place's well-known formulation that "noir is a male fantasy,"[30] it reproduces the film's positioning of Rose as a femme fatale even as it evacuates the historical specificity of Monroe's performance. More to the point, if film noir is not addressed solely to male spectators—if, in other words, the genre is not simply a male fantasy—Rose's character can be said to mobilize certain female fantasies. Consider, for instance, Mrs. Loomis. Living as she is on "lounge time" (unlike Polly, who has a "union card"),[31] Rose is wholly divorced from the domestic sphere and the sort of homemaking duties traditionally associated with '50s femininity such as cooking and cleaning, shopping and child rearing. She's therefore free to do exactly as she pleases.

And what pleases her? Ted Patrick, for one thing. The other thing that gives her pleasure is her own uninhibited sense of sexuality, an *élan vital* that cannot be reduced to a libidinal drive, akin as it is, like Gilda's in Vidor's 1946 film, to a life force. Carl E. Rollyson captures something of this exorbitant force—call it charisma[32]—in his gloss of the pop-music sequence in *Niagara*: "Monroe is isolated in her singing of 'Kiss' dreamily, moodily, and so suggestively that the crowd of young people who have been dancing recede from her in hushed wonder. . . . [Monroe] seems to be caressing herself, to have retreated into the deepest recesses of her private fantasy life."[33]

Yet if Rollyson's reading usefully indexes the performative disjunction between Monroe's image and Rose's character as well as the lability of Mrs. Loomis's psyche, it does so only to box Rose in again like the comic-book strip that he enlists to describe her cartoonish "Betty Boop" character. In this, his interpretation of Rose as a "parodic sexual siren" arguably conforms to the same masculine logic where Monroe's performance in *Niagara* continues to "elicit condemnations of vulgar exhibitionism and self-exploitation from her biographers, reproaches that seem markedly similar to the attitudes formerly held by DiMaggio."[34]

What might it mean, though, to read Rose's character from another, cultural-historical perspective, one that's responsive to both Monroe's "innocent"—that is, Protestant, guilt-free—sexuality and its private, fantasmatic sense of being for itself?[35] In his meditation on Monroe in *Heavenly Bodies*, Richard Dyer observes that in the 1950s, in the aftermath of the 1953 Kinsey report on female sexuality, the sorts of extremes signified by the "red woman"/"white woman" opposition were less current and did not "necessarily carry with them the strict moral association of sexuality = bad, non-sexuality = good."[36] Question: could it be that Rose is neither a "red" nor "white woman"?

The key here, as in *A Kiss before Dying*, is the color pink, which is the color of the dress Rose is wearing when she sings "Kiss," the same color dress that, not so incidentally, Lorelei Lee is wearing when, intimations of Madonna in "Material Girl" (1984), she performs "Diamonds Are a Girl's Best Friend" in *Gentlemen Prefer Blondes*.[37] Put another, more colorful way (and with Marie Robinson's description of female orgasm as "like going over Niagara Falls in a barrel" in mind[38]), Rose may well be pretty in pink, but she appears rather less interested in pleasing men than in pleasing herself. In fine, Rose puts the *femme* back in femme fatale and, as such, incarnates a new notion of femininity, one that's indebted less to male fantasies because engendered more by a flush, robust sense of female sexuality.

This is a rather different moral from the one that George figuratively delivers on a plate to Polly where if a man falls for a "woman in red" like Rose, he's bound to lose his head. As the dramatic conclusion of *Niagara* suggests, Polly herself is no "white woman," no Pollyanna. She survives George's madness—tellingly, by clinging to the sort of rock that, so myth goes, sirens frequented—to tell another tale ("Why hide it?") in which roses are not always red.

THE GLASS WEB

3-D, TV, AND THE BEGINNING OF THE END OF CLASSIC NOIR

NEW SCENE-SATIONS!
YOU ride with death on the roller-coaster!
The walls of the horror-house close in on YOU!
YOU dodge the bullets!
And YOU do the loving!

—from one-sheet poster for *Man in the Dark*
(1953)

While for many fans and critics the notion of color and widescreen, if not stereophonic, noir is downright blasphemous, 3-D noirs appear—depending on
one's perspective or prejudices—as either preposterous or fantastical. 3-D was
originally developed, like Eastmancolor, CinemaScope, and magnetic sound, in
response to the "catastrophic decline of the movie audience,"[1] and was originally
considered to be most compatible, like the former new technologies, with those
genres historically associated with fantasy and spectacle such as the Western
(*Hondo* [1953]) and science fiction (*It Came from Outer Space* [1953]), the musical (*Kiss Me Kate* [1953]) and action adventure (*Bwana Devil* [1953]). However,
studios were eager to exploit three-dimension and apply it to other, less scenic,
episodic, special effects–driven genres such as the "meller" or "thriller."

In fact, the first 3-D films produced at Columbia, Fox, and RKO were crime
films: respectively, *Man in the Dark* (1953), *Second Chance* (1953), and *Inferno*
(1953). The first Mickey Spillane adaptation, *I, the Jury*, was also shot in 3-D, and
Hitchcock, always intrigued by the technical possibilities of the medium (see,
par excellence, *Rope*), made *Dial M for Murder*. If *Dial M for Murder*—which, at
first glance, seems "like the epitome of photographed theatre"[2]—suggests the
cinematic potentiality of the *Kammerspiel*, *The Glass Web* constitutes a different

sort of solution, a distinctive fusion of 3-D and film noir, magic lantern and "black film." Equally or more provocatively, Jack Arnold's picture represents an uncommon mixture of classic Hollywood cinema and TV, a witch's brew of the "silver" and "small screen" that reads, in retrospect, as both retro and prescient, démodé and sibylline.

3-D

In the penultimate chapter of H. Dewhurst's 1954 *Introduction to 3-D*, "The 3-D of Today," the author writes:

> The year of 1953 will not easily be forgotten, if only for the bursting of the "3-D" bombshell upon an ill-prepared and astonished world. The growing mass-audiences of Television and the consequent decline in the astronomical attendance figures in the "legitimate" cinemas of the world triggered off a "spontaneous" appearance of a panacea for all ills in a resuscitation of the dormant "true" three-dimensional stereophonic projection.[3]

The capitalization of the word "Television" and the scare quotes around the word "legitimate," as if cinema had been spontaneously delegitimated, offer typographic evidence of the moribund state of the motion picture industry in the early 1950s. (The concluding chapter of Dewhurst's tome is, appropriately enough, "Stereo Television.") "True" 3-D—"3-D film in *depth*"—was the Next Big Thing, a magical wand to ward off the encroaching medium of television.[4]

In the wake of 3-D's first so-called novelty period (1838–1952), the second era of convergence (1952–1985) began with the "brief but protean" movie boom from 1952 to 1955.[5] On November 26, 1952, the first American feature film in 3-D and color, Arch Oboler's *Bwana Devil*—shot in "Natural Vision" with a dual 35mm Mitchell camera rig—premiered in Hollywood. Although critics were underwhelmed, not to say appalled, two Paramount theaters were filled to capacity, and audiences sporting polarized glasses were thrilled by the tossed spears and snakes hanging like fruit from trees.[6] By December, *Bwana Devil* ("A lion in your lap! A lover in your arms!") was raking in money and breaking attendance records.[7] The now canonical image of the *Bwana Devil* audience, 3-D-glassed heads canted toward the screen, still speaks to the utter novelty of the moment.

Classic film noir is historically associated with a particular film stock, black-and-white, as well as technology, 2-D. However, just as there are color noirs such as *Leave Her to Heaven*, *Niagara*, and *Vertigo*, a number of 3-D noirs appeared in the wake of *Bwana Devil*. The first was *Man in the Dark*, which Harry Cohn, the head of Columbia, halted in mid-production and ordered rewritten for 3-D in order to capitalize on the phenomenon. While Lew Landers's *Man in the Dark*

"SO REAL . . . YOU FEEL <u>YOU</u> CAN <u>TOUCH</u> THEM!": RKO advertisement for 3-D film *Second Chance*, starring Robert Mitchum (Russ Lambert) and Linda Darnell (Clare Shepperd).

employs a classic noir device, amnesia, to tell the story of Steven Rawley (Edmond O'Brien), a reformed ex-con who tries to remember his criminal past in order to recover the loot he stashed before he went under the knife (he willingly underwent brain surgery to purge his criminal instincts), Rudolph Maté's *Second Chance* stars Robert Mitchum as a boxer named Russ Lambert who befriends a woman, Clare Shepperd (Linda Darnell), who has agreed to testify against her former mobster boyfriend.

Harry Essex's *I, the Jury* is a classic noir revenge tale in which private detective Mike Hammer (Biff Elliot) investigates a motley crew of suspects, all of whom—including femme fatale Charlotte Manning (Peggie Castle)—were last seen in the company of his now very dead best friend. Similarly, Roy Baker's *Inferno* starts out as a revenge fantasy when, during a mining expedition in the Mojave Desert, Donald Whitley Carson III (Robert Ryan) is left for dead when his wife, Geraldine (Rhonda Fleming), and her lover, Joseph Duncan (William Lundigan), abandon him after he falls off a horse and breaks his leg.

If *Man in the Dark* is notable for its expressionist dream sequence and roller-coaster special effects, *Second Chance* for its colorful Mexican exoticism and high-wire cable-car theatrics, *I, the Jury* for its salacious Spillane source material and John Alton–directed cinematography, and *Inferno* for the protagonist's indomitable will to live against seemingly insurmountable odds (a rattlesnake striking at the camera is just one of any number of eye-catching 3-D effects), *The Glass Web* is remarkable for its self-reflexivity and televisuality. In this Jack Arnold film, Edward G. Robinson plays Henry Hayes, a detail-obsessed production researcher intent on becoming a writer on the true-crime TV show on which he's gainfully but unhappily employed. However, his literary dreams come true when, after strangling the two-timing starlet with whom he's having an affair, he turns the murder into a riveting episode of "Crime of the Week."

The interest of *The Glass Web* in the context of '50s noir is how it dramatizes the motion picture industry's recourse to 3-D in response to the emerging hegemony of television. At the same time, if the film's backstage reconstruction of a reality-based crime show can be said to anticipate the demise of classic expressionist noir, the recourse to 3-D can also be seen as a form of spectacular expressionism, a cinematic riposte to the competing claims of neorealism advanced by increasingly popular TV series such as *Dragnet*.

TROMPE L'OEIL

The screenplay for *The Glass Web*, Robert Blees and Leonard Lee's relatively faithful adaptation of Max Victor Erlich's *Spin the Glass Web*, is set in the world of early live television.[8] Unlike Erlich's novel, which begins with screenwriter Don

Newell commuting via train from his home in Long Island to the TBC studios in Manhattan, *The Glass Web* opens in medias res on a wide desert shot of a man and woman getting out of a sedan. As they start up a slight incline, the camera pulls back to reveal a mine shaft,[9] the man and woman framed by broken timbers that jut into the air like dark spikes:

> WOMAN: Alright, Ben, so it's a mine. Why drag me to the middle of nowhere to look at a hole in the ground? I'm going back to the car.

However, when the woman turns to go, the man takes out a revolver and shoots her—*bang, bang, bang*—then drags her body back up to the mine, where, after picking her up and holding her in his arms, he drops her legs-first into the hole.

Although the man starts to leave, he returns for her purse (evidence, like her body, to be disposed of) and the camera pulls back for a wider shot, where a camera operator can be seen in the right foreground along with, at the top of the frame, arc lights. On set, the man tries to erase his footprints with a piece of brush as the film pans left for a deep-focus shot of the show's announcer (John Hiestand). Cut to a medium shot of the announcer, backed by the requisite *Dragnet*-like music, standing in front of an advertisement for Colonial cigarettes:

> And so last November 21st Ben Willis of Ogden, Utah, murdered his wife, Eleanor. Willis was certain he had committed the perfect crime, but he was wrong as you will see next week when "Crime of the Week" presented by Colonial brings you a complete story of "The Willis Murder Case."

In the subsequent wide reverse shot, Henry, Don Newell (John Forsythe), and Dave Markson (Richard Denning)—the creative triumvirate behind "Crime of the Week"[10]—sit intently watching the action.

While Dave, directing the show, relays instructions—"Camera one, a little tighter, watch your focus"—the film returns to the announcer, who takes a cigarette out of a prominently placed pack of Colonials:

> Colonial is the favorite cigarette of millions. A wonderful formula designed, tested, and proved to make the last smoke of the day as refreshing as the first from the pack.

Dave's continuing to give directions—"Stand by one, take one"—when the film cuts away to a master shot of the studio arrayed in various, staggered planes: first, the back of Don's and Henry's heads in the left foreground and, in the right, TV monitors; next, in the right middle ground, a cameraman and, in the center of the frame, the announcer backed by a draped advertisement for Colonial cigarettes; and, finally, in the rear, the desert set, deserted now except for the sedan and the matte mountains in the distance.

Dave instructs the second camera to "get on the title track," but it pans instead, as if it has a mind of its own, to the glass-enclosed sponsor's booth, where Don's wife, Louise (Marcia Henderson), flanked by the couple's children, Timmy and Barbara, catches his eye. Don waves back as the announcer continues his spiel:

All cigarette manufacturers buy good tobacco. All manufacturers have modern plants. But the difference between a good cigarette and the best cigarette is the difference in know-how, knowing how to buy not just good tobacco but tobacco at its peak that burns nice and even, that doesn't raw the tongue.

Timmy whispers to his mother, "Hey, Mom, Dad really wrote a swell show this week, didn't he? Two murders!," though Louise quickly shushes him, reminding him that the "commercial's the most important part of the show." Timmy proceeds to mock the announcer, solemnly pretending to take a drag on a cigarette, as the account executive smiles and Louise, the good wife, beams.

The opening sequence of *The Glass Web* concludes with a *plan Américain* shot of the announcer holding up a pack of cigarettes—"So, buy Colonial, try Colonial, and you'll be a Colonial smoker for keeps"—after which, with an exaggerated flourish, he swings a lit cigarette around to the camera and then back to his mouth for one final puff: "Aah!" A sudden segue on the sound track from the saccharine, string-laden commercial music to the percussive crime score signals the end of the advertisement: "Be with us again next week when 'Crime of the Week' brings you the true story, the story exactly as it happened." In the control booth, Dave crisply signs off for the day: "Stand by master control, studio C, fading into black, audio and video."

COLONIAL NEOREALISM

The extended TV show-within-a-film prologue that opens *The Glass Web* is a tour de force and, since it departs substantially from Erlich's novel, demonstrates Arnold's considerable mastery of both 3-D and the conventions of "classic realist cinema."[11] I use the last pejorative term with not a little irony, as *The Glass Web* amply testifies to the extent to which certain classical Hollywood texts do not so much embody as self-reflexively, even satirically, comment on the ideological codes that ostensibly constitute them. In fact, the introductory sequence of *The Glass Web* represents a veritable treasure trove of Brechtian "alienation effects," baring the sort of audiovisual devices typically used to produce '50s TV and, in the process, critically narrativizing the production.

The real twist of *The Glass Web*, though, is its exposé of the show's embedded authorial function: the narrator/announcer. In docu-noir the narration tends to be objective third person, and the narrator—the so-called voice of God—is invisible, not to say omniscient. In *The Glass Web*, by contrast, the narrator begins offscreen but is revealed to be a commercial spokesman. Thus, if in the first, fictional part of the sequence, the narrator's voice is, true to semidocumentary convention, stereotypically stentorian, in the commercial part the intonation abruptly shifts and the narration is unctuous, obsequious. In other words, the film foregrounds the constitutive relation between the show's narration—"And so last November 21st . . ."—and its sponsor, Colonial cigarettes.

Tobacco, of course, was central to the political economy of colonial America and '50s TV.[12] For instance, *Dragnet* (NBC, 1951–1959) famously began with the announcer, backed by the show's familiar, Walter Schumann–composed theme music, "Dragnet March," intoning, "The story you are about to see is real; the names have been changed to protect the innocent. Fatima, best of all king-size cigarettes, brings us *Dragnet*." The cozy relation between programming and sponsor—in this case, the United States Tobacco Company—was even more explicit in another crime drama, *Martin Kane, Private Eye* (NBC, 1949–1954). Created by William Gargan, who appeared in a number of noirs, among them *I Wake Up Screaming* (1941), *Strange Impersonation* (1946), and *Night Editor*, *Martin Kane* was one of the earliest and most popular private eye series on American TV. (Among other things, it was also the first to use the three-camera setup.) In the show, the pipe-smoking Kane's favorite brand is Old Briar ("15 cents a pouch") and he frequents McMann's Tobacco Shop, where the sponsor's products (Dill's Best pipe tobacco, Encore filter-tip and Sano non-filtered cigarettes) are prominently on display.

In *The Television Crime Fighters Factbook*, Vincent Terrace comments on the fluid relation between content and advertising in early shows like *Martin Kane*:

> When Kane discusses a case with shop owner Tucker "Hap" McMann, customers appear to purchase a product, Hap excuses himself and pitches the sponsor's product while Kane, or someone else involved with the case, waits patiently on the side. With the sale concluded, the show picks up from where the customer entered.[13]

Although the relation between content and advertising is not quite as seamless in *Spin the Glass Web* as it is in *Martin Kane*, tobacco plays a crucial role in Arnold's film, which draws extensively on Erlich's novel for its representation of the wonderful world of television.

For example, in *Spin the Glass Web* the TV show is called "New York Homicide," television is figured as "Aladdin's Lamp," and it serves the "Lord of the Lamp," Audience, whose "sacred king" is Market: "The Lord could let the Lamp live, or snuff it out, and let it die. Tonight the Lamp burned brightly with the flames of untold cigarettes. The smoke of billions of Milo cigarettes billowed from its chimney."[14]

In fact, in *Spin the Glass Web* it's option time for "New York Homicide." Another ad agency is pitching a variety format to Milo, and the staff has only three weeks to impress the sponsor or the show will be canceled. The question is: can Don, Dave, and Henry come up with a sufficiently "smoking" script in time to meet the deadline?

Time is a precious commodity in the world of live TV, especially for Don, who must crank out a fifty-page script—divided into a "video" column on the left and an "audio" column on the right—every single week: "Time was his tyrant, he sweated for it, lived by it, and would some day die by it. Time was money, time was a television script, so many minutes, so many seconds on the nose, no more and no less."[15] Time isn't Don's only enemy, however; there's also Henry, a former police reporter who worships the "Great God Detail."[16]

According to Henry, "New York Homicide" is popular with viewers because it's based on facts, because it's real. Don elaborates on this simple truth in *Spin the Glass Web*:

> People liked "New York Homicide." It operated on the simple premise that truth was more dramatic than fiction. The basic idea was to take a current murder that hit the headlines in town and dramatize it for TV, re-enact it just as it happened. The result was that viewers could sit in their living rooms and eavesdrop on a murder they'd read about only very recently, recreated authentically down to the very last detail.[17]

As the show's researcher, Henry's responsible for the show's aura of authenticity, what the narrator of *Spin the Glass Web* refers to as "documentary realism."[18] Accordingly, when Don presents his next, Benzedrine-fueled script for review, Henry—"one part bulldog, one part bloodhound, and one part Sherlock Holmes"[19]—pronounces it "flat" before attacking it for its lack of fidelity: "Now, on page 15, you have Jordan's wrist-watch smashed to establish the time—Jordan wore a gold watch on a chain. Didn't you look at the police pictures?"

Don disagrees—he's more concerned with dramaturgy ("Who the devil cares about that if the scene plays?"), although Henry expatiates in detail and at length on the show's aesthetic:

> What we're selling is realism. The people who watch our show every Wednesday night . . . wanna smell the stink of [murder], they love it, and they watch our show instead of the others because they know I give them the truth. . . . The people buy the little details, the quirks, the idiosyncrasies, the poor slobs in the news. What makes them different? The color of lipstick, the books they read, did the victim wear stockings or go bare-legged, did she love music, did she have jewelry and, if not, why not?

Henry's monologue not only captures his obsessive-compulsive personality but vividly illustrates the transitional space that *The Glass Web* occupies in the historical evolution of film noir.[20] On one hand, as performed by "Eddie" Robinson, Henry's impassioned soliloquy recollects Barton Keyes's speech about suicide statistics in *Double Indemnity*, a Billy Wilder film that's the epitome of classic expressionist noir. On the other hand, in its rhetorical emphasis on the "little details," Henry's speech reflects the rapidly waxing influence of neorealism in postwar American cinema.

While the semidocumentary tradition in film noir can be traced back to 1945 and Henry Hathaway's *The House on 92nd Street*, by 1951 it had migrated to the medium of television in the form of crime series like *Dragnet*. Before *Dragnet*, American TV was dominated by various crime shows featuring private detectives as well as cops, G-men, DAs, lawyers, police reporters, crusading editors, and crime photographers, not to mention husband/wife, father/son, and father/daughter investigative teams.[21] *Dragnet*, conceived and directed by Jack Webb, the "Orson Welles of television," was different, its "terse, everyday dialogue, realistic plotting, and incorporation of legitimate police procedure setting it apart from . . . the private-eye dramas which were then prevalent."[22]

Marked by "rapid, uninflected dialogue," what Webb called a "dramatic monotone" (he allegedly had his actors read their lines cold off cue cards or the teleprompter to speed up production), *Dragnet* originated and perfected true crime neorealism and, in the process, "became one of the longest-running and most critically acclaimed dramatic series in 1950s American television."[23] Unlike hybrid '40s films such as Alfred L. Werker's *He Walked by Night*, in which Webb starred as a lab technician, *Dragnet* eschewed both the stylish expressionism of classic noir and the topical social relevance of Italian neorealism, striving instead for, as Henry exhorts, an "imitative precision."[24]

CLASSIC NOIR: SPIDER-MAN

Despite the overt emphasis on "documentary realism" in *The Glass Web*, another, pre-neorealist phase or cycle of classic noir, as in the film's repeated invocation of *Double Indemnity*, informs Arnold's picture. The classic as opposed to semidocumentary impulse appears in *The Glass Web* in its most full-bodied, full-blooded form in the figure of the femme fatale Paula Ranier ("3-D girl" Kathleen Hughes[25]), who plays Ben Willis's doomed wife, Eleanor, in the film's opening sequence. In *Spin the Glass Web* Henry describes Paula to Don as a "first-class no good bitch. No talent, all body, you know the kind."[26] Henry, needless to say, has biblical knowledge of which he speaks. In return for Paula's affection (their relation is strictly quid pro quo), Henry has promised to feature her in a future episode of

Rock 'n' Shock: Advertisement for *The Glass Web* with—from top to bottom on the left—Henry Hayes (Edward G. Robinson), Don Newell (John Forsythe), and Dave Markson (Richard Denning). On the right, "3-D girl" Kathleen Hughes as femme fatale Paula Ranier.

"Crime of the Week." However, when Henry tells Paula the good news—after having treated her to a romantic dinner, complete with classical music—she glances at her watch and sighs, "It's just that a girl doesn't like falling down mineshafts."

Paula, it's clear, is not exactly enamored with Henry, but she feigns interest in his new Cézanne print—"Oh, yes, it's very interesting . . . an interesting facial concept, I think"—and he eagerly takes the bait: "You've learned a lot the last few months. When I met you, you didn't know an Impressionist from a Surrealist." (Edward G. Robinson was, it's worth noting, a well-known art collector.) The couple's dynamic is now manifest: Paula gives Henry sex, Henry—or so he thinks—gives her class in the form of cultural capital, and together, at least according to him, they'll rise "above the crowd": "You're gonna get the parts you deserve, and I'll be getting credit for the work I do."

The accent in *The Glass Web* on fine art and sex, Cézanne and sugar daddies, has a direct antecedent in *The Woman in the Window* and *Scarlet Street*, classic noirs in which Robinson plays an older man who falls for a younger and, in the latter instance at least, duplicitous woman. The difference between Robinson's characters in the Fritz Lang films and *The Glass Web* is that whereas Professor Wanley in *The Woman in the Window* and Christopher Cross in *Scarlet Street* may be murderers, Henry is unabashedly mercenary and also something of a spider-man. The "spidey" trope is patent in *Spin the Glass Web*:

> The monstrous spider worked on, exuding the sticky liquid from its spinnerets, and from them sprung the strands. The strands were gossamer and delicate. The spider spun the first strand, used it as a kind of suspension bridge, spun the second and third. The web began to take the shape of an orb, a geometric marvel of dainty beauty, the strands radiating outward . . . like the spokes of a wheel.[27]

And yet, if Henry, not Paula, is the real predator, who's the prey?

Henry's dinner date with Paula ends abruptly not because, as she tells him, she has an audition at Le Capitan but because, as he suspects, there's another man (a figure who will become a central part of the next, climactic episode of "Crime of the Week"). Cut to a brightly lit apartment where there's cocktail music on the record player and Paula has changed into a tight, shimmering top—note the 3-D-enhanced décolletage when she bends over a couch to light a cigarette—as she prepares for her rendezvous with Henry's arch nemesis, Don, the head writer of "Crime of the Week."

Don's character is a mainstay of classic noir: like Walter Neff (Fred MacMurray) in *Double Indemnity*, he's the everyman as dupe, the man who thinks he has all the answers but, as Paula caustically reminds him at one point, doesn't even know the questions. Don wants to terminate his affair with Paula; however, she has taken out a little insurance in the form of a pair of pajamas he thought he misplaced in Tahoe. "Now they're in a nice safe place and for sale," Paula purrs, running a fingertip lightly across Don's lips, "for two-five-zero-zero." A big band version of "Blue Moon" plays in the background.

Don, licked, repairs to the Blue Sands, where he nurses a drink and reflects in voice-over—a classic noir moment—on his past history with Paula: "How did I ever get into this? How did I ever get sucked in so far I couldn't get out? Why didn't I have Paula Ranier sized up the first time I met her the way she had me?" The screen suddenly goes out of focus (another classic noir moment) and the film flashes back to the first time that Don met Ms. Ranier, bumping into her—or, more precisely, "accidentally" getting bumped into by her—in the TBC lobby. The scenario is familiar: Don has his head in a script, and Paula's dressed to kill in a white dress offset by a black purse and a black hat with a brim as big as a flying saucer. Proffering one black-gloved hand, Paula blows Don up as big as a soap bubble: "I've always wanted to have a part in one of your shows. I think they're the best on the coast." In retrospect, Don's a whole lot wiser about himself and Paula: "Sure I can be flattered. Sure I liked the barbed-wire dress, the one she said protected the property but didn't hide the view."

Don's voice-over narration is generic—albeit smart, like Paula's repartee—but his take on his second, even more fateful meeting with Paula is even more rueful, assuming the cadences of Steve Thompson's (Burt Lancaster) retrospective narration of his "accidental" encounter with Anna (Yvonne De Carlo) at Union Station in *Criss Cross* (1949): "Maybe if Louise hadn't taken the kids to Tahoe to visit her mother. Maybe if I hadn't been at Blue Sands and dropped in the bar for a drink and just happened to run into Paula." At the Blue Sands, Paula's now dressed all in black, and after placing a hand over Don's, she assures him that she isn't prejudiced against married men: "Some of my best friends are married." A jagged-edged shadow on the wall cries danger, although Don's too busy gazing into Paula's limpid eyes to notice.

Cut to Paula's apartment, where the two are sitting next to each other on the couch, and even Paula's cat, as Don says, seems to be in on the act, "pulling out the light cord right on cue." Kiss kiss. Before too long, Paula's ingenuously asking him for a fifty-dollar loan, then one hundred dollars, and, *bang bang*, Don's got an expensive "habit." When he finally decides to kick, he has to cash in his children's savings account to pay the piper. End of flashback, but not, needless to say, end of story.

Back in the tangled-web present, Paula's ex-husband, Fred Abbott (John Verros), has called to say that he wants to see Paula when, out of the blue, Henry shows up unannounced at her apartment. Unlike Don and Fred, both of whom want out and fast, Henry wants to up the ante, promising Paula that he'll soon be making five hundred dollars a week as a writer on "Crime of the Week," more than enough to keep her in the flush style to which she's become accustomed thanks to all the generous men in her life. Paula laughs the laugh of the Medusa: "You writing the show? You'll never be anything more than an errand boy around the studio. A fussy little character with a tiny little job. 'Above the crowd.'" The record on the phonograph, "Temptation," ends, then automatically begins again.

Don, who has arrived prepared for the long good-bye, is about to knock on Paula's door when he hears her talking to someone inside. There's a party next door and when it spills into the hallway, he ducks into a stairwell, where a high-angle shot shows him pinned against a wall isolated by a crescent of light. When Don returns to Paula's apartment, the record is still playing, but the "black angel" has gone to heaven, strangled to death like Mavis Marlowe in *Black Angel* (1946).

Relieved that his troubles are now behind him, Don returns to his favorite haunt for a postmortem drink. However, after taking a deep drag on a cigarette (Colonial?), he reaches for his pocket handkerchief only to realize, as if the universe were playing some sadistic trick on him, that the name tag he just ripped out of the incriminating pajamas hidden in Paula's bedroom dresser has vanished into thin air. The ensuing sequence—in which Don races back to Paula's apartment before stopping dead in his tracks when he sees two patrol cars, sirens blaring, in front of the building—marries 3-D and film noir in a "real" spectacle of expressionism.

First, Don, walking glass-eyed like a zombie—"Name tag, they'll find the name tag, they'll tie me up with Paula, learn that she was blackmailing me, say I killed her to get rid of her"—steps off the curb and smack into the path of a truck. (A ladder attached to the truck's roof threatens to puncture the screen.) Next, Don's about to walk into a hose that a man's using to wash down the sidewalk when the man, turning away from Don, sprays the water right into the eye of the camera. Finally, Don serenely strolls under a chute extruding from a building that's being demolished ("Danger") just as the rocky debris trundles toward the camera like an avalanche.[28] A policeman, mistaking Don for a drunk, stops him and sends him home.

Although there's good news on the radio the next morning—Paula's ex-husband has been arrested for her murder—Don's reprieve is short-lived. As soon as he walks into Dave's office for a script conference, the producer tells him that the show needs a "smash" episode to ensure that Colonial picks up the option on the show, and, thanks to Henry, he has a "terrific idea": the Paula Ranier murder. Cut to a high wide-angle shot of Don in his wood-paneled office at home, dictating—not unlike Walter Neff in *Double Indemnity*—into a microphone: "The Paula Ranier murder. By Don Newell. First draft script." As the camera slowly dollies in for a medium shot, Don replays what he has just dictated into the tape recorder, then, after seeing a graphic crime photo of Paula, starts over again: "Fade in. Establishing shot of Paula Ranier's apartment. Day. This is apartment 801 in a new building on Wilshire and Fairmont. The apartment is done in California moderne. Attractive enough, with a large couch by the balcony. A record player stands to the right."

Don doesn't seem to realize, however, that Henry now suspects he's the "other man." In fact, Henry arrives at Don's house the next morning just in time for the delivery of a package that, to Don's but not Henry's surprise, contains a pair of pajamas. Don insists on discussing the matter, and during a car ride, Henry explains that he knew Don's script described Paula's apartment from memory because the maid told him that she had moved the furniture the day of the murder. Don violently yanks the car over to the side of a road, the camera cutting to a dizzying overhead shot of Henry and him standing at the edge of a bluff, the waves crashing on the rocks below. Henry's proposal: Don will move to Chicago or New York, while Henry will assume his duties as writer of "Crime of the Week." Don's immediate reaction is to push Henry off the cliff—"These have been the happiest weeks you've spent in your life, better than any your fabulous brain could conceive"—but he's trapped like a fly in the spider-man's "slimy web."

TRUE CRIME TV: "THE PAULA RANIER MURDER CASE"

Although the enhanced, high-angle crane shot is typical of how *The Glass Web* mobilizes the new technology of 3-D to reanimate classic noir, the film's conclusion returns to the real scene of the crime: the TBC studios. It also turns, not unlike classic, pre-neorealist noir, on obsession and repetition-compulsion. The sequence begins when Dave introduces Don to Lieutenant Stevens (Hugh Sanders), the detective investigating the Paula Ranier murder for the LAPD. As Henry's putting the finishing touches on the set decoration for Paula's apartment, a prop man carrying a giant panda doll and silent butler appears: "Where does this junk go?" Henry directs him to put the panda in a chair and takes the butler and places it—just so—on a coffee table. When Don and Lieutenant Stevens walk up, Henry tells the electrician to "hit the lights" and the lieutenant is duly impressed: "Pretty realistic."

While Don heads for the control booth, passing the announcer, who's prepping for the show, and Sonia (Jean Willes), the actress who has been cast to play Paula in the new episode of "Crime of the Week," Lieutenant Stevens joins an account executive in the sponsor's booth, where they watch the series' filmed opening on a television set: "The difference between a good cigarette and the best cigarette. . . ." Dave cues Jake ("Ready to fade music") and the announcer's voice comes on air:

Tonight "Crime of the Week" presents another true story, a story based on fact, the story of a murder. Police files are not yet marked closed, the ending is not yet known, but the beginning is. [Cut to a close-up of the monitors] Most of the facts are a matter of record. ["Stand by, camera three"] Tonight Colonial invites you to be your own jury ["Stand by, Sonia"] on "The Paula Ranier Murder Case."

["Take three, cue Sonja"] This is Paula Ranier, an actress occasionally, a model occasionally [cut to a medium shot of Paula crossing her apartment to primp in a mirror and make a drink], a girl who came to Los Angeles hoping desperately that beauty was enough. Men always looked two and three times at Paula, and for a while Paula Ranier may have felt that the way she looked, the way she walked, just being Paula Ranier, was enough. These were enough to get her murdered.

When Paula crosses the room, cocktail in hand, to turn on the phonograph, Dave cues the music—"Jake, get your music with her action"—and the sound of "Temptation" fades up:

One evening less than a month ago, the buzzer in her West Los Angeles apartment sounded as it had sounded many an evening before and a man was there as there had been many an evening before. His name at present is a matter of doubt, but what he did was as definite and final as death itself.

An actor bearing a distinct resemblance to Paula's ex-husband (this uncanny verisimilitude being Henry's forte as a casting director) strolls through Paula's door as if he lived there. After she lights up a cigarette (another, subliminal ad for Colonial?), Lieutenant Stevens exclaims, "That cigarette lighter's exactly the same!" a sentiment seconded by the account executive: "That's what we mean by realism, lieutenant."

On set, Paula's on one side of a beam, the man's on the other, and a microphone boom cuts a wide diagonal swath across the screen:

PAULA: Big promoter, wheeling and dealing. You think you know all the an-
    swers. You don't even know the questions, buster.
MAN: For instance?
PAULA: For instance, the twenty-five hundred under the table from Sam Mar-
    tin, the payoff for the sale. I think there's a lot of people in this civic center
    who would like the details.
MAN: Paula, you're not gonna tell anybody anything.

The man suddenly grabs Paula by the arm, and although Don can't bear to watch, Henry can. In fact, Henry looks over to Jake, who resets the needle on "Temptation."

An insert shot of the spinning record doubles Don's realization that he may not be trapped in Henry's spun-glass web after all. On set, the man slaps Paula, then, after placing his hands around her neck, begins to strangle her. The camera cuts away, but as she slides to the floor, the announcer resumes his deadpan narra-tion: "And so, Paula Ranier, the girl born Paula Roebuck in Lakewood, Missouri, twenty-five years ago, was dead from strangulation." A foreshortened shot of Paula lying dead at the man's feet, naked to the camera's eye and laid out head-first for full 3-D effect, sutures the narration: "In just one minute you will see the high-lights of Paula's life."

CODA: 3-D/REALITY TV

Although Henry's strangulation of Paula in the first, "real" part of *The Glass Web* occurs offscreen, in the imagined, dramatized version that appears on "Crime of the Week," it's sensational, exploitative. The difference is distinctly audible on the sound track in the abrupt shift from Paula's agonized death throes to the an-nouncer's jaded voice, which is at once alienating and nauseating (in the strong, Sartrean sense). In fact, Paula's murder is meticulously reenacted in all its grisly detail and framed by commercials, as if sponsored by corporate America in the form of Colonial cigarettes ("Ah!").

In Erlich's novel the utter monstrosity of the brave new medium of TV is conveyed, like Henry, in metaphorical terms:

> The cameras stood silent now, inanimate on their rubber-treaded wheels, one-eyed monsters trailing their cabled tails behind them, in weird curled patterns on the floor. . . . In a minute, the magic would begin. . . . The cameras would stir, move, breathe, come to life. They would advance, retreat, turn, pan left, pan right, dolly in and dolly back, swishing their tails in endless designs on the studio floor, the glass eyes pitilessly and accurately recording what they saw.[29]

It's in the above, monstrous sense that the 3-D title sequence of *The Glass Web*, in which an enormous spider's web shatters like glass, the shards flying outward toward the camera, should be understood.

As in *Spin the Glass Web*, the "glass web" alludes both to television (the trades colloquially referred to the TV networks as "webs") and the camera's "pitiless," seemingly veridical glance: "In his passion for realism, in his psychopathic delight in reliving his own experience, Henry had caught himself in the glass eye of the television."[30] This specular scenario is later reprised in the conclusion of *The Glass Web* when a revolver materializes out of the shadows—a shot that's magnified in 3-D—and we see Henry in studio B holding a gun on Don's wife, Louise. However, in yet another turn of the televisual screw (one foreshadowed by Don's superior position in the studio B control booth), Don flips a switch, and because Henry doesn't realize that the camera's rolling, he inadvertently incriminates himself: "After that door was slammed in my face, after the little tramp said she was too good for me, of course I killed her." In the film's climax, Don comes to his wife's rescue and Henry is about to shoot him when Lieutenant Stevens, who has been watching the feed live with Dave in the studio C control booth, arrives and shoots Henry instead: for praying to the false idol of TV, Henry pays in the end with his life.

If the glass web obviously references Henry's fatal obsession with superrealism and his overweening desire to displace Don—to become, that is, the main writer on "Crime of the Week" and thereby reclaim Paula—there's yet another twist to the film's central figure. Thus, in the title sequence of *The Glass Web*, the glass web is projected in 3-D and is associated with the shattering of the two-dimensional screen of TV, which is associated in turn with mimesis understood as a glass or mirror. The complexity of this cinematic figure is reflected in the film's multidimensional relation to classic noir, since if 3-D can be seen as a superior form of mimesis that trumps the "flat" technology of TV, it can also be viewed—as in Don's postmortem, nighttime odyssey—as a form of spectacular expressionism. Put another way, just as the true crime narrative of *The Glass Web* is indebted to classic noir, so much so that the film appears to be a parody of *Double Indemnity*, Arnold's expressive recourse to 3-D pulverizes TV's pretense to realism, simultaneously negating and sublating its documentary thesis.

Live "True Crime" TV: Don Newell (John Forsythe) flipping the audio switch in the TBC studio B control booth as Henry Hayes (Edward G. Robinson) holds a gun on Don's wife, Louise (Marcia Henderson), on the set below in *The Glass Web*. Note the boom, camera, and expressionist façade in the background.

The result is a motion picture that brilliantly reflects the crossroads that film noir faced in the early 1950s, caught as it was between the competing demands of film and television, realism and expressionism.[31] *The Glass Web* suggests that one answer to this historical aporia was true crime TV and the postwar semidocumentary tradition where the cop, not the crook, is supreme and the devil is in the details. At the same time, Arnold's film points in another, rather more devilish direction—toward irony and 3-D, postmodern pastiche and self-reflexivity—a route that would find fruition in later neo-noirs such as *L.A. Confidential* (1997).

It's therefore no accident, I think, that Curtis Hanson's film is set in 1953, the same year that *The Glass Web* was released and that, as H. Dewhurst observed, 3-D exploded like an atomic bomb upon the American mass media landscape. It's also no accident that the pivotal character of *L.A. Confidential*, Jack Vincennes (Kevin Spacey), is a technical advisor on "Badge of Honor," a TV series that not only recalls *Dragnet* and Jack Webb's "memoir," *Badge* (1958), but Whit Masterson's *Badge of Evil* (1951), the source material for Orson Welles's *Touch of Evil*.[32] Indeed, one of the retroactive ironies of *The Glass Web* is that it's only from the latter, meta-cinematic perspective that Arnold's film appears in all its dialectical complication as a "late" 3-D noir, one that signifies both the beginning of the end of the classical era and the genre's future afterlife in the protean form of neo-noir.

CONCLUSION

THE CRIMSON KIMONO

ODDS FOR TOMORROW

There is no end in art.

—Samuel Fuller, "Los Angeles, Mon Amour," *A Third Face* (2002)

Whether the symptomatic film is considered to be *Touch of Evil* or *Odds against Tomorrow*, the critical consensus has been that the historical period of film noir concludes in the late 1950s. Although a number of formal and ideological factors have been adduced for this demise (for example, TV and HUAC, respectively), the end of classic noir, like its advent or origination, is more a matter of degree than kind. For example, if the tricked-out stylistics of *Touch of Evil* can be said to crystallize the classic expressionist strain of '40s noir, its exploration of the Mexican border and the hybrid performative character of racial and national identities, not to mention its uncanny anticipation of Hitchcock's *Psycho*, point to the future. Similarly, *Odds against Tomorrow* looks both forward and backward—backward as the "culmination of the grittily realistic style with which [Robert Wise] had become so clearly identified in the 1940s" and forward in terms of the film's overt engagement with the issue of racial conflict.[1]

Another late classic film noir that not only looks both forward and backward but explicitly tackles the problem of race in the United States is Samuel Fuller's *Crimson Kimono*, which was released, like *Odds against Tomorrow*, in October 1959. However, whereas *Odds against Tomorrow* was Wise's last film noir, *The Crimson Kimono* is the prelude to a trilogy of seminal Fuller films—*Underworld U.S.A* (1961), *Shock Corridor* (1963), and *The Naked Kiss* (1964)—that, together with *Psycho*, redefine the genre. In fact, *The Crimson Kimono* can be said to constitute an implicit critique of '50s "orientalist" noirs like *Macao*, *World for Ransom* (1954), and *The Shanghai Story* as well as a considered revision of Fuller's own *House of Bamboo*, a revision sharpened, paradoxically enough, by the shift in location from Tokyo, Japan, to Little Tokyo, Los Angeles. Subgenre is critical here. While *House of Bamboo* is a gangster noir, *The Crimson Kimono* is a *policier* or, more specifically, a police melodrama. The last subgeneric determination, which is central, like that of the "crime melodrama,"[2] to the origins and formation of classic noir, also captures the peculiar, operatic tonality of *The Crimson Kimono*.[3]

One way to understand the tonality of these late Fuller films is from the perspective of Bertolt Brecht's influential notion of, among other things, the *Lehrstücke* ("learning plays") or what Fuller called "illustrated lectures."[4] Discussing one of the signature components of the director's style, "shock editing," Nicholas Garnham argues that "just as Brecht was forced to destroy the traditional theatre," Fuller regularly deploys the sort of self-reflexive devices and "alienation effects" associated with Douglas Sirk's '50s melodramas. This distanciation is most obvious in *The Crimson Kimono* in the frequently startling discontinuity between the "romantic" and "professional plotlines" as well as the juxtaposition between the "master" long takes and the kinetic, analytical editing.[5] It's apparent as well in Fuller's iconoclastic use of close-ups as "headlines."[6] If in the history of cinema the human face has been invoked since D. W. Griffith as a privileged "vehicle for conveying thoughts and feelings," in *The Crimson Kimono* the face is less a window than a mirror, where the mirror is itself a figure for the cinematic screen.[7]

The opening credit sequence of *The Crimson Kimono*, set in an artist's studio and composed of a series of dissolves of a life-size sketch of a woman in a crimson kimono that metamorphoses into a full-fledged easel painting, foregrounds the importance of process and perception in art and, by extension, life. The sequence concludes with a hand that enters the frame from screen right and signs the painting "Chris." Although we do not know who the artist is, the signature is a self-reflexive gesture and suggests that the artist is a surrogate for the director, as if Fuller, at the very beginning of the "picture," is signing it.

Fuller's signature style of "shock editing," underscored by the dramatic change in Henry Sukman's score from romantic orchestral music to a "sleazy," big band vamp, can be seen in the fade from the close-up of the artist signing the painting to a semidocumentary aerial shot of the city of Los Angeles at night—"Main Street 8:00 P.M."—that's succeeded by a high wide shot of a marquee featuring a blow-up doll and neon burlesque dancer: "BURLESQUE ON STAGE AND IN PERSON / SUGAR TORCH AND NUDIE DOLLS." After the camera tilts up from another, closer shot of the marquee to a shot of a nudie doll, there's a match cut to Sugar Torch (Gloria Pall) on stage performing a striptease and singled out by a spotlight. This transition is, to say the least, jarring and stages a flagrant disjunction between the high, fine art of easel painting and the low, not to say debased, art of burlesque;[8]

it anticipates, moreover, the discontinuousness between the romantic-melodramatic and criminal-investigative plotlines.

Consequently, when a sunglassed figure in a hat and trench coat fires at Sugar Torch after she has just come off stage and then kills her in the middle of Main Street, the murder investigation comes briskly to the fore. Two LAPD officers, Det. Sgt. Charlie Bancroft (Glenn Corbett) and Det. Joe Kojaku (James Shigeta), are assigned to the case and discover that Sugar Torch was working on a new Las Vegas act, "The Crimson Kimono," set in a geisha house and featuring a love triangle. As her manager explains:

> This gorgeous geisha makes her entrance in a crimson kimono. . . . Not an inch of flesh exposed, only her face. She begins dancing to Japanese music and then she starts a real slow peel with this karate brick-smasher watching her. Suddenly, her jealous boyfriend barges in, a samurai warrior with a sword, Hidaka. . . . The two guys begin battling over her, bare hands versus sword. The brick crusher kills Hidaka with one blow, turns to collect Sugar, but she tosses herself on the dead warrior. . . . The brick crusher blows his top, kills her and exits as the curtain slowly comes down on the two dead lovers. Sort of a Romeo and Juliet touch.

There are any number of elements at play here. First, the individual sketches of the *karateka* and samurai warrior resemble nothing so much as storyboards and, as such, reiterate the film's accent on artifice and self-reflexivity. Second, Sugar Torch's exploitation of Japanese culture may be a form of exoticism, but it also bespeaks her desire to "transcend the 'low' art world of burlesque."[9] Finally, the manager's reference to Shakespeare represents, like Chris's painting and Sugar Torch's own "transgressive" recourse to the martial arts and the geisha trope, yet another twist on the film's deconstructive, proto-postmodern take on the relation between elite and mass culture.

The detectives' initial investigative forays reflect these divergent worlds. While Joe interviews "samurai warrior" Willy Hidaka (George Yoshinaga) at a martial arts studio in Little Tokyo, Charlie tracks down the artist who painted the "The Crimson Kimono" to a studio at the University of Southern California, where he discovers that "Chris" is a woman, Christine Downes (Victoria Shaw), and that the painting was commissioned by a man named Hansel (Neyle Morrow), an Asian art expert at the public library. The crucial moment in the sequence occurs when Christine sketches a portrait of Hansel while Charlie, plainly infatuated, gazes at her. The shot is conspicuous because Christine's body is blocked by the easel in the foreground, a composition that emphasizes the act of Charlie reading her face. Later, when an anonymous man tries to shoot Christine at her sorority house, the detectives move her back to their apartment, where, after she reviews a series of mug shots, she breaks down and Charlie kisses her.

In a parallel and reverse movement, while Charlie confers with an informer, Ziggy (Walter Burke), about Hansel's whereabouts, Joe, holding a kendo doll, explains the martial art to Christine, then plays a "little children's song," "Akatombo" ("Red Dragonfly"), on a piano decorated with a bust of Beethoven. As Joe's playing ("Charlie didn't pass me off as a Mozart?"), Christine, curious about why he chose a gun rather than a brush, inquires about a lacquer painting signed "Kojaku" on the wall, and Joe tells her that it was painted by his father. If Joe, unlike his father, has opted for a more practical, financially secure occupation, he reveals his sensitive, artistic side when he critiques Christine's painting and—this is *the* melo-romantic moment—the couple suddenly realizes that there's something special between them. Joe takes Christine by the hands; he does not, however, kiss her. Since Charlie has already announced his intentions (he plans to ask Christine to marry him), Joe's now caught between his growing desire for Christine and his personal and professional bond with his partner.

Joe, troubled, goes to Little Tokyo, where he talks to a sensei about his problem:

SENSEI: Who is she?
JOE: Chris Downes.
SENSEI: What is her Japanese name? Is she Caucasian?
JOE: Yes.
SENSEI: I can see what is the problem.
JOE: That's not what is wrong. I keep asking myself, How do I rate a girl like
    Chris? Me, Joe Kojaku? How do I rate her?

Just as Joe asks his sensei for advice, Christine asks Mac (Anna Lee), a cigar-smoking, bourbon-swilling, skid-row muralist,[10] if she was "ever in love with a man from a different world," "someone of a different race." Mac forthrightly replies, "Joe's not fighting any[thing] racial"; the problem is Charlie. "What those two had together in the war," Mac reflects, "no one can touch": "Joe's blood kept Charlie alive in Korea, and now it's Charlie's friendship that's keeping Joe alive."[11] Here, Fuller uses the trope of painting to describe the mixed "blood" relationship between Joe and Charlie, which, according to Mac, is "like mixing two dabs of paint together."

Although Christine's confident that she can patch things up—"I can straighten this out without any melodrama at all"—when Charlie returns to the apartment, a portrait of Joe that Christine has sketched rests, in an echo of the previous studio scene at USC, on an easel between Charlie and her. It's a dramatically ironic prop: Charlie cannot see that the answer to why his partner has been acting like a zom-

LA COLUMBIA PICTURES *presenta*

IL KIMONO SCARLATTO

con **VICTORIA SHAW** · **GLENN CORBETT** · **JAMES SHIGETA**

Scritto, prodotto e diretto da **SAMUEL FULLER**   *Una produzione* **GLOBE ENTERPRISES**

True Confession/Combat! Italian *fotobusta* for *The Crimson Kimono*. On the left, Roma Wilson (Jaclynne Greene) confesses to Det. Joe Kojaku (James Shigeta). On the right, Joe and Charlie Bancroft (Glenn Corbett) face off in the kendo match.

bie is right before his eyes. The fact that the only other sketch in the film—with the exception, of course, of "The Crimson Kimono"—is of Hansel, the suspected killer of Sugar Torch, also points to a buried connection between Hansel and Joe as well as between the domestic and police detective plots, a subversive one that's revealed in the penultimate scene of the film.

The subsequent kendo sequence, a tour de force of music, editing, and cinematography,[12] mimics and inverts the earlier action sequence in which Joe and Charlie work together as a team—Joe using karate, Charlie throwing punches—to subdue Shuto (Fuji), the *karateka* in Sugar Torch's act. Set in a gymnasium, the match pits "champions" Joe and Charlie as representatives of their respective Nisei and LAPD dojos. The host explains to the audience that kendo "is an art of disciplined assault. It can be dangerous if not executed according to the rules. When a protagonist aims for the head, torso, or the wrists, the targets will be called out. When a combatant is hit in one of these targets that has been called out, he loses the bout." Importantly, the host refers to the LAPD team as "Caucasian," but in fact it's mixed, as is the Nisei team and audience.

Before the match begins, Charlie is identified by his black jacket (*keiko-gi*) and pleated "skirt" (*hakema*) and Joe by his white one. Thus, despite the fact that both masks are black, it's possible—at least initially—to determine which combatant is which, since the scene is photographed primarily in wide shots. As the scene progresses and the fighting becomes more intense, however, close-ups begin to predominate and it's virtually impossible to tell the combatants apart. Only after one of them starts to beat the other one over the head with his bamboo sword (*shinai*) and audience members react in horror do we realize that it's Joe who's violating the rules. In fact, Joe's attack is so furious and relentless that he knocks Charlie, unconscious, to the ground.

The costuming in this scene (supervised by Bernice Pontrelli) is critical. For example, Fuller reverses the usual polarity so that Joe, the "aggressor," is associated with the color white while Charlie, the "victim," wears black, a color scheme that problematizes the conventional, melodramatic coding wherein the Caucasian character is the "good," white one. Similarly, just as the kendo match is constructed "so that the viewer is in the middle of the action,"[13] both aggressor and victim, the masks thwart the stereotypical process of racial identification. The grilles on the masks are, in this context, particularly suggestive as they recall the earlier piano sequence in which Joe—his face uncluttered, like Christine's in the first USC sequence—sits playing the piano in the right foreground of the frame while, in the left background, Christine stands isolated and imprisoned by a cross-hatched music stand. As in the scene where Joe, walking alone and desolate in the city, passes a chain-link fence, the grilles on the kendo masks signify the way racial categories imprison perception so that the face is not so much a window as a mask.

Men (面): Face mask of Joe Kojaku (James Shigeta) after breaking the rules and attacking his partner, Charlie Bancroft (Glenn Corbett), in the kendo sequence in *The Crimson Kimono*.

The transition from the kendo contest—a match shot from a close-up of a stunned Joe to Charlie's unmasked face—prefigures Joe's confession and Charlie's reaction. While Charlie lies recuperating in a dressing room, Joe finally confesses his feelings about Christine: "I'm in love with her, she's in love with me. . . . On account of you, I never even touched her. I wanted to hold her in my arms, but I couldn't." Charlie's response—"You mean you wanna marry her?"—appears innocuous enough, but Joe interprets his reaction as calling into question his prerogative as a Japanese American to marry a Caucasian woman like Christine: "You wouldn't have said it that way if I were white." Even though Charlie's clearly bewildered—"What are you talking about?"—Joe proceeds to read the expression on his face as revulsion: "Look at you! It's all over your face! What burns you is that you lost her to me. . . . The thought makes you sick to your stomach. Look at your face!" The look on Charlie's face is in fact "ambiguous."[14] The question therefore becomes: is Charlie really "sick to [his] stomach" because he has lost Christine to an Asian American, or is Joe projecting his own feelings of racial abjection onto his partner?

Cut to Joe's room, where he's violently packing a suitcase as Christine sits watching on the edge of his bed:

JOE: It wasn't just plain normal jealousy. That's why those words poured out of me.

CHRISTINE: You only saw what you wanted to see.

JOE: You weren't there.

CHRISTINE: I know how [Charlie] feels about those things.

JOE: I saw that look, Chris. It's a look I've never seen before on his face or anybody else's.

Since it's difficult to imagine that Joe has "never experienced racism before,"[15] this plot turn is, it's clear, a melodramatic conceit. Its equivalent in the sphere of romance is the fact that, true to the conventions of the genre, Charlie seems to fall in love with Christine, and Christine with Joe, at first sight.

But if Joe's romance with Christine threatens to detonate his domestic and professional life, it also compels him to recognize his difference from both Charlie and Christine. This difference, gesturing as it does to a collective history "larger and longer than his or her individual history,"[16] exposes an abyss of identity that, as Joe's monologue eloquently attests, neither love nor desire, empathy nor identification, can bridge:

You can't feel for me unless you are me. Take a good look, Chris. Do I look different to you than I did yesterday? [Christine turns away] Did my face change? . . . I never felt this in the army, in the police. Maybe it's five thousand years of blood behind me busting to the front. For the first time I feel different. I taste it right through every bone inside me.

Joe's experience of radical difference is a direct result of the hurt and pain that he feels as a "socially disprized subject" who, by virtue of his race, doesn't "rate" a white woman who happens to be the object of desire of another, white male.[17] That this man happens to be his partner and roommate only adds to the confusion. As Joe puts it before he says good-bye to Christine: "I was born here. I'm American. I feel it, live it, and love it. But down deep, what am I? Japanese American? American Japanese? Nisei?"

Joe's identity crisis is registered in a fraught sequence set at a restaurant where Japanese American girls and women are dressing for the Nisei Week Festival. A little girl tugs at Joe's sleeve, and as the other girls and women look on, giggling, she gives him a fortune cookie. The atmosphere is festive and both the girls and women are smiling, yet the mere fact that Joe is the object of their gaze reinforces his continuing anxiety about whether he is Japanese American or American Japanese. When Charlie arrives, he tries to talk to Joe, although he resolutely refuses to apologize for what he calls "normal healthy jealous hate," reminding Joe that he's "carrying a pint of [his] blood inside of [him.]"

Christine is encouraging Joe not to resign from the police force when she recognizes Hansel. Joe, Charlie, and Christine race after Hansel, trailing him to a back room at a Japanese doll exhibit where he insists that his relationship with Sugar Torch was "strictly business." (Note the silhouetted shadows of Christine and a policeman on the wall behind Joe, Hansel, and Charlie, which point up, as in a caricature, the stock, programmatic nature of the characters.) Suddenly, a Caucasian woman who makes wigs for the dolls, Roma Wilson (Jaclynne Greene), materializes with a .32 Smith & Wesson and shoots at Hansel, then flees.

The ensuing chase through Little Tokyo as the Grand Parade's in progress is a stunning instance of audiovisual montage as "collision."[18] While traditional Japanese music accompanies the ceremoniously dressed female Ondo dancers, American martial music plays under the troops of Nisei boy scouts. Equally importantly, the film continually crosscuts between Roma, who's running, and Joe, who's chasing her, so that the music rapidly changes from "Japanese" to "American" and back again. The effect is highly discordant and performatively mirrors Joe's identity crisis.

An even more striking "alienation effect" punctuates the chase sequence. After Roma shoots at Joe and Joe, returning fire, downs her with one shot, she confesses that she killed Sugar Torch because she thought that her boyfriend, Paul Sand, aka Hansel, was romantically involved with the burlesque dancer: "I was sure she took him from me." As the sound of an ambulance siren grows closer, the camera periodically cuts away to low-angle shots of Japanese American girls and women,

"Oriental" *Entfremdungseffekt*: Cutaway to black Noh masks in the climactic, penultimate sequence of *The Crimson Kimono*.

brilliantly costumed in spangled headdresses and multicolored kimonos, solemnly looking down at her.

The real coup de maître occurs, however, when Roma, anguished, keens—"I was wrong. I was so wrong. He never even looked at her"—and the camera cuts away to a series of Noh masks, black, impassive, contorted. These masks, which constitute a site of extraordinary overdetermination, not only recollect the black masks in the kendo sequence but evoke the "cliché of Oriental inscrutability,"[19] graphically accentuating how the Asian face has historically been figured as a mask.

The coda to *The Crimson Kimono* is surprisingly free of ambiguity. When Joe catches up with Charlie, he rehearses why Roma killed Sugar Torch—"She only saw in his face what she wanted to"—and then apologizes: "I don't know how to tell you how I feel." "You don't have to," Charlie snaps. "It's all over your face." While Charlie's happy that Joe has "wrapped up [his] own case," his answer to Joe's question about whether they're still partners is a flat negative: "As far as Chris is concerned, it'll always be rough for me." Joe and Charlie's partnership and "homosocial" domestic arrangement will not survive this particular homicide case.[20]

But even as the two men are working out the end of their partnership, Christine calls out to Joe. When he turns and sees her running toward him, he runs to her and, lifting her up, twirls her around in the air, their bodies silhouetted against the lantern-lit, banner-decorated skyline of Little Tokyo. The camera cuts away to Mac consoling Charlie—"C'mon, Charles, let's belt a few"—then back to Joe and Christine, who, standing in a river of silently gesticulating dancers, share a kiss that's deep as it is long.

* * *

In the twinned, staggered climaxes of *The Crimson Kimono*, the detective-in-vestigative plot is resolved, then the interracial romantic triangle "with the Nisei getting the Caucasian girl."[21] To fully appreciate this dénouement, though, which was "incredibly bold for 1959,"[22] one must see it in the context of the history of both classical Hollywood cinema and film noir.

Although classical Hollywood cinema has been indelibly marked by the rapacious subtext of Cecil B. DeMille's *The Cheat* (1915), the specific pretext for *The Crimson Kimono* is the romance between Cheng Huan (played in "yellowface" by Richard Barthelmass) and Lucy (Lilian Gish) in *Broken Blossoms* (1919). In *A Third Face* Fuller remembers that, "as a boy," he "wanted Lilian Gish's heroine to end up with the sweet Chinese guy in D. W. Griffith's *Broken Blossoms*."[23] It's in this sense that *The Crimson Kimono* is a signature film for Fuller—which is to say, it's personal. Hence Fuller's dismay at the studio's marketing of the film: "[Columbia] went against my wishes and *slanted* the campaign with phrases such as.... WHY DOES SHE CHOOSE A JAPANESE LOVER? "I complained bitterly about how they'd cheapened the movie."[24]

If classical Hollywood cinema is one lens with which to view *The Crimson Kimono*, it's also important to see Fuller's film from the perspective of film noir, where, as I remarked at the beginning of this chapter, continuity is as consequential as difference or disjunction. Thus, in the 1930s and 1940s, in the aftermath of the "Yellow Peril" films of the 1910s and 1920s like *The Cheat*, not to mention "Master Oriental Criminals" like Long Sin, Wu Fang, and Fu Manchu,[25] Asian detective films featuring Charlie Chan, Mr. Wong, and Mr. Moto flourished. For instance, the Charlie Chan series, which debuted in 1926 with *The House without a Key*, bridges not only the silent and sound eras but, like *The Thin Man* pictures, the proto- and classical periods of film noir.[26]

Still, one of the ironies of the Hollywood Asian detective film is that even as it provided a positive, non-villainous representation of an Asian character (who possessed superior, if "mysterious," deductive skills), it did so in contradistinction to the white, quintessentially American private detective (since the Asian detective's wisdom was a function of an "inscrutable" culture). In other words, if the Asian detective was, as it were, affirmatively "othered"—not unlike Sherlock Holmes (consider the eccentric British private detective's penchant for opium)—this same process of othering effectively "functioned to prevent . . . overidentification."[27] *The Crimson Kimono* subtly inverts this process, eliciting an identification with Joe Kojaku before melodramatically distancing his character in order to facilitate a romantic happy ending.

At the beginning of Fuller's film, Joe flaunts his assimilated status as a Nisei or second-generation Japanese American. Charlie has just woken him up with a lead about the "author" of "The Crimson Kimono."[28] While Joe talks in Japanese to a source in the community, Sister Gertrude (Aya Oyama), about where Shuto lives, Charlie reminds him about his Sunday date with the "Gardena babe." Joe wants to put it off in order to wrap up the case (his ambition is to make sergeant sooner rather than later), but when Charlie mentions that the "grapevine" has it that the "Gardena beauty" wants him to meet her family, Joe grouses: "We never agree on anything. All we do is get into beefs about the old country."

Unlike Joe's female friend, who as a *Kibei* was born in Japan and, to recollect Joe's own self-interrogative terms, is more Japanese than American, Joe is emphatically Japanese *American*. At the same time, if Joe's momentarily othered in the kendo sequence when he violates the rules of the game, his character's aggression counters the stereotypical representation of Asian men in classical Hollywood cinema as meek, submissive or, in a word, castrated. Accordingly, Joe's violation of the rules of kendo in conjunction with his romantic confession and subsequent denunciation of Charlie as racist both "sames" *and* "others" him. One consequence of the former self-assertive acts is that just as Christine becomes a "desiring figure in her own right" when she declares her love for Joe,[29] Joe's aggression and declaration of love represent an alternative, more integrated model of Japanese American masculinity, "a complex Asian ethnic male" who not only "maintains ties to his community" but solves the case and openly "pursues his sexual desires."[30] Another consequence of this dialectical process of identification, at once positive and negative, is a new position or synthesis in the form of the film's ecstatic happy ending.

This happy ending is significant because if *The Crimson Kimono*, like *Touch of Evil* and *Odds against Tomorrow*, does not avail itself of 3-D, color, or widescreen, it nevertheless conforms to the stereotypical portrait of '50s noir in which the investigative figure is a policeman rather than private detective. In "The McCarthyite Crime Film" (the title is indicative), Dennis Broe writes that the "outstanding feature" of the '50s crime film is the "focalization of the audience through the perspective of the cop."[31] Broe is specifically referring to the period from 1950 to 1955, the "time of the toad" and "conformist cop" as "fascistic enforcer of the law,"[32] but this interpretation, as I've argued, has colored the critical appreciation of '50s noir as a whole.

In this interpretive context, it's important to note that neither *Touch of Evil* nor *Odds against Tomorrow* features a conventional policeman. In *Touch of Evil* Hank Quinlan (Orson Welles) is certainly, as brothel owner Tanya (Marlene Dietrich) says, a "lousy cop," and he may well be fascistic, but as performed by Welles, he's also "childlike, almost Falstaffian."[33] While the "nominal hero" of *Touch of Evil*, Ramon Miguel Vargas (played in "brownface" by Charlton Heston), is clearly the "good cop" to Quinlan's "bad cop," by the conclusion of Welles's film "Mike," for all his stiff-necked sanctimoniousness, ends up resorting to the same dirty tricks as his nemesis. As for *Odds against Tomorrow*, the character of David Burke (Ed Begley) is the mastermind of a bank heist; however, he's also an ex-cop who spent a year in prison for refusing to testify before a state crime commission, an act of resistance that reflects—in displaced form—the sensibility of the film's blacklisted screenwriter, Abraham Polonsky.

Unlike *Touch of Evil* and *Odds against Tomorrow*, *The Crimson Kimono* is less a product of late classic expressionism or post-HUAC cultural politics than the atomic "structure of feeling" that pervaded quotidian American life in the 1950s and beyond. One determinate element of this mood or climate was Americans' considerable ambivalence about Japanese Americans in the wake of the Second World War. In other words, the law in Fuller's film is not so much about "surveillance, investigation, order, control" as the law of the genre where classic film noir has simultaneously probed and policed the issue of race.[34] Thus, it's not insignificant that Quinlan in *Touch of Evil* is haunted by his long-standing hatred of a "half-breed" who murdered his wife, or that the heist in *Odds against Tomorrow* ultimately fails because of the racial antagonism between Johnny Ingram (Harry Belafonte) and Earl Slater (Robert Ryan). It's also significant, I think, that the elaborate tracking shot that announces Welles's film concludes with a kiss between Vargas and his wife, Suzy (Janet Leigh), that can be said to ignite the explosion of Rudy Linnekar's automobile that precipitates, in turn, the "film's central investigation."[35] (Ever the racist, Quinlan thinks that the culprit is Linnekar's "Mexican shoe clerk son-in-law," Sánchez [Victor Millan].) Similarly, in an echo of the incendiary conclusion of both *White Heat* and *Kiss Me Deadly*, *Odds against Tomorrow* climaxes with a spectacular, sky-high explosion that leaves Earl's and Johnny's bodies so charred as to be indistinguishable.

The bomb in *The Crimson Kimono* may be metaphorical, but the interracial romance between Joe Kojaku and Christine Downes is no less explosive. In the "Akatombo" piano sequence, Joe and Christine are about to kiss when he warns her, "Let's not trigger a bomb."[36] Compared to the bleak dénouement of *Odds against Tomorrow*, which concludes with a sign that reads "Stop / End," and the tacked-on ending of *Touch of Evil*, in which Mike and Suzy embrace before they drive off into the sunset in a car that looks suspiciously like Rudy Linnekar's,[37] the happy ending of *The Crimson Kimono*, exploding as it does the "limits of the crime film," constitutes a moment of "political ecstasy."[38] Indeed, the finale of *The Crimson Kimono*—a series of aerial shots of the glittering lights of Little Tokyo and, beyond, the city of Los Angeles[39]—intimates that, for the moment at least, the odds are not against but *for* tomorrow.

NOTES

PRISE DE POSITION

1. On "Disney Noir," see J. P. Telotte, "Disney Noir: 'Just Drawn That Way,'" in *Kiss the Blood Off My Hands: On Classic Film Noir*, ed. Robert Miklitsch (Urbana: University of Illinois Press, 2015), 99–112.

2. Paul Schrader, "Notes on Film Noir," in *Perspectives on Film Noir*, ed. R. Barton Palmer (New York: G. K. Hall, 1996), 109.

3. Jean-Luc Godard, *Godard on Godard*, ed. Jean Narboni and Tom Milne (New York: Viking, 1972), 171.

PREFACE

1. Raymond Borde and Étienne Chaumeton, *A Panorama of American Film Noir*, trans. Paul Hammond (San Francisco: City Lights, 2002), 83.

2. Paul Schrader, "Notes on Film Noir," in *Perspectives on Film Noir*, ed. R. Barton Palmer (New York: G. K. Hall, 1996), 106.

3. Andrew Spicer, *Film Noir* (Harlow, England: Longman, 2002), 59. In fact, elsewhere in his study Spicer notes that the "classical period" extends from 1940 to 1959—from, that is, *Stranger on the Third Floor* to *Odds against Tomorrow* (ibid., vii)—a determination that accords with the current periodization of the genre. See also "Conditions of Production and Reception" (ibid., 27).

4. For a discursive history of the periodization of classic noir, see Robert Miklitsch, "Periodizing Classic Noir: From *Stranger on the Third Floor* to the 'Thrillers of Tomorrow,'" in *Kiss the Blood Off My Hands: On Classic Film Noir*, ed. Robert Miklitsch (Urbana: University of Illinois Press, 2015), 193–218.

5. For my take on the genre, see "Cues," in Robert Miklitsch, *Siren City: Sound and Source Music in American Film Noir* (New Brunswick, NJ: Rutgers University Press), xi–xv; and "Back to Black: 'Crime Melodrama,' Docu-Melo-Noir, and the 'Red Menace' Film," in Miklitsch, *Kiss the Blood*, 1–15.

6. Brian Neve, *Film and Politics in America: A Social Tradition* (London: Routledge, 1992), 149.

7. The classic account is Dorothy Jones, "Communism and the Movies: A Study of Film Content," in John Cogley, *A Report on Blacklisting* (New York: Fund for the Republic, 1956), 196–233. See also Peter Roffman and Jim Purdy, "The Decline of the Social Problem Film," in *The Hollywood Social Problem Film: Madness, Despair, and Politics from the Depression to the Fifties* (Bloomington: Indiana University Press, 1981), 296–99; and Brian Neve, "HUAC, the Blacklist, and the Decline of Social Cinema," in *Transforming the Screen, 1950–1959*, ed. Peter Lev (New York: Charles Scribner's Sons, 2003), 65–86.

8. Frank Krutnik, *In a Lonely Street: Film Noir, Genre, Masculinity* (London: Routledge, 1991), 204; Spicer, *Film Noir*, 60.

9. For a recent, synoptic example, see Robert Porfirio's "The Strange Case of Film Noir": "This was about the time [circa 1948] the social problem films of the cycle began to be displaced by the semi-documentaries, and these in turn began to be formulaic as the police procedurals became more dominant. . . . By the early 1950s, this type of film was hardly transgressive. If anything, it tended to reinforce conservative American values." *A Companion to Film Noir*, ed. Helen Hanson and Andrew Spicer (Malden, MA: Wiley Blackwell, 2013), 60.

10. Alexander Ballinger and Danny Graydon, *The Rough Guide to Film Noir* (London: Rough Guides, 2007), 27.

11. Ibid.

12. Schrader, "Notes on Film Noir," 107; Borde and Chaumeton, *Panorama*, 155.

13. Ballinger and Graydon, *Rough Guide to Film Noir*, 33.

14. Schrader, "Notes on Film Noir," 107.

15. Thom Andersen, "Red Hollywood," in *"Un-American" Hollywood: Politics and Film in the Blacklist Era*, ed. Frank Krutnik, Steve Neale, Brian Neve, and Peter Stanfield (New Brunswick, NJ: Rutgers University Press, 2007), 225–63.

16. Joshua Hirsch, "Film Gris Reconsidered," *Journal of Popular Film and Television* 34, no. 2 (2006): 84.

17. Krutnik, *In a Lonely Street*, 191.

18. Alain Silver and Elizabeth Ward, Introduction to *Film Noir: An Encyclopedic Reference to the American Style*, ed. Silver and Ward (Woodstock, NY: Overlook, 1992), 2.

19. Nicholas Christopher, *Somewhere in the Night* (New York: Free Press, 1997), 49.

20. Ibid., 50.

21. Ibid.

22. Silver and Ward, *Film Noir*, 52.

23. Walter Metz, "'Keep the Coffee Hot, Hugo': Nuclear Trauma in Fritz Lang's *The Big Heat*," *Film Criticism* 21, no. 3 (1997): 54.

24. Ibid., 44–45.

25. Ibid.

26. On *Touch of Evil* as "noir's epitaph," see Miklitsch, "Periodizing Classic Noir," in *Kiss the Blood*, 200–202.

27. Spicer, *Film Noir*, 62.

28. Schrader, "Notes on Film Noir," 107.

29. Spicer, *Film Noir*, 63.

30. See, for example, Kelly Oliver and Benigno Trigo, "The Borderlands of *Touch of Evil*," in *Noir Anxiety* (Minneapolis: University of Minnesota Press, 203), 115–36; Jennifer Fay and Justus Nieland, *Film Noir: Hard-Boiled Modernity and the Cultures of Globalization* (New York: Routledge, 2010), 173–75; and Jonathan Auerbach, *Dark Borders: Film Noir and American Citizenship* (Durham, NC: Duke University Press, 2011), 200–203.

31. For my reading of *Odds against Tomorrow* as a terminal classic noir, see Miklitsch, "Omega: *Odds against Tomorrow*," in *Kiss the Blood*, 205–212.

32. Schrader, "Notes on Film Noir," 107.

33. Raymond Durgnat, "Paint It Black," in Palmer, *Perspectives on Film Noir*, 92, 94.

34. David J. Hogan, *Film Noir FAQ* (Milwaukee: Applause, 2013), 308.

35. See Brad Stevens, "Mob Rules: *Party Girl* and the Blacklist," *BFI Film Forever*, May 26, 2015, http://www.bfi.org.uk/news-opinion/sight-sound-magazine/comment/bradlands/mob-rules-party-girl-blacklist.

36. See my "Hollywood Noir," forthcoming in *Film Noir: Light and Shadow*, ed. Alain Silver and James Ursini (Montclair, NJ: Applause/Hal Leonard, 2016).

37. For some recent examples of the mass popular-cultural remediation of classic noir, see the preface to *Kiss the Blood Off My Hands*, "Noir Futures," xii.

INTRODUCTION

1. Richard Jewell, *The RKO Story* (New York: Arlington House, 1982), 143.

2. Ibid., 260.

3. Wheeler Winston Dixon, *Film Noir and the Cinema of Paranoia* (New Brunswick, NJ: Rutgers University Press, 2009), 83.

4. Raymond Borde and Étienne Chaumeton, *A Panorama of American Film Noir*, trans. Paul Hammond (San Francisco: City Lights, 2002), 97.

5. See J. Hoberman, *An Army of Phantoms: American Movies and the Making of the Cold War* (New York: Free Press, 2011), 197.

6. Ibid., 201.

7. Ibid., 202.

8. Ibid.

9. According to Brenda Murphy, *Big Jim McLain* earned $2,600,000 in domestic rentals on production costs of $825,554. *Congressional Theatre* (Cambridge: Cambridge University Press, 1999), 84. In his review of *Big Jim McLain* in the *New York Herald Tribune* (September 18, 1952), Otis L. Guernsey wrote that the film was "part travelogue, part documentary-type melodrama, and part love story" (cited by Brenda Murphy in *Congressional Theatre*, 85).

10. Ibid.

11. Barry Gifford, *Out of the Past: Adventures in Film Noir* (Jackson: University Press of Mississippi, 2001), 133.

12. Peter Lev, "Anticommunist Noir," in *Transforming the Screen, 1950–1959*, ed. Peter Lev (New York: Charles Scribner's Sons, 2003), 53.

13. Eddie Muller, *Dark City: The Lost World of Film Noir* (New York: St. Martin's Griffin, 1998), 37.

14. Hoberman, *Army of Phantoms*, 226.

15. Alexander Ballinger and Danny Graydon, *The Rough Guide to Film Noir* (London: Rough Guides, 2007), 153.

16. Samuel Fuller, *A Third Face* (New York: Knopf, 2002), 293.

17. Muller, *Dark City*, 116.

18. Elaine Tyler May, *Homeward Bound: American Families in the Cold War Era* (New York: Basic Books, 1988), 154.

19. Cyndy Hendershot, *Anti-Communism and Popular Culture in Mid-Century America* (Jefferson, NC: McFarland, 2003), 70.

20. Mick Broderick, *Nuclear Movies* (Jefferson, NC: McFarland, 1988), 10.

21. Michael F. Keaney, *Film Noir Guide* (Jefferson, NC: McFarland, 2003), 430.

22. Broderick, *Nuclear Movies*, 11.

23. Hendershot, *Anti-Communism*, 102.

24. Charles Flynn and Todd McCarthy, "The Economic Imperative: Why Was the B Movie Necessary?," *Kings of the Bs: Working within the Hollywood System*, ed. Charles Flynn and Todd McCarthy (New York: Dutton, 1975), 42.

25. Chris Hugo, "*The Big Combo*: Production Conditions in the Film Text," in *The Book of Film Noir*, ed. Ian Cameron (New York: Continuum, 1993), 248.

26. Flynn and McCarthy, "Economic Imperative," 42.

27. Karl Marx, *The Eighteenth Brumaire of Louis Bonaparte* (1852), in *Marx: Later Political Writings*, ed. and trans. Terrell Carver (Cambridge: Cambridge University Press, 1996), 77.

28. R. Emmet Sweeney, "Off the Beaten Track: *Shack Out on 101* and *Plunder Road*," October 1, 2013, *Movie Morlocks*, http://moviemorlocks.com/2013/10/01/off-the-beaten -track-shack-out-on-101-and-plunder-road.

29. Roger Westcombe, "*City of Fear*," *Film Noir: The Encyclopedia*, ed. Alain Silver at al. (New York: Overlook, 2010), 70.

30. Robert Kleyn, "*Kiss Me Deadly*," *Framework* 54, no. 1 (2013): 114.

31. Robert Aldrich, "Aldrich Interview," interview conducted by Pierre Sauvage, *Movie* 23 (Winter 1976–1977), in *Robert Aldrich: Interviews*, ed. Edwin T. Arnold and Eugene L. Miller (Jackson: University Press of Mississippi, 2004), 101.

32. David Bordwell, Janet Staiger, and Kristin Thompson, *The Classical Hollywood Cinema: Film Style and Mode of Production to 1960* (New York: Columbia University Press, 1985), 357.

33. Ibid.

34. Richard Maltby, *Hollywood Cinema* (Oxford: Blackwell, 1995), 159.

35. Charles G. Clarke, cited by Anthony Slide, "Charles G. Clarke," *Film Reference*, www .filmreference.com; Darryl Zanuck, *Memo from Darryl F. Zanuck: The Golden Years at Twentieth Century-Fox*, ed. Rudy Behlmer (New York: Grove, 1993), 234.

36. Nicholas Garnham, *Samuel Fuller* (New York: Viking, 1971), 71.

37. Lisa Dombrowski, *The Films of Samuel Fuller: If You Die, I'll Kill You!* (Middletown, CT: Wesleyan University Press, 2008), 87.

38. Ibid.

39. See, in this transnational context, Jennifer Fay and Justus Nieland, *Film Noir: Hard-Boiled Modernity and the Cultures of Globalization* (New York: Routledge, 2010), 60–62.

40. Fuller, *Third Face*, 323.

41. Ibid., italics mine.

42. Todd McCarthy, Introduction to John Alton, *Painting with Light* (Berkeley: University of California Press, 1995), xviii.

43. Frederic Lombardi, *Alan Dwan and the Rise and Decline of the Studios* (Jefferson, NC: McFarland, 2014), 285.

44. Alton, *Painting with Light*, 163.

45. Blake Lucas, "Slightly Scarlet," in Silver et al., *Film Noir: The Encyclopedia*, 383.

46. Nicholas Christopher, *Somewhere in the Night: Film Noir and the American City* (New York: Free Press, 1997), 225.

47. Robert Ottoson, *The American Film Noir* (Metuchen, NJ: Scarecrow Press, 1981), 96.

48. James Crawford, "Bedroom Eyes," *Reverse Shot* (Summer 2006), http://reverseshot.org/archive/entry/213/kiss_before_dying.

49. Christopher, *Somewhere in the Night*, 226.

50. R. Barton Palmer, "Henry Hathaway," in *Film Noir: The Directors*, ed. Alain Silver and James Ursini (Milwaukee: Limelight, 2012), 127.

51. Alain Silver and Meredith Brody, "Niagara," in Silver et al., *Film Noir: The Encyclopedia*, 204.

52. Ray Zone, "Deep Black and White: 3-D Film Noir of the 1950s," March 2004, *Film Noir Foundation*, http://www.filmnoirfoundation.org/noircitymag/3D-Noir.pdf.

53. Dana Reemes, *Directed by Jack Arnold* (Jefferson, NC: McFarland, 1988), 38.

54. Suzanne Arakawa, "The Japanese Los Angeles of *The Crimson Kimono* and *Brother*," in *East Asian Film Noir: Transnational Encounters and Intercultural Exchange*, ed. Chi Yun Shin and Mark Gallagher (London: I. B. Tauris, 2015), 58–59.

55. Garnham, *Samuel Fuller*, 37.

56. Fuller, *Third Face*, 375.

57. On Joe Kojaku as the "hero" or "rightful contender for carrying the narrative" of *The Crimson Kimono*, see Celine Parreñas Shimizu, *Straitjacket Sexualities: Unbinding Asian American Manhoods in the Movies* (Stanford, CA: Stanford University Press, 2012), 210.

58. On the "Shanghai gesture," see Homay King, *Lost in Translation: Orientalism, Cinema, and the Enigmatic Signifier* (Durham, NC: Duke University Press, 2010), 49–74.

CHAPTER 1. *THE WOMAN ON PIER 13*

1. Russell Campbell, "The Red Scare Film Cycle," in *Celluloid Power: Social Film Criticism from The Birth of the Nation to Judgment at Nuremberg*, ed. David Platt (Metuchen, NJ: Scarecrow, 1992), 101–109.

2. Daniel Leab, "How Red Was My Valley: Hollywood, the Cold War Film, and *I Married a Communist*," *Journal of Contemporary History* 19, no. 1 (1984): 66.

3. Tony Thomas, *Howard Hughes in Hollywood* (Secaucus, NJ: Citadel Press, 1985), 104.

4. Ibid., 106.

5. Bernard Eisenschitz, *Nicholas Ray: An American Journey*, trans. Tom Milne (London: Faber and Faber, 1993), 121. For the Losey quote, see *Losey on Losey*, ed. Tom Milne (Garden City, NY: Doubleday, 1968), 75–76. Leab, however, disputes Losey's claim that Hughes used *I Married a Communist* as a "litmus test" for directors; see "How Red Was My Valley," 78–79.

6. Daniel Mainwaring, "Daniel Mainwaring," interview conducted by Robert Porfirio, in *Film Noir Reader 3: Interviews with Filmmakers of the Classic Noir Period*, ed. Robert Porfirio, Alain Silver, and James Ursini (New York: Limelight, 2002), 155.

7. Eisenschitz, *Nicholas Ray*, 123.

8. Ibid., 124.

9. Brian McFarlane, "Jack of All Trades: Robert Stevenson," in *The Unknown 1930s: An Alternative History of the British Cinema, 1929–1939*, ed. Jeffrey Richards (London: I. B. Tauris, 1998), 161–79.

10. Robert Ottoson, *A Reference Guide to the American Film Noir, 1940–1958* (Metuchen, NJ: Scarecrow Press, 1981), 194.

11. Peter Lev, "Anti-Communism and Film Noir," in *Transforming the Screen: 1950–1959*, ed. Peter Lev (New York: Charles Scribner's Sons, 2003), 53.

12. Ibid., 51.

13. See Dalton Trumbo, *The Time of the Toad: A Study of Inquisition in America* (West Nyack, NY: Journeyman Press, 1982).

14. Philip Kemp, "From the Nightmare Factory: HUAC and the Politics of Noir," in *The Big Book of Noir*, ed. Edward Gorman, Lee Server, and Martin H. Greenberg (New York: Carroll and Graf, 1998), 78.

15. Richard Jewell, *The RKO Story* (New York: Arlington, 1982), 242.

16. Consider, for example, the script of *The Woman on Pier 13*, on which at least seven writers worked, including George F. Slavin and George W. George (who are credited with the story), Art Cohn, James Edward Grant, and Herman Mankiewicz, as well as Charles Grayson and Robert Hardy Andrews (the latter two of whom are credited with the screenplay).

17. Art Cohn not only labored on the screenplay from August 31, 1948, to December 29, 1948, but also protested the studio's determination of the screen credits and appealed the matter to the Screen Writers Guild. On Cohn's contributions to the screenplay of *The Woman on Pier 13*, see Leab, "How Red Was My Valley," 69–72.

18. For Ray's and Mankiewicz's involvement in the production of *I Married a Communist*, see Eisenschitz, *Nicholas Ray*, 123.

19. Leab, "How Red Was My Valley," 76.

20. Ellen Schrecker, *The Age of McCarthyism: A Brief History with Documents* (1994; Boston: Bedford/St. Martin's, 2002), 217 and 55. As an active member of HUAC, Nixon was also of course involved in the investigation of Alger Hiss, eventually compelling Whittaker Chambers to produce documents that would incriminate Hiss. In a scenario straight out of a Hollywood thriller, Chambers famously led two HUAC staff members to a Maryland farm where he had stashed the microfilm in a pumpkin.

21. Franklin Jarlett, *Robert Ryan: A Biography and Critical Filmography* (Jefferson, NC: McFarland, 1990), 202.

22. James Naremore, *More Than Night: Film Noir in Its Contexts* (Berkeley: University of California Press, 1998), 175. For the Alton, see *Painting with Light* (New York: Macmillan, 1949).

23. All quotations are from the screenplay by Charles Grayson and Robert Hardy Andrews, *The Woman on Pier 13* (New York: Frederick Ungar, 1976).

24. Raymond Chandler, *Farewell, My Lovely* (New York: Library of America, 1995), 767.

25. As Jeff Smith notes: "Unlike the Collins home which is initially treated as a kind of domestic sanctuary, Christine's apartment collapses the distinction between public and private spheres in that it functions as both her home and her workplace." Jeff Smith, in *Film Criticism, the Cold War, and the Blacklist: Reading the Hollywood Reds* (Berkeley: University of California Press, 2014), 74. Hence Christine's kitchenette is used both for "food preparation" and for "purposes of espionage" (75).

26. Paul Schrader, "Notes on Film Noir," in *Perspectives on Film Noir*, ed. R. Barton Palmer (New York: G. K. Hall, 1996), 104.

27. The "maze-like" character of the communist warehouse is accented in the script in both the early and closing sequences set there: "Through a maze of cranes, the sedan swings around and comes to rest in front of a metal door." Grayson and Andrews, *Woman on Pier 13*, 20; "Brad drives his car through a maze of cranes" (75).

28. On the resemblance between *Out of the Past* and *The Woman on Pier 13*, see also Smith, *Film Criticism*, 61 and 63.

29. Richard Maltby, "Made for Each Other: The Melodrama of Hollywood and the House Committee on Un-American Activities, 1947," in *Cinema, Politics and Society in America*, ed. Philip Davies and Brian Neve (Manchester: University of Manchester Press, 1981), 77.

30. Jarlett, *Robert Ryan*, 201; Leab, "How Red Was My Valley," 81.

31. Michael Walker, Introduction to *The Book of Film Noir*, ed. Ian Cameron (New York: Continuum, 1993), 23.

32. Richard Maltby, "The Politics of the Maladjusted Text," in Cameron, *Book of Film Noir*, 39; italics mine. In Robert Hardy Andrews's penultimate draft of the script, Nixon aka Vanning interrogates Brad and, in the process, produces his Communist Party card, a scenario that establishes an "implicit parallel" between HUAC and the Communist Party. Smith, *Film Criticism*, 70.

33. See, in addition, *The Man I Married* (1940), which was originally titled *I Married a Nazi*.

34. Nora Sayre, *Running Time: Films of the Cold War* (New York: Dial Press, 1982), 81. On the historical role as opposed to cinematic representation of women in communism, see Kate Weigand, *Red Feminism: American Communism and the Making of Women's Liberation* (Baltimore: Johns Hopkins University Press, 2001). For a remarkable memoir about, among other things, women, Hollywood, and the Communist Party, see Norma Barzman, *The Red and the Blacklist* (New York: Thunder's Mouth, 2003). On the "web of subversion," see James Burnham, *The Web of Subversion: Underground Networks in the U.S. Government* (New York: John Day Company, 1954).

35. Consider how Vanning is described in the script after Don punches him: "[Vanning] produces a snowy handkerchief—dabs fastidiously at mouth." Grayson and Andrews, *Woman on Pier 13*, 54. The word "fastidious" is also repeated right before he leaves Christine's

apartment: "Fastidiously, [Vanning] drops handkerchief in wastebasket" (55). However, if Vanning can be said to be feminized, Christine is figuratively masculinized—at least on the phone. In addition to invoking the figure of the prostitute ("working girl"), the scene points up the discrepancy between what she tells Don she's wearing ("overalls") and what she really has on ("smart negligee"), thereby reinforcing the notion that communists are deceptive or, not to put too fine a point on it, liars.

36. J. Edgar Hoover, *Masters of Deceit: The Story of Communism in America and How to Fight It* (New York: Holt, Rinehart, and Winston, 1958), 214.

37. Smith, *Film Criticism*, 71.

38. Ibid., 78.

39. On the Advertising Code Administration's concern about the explicit nature of this language, Smith records: "The Administration Code appeared to have no problem with the insinuation of prostitution . . . as long as it did not imply the woman's profiting from her activities." Smith, *Film Criticism*, 71.

40. Leab, "How Red Was My Valley," 82.

41. Hoover, "Testimony before HUAC," in Schrecker, *Age of McCarthyism*, 130. *The Woman on Pier 13* was inspired by the case of Harry Bridges, "the leader of the West Coast longshoremen whom the government spent some thirteen years and millions of dollars futilely trying to convict of having allowed Reds to infiltrate his union." See Michael Barson and Steven Heller, *Red Scared!: The Commie Menace in Propaganda and Popular Culture* (San Francisco: Chronicle Books, 2001), 75. The truth, as Sayre recounts, is that Bridges "actually ejected the gangsters from his branch of the International Longshoremen's and Warehousemen's Union." Sayre, *Running Time*, 153. On the San Francisco waterfront strikes of 1934, 1936, and 1948, see Charles P. Larrowe, *Harry Bridges: The Rise and Fall of Radical Labor in the United States* (New York: Lawrence Hill, 1972), 32–94, 114–16, and 293–99. It's worth noting that the 1948 strike turned on the ship owners' unsuccessful demand that union officers sign noncommunist affidavits.

42. Sayre, *Running Time*, 153. Harry Cohn initially agreed to make *The Hook*, but since the script revolved around union activity, he first sent it to Roy Brewer to be vetted. (Brewer was, at the time, the head of the International Alliance of Theatrical Stage Employees and the "toughest anti-communist in town"—the town, of course, being Hollywood). Brewer found the depiction of union corruption in *The Hook* so "appalling" that he passed it on to the FBI. The bureau's recommendation to Arthur Miller: "'all' he had to do was to rewrite the story so that instead of racketeers terrorizing the dockworkers, it would be the communists." Sayre, *Running Time*, 153. See also Reynold Humphries, who maintains that in *The Woman on Pier 13* the character of Jim Travis—"a unionist determined to defend the workers against greedy bosses" transformed by the end of the film into a "good anti-communist"—is a double of Roy Brewer. Humphries, "The Woman on Pier 13," in *Film Noir: The Encyclopedia*, ed. Alain Silver et al. (New York: Overlook, 2010), 338.

43. Frank Krutnik, "'A Living Part of the Class Struggle': Diego Rivera's *The Flower Carrier* and the Hollywood Left," in *"Un-American" Hollywood: Politics and Film in the Blacklist Era*, ed. Frank Krutnik, Steve Neale, Brian Neve, and Peter Stanfield (New Brunswick, NJ: Rutgers University Press, 2007), 56–57. The woman who helps the "flower carrier" in Ri-

vera's painting may or may not be his wife, but there's an unmistakable air of communion between the two figures. That is to say, in the public space depicted in the painting, the relation between the sexes is harmonious, a relation that's emphatically at odds with the representation of marriage in *The Woman on Pier 13*. The motif of marital discord that runs like a red thread throughout *The Woman on Pier 13* is epitomized by the drunk at the Gay Paree who, with one arm around another woman, concludes a phone conversation with his wife by slurring, "Ah—shaddup!"

44. Ibid., 57–58.

45. Ibid., 61.

46. For example, when Nan tries to help Brad when he returns home after sustaining a gunshot wound at the warehouse, his harsh reaction speaks volumes: "Please go back to bed." Nan: "But Brad. . . ." Brad: "You heard me, go on." An even more blatant example occurs when Jim Travis comes to the Collinses' apartment to talk to Brad and Nan interjects: "Why won't you reopen negotiations? You don't want to put a lot of men out of work, some of them your old friends." The script records Brad's response: "Brad: (interrupts harshly) *Nan, do you mind?* It's like a slap in her face" (46; italics in original).

47. As a result of this exchange, *The Woman on Pier 13* problematizes the simple, stable "binarism" between the femme fatale and the nurturing woman that structures so many classic film noirs. Smith, *Film Criticism*, 77.

48. Nan's relationship with management is conveyed via the trope of the Ming vase. The figure first appears when Nan notices a Ming vase in her and Brad's honeymoon hotel: "Ming dynasty, Chinese. Of course, it isn't real." (Brad, who's a red-blooded male despite his "red" past, is, of course, clueless: "Ming who?") The trope then reappears in the context of the Cornwalls' wedding present to Brad and Nan. Nan: "Ming! And it's real this time!" As the script details, the final appearance of the figure amplifies its symbolic import as well as ideological heterogeneity: "Close up of the Ming vase—held in frail, aristocratic hands of Cornwall" (*Woman on Pier 13*, 17). In the film Cornwall himself says about the vase: "Very ornamental but quite useless." Unlike Cornwall, who is, as he himself remarks, a "product of an outmoded feudal system," Brad is the "product of a new system, a new world"; unlike Cornwall, he has risen up through the ranks from stevedore foreman to "executive vice-president" of Cornwall Shipping. Nan, who worked for "Masson and Co., Decorators" and opened her own establishment in 1947 before marrying Brad (*Woman on Pier 13*, 6), is part of this brave new world. Her profession, interior decorating, may be gendered feminine, but she is also—no mean thing—a small businesswoman in her own right.

CHAPTER 2. THE RED AND THE BLACK

1. Andrew Spicer, *Film Noir* (Harlow, England: Pearson, 2002), 70.

2. Nicholas Christopher, *Somewhere in the Night* (New York: Free Press, 2002), 50.

3. Wheeler Winston Dixon, *Film Noir and the Cinema of Paranoia* (New Brunswick, NJ: Rutgers University Press, 2010), 86.

4. Frank Krutnik, for example, cites *The Woman on Pier 13*, *I Was a Communist for the F.B.I.*, and *Big Jim McLain*. Frank Krutnik, *In a Lonely Street* (New York: Routledge, 1991), 191. For Nicholas Christopher, the "obvious Red-scare noir films" are *The Woman on Pier*

13, The Whip Hand, I Was a Communist for the F.B.I., and *Walk East on Beacon!* Christopher, *Somewhere in the Night,* 52. Andrew Spicer, in his brief survey, discusses *Walk East on Beacon!, The Thief, Suddenly* (1954), and *Pickup on South Street.* Spicer, *Film Noir,* 70. Dixon, in a brief but wide-ranging survey, analyzes *The Woman on Pier 13, The Whip Hand, Red Planet Mars, Big Jim McLain, Red Snow* (1952), *Invasion U.S.A.* (1952), *Pickup on South Street, Jet Pilot,* and *The Girl in the Kremlin* (1957). Dixon, *Film Noir and the Cinema,* 82–85. In the entry for *I Was a Communist for the F.B.I.* in *Film Noir: An Encyclopedic Reference to the American Style,* Robert Porfirio mentions *The Red Menace; The Iron Curtain* (1948); *I Married a Communist,* aka *The Woman on Pier 13; The Whip Hand;* and *I Was a Communist for the F.B.I.* Porfirio, *Film Noir: An Encyclopedic Reference to the American Style,* ed. Alain Silver and Elizabeth Ward (Woodstock, NY: Overlook, 1992), 144.

5. Reynold Humphries, "The Anti-Communist Crusade on Screen," *Hollywood's Blacklists: A Political and Cultural History* (Edinburgh: Edinburgh University Press, 2010), 139.

6. Ibid.

7. Ibid.

8. Tony Thomas, *Howard Hughes in Hollywood* (Secaucus, NJ: Citadel Press, 1985), 106.

9. Ibid.

10. Ibid.

11. Donald L. Bartlett and James B. Steele, *Empire: The Life, Legend, and Madness of Howard Hughes* (New York: Norton, 1981), 175.

12. Ibid., 176.

13. Richard B. Jewell with Vernon Harbin, *The RKO Story* (New York: Arlington, 1982), 260.

14. Norman Cameron, cited by Cyndy Hendershot, *Anti-Communism and Popular Culture in Mid-Century America* (Jefferson, NC: McFarland, 2003), 18–19.

15. On Menzies's career, see Cathy Whitlock, *Designs on Film: A Century of Hollywood Art Direction* (New York: itbooks, 2010), 12–17, 46–48, and 76.

16. Hendershot, *Anti-Communism and Popular Culture,* 20.

17. Michael Paul Rogin, *"Ronald Reagan," the Movie: And Other Episodes in Political Demonology* (Berkeley: University of California Press, 1987), 247.

18. Ibid.

19. Ibid.

20. Paul Buhle and Dave Wagner, *Radical Hollywood* (New York: Free Press, 2002), 211; James J. Lorence, "The 'Foreign Policy of Hollywood': Interventionist Sentiment in the American Film, 1938–1941," in *Hollywood as Mirror,* ed. Robert Brent Toplin (Westport, CT: Greenwood, 1993), 100.

21. Lorence, "'Foreign Policy,'" 100.

22. Buhle and Wagner, *Radical Hollywood,* 211.

23. Ibid., 212.

24. J. Hoberman, *An Army of Phantoms: American Movies and the Making of the Cold War* (New York: Free Press, 2011), 275.

25. Nathaniel Rich, *San Francisco Noir* (New York: Little Bookroom, 2005), 44.

26. For one of the few entries on *Walk a Crooked Mile* in the extant "encyclopedic" litera-

ture on noir, see Michael F. Keaney's *Film Noir Guide* (Jefferson, NC: McFarland, 2003), 458–59.

27. Hendershot, *Anti-Communism*, 115; Hoberman, *Army of Phantoms*, 165.

28. Cvetic's memoir was preceded by John Roy Carlson's *Under Cover* (Cleveland: World Publishing Company, 1943), the hyperextended title of which—*My Four Years in the Nazi Underworld of America: The Amazing Revelation of Axis Agents and How Our Enemies within Are Now Plotting to Destroy the United States*—captures the melodramatic cast of the genre.

29. On Eisler, see, for example, Reynold Humphries, "'Documenting' Communist Subversion," *Docufictions: Essays on the Intersection of Documentary and Fictional Filmmaking*, ed. Gary Rhodes and John Parris Springer (Jefferson, NC: McFarland, 2006), 106–107.

30. Matt Cvetic, *The Big Decision: Based on the Experiences of Matt Cvetic, Former FBI Counterspy* (Hollywood: Big Decision, 1959), 5.

31. Blandon has generally been read as a not so disguised semblance of communist leader Steve Nelson. For example, Humphries notes that Cvetic not only "testified against [Nelson]; [Nelson's] trial for sedition was under way in Pittsburgh at the same time as the release of *I Was a Communist for the F.B.I.*" Humphries, "'Documenting' Communist Subversion," 106. For a detailed discussion of Steve Nelson in the larger social and political contexts of *I Was a Communist for the F.B.I.*, see Daniel Leab, *I Was a Communist for the F.B.I.* (University Park: Pennsylvania State University Press, 2000), 18–19, 21–23, 56–58, 68–69, and 82–87.

32. Although, as Jeff Smith points out, the Freedom Hall scene shows that "large numbers of African Americans may join the Communist Party," the same scene also shows that "they remain marginalized and excluded from the central power symbolized by the small cadre of whites in the center of the dais." Jeff Smith, *Film Criticism, the Cold War, and the Blacklist: Reading the Hollywood Reds* (Berkeley: University of California Press, 2014), 105.

33. Humphries, *Hollywood's Blacklists*, 133. As Humphries notes elsewhere, Rankin was "notorious for blocking all attempts to introduce anti-lynching laws in Congress and his refusal to condemn the Ku Klux Klan." Humphries, "'Documenting' Communist Subversion," 114. In this racial-political context, see also Tom Wright's (Napoleon Simpson) rebuttal of his son Sam's (Duke Williams) defense of the Communist Party ("You know what the Party is doing for your race?") in *The Red Menace*.

34. Humphries, *Hollywood's Blacklists*, 134.

35. Smith, *Film Criticism*, 107.

36. Cvetic, *Big Decision*, 24.

37. Although baseball is also referenced in *The Thief* and *The Atomic City*, see, for a paradigmatic instance, the fantastic "football" conceit in *My Son John*.

38. Thomas Doherty observes that Sheen represented a kind of "normative anticommunism": "Like a medieval monk battling a terrible heresy, he took to the task with a Thomistic zeal, giving line-for-line refutations of the false prophets Marx and Lenin and their agent on earth, Stalin." Thomas Doherty, *Cold War, Cool Medium: Television, McCarthyism, and American Culture* (New York: Columbia University Press, 2003), 157.

39. Cvetic: "I knew quite well what [was] meant by the RED KNOCK on my door—that the Reds had over-run the country and seized control." Cvetic, *Big Decision*, 5.

40. Hoberman, *Army of Phantoms*, 164.

41. Porfirio, "*I Was a Communist for the F.B.I.*," in *Film Noir*, 144.

42. The train tunnel sequence recalls the concluding, sewer sequence in Alfred L. Werker's *He Walked by Night*, which, as Humphries notes, was based on a story by Crane Wilbur, who co-authored the script. Humphries, "'Documenting' Communist Subversion," 117.

43. Rogin, *Ronald Regan*, 260.

44. On the German American Bund in the context of *Confessions of a Nazi Spy*, see Jonathan Auerbach, *Dark Borders: Film Noir and American Citizenship* (Durham, NC: Duke University Press, 2011), 27–40.

45. Cvetic, *Big Decision*, 214.

46. Humphries, "'Documenting' Communist Subversion," 114.

47. On the contradictory discourse of racial discrimination in *The Red Menace*, see Smith, *Film Criticism*, 95–100.

48. J. Edgar Hoover, *Masters of Deceit: The Story of Communism and How to Fight It* (New York: Holt, Rinehart and Winston, 1958), 246. Although it's true the Communist Youth League played an instrumental role in the Harlem race riot of 1935, the causal link advanced by Crowley between the Communist Party and the Detroit and Harlem race riots of 1943 is, in fact, spurious. The remote cause of the Detroit race riot that year was the lack of adequate housing for the African Americans who had streamed into the city from the South to work in the war-mobilized manufacturing sphere. The riot itself originated at the popular, integrated amusement park Belle Isle and spilled over to the bridge back to the mainland, where a fight broke out between blacks and white sailors. As for the 1943 Harlem race riot, the immediate cause was the shooting of a black soldier by a white policeman. (According to the soldier, he was coming to the aid of a black woman; according to the policeman, he was interfering with an arrest.) Although the soldier was only wounded, the riot-inciting rumor was that he had been killed.

49. Writing about the congressional debate about the Fair Employment Practices Commission (FEPC) in May 1950, Mary Dudziak captures the tenor of the times: "In a political and cultural climate steeped in anticommunism, arguing that civil rights reform would be a capitulation to communists, who themselves must clearly be pursuing ulterior motives to undermine American society, proved to be an effective strategy. Anticommunism was more important to Congress than civil rights." Mary Dudziak, *Cold War Civil Rights: Race and American Democracy* (Princeton, NJ: Princeton University Press, 2000), 89.

50. Humphries, "'Documenting' Communist Subversion," 114.

51. Ibid., 118.

52. Thus, as Leab recounts, a Warner Bros. script person, reading Crane Wilbur's first draft of *I Was a Communist for the F.B.I.*, wrote on its cover, "tell as 92nd St." Leab, *I Was a Communist*, 79. See also Spicer's entry in *Historical Dictionary of Film Noir* on the "Right-Wing Cycle," which begins with *The House on 92nd Street* and concludes with *Walk East on Beacon!*, producer Louis de Rochemont's semidocumentary anticommunist sequel to the former film. Andrew Spicer, *Historical Dictionary of Film Noir* (Lanham, MD: Scarecrow Press, 2010), 261–62.

53. Tony Shaw, *Hollywood's Cold War* (Edinburgh: Edinburgh University Press, 2007), 54.

54. Robert Ottoson, *A Reference Guide to the American Film Noir: 1940–1958* (Metuchen, NJ: Scarecrow Press, 1981), 86.

55. Shaw, *Hollywood's Cold War*, 58.

56. Ibid., 54.

57. Ibid., 64.

58. As Shaw notes, Gold "implicated a Los Alamos atomic machinist, David Greenglass, who in turn implicated his sister and brother-in-law, Ethel and Julius Rosenberg." Ibid., 69n51.

59. Leo Rosten, quoted in Shaw, *Hollywood's Cold War*, 57.

60. Ibid., 58.

61. Ibid.

62. Ibid., 63.

63. Kafer's description of his work sounds grandiloquent; however, it presages not only the space race precipitated by Sputnik in 1957 but also the Strategic Defense Initiative (SDI), so-called Star Wars, promulgated by the Reagan administration in the 1980s. Since the professor is seen testing his theory on the "newly developed high-speed calculators" (the footage is actually of IBM's Selective Service Electronic Calculator located at the time in New York City), Kafer's peroration also anticipates the language used to describe the Internet—that is, the "information superhighway."

64. Shaw, *Hollywood's Cold War*, 61.

65. Ibid., 60.

66. Manny Farber, quoted by Hoberman in *Army of Phantoms*, 198.

67. Humphries, *Hollywood's Blacklists*, 137.

68. David Bordwell, Janet Staiger, and Kristin Thompson, *The Classical Hollywood Cinema: Film Style and Mode of Production to 1960* (New York: Columbia University Press, 1985), 359.

69. Bosley Crowther, "*Big Jim McLain*: Film Study of Congressional Work against Communism, at Paramount," *New York Times*, September 18, 1952, http://www.nytimes.com/movie/review?res=9805E2D9133AE23BBC4052DFBF668389649EDE.

70. Richard English not only wrote "We Almost Lost Hawaii to the Reds" for the *Saturday Evening Post* but also authored an article titled "What Makes a Hollywood Communist?" According to Brenda Murphy, "HUAC's chief investigator in Hollywood," William Wheeler, helped English write the screenplay for *Big Jim McLain*. Brenda Murphy, *Congressional Theatre: Dramatizing McCarthyism on Stage, Film, and Television* (Cambridge: Cambridge University Press, 1999), 78. English, John Wayne, and James Edward Grant were all members of the MPAPAI.

71. Thomas W. Benson, "Looking for the Public in the Popular: The Hollywood Blacklist and the Rhetoric of Collective Memory," in *The Terministic Screen: Rhetorical Perspectives on Film*, ed. David Blakesley (Carbondale: Southern Illinois Press, 2003), 134.

72. Jeff Smith, *Film Criticism*, 110–11.

73. Ibid., 59.

74. Benson, "Looking for the Public," 133. Thomas Doherty observes that *Big Jim McLain* "enacts another kind of reconciliation: international Communism itself has been absorbed and domesticated by Hollywood convention." Thomas Doherty, "Hollywood Agit-Prop: The Anti-Communist Cycle, 1948–1954," *Journal of Film and Video* 40, no. 4 (1988): 24. To wit, entertainment—and *Big Jim McLain*, its retrograde politics aside, is pretty entertaining—trumps ideology.

75. Hoberman, *Army of Phantoms*, 204.

76. On tourism and visual spectacle in *Big Jim McLain*, see Russell Meeuf, who argues (and here it's worth noting that Hawaii was a "U.S. territory and not a state" when Ludwig's picture was being shot) that the film implicitly promotes an "ideology of cosmopolitan travel, leisure, and consumption as the real spaces that need to be saved from the taint of Communism." Russell Meeuf, *John Wayne's World: Transnational Masculinity in the Fifties* (Austin: University of Texas Press, 2013), 78–79.

77. Benson, "Looking for the Public in the Popular," 131.

78. Ibid., 134.

79. Patricia Highsmith, *The Talented Mr. Ripley* (New York: Vintage, 1992), 123.

80. Benson, "Looking for the Public," 136.

81. Ibid., 131.

82. Smith, *Film Criticism*, 116.

CHAPTER 3. *PICKUP ON SOUTH STREET*

1. Jeff Smith, *Film Criticism, the Cold War, and the Blacklist: Reading the Hollywood Reds* (Berkeley: University of California Press, 2014), 147.

2. Ibid.

3. Lisa Dombrowski, *The Films of Samuel Fuller: If You Die, I'll Kill You!* (Middleport, CT: Wesleyan University Press, 2008), 9.

4. J. Hoberman, *An Army of Phantoms: American Movies and the Making of the Cold War* (New York: Free Press, 2011), 238.

5. Emilie Pickerton, *A Short History of* Cahiers du Cinéma (London: Verso, 2009), 9; Georges Sadoul, letter to Jacques Doniol-Valcroze, September 25, 1955, cited in Pickerton, *Short History*, xviii.

6. Lou Moullet, "Sam Fuller: In Marlowe's Footsteps," *Cahiers du Cinéma*, vol. 1, *The 1950s: Neo-Realism, Hollywood, New Wave*, ed. Jim Hillier (New York: Routledge, 1985), 147.

7. Ibid., 154. For the Godard, see "Hiroshima, notre amour," *Cahiers du Cinéma* (July 1959): 62.

8. Peter Stanfield, *Maximum Movies—Pulp Fictions: Film Culture and the Worlds of Samuel Fuller, Mickey Spillane, and Jim Thompson* (Brunswick, NJ: Rutgers University Press, 2011), 127.

9. Samuel Fuller, *A Third Face: My Tale of Writing, Fighting, and Filmmaking* (New York: Knopf, 2002), 262.

10. Ibid., 523.

11. Ibid., 295.

12. Ibid., 264.

13. Ibid., 269.

14. Ibid., 273.

15. Michael Rogin, "Kiss Me Deadly," in *"Ronald Reagan," the Movie: And Other Episodes in Political Demonology* (Berkeley: University of California Press, 1987), 267.

16. Ibid., 221.

17. Fuller, *Third Face*, 303.

18. Ibid.

19. Rogin, "Kiss Me Deadly," 268.

20. For an incisive reading of the microfilm as, among other things, a cinematic figure, see Jonathan Auerbach, *Dark Borders: Film Noir and American Citizenship* (Durham, NC: Duke University Press, 2011), 165–88.

21. Dombrowski, *Films of Samuel Fuller*, 71.

22. Jack Shadoian, *Dreams and Dead Ends: The American Gangster Film* (New York: Oxford University Press, 2003), 193.

23. Ibid.

24. Ibid., 192.

25. If, as Smith argues in the most nuanced reading of the "politics of naming names" in *Pickup on South Street*, "Moe's activities and motivations" in the first part of the film "parallel those of HUAC informers," her refusal to sell out Skip to the communists "links her to those HUAC witnesses who were ultimately blacklisted for failing to play the role of informer." Smith, *Film Criticism*, 157, 159.

26. Ibid., 186.

27. Fuller, *Third Face*, 304.

28. Ibid.

29. Dombrowski, *Films of Samuel Fuller*, 70; italics in original.

30. Shadoian, *Dreams and Dead Ends*, 194.

31. Ibid., 189.

32. Auerbach, *Dark Borders*, 170.

33. Dombrowski, *Films of Samuel Fuller*, 75–76.

34. J. Hoberman, "Three American Abstract Sensationalists" (1981), in *Vulgar Modernism* (Philadelphia: Temple University Press, 1991), 22–40.

35. Shadoian, *Dreams and Dead Ends*, 193.

36. Dombrowski, *Films of Samuel Fuller*, 75–76.

37. Frank D. McConnell, "*Pickup on South Street* and the Thriller," in *The Spoken Seen: Film and the Romantic Imagination* (Baltimore: Johns Hopkins University Press, 1975), 133.

38. Fuller, *Third Face*, 431.

39. Ibid.

40. Ibid., 297.

41. McConnell, "*Pickup on South Street* and the Thriller," 135.

CHAPTER 4. *D.O.A.*

1. Jerome F. Shapiro, *American Bomb Cinema* (New York: Routledge, 2002), 61.

2. Paul Boyer, *By the Bomb's Early Light: American Thought and Culture* (Chapel Hill: University of North Carolina Press, 1994), 11.

3. Jack Shadoian, *Dreams and Dead Ends* (New York: Oxford University Press, 2002), 181.

4. R. Barton Palmer, *Hollywood's Dark Cinema* (New York: Twayne, 1994), 88.

5. Nicholas Christopher, *Somewhere in the Night* (New York: Free Press, 1997), 54.

6. Ibid.

7. Austin M. Brues, quoted by Boyer in *By the Bomb's Early Light*, 308.

8. Shadoian, *Dreams and Dead Ends*, 189.

9. Laurence E. MacDonald, *The Invisible Art of Music* (Lanham, MD: Scarecrow Press, 2013), 131.

10. Beverley Carter, "The War of the Sexes: Men in Film Noir and *D.O.A.*," *Film Noir Reader 4*, ed. Alain Silver and James Ursini (New York: Limelight, 2004), 90.

11. David Butler, *Jazz Noir* (Westport, CT: Praeger, 2002), 69.

12. See, in the context of African American singers and musicians, Robert Miklitsch, "Singing Detectives and Bluesmen, Black Jazzwomen and Torch Singers," *Siren City: Sound and Source Music in Classic American Noir* (New Brunswick, NJ: Rutgers University Press), 164–92.

13. Ibid., 70.

14. Robert Porfirio, "Dark Jazz: Music in Film Noir," *Film Noir Reader 2*, ed. Alain Silver and James Ursini (New York: Limelight, 1999), 179.

15. "Within hours of Eben Ayres' announcement, the bar of the Washington Press Club offered an 'Atomic Cocktail'—a greenish blend of pernod and gin." Boyer, *By the Bomb's Early Light*, 10. The "atomic cocktail"—equal parts vodka, brandy, and champagne—was also a "big seller" on the Las Vegas Strip. A. Costandina Titus, *Bombs in the Backyard: Atomic Testing and American Politics* (Reno: University of Nevada Press, 1986), 93.

16. Mark Osteen, *Nightmare Alley: Film Noir and the American Dream* (Baltimore: Johns Hopkins University Press, 2012), 161.

17. Palmer, *Hollywood's Dark Cinema*, 87.

18. For a gloss of a still from this scene, see Alain Silver and James Ursini, *The Noir Style* (New York: Overlook, 1999), 174–75. On the scene's racial logic, see Kelly Oliver and Benigno Trigo, *Noir Anxiety* (Minneapolis: University of Minnesota Press, 2003), 232.

19. See Eddie Muller, *Dark City* (New York: St. Martin's Griffin, 1998), 116.

20. Boyer, *By the Bomb's Early Light*, 8.

21. Titus, *Bombs in the Backyard*, 17.

22. See Alexander Ballinger and Danny Graydon, *The Rough Guide to Film Noir* (London: Rough Guides, 2007), 82.

23. Ibid., 83.

24. Jon Tuska, *Dark Cinema: American Film Noir in Cultural Perspective* (Westport, CT: Greenwood, 1984), 165.

25. Shadoian, *Dreams and Dead Ends*, 184.

26. On *D.O.A.*'s "exploitation" of orientalism, see Stanley Orr, *Darkly Perfect World: Colonial Adventure, Postmodernism, and American Noir* (Columbus: Ohio State University Press, 2010), 100–102.

27. Elaine Tyler May, *Homeward Bound* (New York: Basic, 1988), 91.

CHAPTER 5. "BLACK FILM" AND THE BOMB

1. See Glenn Scott Allen, *Master Mechanics and Wicked Wizards: Images of the American Scientist as Hero and Villain from Colonial Times to the Present* (Amherst: University of Massachusetts Press, 2009).

2. Jessica Wang, *American Science in an Age of Anxiety: Scientists, Anticommunism, and the Cold War* (Chapel Hill: University of North Carolina Press, 1999), 11.

3. Ibid., 224.

4. Ibid.

5. Ibid., 240.

6. Ibid., 260.

7. Richard G. Hewlett and Oscar E. Anderson Jr., *Atomic Shield: A History of the United States Atomic Energy Commission*, vol. 2, *1947–1952* (Berkeley: University of California Press, 1990), 472.

8. Ibid., 264–65.

9. Wheeler Winston Dixon, *Film Noir and the Cinema of Paranoia* (New Brunswick, NJ: Rutgers University Press, 2009), 73.

10. Robert Porfirio, "The Thief," in *Film Noir: An Encyclopedia Reference to the American Style*, ed. Alain Silver and Elizabeth Ward (Woodstock, NY: Overlook Press, 1992), 287.

11. Dixon, *Film Noir and the Cinema*, 73.

12. Porfirio, "Thief," 287.

13. Mark Osteen, "The Big Secret," *Journal of Popular Film and Television* 22, no. 2 (1994): 7.

14. Joyce A. Evans, *Celluloid Mushroom Clouds: Hollywood and the Atomic Bomb* (Boulder, CO: Westview, 1998), 126.

15. Ibid.

16. See Alain Silver: "*The Thief* was considered an early Cold War, anti-Communist drama. However, why [Fields] is spying is a question that is never asked nor answered." Alain Silver, "The Thief," *Film Noir: 100 All-Time Favorites*, ed. Paul Duncan and Jürgen Müller (Köln: Taschen, 2014), 329.

17. Robert Corber, *Homosexuality in Cold War America: Resistance and the Crisis of Masculinity* (Durham, NC: Duke University Press, 1997), 11.

18. Ibid.

19. Evans, *Celluloid Mushroom Clouds*, 128.

20. Jon Hunner, *Inventing Los Alamos: The Growth of an Atomic Community* (Norman: University of Oklahoma Press, 2004), 6. The AEC took control of Los Alamos on January 1, 1947 (125).

21. As Hunner recounts, Ellen Reid "recalled discussing the hydrogen bomb at home" with her father, who worked with "high explosives" and "worried that maybe they didn't know what they were doing." Hunner, *Inventing Los Alamos*, 164.

22. As Hunner documents, these "non-nuclear" explosions were in fact routine at Los Alamos. See Hunner, *Inventing Los Alamos*, 143.

23. Ibid., 56–57.

24. Cyndy Hendershot, *Anti-Communism and Popular Culture in Mid-Century America* (Jefferson, NC: McFarland, 2003), 102.

25. Ibid.

26. A. Costandina Titus, *Bombs in the Backyard: Atomic Testing and American Politics* (Reno: University of Nevada Press, 1986), 90.

27. It's worth noting that the hydrogen bomb detonated at Yucca Flats at the Nevada Test Site in the spring of 1952 was telecast live across the United States by KTLA. Hunner, *Inventing Los Alamos*, 184.

28. Mick Broderick, *Nuclear Movies* (Jefferson, NC: McFarland, 1991), 11; Colin Shindler, *Hollywood Goes to War: Films and American Society, 1939–1952* (New York: Routledge and Kegan Paul, 1979), 137.

29. Hunner, *Inventing Los Alamos*, 149.

30. Although the square dance suggests that the Native Americans have been integrated into the Los Alamos community, the fact that the communists use their cliff dwellings to hold Tommy hostage also suggests the Indians are guilty by association.

31. Osteen, "Big Secret," 7.

32. Hendershot, *Anti-Communism and Popular Culture*, 103.

33. Osteen, "Big Secret," 7.

34. Hendershot, *Anti-Communism and Popular Culture*, 103.

35. Leonard Maltin, ed., *Leonard Maltin's Classic Movie Guide* (New York: Plume, 2010), 587.

36. Bolesroor (New York), March 15, 2009, Internet Movie Database, user reviews of *Shack Out on 101*, www.imdb.com/title/tt0048607/reviews?start=20.

37. Barry Gifford, *Film Noir: Adventures in Film Noir* (Jackson: University Press of Mississippi, 2001), 142.

38. Thomas Cole, "(The) Bikini: Embodying the Bomb," *Genders* 53 (Spring 2011): 7. On Réard and the "invention" of the bikini, which appeared after couturier Jacques Heim's two-piece Atome, see Patrick Alac, "The Birth of the Bikini," *The Bikini: A Cultural History* (New York: Parkstone, 2002), 26–42.

39. Stephanie A. Smith, *Household Words* (Minneapolis: University of Minnesota Press, 2006), 76; Cole, "Bikini," 7.

40. Andrew Sarris, *American Cinema: American Directors and Directions* (New York: Dutton, 1968), 215.

41. John Earl Hayes and Harvey Klehr, *Venona: Decoding Soviet Espionage in America* (New Haven, CT: Yale University Press, 1999), 325.

42. "Co-60 occurs as a solid material and might appear . . . in a tube, enclosed at both ends. . . . Co-60 can occur as a powder if the solid sources have been ground." "Radioisotope Cobalt-60," Department for Health and Human Services, Centers for Disease Control and Prevention, August 18, 2004, www.epa.gov/radiation/radionuclides/cobalt.html.

43. Edward Dimendberg, *Film Noir and the Spaces of Modernity* (Cambridge: Harvard University Press, 2014), 252.

44. Roger Westcombe, "City of Fear," in *Film Noir Encyclopedia*, 70.

45. Ibid.

46. Ibid.

47. Ibid.

48. Jonathan Benair, "*Panic in the Streets*," in Silver and Ward, *Film Noir: An Encyclopedic Reference*, 222.

49. Alexander Ballinger and Danny Graydon, *The Rough Guide to Film Noir* (London: Rough Guides, 2007), 77. About *City of Fear*, Dimendberg concludes that the film "functions as a striking allegory of the disappearance of the city, the urban subject, and the semi-documentary impulse in the age of nuclear war." Dimendberg, *Film Noir*, 158.

CHAPTER 6. *KISS ME DEADLY*

1. On Mickey Spillane's early career in the "slicks," "pulps," and comic books ("Sub-Mariner, the Human Torch, Blue Bolt, Captain America," etc.), see Mickey Spillane, "Mickey Spillane in His Own Words," in Max Allan Collins and James L. Traylor, *Mickey Spillane on Screen: A Complete Study of the Television and Film Adaptations* (Jefferson, NC: McFarland, 2012), 188.

2. For Hammer as the laureate of the Eisenhower era, see J. Kenneth Van Dover, *Murder in the Millions* (New York: Frederick Ungar, 1984), 91.

3. Max Décharné, *Hardboiled Hollywood: The True Crime Stories behind the Classic Noir Films* (New York: Pegasus, 2010), 80.

4. Ibid., 81.

5. Geoffrey O'Brien, *Hardboiled America: Lurid Paperbacks and the Masters of Noir* (New York: Da Capo, 1997), 104.

6. Mickey Spillane, cited in Peter Stanfield, *Maximum Movies—Pulp Fictions: Film Culture and the Worlds of Samuel Fuller, Mickey Spillane, and Jim Thompson* (New Brunswick, NJ: Rutgers University Press, 2011), 94.

7. Mickey Spillane, *Kiss Me, Deadly* (Thorndike, ME: G. K. Hall, 1980), 30.

8. Ibid., 157.

9. Ibid., 58.

10. Ibid., 211 and 264.

11. Stanfield, *Maximum Movies*, 84.

12. Victor Saville quoted in ibid., 97.

13. Robert Aldrich, quoted in Edwin T. Arnold and Eugene L. Miller, *The Films and Career of Robert Aldrich* (Knoxville: University of Tennessee Press, 1986), 36.

14. Richard Maltby, "'The Problem of Interpretation . . .': Authorial and Institutional Intentions in and around *Kiss Me Deadly*," *Screening the Past* 10 (June 30, 2000), www.latrobe.edu.au/screening.

15. Ibid.

16. Ibid.

17. On the "atomic MacGuffin," see Collins and Traylor, *Mickey Spillane on Screen*, 45. A. I. Bezzerides, "The Thieves' Market: A. I. Bezzerides in Hollywood," interview with Lee Server, in *The Big Book of Film Noir*, ed. Lee Server, Ed Gorman, and Martin H. Greenberg (New York: Carroll and Graf, 1998), 121.

18. Ibid.

19. Robert Aldrich, "Interview with Robert Aldrich," conducted by Joel Greenberg, *Sight and Sound* 37, no. 1 (1968–1969), in *Robert Aldrich: Interviews*, ed. Edwin T. Arnold and Eugene L. Miller (Jackson: University of Mississippi Press, 2004), 45.

20. On the similarity between the novel and film, which has "often been understated," see, for example, Eddie Robson, "*Kiss Me Deadly* (1955)," in *Film Noir* (London: Virgin, 2005), 187.

21. Aldrich, cited in Arnold and Miller, *Films and Career of Robert Aldrich*, 37.

22. Maltby, introduction to Peter Stanfield, *Maximum Movies*, ix.

23. Aldrich, cited in Maltby, "Problem of Interpretation."

24. Elizabeth Willis, "Christina Rossetti and Pre-Raphaelite Noir," *Textual Practice* 18, no. 4 (2004): 532. On Bezzerides's relation to the blacklist (he was placed on it, according to the author himself, after teaching at "Hollywood's famous 'Little Red Schoolhouse'" in the late 1940s"), see Garrett White, foreword to A. I. Bezzerides, *Thieves' Market* (Berkeley: University of California Press, 1997), xiv.

25. Aldrich, "Interview with Robert Aldrich," in Alain Silver and James Ursini, *What Ever Happened to Robert Aldrich?: His Life and His Films* (New York: Limelight, 1995), 347; Geoffrey Shurlock, quoted in Maltby, "Problem of Interpretation."

26. Aldrich, "You Can't Hang Up the Meat Hook," cited in Arnold and Miller, *Films and Career of Robert Aldrich*, 38; anonymous review of *Kiss Me Deadly*, *Variety* (April 20, 1955), cited by Robson in *Film Noir*, 192.

27. Aldrich, "You Can't Hang Up the Meat Hook," 38.

28. Alain Silver, "Evidence of a Style," *Film Noir Reader*, ed. Alain Silver and James Ursini (New York: Limelight, 1996), 221.

29. Jack Shadoian, *Dreams and Dead Ends: The American Gangster Film* (New York: Oxford University Press, 2003), 234.

30. On the "X" motif in *Kiss Me Deadly*, see Collins and Traylor, *Mickey Spillane on Screen*, 50.

31. Ibid., 59.

32. For a comparison of Christina Rossetti's "Remember" and the recitation of the poem in *Kiss Me Deadly*, see Willis, "Christina Rossetti and Pre-Raphaelite Noir," 521–40; and Rodney F. Hill, "Remembrance, Communication, and *Kiss Me Deadly*," *Literature/Film Quarterly* 32, no. 2 (1995): 146–49.

33. Hill, "Remembrance, Communication," 148.

34. Leopold Kawolsky is one of the names—like Harvey Wallace, Nicholas Raymondo, and Carmen Trivago—that Ray Diker, via Velda, tells Hammer to investigate. Mike learns that Wallace drove the truck that supposedly killed Kawolsky. The engineer/scientist Raymondo also died in a "traffic accident," Trivago tells Hammer, because he discovered a "little secret."

35. Stanfield notes that the pictures in Mist's gallery are by "Giorgio Morandi, Carlo Carra, and Massimo Campigli." Stanfield, *Maximum Movies*, 205n76.

36. Soberin's rebuke to his underlings underscores the motif of resurrection that has previously been introduced in the film. After Hammer's car is pushed off the cliff at the beginning of the film and explodes into flames (foreshadowing the film's pyrographic conclusion), he wakes up in the hospital—it's an out-of-focus POV shot from his woozy perspective—to a nurse and Velda, then to Pat Murphy, who remarks, "Three days ago I was figuring I'd have to finance a new tux to bury the corpse." Later, Mike goes to Nick's garage and Nick—"risen from his grease pit as if from the grave"—exclaims to his partner, "Hey, look, Sammy, my friend just return [*sic*] from the grave. Like Lazarus." The same wing-tipped, white-stitched shoes also appear in the scene set at Nick's garage where Nick is working underneath a car and the man in the distinctive shoes releases the hydraulic jack, crushing Nick's body.

37. Paula James, "*Kiss Me Deadly* (1955): Pandora and Prometheus in Robert Aldrich's Cinematic Subversion of Spillane," in *Screening Love and Sex in the Ancient World*, ed. Monica

S. Cyrino (New York: Palgrave Macmillan, 2013), 26. See also Laura Mulvey, "The Myth of Pandora: A Psychoanalytical Approach," in *Feminisms in the Cinema*, ed. Laura Pietropaolo and Ada Testaferri (Bloomington: Indiana University Press, 1995), 3–19.

38. Hill, "Remembrance, Communication," 147.

39. Stanfield, *Maximum Movies*, 205n76.

40. J. Hoberman, *An Army of Phantoms: American Movies and the Making of the Cold War* (New York: New Press, 2011), 296.

41. Charles J. Rollo, "Simenon and Spillane: The Metaphysics of Murder for the Millions," in *Mass Culture: The Popular Arts in America*, ed. Bernard Rosenberg and David Manning White (Glencoe, IL: Free Press, 1957), 171.

42. Russell Meeuf, "Nuclear Epistemology: Apocalypticism, Knowledge, and the 'Nuclear Uncanny' in *Kiss Me Deadly*," *LIT: Literature Interpretation Theory* 23, no. 3 (2012): 282.

43. A number of critics have seen a communist subtext in Soberin and his cohorts' un-American activities, but both Aldrich's and Bezzerides's political inclinations militate against such a reading. More likely, Soberin is a hyperbolic double of Hammer before the latter is "enlightened." As Jonathan Auerbach argues, Soberin's "allegiances are unclear—no Soviet agent, he. All we learn in the end is that he plans to take the radioactive treasure out of the country and sell it to the highest bidder." Jonathan Auerbach, *Dark Borders: Film Noir and American Citizenship* (Durham, NC: Duke University Press, 2011), 198.

44. Carol Flinn, "Sound, Woman, and the Bomb: Dismembering the 'Great Whatsit' in *Kiss Me Deadly*," *Wide Angle* 8, nos. 3–4 (1986): 124.

45. Jans Wager, *Dames in the Driver's Seat: Rereading Film Noir* (Austin: University of Texas Press, 2005), 70.

46. Meeuf, "Nuclear Epistemology," 298.

47. Ibid.

48. On an "uncontainable nuclear reaction" in the context of *Kiss Me Deadly*, see William Luhr: "By the time of *Kiss Me Deadly*, the prospect of a never-ending explosion was no longer science fiction; it had assumed the mantle of a 'real world' version of biblical Apocalypse." William Luhr, *Film Noir* (Malden, MA: Wiley-Blackwell, 2012), 136. About the ending of *Kiss Me Deadly*, Aldrich commented: "Mike was left alive long enough to see what havoc he had caused, though certainly he and Velda were both seriously contaminated." Quoted in Arnold and Miller, *Films and Career of Robert Aldrich*, 245 n36.

49. Raymond Borde and Étienne Chaumeton, *A Panorama of American Film Noir*, trans. Paul Hammond (San Francisco: City Lights, 2002), 155.

50. Collins and Traylor, *Mickey Spillane on Screen*, 61.

51. On *Kiss Me Deadly* as an "apocalyptic noir," see Tony Williams, *Body and Soul: The Cinematic Vision of Robert Aldrich* (Lanham, MD: Scarecrow Press, 2004), 126–33; and Meeuf, "Nuclear Epistemology," 283–304.

52. Claude Chabrol, "Evolution of the Thriller" (1955), in *Cahiers du Cinéma: The 1950s*, ed. Jim Hillier (Cambridge: Harvard University Press, 1985), 163; Robert Aldrich, "Interview with Robert Aldrich," conducted by Ian Cameron and Mark Shivas, *Movie* 8 (April 1963), in *Robert Aldrich: Interviews*, 25.

53. Ibid.

CHAPTER 7. *NOIR EN COULEUR*

1. John Belton, *Widescreen Cinema* (Cambridge: Harvard University Press, 1992), 195.

2. Alexander Ballinger and Danny Graydon, *The Rough Guide to Film Noir* (London: Rough Guides, 2007), 131.

3. John Alton, cited in Todd McCarthy, "Through a Lens Darkly: The Life and Films of John Alton," in John Alton's *Painting with Light* (Berkeley: University of California Press, 1995), ix.

4. Raymond Borde and Étienne Chaumeton, *A Panorama of American Film Noir*, trans. Paul Hammond (San Francisco: City Lights, 2002), 47.

5. Cited in James Naremore, *More than Night* (Berkeley: University of California Press, 1998), 187.

6. Ibid., 198.

7. Ibid., 188.

8. Patrick Keating, *Hollywood Lighting: From the Silent Era to Film Noir* (New York: Columbia University Press, 2010), 218.

9. Richard W. Haines, *Technicolor: The History of Dye Transfer Printing* (Jefferson, NC: McFarland, 1993), 149. The net result was that from 1950 to 1955, the percentage of Hollywood films produced in color increased from roughly 15 to 50 percent.

10. Steve Neale, *Cinema and Technology: Image, Sound, Colour* (London: BFI/Macmillan, 1985), 147.

11. Katherine Glitre, "Under the Color Rainbow," in *Neo-Noir*, ed. Mark Bould, Katherine Glitre, and Greg Tuck (London: Wallflower, 2009), 15. For the definitive book on Technicolor, which has informed my reading of '50s color noirs in general and, in particular, the rainbow-graced *Niagara*, see Scott Higgins, *Harnessing the Technicolor Rainbow: Color Design in the 1930s* (Austin: University of Texas Press, 2007).

12. Darryl Zanuck, *Memo from Darryl Zanuck: The Golden Years of Twentieth Century-Fox*, ed. Rudy Behlmer (New York: Grove Press, 1993), 223. On the "Theatrical Metaphor" and "Theatre and CinemaScope," see, respectively, Belton, *Widescreen Cinema*, 190–96, and James Spellerberg, *Technology and the Film Industry: The Adoption of CinemaScope* (Ann Arbor, MI: University Microfilms International, 1980), 228–34.

13. Belton, *Widescreen Cinema*, 192; *Hollywood Reporter*, June 28, 1954, cited by Spellerberg, *Technology and the Film Industry*, 232.

14. For instance, in "The Techniques of CinemaScope Pictures" (1955), Clarke writes that in "CinemaScope pictures the technique is like that of the theatre with the added advantage of being able to move in with the camera to accentuate the most important parts of the scene." http://www.widescreenmuseum.com/widescreen/page0-1.htm.

15. Zanuck, *Memo from Darryl Zanuck*, 22.

16. Donald Spoto, *Marilyn Monroe: The Biography* (New York: HarperCollins, 1993), 282.

17. Richard Strauss, "Reminiscences of the First Performances of My Operas," cited by Linda Hutcheon and Michael Hutcheon in "Staging the Female Body," in *Siren Songs: Representations of Gender and Sexuality in Opera*, ed. Mary Ann Smart (Princeton, NJ: Princeton University Press, 2000), 284. On the discourses of hysteria, orientalism, and nymphomania in *Salome*, see also Hutcheon and Hutcheon, "Staging the Female Body," 216 and 214.

18. I can only gesture to the extensive literature on Salome. On Strauss's opera, see, for example, Lawrence Kramer, "Modernity's Cutting Edge: The Salome Complex," *Opera and*

Modern Culture: Wagner and Strauss (Berkeley: University of California Press, 2004), 128–66; and Derrick Puffett, "Postlude: Images of Salome," in *Richard Strauss: Salome* (Cambridge: Cambridge University Press, 1989), 161–64.

19. Julie Grossman, *Rethinking the Femme Fatale: Ready for Her Close-Up* (London: Palgrave Macmillan, 2010), 139–40.

20. Patrick Quentin, *Black Widow* (New York: Simon and Schuster, 1952), 128.

21. Ibid., 211.

22. For brief critiques of Fuller's take on Japan in *House of Bamboo,* see Michael Richardson, *Otherness in Hollywood Cinema* (New York: Continuum, 2010), 117–18; and James King, *Under Foreign Eyes: Western Cinematic Adaptations of Postwar Japan* (Winchester, UK: Zero, 2012), 114–19.

23. Samuel Fuller, *A Third Face* (New York: Knopf, 2002), 315; Blake Lucas and Alain Silver, "House of Bamboo," in *Film Noir: The Encyclopedia,* ed. Alain Silver and James Ursini (New York: Overlook Press, 2010), 139.

24. See, in this context, Keith Uhlich's review of the DVD release of Fuller's *House of Bamboo*: "Quite simply, *House of Bamboo* has some of the most stunning examples of widescreen photography in the history of cinema." *Slant,* June 6, 2005, http://www.slantmagazine.com/dvd/review/house-of-bamboo.

25. Fuller, *Third Face,* 23.

26. Samuel Fuller, "Samuel Fuller (1912–1997)," interviewed by Robert Porfirio and James Ursini, in *Film Noir 3: Interviews with Filmmakers of the Classic Noir Period,* ed. Robert Porfirio, Alain Silver, and James Ursini (New York: Limelight, 202), 43.

27. See Nicholas Garnham, *Samuel Fuller* (New York: Viking, 1971), 90.

28. Lisa Dombrowski, *The Films of Samuel Fuller: If You Die, I'll Kill You!* (Middletown, CT: Wesleyan University Press, 2008), 84.

29. Samuel Fuller, "Samuel Fuller," interviewed by Eric Sherman and Martin Rubin, in *Samuel Fuller: Interviews,* ed. Gerald Peary (Jackson: University of Mississippi Press, 2012), 23.

30. Samuel Fuller, "Samuel Fuller (1912–1999)," in *Film Noir Reader 3,* ed. Robert Porfirio, Alain Silver, and James Ursini (New York: Limelight, 2002), 43.

31. See Phil Hardy, *Samuel Fuller* (New York: Praeger, 1970), 112.

32. Nicholas Christopher, *Somewhere in the Night* (New York: Free Press, 1997), 224.

33. James M. Cain, *Love's Lovely Counterfeit* (New York: Knopf, 1947), 137.

34. Blake Lucas, "Slightly Scarlet," in *Film Noir: An Encyclopedic Reference to the American Style,* ed. Alain Silver and Elizabeth Ward (Woodstock, NY: Overlook, 1992), 259.

35. Charles G. Clarke, *Professional Cinematography* (Hollywood, CA: American Society of Cinematographers, 1964), 150; italics in original. See also Clarke's *Highlights and Shadows: The Memoirs of a Hollywood Cameraman* (Metuchen, NJ: Scarecrow Press, 1989).

36. McCarthy, "Through a Lens Darkly," xxviii.

37. Lucas, "Slightly Scarlet," 260.

38. Ibid.

39. The reference is, of course, to "Jimmy Valentine lighting," which Alton discusses in *Painting with Light,* 54.

40. Naremore, *More than Night,* 189.

41. Cain, *Love's Lovely Counterfeit,* 218.

42. Ibid., 259–60.

43. Geoff Mayer, "*Slightly Scarlet*," in Geoff Mayer and Brian McDonnell, *Encyclopedia of Film Noir* (Westport, CT: Greenwood Press, 2007), 383.

44. Fred Basten, *Glorious Technicolor: The Movies' Magic Rainbow* (Camarillo, CA: Technicolor, 2005), 100 and 103.

45. Christopher, *Somewhere in the Night*, 224.

46. Ibid.

47. Otto Penzler, Introduction to Ira Levin, *A Kiss before Dying* (New York: Carroll and Graf, 2003), ix.

48. Robert Ottoson, *American Film Noir* (Metuchen, NJ: Scarecrow, 1981), 96.

49. Christopher, *Somewhere in the Night*, 226.

50. Lee Sanders and Meredith Brody, "*Leave Her to Heaven*," in Silver and Ward, *Encyclopedic Reference*, 224.

51. Ballinger and Graydon, *Rough Guide to Film Noir*, 129.

52. Keating, *Hollywood Lighting*, 220.

53. Ibid.

54. Levin, *Kiss before Dying*, 15.

55. Ibid.

56. Ibid., 27.

57. Ibid., 156.

58. Ibid., 127.

59. Ibid., 241.

60. Patricia Highsmith, *The Talented Mr. Ripley* (1955; New York: Vintage, 1992), 81. On the homme fatal, see, for example, Vincent Brook, *Driven to Darkness: Jewish Émigré Directors and the Rise of Film Noir* (New Brunswick, NJ: Rutgers University Press, 2009), 133–34.

61. See Sarah Street, *Costume and Cinema: Dress Codes in Popular Film* (London: Wallflower, 2001), 35–54.

62. On the female detective in film noir, see, for example, Helen Hanson, *Hollywood Heroines: Women in Film Noir and the Female Gothic* (London: I. B. Tauris, 2007) and Philippa Gates, *Detecting Women: Gender and the Hollywood Detective Film* (Albany: State University of New York Press, 2011).

CHAPTER 8. *NIAGARA*

1. Polly Platt, *Henry Hathaway: A Directors Guild of America Oral History*, ed. Rudy Behlmer and interviews conducted by Polly Platt (Lanham, MD: Scarecrow Press, 2001), ix; Ephraim Katz, "Henry Hathaway," *The Film Encyclopedia* (New York: HarperCollins, 2008), 628. For a revisionist account of Hathaway's noir films ("Hathaway's . . . noir projects constitute one of the most consistently fine bodies of work in the [noir] series, rivaled only by such more widely acclaimed masters as Fritz Lang, Billy Wilder, and Alfred Hitchcock"), see R. Barton Palmer, "Henry Hathaway," *Film Noir, the Directors*, ed. Alain Silver and James Ursini (Milwaukee: Limelight, 2012), 114–29.

2. Maurice Zolotow, *Marilyn Monroe* (London: W. H. Allen, 1961), 48.

3. André Bazin, "*Niagara*" (September 17, 1953), in *Bazin at Work: Major Essays and Reviews from the Forties and Fifties*, ed. Bert Cardullo and trans. Alain Piette (New York: Routledge,

1997), 125. On François Truffaut's review of *Niagara*—written under the nom de plume Robert Lachenay—see "*Niagara*'s Underpinnings," in Wheeler Winston Dixon, *The Early Film Criticism of François Truffaut*, trans. Ruth Cassel Hoffman, Sonja Kropp, and Brigitte Formentin-Humbert (Bloomington: Indiana University Press, 1993), 5–7.

4. Bazin, "*Niagara*," 127.

5. Ann Reynolds, "Curving into a Straight Line," in Zoe Leonard, *You See I Am Here after All* (New York: Dia Art Foundation, 2010), 161.

6. Ibid.

7. Merrill Schleier, "Fatal Attractions: 'Place,' the Korean War, and Gender in *Niagara*," *Cinema Journal* 51, no. 4 (2012): 28. On the border setting in *Niagara* as a site of "disruption, transgressive sexuality, and psychological ambiguity," see Dominque Brégent-Heald, "Dark Limbo: *Film Noir* and the North American Borders," *The Journal of American Culture* 29, no. 2: 128–29.

8. Bazin, "*Niagara*," 127.

9. Zolotow, *Marilyn Monroe*, 150.

10. Donald Spoto, *Marilyn Monroe* (New York: Cooper Square Press, 1993), 221.

11. Schleier notes that the pollution produced by Niagara Falls' industries are displaced onto the "lower-class Loomises" and, moreover, that their cabin, littered with clothing, newspapers, and cigarette butts, displays—as the script puts it—"a startling lack of neatness." "Fatal Attractions," 33.

12. Alain Silver and Meredith Brody, "*Niagara*," in *Film Noir: An Encyclopedic Reference to the American Style*, ed. Alain Silver and Elizabeth Ward (New York: Overlook Press, 2002), 199.

13. Ibid.

14. Rachel Chambers, "*Niagara*: Bust Out the Firehose, Here Comes Marilyn," *On This Day in Fashion*, January 11, 2011, http://onthisdayinfashion.com/?p=10172.

15. Spoto, *Marilyn Monroe*, 221. For a close reading of Rose Loomis's sirenic, autoerotic performance of "Kiss," in which Rose is "lost in her own remembered, desired or imagined pleasure," see Griselda Pollock, "Ecoutez la *Femme*: Hear/Here Difference," *The Femme Fatale: Images, Histories, Contexts*, ed. Helen Hanson and Catherine O'Rawe (Basingstoke, UK: Palgrave Macmillan, 2010), 13–18.

16. Bazin, "*Niagara*," 126.

17. Silver and Brody, "*Niagara*," 199.

18. "In the Gloaming" is an English song composed in 1877 by Annie Fortescue Harrison and Meta Orred.

19. Barbara Leaming, *Marilyn Monroe* (New York: Crown, 1998), 76.

20. Spoto, *Marilyn Monroe*, 222.

21. Ibid., 220.

22. In this context, note the car whose horn George rigs in order to steal onto the Ketterings' fishing boat near the conclusion of the film. For an evocative reading of the Korean War as a constitutive "structure of feeling" in *Niagara*, see Schleier, "Fatal Attractions," 36–40.

23. See, for example, Zolotow: "Marilyn . . . has been called the actress with the horizontal walk." *Marilyn Monroe*, 130. See also Lisa Cohen, "The Horizontal Walk: Marilyn Monroe, CinemaScope, and Sexuality," *Yale Journal of Criticism* 11, no. 1 (1998): 259–88.

24. As Palmer notes, this shot is extraordinarily "abstract" given the otherwise naturalistic tenor of the film: "An overhead shot from the point of view of the carillons shows us the murder in a now abstract set, crossed by swirling shadows." Palmer, "Henry Hathaway," 127.

25. Spoto, *Marilyn Monroe*, 222.

26. See, for example, Klaus Theweleit, "The Red Nurse" and "The White Nurse," *Male Fantasies*, vol. 1: *Women, Floods, Bodies, History*, trans. Stephen Conway (Minneapolis: University of Minnesota Press, 1987), 4 and 90–100.

27. Clara Juncker, *Circling Monroe: Text Body Performance* (Odense: University Press of Southern Denmark, 2010), 93.

28. Graham McCann, *Marilyn Monroe* (New Brunswick, NJ: Rutgers University Press, 1988), 20.

29. Ibid., 95.

30. Janey Place, "Women in Film Noir," in *Women in Film Noir*, ed. E. Ann Kaplan (London: BFI, 1998), 47.

31. See Vivian Sobchack's "Lounge Time: Postwar Crises and the Chronotope of Film Noir," in *Refiguring American Film Genres*, ed. Nick Browne (Berkeley: University of California Press, 1998), 129–70.

32. I'm alluding here to Richard Dyer's "Resistance through Charisma: Rita Hayworth and *Gilda*," in which Dyer remarks upon the performativity of Hayworth's star persona. Dyer, in *Women in Film Noir*, 115–22.

33. Carl E. Rollyson, *Marilyn Monroe: A Life of the Actress* (Ann Arbor, MI: UMI Research Press, 1986), 58.

34. Ibid. Sarah Churchwell, *The Many Lives of Marilyn Monroe* (London: Granta, 2004), 234.

35. "The weight of the Monroe image . . . is on innocence. She is certainly aware of her sexuality, but she is guiltless about it and it is moreover presented primarily in terms of narcissism—i.e., sexuality for herself rather than for men." Richard Dyer, *Stars* (London: BFI, 1998), 13.

36. Richard Dyer, *Heavenly Bodies: Film Stars and Society* (New York: St. Martin's, 1986), 44.

37. The "Diamonds Are a Girl's Best Friend" sequence from *Gentlemen Prefer Blondes* was featured, together with *The Robe* and *How to Marry a Millionaire*, in a fifty-minute promotional demonstration that Fox, wedding "star" (Monroe) and "star" (CinemaScope), presented to the press and motion picture industry on March 18, 1953.

38. Dyer, *Heavenly Bodies*, 51 and 50.

CHAPTER 9. *THE GLASS WEB*

1. Richard Maltby, *Hollywood Cinema* (Malden, MA: Blackwell, 1995), 154.

2. David Bordwell, "*Dial M for Murder*: Hitchcock Frets Not at His Narrow Room," September 7, 2012, http://www.davidbordwell.net/blog/2012/09/07/dial-m-for-murder-hitchcock-frets-not-at-his-narrow-room.

3. H. Dewhurst, *Introduction to 3-D* (New York: Macmillan, 1954), 124. The seminal text on 3-D is Raymond Spottiswoode and Nigel Spottiswoode, *The Theory of Stereoscopic Trans-*

mission and Its Application to the Motion Picture (Berkeley: University of California Press, 1953).

4. Dewhurst, *Introduction to 3-D*, 131.

5. "Imitating the movement of the human eye, the 3-D motion picture cinemas of the 1950s converged on subject matter, whether near or distant, and set the action within the confines of the contemporary motion picture frame of the time (1:33 to 1, or Academy Aperture)." Ray Zone, *Stereophonic Cinema and the Origins of 3-D Film, 1838–1952* (Lexington: University Press of Kentucky, 2007), 2.

6. I'm drawing here on Hal Morgan and Dan Symmes's *Amazing 3-D*, in particular "Hollywood Takes the Plunge: The Movies Go 3-D" (Boston: Little, Brown, 1982), 52–105. *Amazing 3-D*, which comes equipped with red-and-blue tinted glasses as well as 3-D comics, trading cards, movie stills, and View-Master excerpts, is a real must-see. On "Natural Vision," see Lenny Lipton, *Foundations of Stereoscopic Cinema: A Study in Depth* (New York: Van Nostrand Reinhold, 1982), 149–52.

7. Zone, *Stereophonic Cinema*, 185.

8. *The Glass Web* also appeared on the Lux Video Theatre on November 15, 1956. It was adapted from Blees and Lee's screenplay by Harry Kronman, directed by Richard Goode, and starred Dan O'Herlihy as Henry Hayes, George Nader as Don Newell, and Lawrence Dobkin as Dave Markson.

9. The opening of *The Glass Web* echoes the sequence in Arnold's *It Came from Outer Space* in which an alien lures George Putnam (Richard Carlson) across the desert to a mine shaft by assuming the appearance of his fiancée.

10. While Richard Denning, a "blond, handsome, athletic leading man and supporting player," appeared in numerous Hollywood films in the 1940s and '50s, including the noirs *The Glass Key* (1942), *No Man of Her Own* (1950), and *The Crooked Web* (1955), by the time *The Glass Web* was released, he was already starring as the amateur detective and crime publisher in *Mr. and Mrs. North* (CBS/NBC, 1952–1953, 1954). For the Denning, see Ephraim Katz, *The Film Encyclopedia* (New York: Harper Collins, 2008), 375. John Forsythe, "a tall handsome, Madison Avenue type," appeared in *The Captive City* (1952), but later became well-known as the star of the popular family sitcom, *Bachelor Father* (CBS, 1957–1962). Katz, *Film Encyclopedia*, 495.

11. Jack Arnold began his career in the Signal Corps as an assistant cameraman for famed documentary filmmaker Robert Flaherty, then became a contract director for Universal-International, where he "developed a particularly lean, efficient narrative style, typified by extreme deliberation" (he storyboarded all his scripts) and "fluid camerawork with an eye to 'one take' economy." Dana Reemes, *Directed by Jack Arnold* (Jefferson, NC: McFarland, 1988), 5. Before directing *The Glass Web*, Arnold had completed *Girls in the Night* (1953), a classic "bad girl" film for Albert J. Cohen, and the 3-D science-fiction classic *It Came from Outer Space*. Together with Clifford Stine of Universal-International's camera department, Arnold devised a 3-D system for the latter film that utilized "two Mitchell cameras side-by-side with one upside down so that the lenses were near each other. The upside down camera was accordingly altered to run backwards in synchronization with the other." Reemes, *Directed by Jack Arnold*, 30. Although Arnold would go on to helm a number of B noirs such as *Outside the Law* (1956) and *The Tattered Dress* (1957), he remains most famous today for the

creature features *Creature from the Black Lagoon* (1954) and *Revenge of the Creature* (1955), as well as the sci-fi classic *The Incredible Shrinking Man* (1957).

12. Steve Craig and Terry Moellinger, "'So Rich, Mild, and Fresh': A Critical Look at TV Cigarette Commercials: 1948–1971," *Journal of Communication Inquiry* 25, no. 1 (2001): 55–71.

13. Vincent Terrace, *The Television Crime Fighters Factbook* (Jefferson, NC: McFarland, 2003), 70.

14. Max Erlich, *Spin the Glass Web* (New York: Harper, 1952), 171 and 173.

15. Ibid., 3.

16. Ibid., 16.

17. Ibid., 9–10.

18. Ibid., 47.

19. Ibid., 43.

20. The cast, like the film's look, straddles '40s and '50s noir. For example, the "classic" aspect of *The Glass Web* is represented by the iconic presence of Edward G. Robinson. Having made a series of classic gangster pictures and film noirs in the 1930s and 1940s—from *Little Caesar* (1931) to *House of Strangers* (1949)—Robinson continued to be associated with the noir-gangster genre in the 1950s, albeit, due to the impact of HUAC, in a minor key: *Vice Squad* (1953), *Illegal* (1955), *Black Tuesday* (1955), *Tight Spot* (1955), *Bullet for Joey* (1955), *Nightmare* (1956), and *Hell on Frisco Bay*. Although Robinson was not officially blacklisted, in 1950 *Red Channels* "named him as a contributor to a number of Communist-front organizations." Robert Beck, *The Edward G. Robinson Encyclopedia* (Jefferson, NC: McFarland, 2002), 82. Like Bogart, Robinson had been a signatory of the Committee for the First Amendment and, like Bogart, he admitted he had been a "very choice sucker" (ibid., 83).

21. For examples of these early '50s TV shows, see Everett Aaker, "Appendix: Television Catalog," in *Encyclopedia of Early Television Crime Fighters* (Jefferson, NC: McFarland, 2006), 607–618.

22. R. Barton Palmer, "*Dragnet*, Film Noir, and Postwar Realism," in *The Philosophy of TV Noir*, ed. Steven M. Sanders and Aeon J. Skoble (Lexington: University Press of Kentucky, 2008), 45 and 33.

23. Ibid., 42.

24. For example, "an exact replica of the LAPD squad room was constructed on the lot," per Webb's instructions, "accurate down to the calendars and the extension numbers of the telephone." Aaker, *Encyclopedia of Early Television Crime Fighters*, 576.

25. Kathleen Hughes was a contract player at Fox before making her mark at Universal in *It Came from Outer Space*. In addition to the latter film, about which *Variety* wrote that "sticks and stones are not the only things that can be projected out into the auditorium" (Reemes, *Directed by Jack Arnold*, 232n4), Hayes is most memorable as the "good girl" Julia Thompson in the cult classic *Cult of the Cobra* (1955) and as the baddest sister, Valerie Craig, in the "bad girl" feature *Three Bad Sisters* (1956).

26. Erlich, *Spin the Glass Web*, 116.

27. Ibid., 153. In Erlich's *Spin the Glass Web*, the narrator also reprises the "spider-man" conceit to record Don's sudden reversal of fortune: "*suddenly, one of the spider's legs became caught in a strand, which it did not see. . . . And for the first time there was fear in its many eyes*

and incredulous astonishment. Its prey was galvanized by what it saw" (ibid., 182–83; italics in original).

28. This effect echoes a similar one in Arnold's *It Came from Outer Space* when there's an avalanche inside the crater where the alien spaceship has landed. "For the world premiere at the Pantages theatre in Hollywood," Reemes notes, an "additional effect was added": as the massive boulders began to tumble, "Arnold gave the cue to trip the catapults set up at the sides of the screen, scattering styrofoam rocks into the audience." Reemes, *Directed by Jack Arnold*, 33.

29. Erlich, *Spin the Glass Web*, 182–83.

30. Ibid., 195.

31. See also the final scene of *The Glass Web,* where the set, composed of a house and sunflowers, leafless tree and wooden fence, has an antic, German Expressionist cast.

32. On Webb's *Badge* and the TV show *Badge of Honor*, see Mahnola Dargis, *L.A. Confidential* (London: BFI, 2003), 27–28.

CONCLUSION

1. Robert Porfirio, "*Odds against Tomorrow,*" *Film Noir: The Encyclopedia*, ed. Alain Silver, Elizabeth Ward, James Ursini, and Robert Porfirio (Woodstock, NJ: Overlook Press, 2010), 217.

2. On the relation between the "crime melodrama" and classic noir, see my introduction, "Back to Black: 'Crime Melodrama,' Docu-Melo-Noir, and the 'Red Menace' Film," to *Kiss the Blood Off My Hands*, ed. Robert Miklitsch (Urbana: University of Illinois Press, 2014), 1–15.

3. Samuel Fuller, *A Third Face* (New York: Knopf, 2002), 326.

4. For some provocative remarks on the resemblance between Bertolt Brecht and Fuller, see Nicholas Garnham, *Samuel Fuller* (New York: Viking, 1971), 37–38. On Brecht's notion of the *Lehrstück*, see, for instance, "An Example of Paedagogics," in *The Development of an Aesthetic*, ed. John Willet (New York: Hill and Wang, 1964), 31–33. On Fuller's notion of his films as "illustrated lectures," see Lisa Dombrowski, *The Films of Samuel Fuller: If You Die, I'll Kill You!* (Middletown, CT: Wesleyan University Press, 2008), 10–17.

5. Dombrowski, *Films of Samuel Fuller*, 125–28.

6. On Fuller's "tabloid poetics," see Grant Tracey, "*Film Noir* and Samuel Fuller's Tabloid Cinema: Red (Action), White (Exposition), Blue (Romance)," in *Film Noir Reader 2*, ed. Alain Silver and James Ursini (New York: Limelight, 1999), 160.

7. Garnham, *Samuel Fuller*, 37.

8. Gina Marchetti, *Romance and the "Yellow Peril": Race, Sex, and Discursive Strategies in the Hollywood Fiction Film* (Berkeley: University of California Press, 1994), 156. Marchetti poses some intriguing questions about the relation between the "'high' art world of academic painting" and the "'low' art milieu of a Los Angeles burlesque theatre" (143), but her reading is compromised by preconceptions about both the "B movie" and the "B moviegoers' taste and sensibility" (148). These sorts of preconceptions are, it seems to me, fatal when talking about film noir, not to say Fuller's films.

9. Ibid., 146.

10. See also the scene earlier in the film where Charlie visits Mac in her studio and, as she's working on a painting titled "Nude Ascending Celestial Bodies" à la Duchamp, she's lustily singing "Figaro" and splashing beer, Pollock-like, on the canvas.

11. It's important to note that Joe and Charlie bonded, as Mac's remarks indicate, in Korea, where the two men would have been allied as Americans against the communist threat. Fuller's "combat" films—*China Gate* (1957), *Merrill's Marauders* (1962), and, in particular, the two relating to the Korean War, *The Steel Helmet* (1951) and *Fixed Bayonets* (1951)—are pertinent here. See, for example, "Asia," in Phil Hardy, *Samuel Fuller* (New York: Praeger, 1970), 95–121. See also the scene in *The Crimson Kimono* set at the Evergreen Cemetery featuring the Nisei Veterans Memorial, where an Issei, Yoshinaga (Bob Okazaki), visits the grave of his son, who was killed in the Korean War.

12. See Dombrowski, *Films of Samuel Fuller*, 129–30.

13. Ibid., 129.

14. Celine Parreñas Shimizu, *Straitjacket Sexualities: Unbinding Asian American Manhoods in the Movies* (Stanford, CA: Stanford University Press, 2012), 210.

15. Marchetti, *Romance and the "Yellow Peril,"* 156.

16. Shimizu, *Straitjacket Sexualities*, 212.

17. Ibid., 204.

18. On the relation between Fuller's "crosscut collisions" and Soviet—in particular, Eisensteinian—montage, see Tracey, "Film Noir," 162–63.

19. Garnham, *Samuel Fuller*, 37.

20. It's not immaterial that Joe and Charlie's homosocial relationship is mirrored in the spatial dynamics of their apartment, such as the mise-en-scène (for example, East-meets-West décor) and the layout ("too distinct bedrooms that open onto a central living room"). Dombrowski, *Films of Samuel Fuller*, 123. On the homosocial character of Joe and Charlie's relationship, see Marchetti, *Romance and the "Yellow Peril,"* 151; and Shimizu, *Straitjacket Sexualities*, 205. See also note 28 below.

21. Dombrowski, *Films of Samuel Fuller*, 124.

22. Ibid.

23. Fuller, *Third Face*, 376.

24. Ibid., 381; italics mine.

25. On the silent-film Asian serial characters, the "monstrous Mandarin" Long Sin, the even "more sinister" Wu Fang, as well as the "epitome of Asian treachery and cunning," Fu Manchu, see Eugene Franklin Wong, "The Early Years: Asians in the American Films Prior to World War II," in *Screening Asian Americans*, ed. Peter X. Feng (New Brunswick, NJ: Rutgers University Press, 2002), 56–58.

26. Indeed, as Philippa Gates has shown, the "Charlie Chan" series "is second only to Sherlock Holmes in the number of films made with the detective-hero" and inspired, among other things, "a radio series, a television series, [and] a comic strip." Philippa Gates, *Detecting Men: Masculinity and the Hollywood Detective Film* (Albany: SUNY Press, 2006), 76. On the *Thin Man* series as a bridge between proto- and classic noir, see my "Dashiell Hammett at the Movies," *Literature/Film Quarterly* 43, no. 3 (2015): 236–40.

27. Gates, *Detecting Men*, 77.

28. The passage in which Charlie, still in his robe and pajamas, strolls into Joe's bedroom, then watches him as he begins his morning toilette contributes to the impression of homosociality, although the romantic agon "between men" over Christine remains the most significant, because structural, aspect.

29. Shimizu, *Straitjacket Sexualities*, 209.

30. Suzanne Arakawa, "The Japanese Los Angeles of *The Crimson Kimono* and *Brother*," in *East Asian Film Noir: Transnational Encounters and Intercultural Exchange*, ed. Chi Yun Shin and Mark Gallagher (London: I. B. Tauris, 2015), 63. Philippa Gates, "The Assimilated Asian American Action Hero: Anna May Wong, Keye Luke, and James Shigeta in the Classical Hollywood Detective Film," *Canadian Journal of Film Studies* 22, no. 2 (2013): 36.

31. Dennis Broe, *Film Noir, American Workers, and Postwar Hollywood* (Gainesville: University Press of Florida, 2009), 87.

32. Ibid., 88.

33. James Naremore, *The Magic World of Orson Welles* (Dallas, TX: Southern Methodist University Press, 1989), 152.

34. Broe, *Film Noir, American Workers*, 89.

35. Kelly Oliver and Benigno Trigo, *Noir Anxiety* (Minneapolis: University of Minnesota Press, 2003), 123.

36. Joe's response here—"Let's not trigger a bomb"—alludes to the atomic bombing of Hiroshima and Nagasaki. More specifically, Joe is responding to the potential aggressivity of Charlie, who, as the white, all-American character, is associated with the United States.

37. See Naremore, who comments that the "final embrace between Mike and Suzy looks out of place, too obviously a Hollywood device" and that "their convertible. . . . looks very like the one Rudy Linnekar was driving at the beginning of the film." Naremore, *Magic World of Orson Welles*, 165.

38. On the notion of "political ecstasy" in relation to *The Crimson Kimono*, see Shimizu, *Straitjacket Sexualities*, 213. On the "limits of the crime picture," see Garnham, *Samuel Fuller*, 37.

39. On Little Tokyo as a "robust community space" rather than an "exotic tourist" one, see Arakawa, "Japanese Los Angeles," 58–59.

INDEX

ROBERT MIKLITSCH is a professor in the department of English language and literature at Ohio University. He is the editor of *Kiss the Blood Off My Hands: On Classic Film Noir*.

The University of Illinois Press
is a founding member of the
Association of American University Presses.

Composed in 10.75/13 Arno Pro
with Bebas Neue display
by Lisa Connery
at the University of Illinois Press
Cover designed by Jennifer S. Holzner
Cover illustration: 20th Century-Fox / Photofest
Manufactured by Cushing-Malloy, Inc.

University of Illinois Press
1325 South Oak Street
Champaign, IL 61820-6903
www.press.uillinois.edu